Problems of Dostoevsky's Poetics

Theory and History of Literature
Edited by Wlad Godzich and Jochen Schulte-Sasse

Problems

of Dostoevsky's

Poetics

Mikhail Bakhtin

Edited and Translated by Caryl Emerson

Introduction by Wayne C. Booth

Theory and History of Literature, Volume 8

 University of Minnesota Press
Minneapolis
London

**Publication of this book was assisted by a grant
from the publications program of the National Endowment
for the Humanities, an independent federal agency.**

Published by the University of Minnesota Press,
2037 University Avenue Southeast, Minneapolis, MN 55455-3092
Printed in the United States of America on acid-free paper

Sixth printing, 1994

Library of Congress Cataloging in Publication Data

Bakhtin, M. M. (Mikhail Mikhaïlovich), 1895–1975.
 Problems of Dostoevsky's poetics.
 (Theory and history of literature; v. 8)
 Translation of: Problemy poetiki Dostoevskogo.
 Includes index.
 1. Dostoevsky, Fyodor, 1821–1881 – Criticism and
interpretation. I. Emerson, Caryl. II. Title.
III. Series.
PG3328.Z6B2413 1984   891.73'3   83–12348
ISBN 0-8166-1227-7
ISBN 0-8166-1228-5 (pbk.)

Contents

Acknowledgments

Translation is a difficult, time-consuming art, and it fares best when there is no limit to the generosity of one's colleagues and friends. Of the many who have helped, several deserve special mention. Michael Holquist and Katerina Clark, both of Indiana University and long-term colleagues in the task of bringing Bakhtin to the English-speaking public, are a continual inspiration and background presence in this book. Sidney Monas of the University of Texas caught many an awkward phrase or inaccurate reference in the early drafts, and so often came up with just the right solution (it was he who pointed me toward the perfect "joyful relativity"). Gary Saul Morson of the University of Pennsylvania was, here as always, my most unsentimental and rigorous reader; whenever we have shared an idea or a text he has never failed to turn it into a dialogue, and one by which I am always greatly enriched. My largest debt, however, is owed to Nina Perlina of Rutgers University, whose sojourn at Cornell University as a Mellon Postdoctoral Fellow fortunately coincided with my two years' work on this translation. Herself an authority on Bakhtin and a Dostoevsky scholar of the highest caliber, she was unstinting in her generosity toward this project. It was never too late at night to call with a list of impossible words; she was rarely at a loss for a reference or a hypothesis. Our many sessions over the problem areas in this text were a model of scholarly symbiosis, in the best spirit of a Bakhtin circle.

Wayne Booth, Robert Louis Jackson, and Anatoly Liberman read portions of the manuscript and made many helpful suggestions. Marilyn Kann, Slavic Librarian at Cornell University, efficiently tracked down various texts necessary for annotating this edition. For certain details in the apparatus I am grateful to John Bennett, Stephen Farrand, George Gibian, Sander Gilman, Robin Feuer Miller, and Richard Ruppel, all of Cornell University. A special thanks to Philip Holland, who went through every page of the final manuscript with a critical eye, checking all the menippean references for accuracy and placing at my disposal his own work "Robert Burton's *Anatomy of Melancholy* and Menippean Satire, Humanist and English" (Ph.D. dissertation, University of London, 1979)—a fine integration of Bakhtin's ideas on the menippea into Western scholarship. Holland's chapter 2 ("Menippean Satire in Antiquity") provides helpful information on many of the writers Bakhtin discusses in his chapter 4.

The staff of the University of Minnesota Press made work on this book a pleasure with their friendly patience and encouragement. Cornell University generously awarded me a Humanities Grant to cover typing costs; Diane Williams produced a beautiful manuscript. Linda Noble and David Sherman worked long hours with me to proofread the text; the latter also expertly compiled the index. And then there are the people less directly concerned with this book who were nevertheless indispensable to its realization: my parents, whose loving intelligence saw me through many difficult moments, and my husband, Ivan Zaknic, whose own passion for translation (although in a different field and from different languages) equals my own, and whose energy and companionship in this project have been at all times sustaining.

This book has been previously translated into English, both in full and in part. The entire 1963 text was translated by R. William Rotsel (*Problems of Dostoevsky's Poetics*, Ardis, 1973), but his version was seriously flawed and is now out of print. Chapter Five, section Two of the Rotsel translation was revised by Priscilla Meyer and Stephen Rudy as "The Hero's Monologic Discourse and Narrational Discourse in Dostoevsky's Early Novels" in their *Dostoevsky & Gogol: Texts and Criticism* (Ardis, 1979). In addition, Richard Balthazar and I. R. Titunik rendered into English a portion of the 1929 text ("Tipy prozaicheskogo slova") as "Discourse Typology in Prose," in *Readings in Russian Poetics*, ed. Ladislav Matejka and Krystyna Pomorska (The MIT Press, 1971). I would like to thank my fellow translators for their versions of this difficult text. While my solutions rarely coincide with theirs, they did make possible an occasional dialogue over particularly complex sentences and terms. Thanks to their efforts,

Bakhtin's text has generated the interest and reputation in the English-speaking world that it so clearly deserves. It is my hope that this present fully annotated edition will help win for Bakhtin's voice a permanent place in Dostoevsky criticism, and in the broader area of literary scholarship as well.

Note on the Apparatus

This English-language edition of *Problems of Dostoevsky's Poetics* offers three levels of explanatory apparatus: (1) Bakhtin's own footnotes, which are numbered, are reproduced at the end of each chapter. (2) Translator's notes, which are lettered, appear at the bottom of the relevant page and cover such problems as critical or generic terminology, puns, untranslatable terms, and the occasional identification of important literary contexts. (3) An asterisk (*) after a proper name or work indicates that biographical information or an explanatory note can be found in the "Glossary of Proper Names and Works" at the end of the volume.

When Bakhtin quotes Dostoevsky, he does so from the following standard Soviet sources: For fictional and journalistic works: *Sobranie sochinenii* in 10 volumes (Moscow: Goslitizdat, 1956-58) [referred to in footnotes as *SS*] or *Polnoe sobranie khudozhestvennykh proizedenii* in 13 volumes, edited by B. V. Tomashevskii and K. I. Khalabayev (Moscow-Leningrad: Gosizdat, 1926-30) [referred to in footnotes as *PS*]. For Dostoevsky's letters: F. M. Dostoevskii, *Pis'ma* in four volumes, edited by A. S. Dolinin (Moscow: 1928-59) [referred to in footnotes as *Pis'ma*].

Wherever possible I have replaced these quotations with passages from standard translations of Dostoevsky's works. References to these English-language versions are appended to Bakhtin's footnotes or, in the text itself, to the quotation. There is no complete or authoritative English edition of Dostoevsky's correspondence, so all translations from the letters are mine. If there do exist English versions of the critical literature mentioned by Bakhtin in chapter 1, I have so indicated and provided page references. Listed below are the standard translations of Dostoevsky's work used in the text:

The Adolescent [*Podrostok*], trans. Andrew MacAndrew (New York: Norton, 1981).

"Bobok," trans. Constance Garnett, in *The Short Stories of Dostoevsky*, ed. William Phillips (New York: Dial Press, 1946).

The Brothers Karamazov [*Brat'ja Karamazovy*], The Garnett Translation revised by Ralph E. Matlaw (New York: Norton Critical Edition, 1976).

Crime and Punishment [*Prestuplenie i nakazanie*], trans. Constance Garnett (New York: Bantam Books, 1958).

The Diary of a Writer [*Dnevnik pisatelja*], trans. Boris Brasol (Santa Barbara: Peregrine Smith, Inc., 1979).

"The Double" [*Dvoinik*], trans. Jessie Coulson, in *Dostoyevsky: Notes from Underground and the Double* (London: Penguin Classics, 1972).

"The Dream of a Ridiculous Man" [*Son smeshnogo cheloveka*], trans. Olga Shartse, in *Fyodor Dostoyevsky: Stories* (Moscow: Progress Publishers, 1971).

The Idiot [*Idiot*], trans. Constance Garnett (New York: Dell, 1959).

"The Landlady" [*Khozaika*], trans. Constance Garnett, in *The Short Stories of Dostoevsky* (1946).

"A Meek One" [*Krotkaya*], trans. Olga Shartse, in *Fyodor Dostoyevsky: Stories* (1971).

"Notes from Underground" [*Zapiski iz podpol'ia*], The Garnett Translation revised by Ralph E. Matlaw, in *Fyodor Dostoevsky: Notes from Underground and the Grand Inquisitor* (New York: Dutton, 1960).

Poor Folk or *Poor People* [*Bednye liudi*], trans. Constance Garnett, in *Three Short Novels by Fyodor Dostoyevsky: Notes from Underground, Poor People, The Friend of the Family* (New York: Dell, 1960).

The Possessed [*Besy*], trans. Constance Garnett (New York: Dell, 1961). This edition contains a translation of "Stavrogin's Confession" (the chapter "At Tikhon's") by F. D. Reeve. His text differs significantly in detail—although not in tone—from the variant Bakhtin cites. I have adjusted the Reeve translation to approximate more closely the Russian, and noted the major discrepancies.

"Uncle's Dream" [*Diadushkin son*], trans. Ivy Litvinova, in *My Uncle's Dream* (Moscow: Foreign Language Publishing House, n.d.).

Quotations from translated versions of Dostoevsky's works have been amended, when necessary, for accuracy and tone. Bakhtin's own translations from other languages (largely the German) have been checked against the original and any discrepancies noted.

Introduction
Wayne C. Booth

To understand why Bakhtin's work fully justifies the recent explosion of Western interest in it, we must back into the topic. What were we in the West saying about the relations of ideology and form while Bakhtin was writing and rewriting, losing and finding again, his thousands of astonishingly various yet curiously harmonious pages?

Formal critics all begin with a truth that ideological critics too often neglect: form is in itself interesting, even in the most abstract extreme. Shape, pattern, design carry their own interest—and hence meaning—for all human beings. What some critics have called "human meanings" are not required; nothing is more human than the love of abstract forms. The relations discovered or invented in pure mathematics, like the forms we find, or think we find, in the physical world, are felt by all who pursue them to be more worthy of pursuit than sheer chaos would be, even if there were any sense in which a genuine chaos could be pursued, studied, "formulated."

Our "pure," "abstract," "disinterested" interest in forms has proved confusing to formal critics when they have turned to forms made by human beings. Works of art still obviously respond to our love of abstract, or "meaningless" form, but they often come laden with other interests. Abstract painting and sculpture, primitive and modern; non-programmatic music, whether by Bach or by recent mathematical explorers; complex word games; patchwork quilts;

computer "art" based on elaborate equations—all testify to our capacity to enjoy patterns disconnected from any obvious meanings that seem attachable to ideologies. Yet the very act of making even the most dessicated work of art imports into it meanings that carry both maker and receiver into territory other than a pure contemplation of pattern. Sooner or later every formal critic must therefore struggle with the problem of how to deal with the scandal of what is often called "content."

One way is to fight meaning openly, as a taint on pure form. In our century an astonishing number of critics have equated art with the purgation of meanings. Is it not obvious that the closer we can come to a simple, pure vision of form, uncontaminated by the practical interests that clutter our non-artistic lives, the closer we come to what is properly called art? Countless manifestoes have declared for purity and against the philistines who naively import human interests into their responses: "It matters not what artists paint, so long as they paint beautiful forms." "The listening public is the enemy, insisting on sentiment and on melodies that can be sung." "Do not ask whether a given literary character or work is moral or immoral, only whether the design is right."

In the late nineteenth century Pater and others were already telling us that all art aspires to the condition of music, in which form and content are so subtly intertwined that no critic can draw a line between them. In our time we are told that even Pater's terms were not austere enough: art is not a question of beautiful intertwining, for there should be no "content" to intertwine. Music itself properly aspires to the condition of pure mathematics—or alternatively, to the undoctored, inartificial forms of natural sounds. Form is all—or, as the newest version has it, language is all.

Everyone who has pronounced thus boldly for a purified form has been confronted by the scandalous fact that all actual works of art are loaded with ideology. The scandal is most pressing when the "messages" are as blatantly obvious as the religious passion of *Paradise Lost* and the *B-Minor Mass* and *The Waste Land*, or the programmatic, existentialist urgency of most of the best twentieth-century fiction. But it is equally embarrassing when art works more fully disguise their ideology; discerning critics can easily show that if purification is the goal, the artist had better turn the whole business over to indifferent machines. And even that surrender can be probed for its ideology. A whole history of art in our century, not too badly distorted as such histories go, could be written as a grand competition for the position of chief purifier, artists and critics catching each other out for failing to expunge lingering impurities.

Of all the arts, fiction has been most resistant to the drive for purification. It is so obviously built of impurities that some artists have simply repudiated it as a faulty enterprise from the beginning: poets in their credoes often take swipes at mere storytellers who are stuck with the task of providing a "good read." And many a novelist has aspired to the condition of story-free poetry. Since to tell a *story* is in itself to confess a betrayal of pure form, the thing to do is to frustrate story in some way: by leaving the pages unbound, to be shuffled by the reader; by telling everything in alphabetical order; by imposing various word games and tricks with point of view, reminding everyone that structural intricacy is the only legitimate interest; by commenting explicitly to remind readers that your fictions are "generated" not by any interest in characters and how they relate but rather by number systems or stochastic devices like shuffled cards or computers. But the shameful fact is that as soon as you *name* a character and allow even one *event*, readers will, in truculent naiveté, treat them like people in human situations, and all the effort at pure form has gone down the drain.

The obvious failure of pure formalism to deal adequately with even the simplest fictions has led to various attempts to treat ideology not as scandal but as mystery. Engaging stories present us with a complex truth: while human events are not in themselves art, fiction, unlike double acrostics, is clearly an art that is somehow *made of* human events. If art is somehow concerned with form, if form is what distinguishes art from life, and if fictional forms are embedded in the materials of life, how can we talk about the *art* of fiction?

A second way of dealing with the scandal, then, is to embrace it, to downgrade formal interests and to identify a work's art with its ideology, judging works according to their surface truth or falsehood. In effect, one can thus simply delete the boundary between art and life and treat every art work as if it were direct, primary experience. Despite the discrediting of this "philistine" view by centuries of attack, it still persists: in censorship programs directed at our schools; in some political criticism, not only in totalitarian regimes; in some hasty attacks on sexist or racist works—attacks launched with inadequate attention to the targets; in the programs of certain moral and religious critics who, like John Gardner in *On Moral Fiction*, often forget their own claims to respect the distinctive values of art. And many a new sociological or "neo-Marxist" critic has embraced new sophisticated forms of antiformalism. For them, all art and all criticism is "political." And it is easy for them to show that any work of art, when *probed* for ideology, will reveal ideology. Even the blank canvases, the 4½-minute silences, the self-destroying machines, the pure circles and spheres and triangles of the most minimal art cannot escape their meanings: these seemingly innocuous games are offered by human beings to other human beings, and they thus carry the meanings of their situations and of the makers' acts in those situations. Thus even the purest form itself becomes ideology, and in a curious way left-wing and right-wing critics join hands in judging art by ideological standards alone.

A third way is to move unsystematically back and forth, in an uneasy compromise between talk about form and talk about meanings, depending on what the work itself forces on our attention. Form in this eclectic view comes to seem like a kind of easily removable envelope, one that contains the content. This was one chief classical way of thinking, based on the *res/verba* distinction: "things," as content, offer all the "meaning," and "words" or language, as form, do the carrying job, like some delivery service that doesn't much care what is in the packages. The New Critics, at least when they turned to fiction, tended to treat its form this way.

A fourth way might be called "Aristotelian," or perhaps, to avoid the claim of really having understood Aristotle, "neo-Aristotelian." Here we reject the notion of a separable "content" altogether, and rely instead on a form/*matter* pairing, in which neither form nor matter can be distinguished in separation from its twin. When torn from its form, any matter simply becomes inchoate, or is placed into another form that changes its fundamental nature. This kind of formal method sees both language and the ideologies that language inescapably embodies as shaped by some conception of a human action, or by an idea to be taught, or by some attitude to be promulgated in the world. Works of art are, like everything else that really *exists*, analyzable as both form and matter, but *qua* existing things they exhibit an identity of the two; what the matter has become *is* this shaped thing.

In this view, you cannot even describe the form, say, of *Oedipus Rex*, without describing with great precision the moral and intellectual qualities of the characters who act and suffer; their action *is* the form. A statement of the plot that did not include a precise appraisal of Oedipus's full character—in modern jargon, his "values," including his "ideology"—would have no formal validity at all, and a statement about "content" that extracted moral views from the shape they are given in the play would be almost as pointless. Similarly, in "Leda and the Swan" the intellectual convictions expressed are not a content formed by the words but a formed idea: a specific form imposed on words that in themselves could express a great many different ideas. *Form* in this view is thus shattered into innumerable *forms*—all of the "things" in this domain, the substances that have been made by artists. These substances, unlike those that occur in nature, are steeped in values; there is no such thing as a fictional form that is value-free, abstracted from the commitments of the characters and their author.

We can see why Aristotelians prefer to speak of many forms rather than of form when we observe how they deal with the notion of plot. In most of the attacks on plot made by those who were interested in a higher or purer fictional form, it became synonymous with intrigue, and intrigue became abstracted from the human value of characters involved in it. When E. M. Forster chose to summarize the structure of Anatole France's *Thaïs*, what occurred to him was — since the priest and the prostitute each ends where the other began — that the *plot* might be represented in the form of an hourglass, or, for even greater simplicity, as an "X." Working at that level of abstraction, we could say that, since *Macbeth* is the story of how a regicide and his wife get caught, after initial successes, then the plot amounts to the shape of a circonflex, or perhaps, to dramatize the fall, an inverted checkmark. Innumerable "structural" analyses of literature have worked at about that level of abstraction, a level which leads to the provocative claim, often made by Northrop Frye and his students, that all literary works have the same story: "the loss and regaining of identity" (*The Educated Imagination*, Bloomington, Indiana, 1964, p. 55). If such a claim is true — and for all I know it may be — it is not very useful, from the point of view of anyone trying to talk about how ideology and form relate.

The key word in this mode is "useful." What can it mean to seek a *useful* language for talking about a story, about its plot, about its "essence" or "unity" or "soul?" Useful to whom? Well, why not useful to everyone? "Aristotelian" critics have always aspired to be, like Aristotle, useful not only to readers and spectators and other critics but useful to creative artists as well. The *Poetics* has often been called a "handbook" for *writing* tragedy; it tells us, in its detailed analysis of the ingredients of existing tragedies, and its strongly evaluative account of the best ways of mixing those ingredients, just how we might go about making, or improving, other objects of the same kind.

It does not do so, however, by offering any simple rule book or algorithm. Its analyses are all steeped in value judgments, not of technical or formal beauty separable from moral qualities but of a shaped action, a "synthesis of incidents" or events that represent choices made by moral or immoral agents, and thus in consequence deserve, as "plot," to be called the "soul" of the work. Thus what Bakhtin calls ideology is an essential part of the Aristotelian analysis; the forms Aristotle treats are made not of abstract shapes but of values: values sought, values lost, values mourned, values hailed. There is no more of a hint in Aristotle's formalism than in Bakhtin's dialogism of pursuing designs like hourglass shapes or spiraling curves or abstract symmetries or asymmetries of any kind. People in action cannot be reduced to mathematical figures or equations, and neither can "imitations of action."

The unity sought in every version of genuinely Aristotelian formal criticism is thus an *ideological* unity, a unity of action that is implicated in ideological matters, whether overtly, as in epithets conferring a good or bad quality on a character, or implicitly, in the ordering of values conferred by any plot sequence. The significant point, as we move toward a comparison with Bakhtin's version of "ideological formalism," is that here the unity *is* sought; it is a unity of effects pursued by an artist, an artist whose artistry is defined as a skill with architectonics. Effect (whether tragic, or comic, or satiric, or horrific, or mystifying, or celebrating—different Aristotelianisms produce different catalogues of the possible or admirable effects) is everywhere the end, and technical problems are discussed as means to given ends. Such functionalism comes to a point of caricature in Edgar Allen Poe's "The Philosophy of Composition," in which every choice by the artist is described as if calculated by a mathematician toward a single, named emotion. But even in the subtler functionalists, among whom I count my own mentors, Ronald Crane, Elder Olson, and their associates, there was never any question but that the key word was "unity" and that the unity we should seek is that of effect. The "perfected" work could thus be reconstructed and accounted for, by the acute critic, as an organic whole, with a kind of "soul," or essential informing principle, by reference to which one could explain, ideally, every choice the author had made.

The author, like the work itself, was implicated in ideology from the beginning. Since authors found themselves addressing audiences who shared some values and did not share others, they had to find effective ways to embody values in fiction and drama, values that would make the work *work*. Authors were thus in charge of created unities that consisted of choices exemplified and judged (though from quite another viewpoint they were not in charge, because their culture imposed norms upon author, work, and audience).

Any critic who begins to study fictional technique from such a base, as I did at mid-century, will of course attempt to see every artistic stroke according to its function in a whole. Even the norms that a novel embodies—its ideology—will be understood to serve the unity that, for any reader, is realized not in a conceptual scheme or "meaning" but in a given effect (however complex that effect may be). Thus when I turned, in the fifties, to reconsider the "objectivity" that critics were touting at the time as a major achievement of all good fiction, it was natural for me to ask whether objectivity was in fact a supreme goal of all good fiction, whether an *air* of objectivity was in fact functional toward all important fictional ends, and whether any kind of genuine objectivity was in fact possible for an author, regardless of how much technical purification was achieved. Working as what might be called a "constructive formalist," it was inevitable that I should answer "no" to all three questions. Objectivity is not a supreme goal. It is unattainable, in itself, because the author's voice is always present, regardless of how thoroughly it is disguised. And even an *air* of objectivity is only on *some* fictional occasions helpful: many of our finest moments with novels are realized by illusions of quite "unobjective" kinds.

My opponents, as I saw it, were all those who had demanded a kind of "point-of-voyeurism" in all good fiction, inventing abstract and absolute rules about how this or that sign of the author's presence should be purged. I thought of myself in part as correcting, from within a rigorously formalist school, a gross but fashionable error of pursuing objectivity at all costs, an objectivity that was in most accounts reduced to surface matters of point of view. Critics had insisted that if an author violated certain rules against "telling," if an author failed to "show," to "dramatize," the result was not "objective" and was therefore somehow bad. About the furthest anyone at the time had gone beyond such useless rule-making was the claim, often referring to Keats on Shakespeare and the ideal of the "chameleon poet," that the novelist should take on the coloration of every character, without imposing heavy moral judgment. Some few critics had extended this notion to the very structure of the novel, claiming that "justice" to all characters was the supreme fictional goal. But most critics, and especially the practical critics, had reduced the question to one of technical purification: an author should create a *surface* that would be, or seem, objective.

As I see it now, my own replies to such arguments were often almost as superficial as were those of my targets. If I had not been ignorant, like almost everyone else, of the work of Bakhtin and his circle, I might have grappled with a much more sophisticated attack on the "author's voice" in fiction, one that would have forced me to reformulate, if not fundamentally to modify, my claim that "the author's judgment is always present, always evident to anyone who knows how to look for it. . . . The author cannot choose whether to use rhetorical heightening [in the service of his authority and of the reader's effective re-telling of the story]. His only choice is of the kind of rhetoric he will use." So far as this argument goes, my debate with the critics I knew still seems to me sound. But the challenge presented in full force by Bakhtin requires an entirely different level of encounter.

That challenge has little to do with whether or not the author claims privileges of omniscience or exercises inside views. Indeed it has nothing at all to do with the author's effort to produce a single unified effect. Its subject is not the ordering of technical means toward certain effects so much as the quality of the author's imaginative gift—the ability or willingness to allow voices into the work that are not fundamentally under the "monological" control of the novelist's own ideology.

"This problem lies deeper than the question of authorial discourse on the superficial level of composition, and deeper than a superficially compositional device for eliminating authorial discourse by means of the *Ich-Erzählung* form (first-person narration), or by a narrator's introduction, or by constructing the novel in scenes and thus reducing authorial discourse to the status of a stage direction. All these compositional devices for eliminating or weakening authorial discourse at the level of composition do not in themselves tackle the essence of the problem; their underlying artistic meaning can be profoundly different, depending on the different artistic tasks they perform" (pp. 56-57).

This statement might at first sound like the "functionalism" I have ascribed to the neo-Aristotelians. For them as well the essence of the problem depends on "the different artistic tasks" performed by different works. And the different formal achievements that Bakhtin would account for are again, like those addressed by Aristotle, "formed ideologies"—not value-free forms imposed on a "content" that alone contains the taint of value judgments or ideology, but rather formed values, formed ideologies. The form itself, in both views, is inherently ideological.

But for Bakhtin the notion of diverse *tasks* is quite different from a collection of literary effects, like tragedy or comedy, satire or eulogy. The artist's essential task is not simply to make the most effective work possible, as viewed *in* its kind. It is rather to achieve a view of the world superior to all other views; fiction of the right kind, pursuing the right tasks, is the best instrument of understanding that has ever been devised. It is indeed the only conceptual device we have that can do justice, by achieving a kind of objectivity quite different from that hailed by most western critics, to the essential, irreducible multi-centeredness, or "polyphony," of human life. In freeing us from narrowly subjective views, the best novels achieve a universally desirable quality, regardless of the particular effects that in an Aristotelian view might be considered their ends. Like the universally desirable "sublime" pursued by Longinus, the quality pursued by Bakhtin is a kind of "sublimity of freed perspectives" that will always, on all fictional occasions, be superior to every other.

His defense of Dostoevsky as the supreme master of such sublimity always depends on larger views that are more fully developed elsewhere (see especially *The Dialogic Imagination: Four Essays by M. M. Bakhtin*, ed. Michael Holquist, trans. Caryl Emerson and Michael Holquist [Austin: The University of Texas, 1981]). Commentators dispute about just *how* large those views are — that is, about the degree to which Bakhtin's unsystematic system is religious or metaphysical. To me it seems clearly to rest on a vision of the world as essentially a collectivity of subjects who are themselves social in essence, not individuals in any usual sense of the word; to this degree it is definitely incompatible with all but the subtlest of materialisms. His "God-term" —though he does not rely on religious language—is something like "sympathetic understanding" or "comprehensive vision," and his way of talking about it is always in terms of the "multi-voicedness" or "multi-centeredness" of the world as we experience it. We come into consciousness speaking a language already permeated with many voices—a social, not a private language. From the beginning, we are "polyglot," already in process of mastering a variety of social dialects derived from parents, clan, class, religion, country. We grow in consciousness by taking in more voices as "authoritatively persuasive" and then by learning which to accept as "internally persuasive." Finally we achieve, if we are lucky, a kind of individuality, but it is never a private or autonomous individuality in the western sense; except when we maim ourselves arbitrarily to monologue, we always speak a chorus of languages. Anyone who has not been maimed by some imposed "ideology in the narrow sense," anyone who is not an "ideologue," respects the fact that each of us is a "we," not an "I." Polyphony, the miracle of our "dialogical" lives together, is thus both a fact of life and, in its higher reaches, a value to be pursued endlessly.

It will be obvious to any literary historian that literary works have tended *not* to do justice to our dialogical natures in this sense. Just as in our individual lives we are tempted to close out voices prematurely, in order to keep things simple and to dominate the world, authors have generally experienced an irresistible temptation to impose monological unities upon their works. Many of the greatest achievements, great when viewed from the perspective of Aristotelian formalism, will thus appear seriously maimed when we ask whether their forms reflect dialogue or monologue.

Bakhtin puts the point another way. Human existence, created as it is *in* many languages, presents two opposing tendencies. There is a "centrifugal" force dispersing us outward into an ever greater variety of "voices," outward into a seeming chaos that presumably only a God could encompass. And there are various "centripetal" forces preserving us from overwhelming fluidity and variety. The drive to create art works that have some kind of coherence — that is, formal unity — is obviously a "centripetal" force; it provides us with the best experience we have of what Coleridge called "multeity in unity," unity that does justice to variety. But we are always tempted to follow that drive too far in the direction of imposing a monologic unity. Lyric poems, for example, marvelous as they can be, tend toward becoming monologues — the poet inventing a single voice, one that belies the actual polyphony of his own inner chorus. Even drama, which on its surface seems polyphonic, and which became for Western objectivists a kind of model to be emulated by fiction, is by nature monologic, because the dramatist is always imposing upon his characters what they must say, rather than allowing their *personalities* the freedom to say what they will, in their own way.

The one grand literary form that is for Bakhtin capable of a kind of justice to the inherent polyphonies of life is "the novel." If we think of "the novel" not as some formalists would do, not as the actual works that we ordinarily *call* novels but rather as a tendency or possibility in literature, one that is best realized only in certain novels and is entirely lacking in others, we can begin to study with some precision the conditions for achieving the elusive quality we have in mind. What we seek is a representation, at whatever time or place and in whatever genre, of human "languages" or "voices" that are not reduced into, or suppressed by, a single authoritative voice: a representation of the inescapably dialogical quality of human life at its best. Only "the novel," with its supreme realization of the potentialities inherent in prose, offers the possibility of doing justice to voices other than the author's own, and only the novel invites us to do so. This is not a matter only of length; epics have all the space in the world but they still tend to be monologic. It is more a matter of the technical resources of narrative in prose — the inherent capacity of narrative to incorporate languages other than the author's (or reader's) own. In various kinds of indirect discourse, novelists can maintain a kind of choral vitality, the very same words conveying two or more speaking voices.

They can, but of course many actual novelists do not. Turgenev, Tolstoy, indeed most who are called novelists, never release their characters from a dominating monologue conducted by the author; in their works, characters seldom escape to become full *subjects*, telling their own tales. Instead they generally remain as objects *used* by the author to fulfill preordained demands.

It is in Dostoevsky and in Dostoevsky alone that Bakhtin finds the polyphonic ideal realized. The greatest of all contrapuntalists genuinely surrenders to his characters and allows them to speak in ways other than his own. Heroes are no longer diminished to the dominating consciousness of the author; secondary characters are no longer encompassed by and diminished to their usefulness to heroes—or to the author. Characters are, in short, respected as full subjects, shown as "consciousnesses" that can never be fully defined or exhausted, rather than as objects fully known, once and for all, in their roles—and then discarded as expendable.

It is clear that any rhetoric of fiction becomes transformed, in this view, from what it will be if we begin with an Aristotelian interest in form and function. In the finest fiction, the author's technique will not be marshaled to harmonize everything into a single unified picture and to aid the reader to see that picture; the unity of the work will not be identified with the total choices of the implied author—the sum of James's choices, the ultimate impact of Austen's voice. The author will have "disappeared" from the work in a manner far different from what was meant by James Joyce when he described that poseur backstage, like God impassively viewing his handiwork and presenting his drama with pretended indifference, "silently paring his fingernails." Techniques will be viewed as performing their highest service by preserving the autonomy of the novel's characters. Raskolnikov in *Crime and Punishment* speaks for Raskolnikov as an inexhaustible personality; he does not speak either as a mouthpiece for Dostoevsky or as a negative example of how we should *not* speak. Svidrigailov, Ivan, Lisa, Sonya—all are treated not as objects serving the author's plans, but as subjects, ends in themselves, defying any temptation the author may have to fit them into his superior plans.

Of course Dostoevsky did not carry out this impulse of his genius to the full; practical demands of publication, his readers' need for some sort of closure, the need for a plot, led him to cheat on occasion, as when he tries to give a clearly monological, conventional Christian epilogue to *Crime and Punishment* (p. 92). But the reader has long since found that every main character pursues independently his or her "idea," that idea being not anything definable in propositions, overtly stated or covertly believed by the author; just as the author exhibits a kind of disinterestedness in allowing characters their freedom, so there is an unlimited openness of the characters to developments out of their "idea" into unpredictable futures (see especially chapter 3).

It is not that the author's voice is entirely absent in "the novel's" highest manifestations.

The consciousness of the creator of a polyphonic novel is constantly and everywhere present in the novel, and is active in it to the highest degree. But the function of this consciousness and the forms of its activity are different than in the monologic novel: the author's consciousness does not transform others' consciousnesses . . . into objects, and does not give them secondhand and finalizing definitions (pp. 67-68)

The challenge of such views to my own about the author's voice is clear and deep. Again and again I have sought, like most of my Western colleagues, to put into propositional form my summaries of what an *author* is up to, and of how a given character's role *contributes* to the author's overall plan. At times I have even allowed myself to talk as if characters could be reduced to pawns in a huge game of chess of which the author alone knows all the rules. I have in fact never until recently, goaded by Bakhtin (and earlier softened up by Burke), confronted fully the possibility he raises of an ideology that "knows neither the separate thought nor systemic unity" of any kind.

For him [Dostoevsky] the ultimate indivisible unit is not the separate referentially bounded thought, not the proposition, not the assertion, but rather the integral point of view, the integral position of a personality. For him, referential meaning is indissolubly fused with the position of a personality. . . . Dostoevsky—to speak paradoxically—thought not in thoughts but in points of view, consciousnesses, voices (p. 93).

Thus any effort to deal with "objectivity" in the western sense, like mine in *The Rhetoric of Fiction*, will not serve as a reply to Bakhtin's case. I argued, I still think rightly, that there is no such thing as objectivity in fiction, because the author's voice is always with us, whether open or disguised. And I used that argument to defend certain open forms of control, as one legitimate expression of the author's voice. But the challenge of Bakhtin is quite different: granted the legitimacy of a wider variety of technical ways of expressing beliefs and values (or "ideology," including direct commentary), must we not agree that "objectivity" in Bakhtin's quite different sense makes for an art superior in kind to the art of most novelists, regardless of whether their techniques are "objective" or not? Is it not true, as Bakhtin claims, that the techniques for freeing characters from the author's direct control are inherently superior to those that make it easy for the author to dominate?

It should be clear by now that what is at stake, in reading Bakhtin, is far more than the question of how we read, or even how we evaluate, fiction. The effort to transcend the author's voice in this book is not a handbook treatment of the technical means to specific artistic effects; it is rather part of a lifetime inquiry into profound questions about the entire enterprise of thinking about what human life means. How are we to know and to say anything to each other about what our lives mean, without reduction to destructive or irrelevant simplicities? When novelists imagine characters, they imagine worlds that characters inhabit, worlds that are laden with values. Whenever they reduce those multiple worlds to one, the author's, they give a false report, an essentially egotistical distortion that tells lies about the way things are. Bakhtin's ultimate value—full acknowledgment of and participation in a Great Dialogue—is thus not to be addressed as just one more piece of "literary criticism"; even less is it a study of fictional technique or form (in our usual sense of form). It is a philosophical inquiry into our limited ways of mirroring—and improving—our lives.

Its challenge can thus be thought of as addressed to three main groups engaged in quite different projects today. The first group consists of all who think that the way to understand human behavior is to base literal propositions on studies of individuals as isolated countable units. If I am fundamentally constituted as polyphonic, then everything that any scientist, of whatever persuasion, might say about "me," in isolation from the many voices that constitute me and with which I speak, will be *essentially* faulty. Bakhtin is generally careful not to name his main enemies, and I don't think the reason is merely political caution. To name enemies—"scientific materialists," "positivists," "naive Marxists"—would be already to risk freezing the hoped-for dialogue. The "enemy," whoever they may be, are surely somehow *in* us as well as *out there*, and whatever literal propositions they may want to offer us about our lives should not be flatly dismissed but rather heard and incorporated.

The second challenged group would be all those who, like myself, care greatly about the literal formal construction of individual works of art. Does the success or failure of any work, as a whole, really matter as much as the "tonal" or "qualitative" life we live as we read its parts? How a work is put together, or how it falls apart, can lead to interesting inquiry, but are such questions about it really as important as whether it educates us to the best possible avenues to truth? I have often scoffed about modes of criticism that care so little about formal construction that they would be unaffected if the works discussed had been written backward. Yet most of what Bakhtin has to say would not be affected if we discovered new manuscripts that scrambled the order of events, or the handling of flashbacks and foreshadowings, or the manipulations of point of view. It is not linear sequence but the touch of the author at each moment that matters. What we seek is what might be called the best *vertical* structure, rather than a given temporal structure and its technical transformations. If Bakhtin is right, a very great deal of what we western critics have spent our time on is mistaken, or trivial, or both.

A third challenge I have already suggested; it is presented to all those who seek language, and especially the language of literature, as having no reference to any kind of reality other than itself. Bakhtin is not a naive representationalist, but he never leaves any doubt that for him the languages employed in fictions are to be judged as they succeed or fail in representing our "linguistic" life in its highest forms. On this one point there is simply no way to reconcile what he is up to with much of what is said these days in the name of "deconstruction." (On many other points he will reinforce the deconstructionists' critique of naive realisms and individualisms.) His claim is that Dostoevsky's languages do a kind of justice to life itself that other novelists have not achieved. Whether Bakhtin is right or not, his challenge should not be obscured, as has sometimes recently happened, by simply lumping him with other innovations from abroad.

Finally—and here I find my own greatest challenge—he makes enormous claims about history and the nature of intellectual milieus on artistic development. Like other "lumping" historians, he thinks in epochs and dialectical sweeps (though we should remember that for him the *word* "dialectical," like the word "rhetoric," generally has pejorative overtones). Art and artistic techniques have a history, a history inextricably tied to social, political, and economic history. Although he is no economic determinist, he still sees novels as constructing "chronotopes," pictures of timed-places and placed-times that would make any effort like mine to do an ahistorical treatment of forms absurd. At times he even seems to suggest that the history of literature progresses; certainly "the novel" has progressed, and he often implies that it continues to do so, though never with any clear statement of what it might be progressing *toward*. After all, to *state* the future would belie its openness, in direct contradiction of the central point of this critic whom Caryl Emerson has called "the apostle of the next chance."

My sense of Bakhtin's unique value does not, of course, leave me with a vision of perfection. To my taste the repetitiousness, disorganization, and reliance on neologisms that Emerson describes in her Preface often impose unnecessary obstacles. He often seems to lapse into a hortatory mode that has little to do with the critical work in hand. Most seriously, his failure to settle into sustained study of any one of Dostoevsky's works and his persistently high level of generality often make me impatient for more of the sort of analysis he is capable of. Whenever an author dwells at great length on general theories about huge lumps of literature called "the novel" or even about smaller piles called "Dostoevsky's works," without settling into detailed efforts at exemplification, I grow restless. The temptation to resist becomes especially great when the generalizations are vague, as they often are in Bakhtin.

But every thinker must pay a price for every virtue, and I find that most of what look like weaknesses are the inevitable consequences of his strengths. If he is "vague," so is every thinker who attempts to approach difficult and general concepts that stand for ultimate and thus ultimately elusive concerns. What is vague from a hostile point of view is wonderfully "suggestive" when we consider it from inside the enterprise. If he is repetitive, why should he not be, when what he is saying will surely not be understood the first, or third, or tenth time? When talking about truths like these, once said is not enough said, because no statement can ever come close enough and no amount of repetition can ever overstate the importance of elusive yet ultimate truth. (See also Emerson's comments on the impossibility of true repetition.) If he creates huge heaps of works and calls them "the novel," leaving out of the heap many works that you and I call novels, why, so does everyone who tries to think not literally but analogically or dialogically.

In any case, I can think of no critic of recent years—and of course he is recent only as translated for us—who more effectively performs that essential task of all criticism: prodding readers to think again about critical standards as applied to the various canons and anti-canons those standards lead to. It is true that for most of us in the West, Dostoevsky himself needs no act of rehabilitation or defense of the kind that was needed in the Soviet Union during most of Bakhtin's lifetime. What requires defense, for us, is the very idea of superlative genius and of a criticism that claims to demonstrate, with reasoned discourse rather than mere assertion, the grounds for greatness. Even if he had written nothing else—and my brief account of this book does great injustice to his astonishingly broad enterprise—his passionately reasoned celebration of what the novel can do would place our crisis-ridden criticism in his debt.

Editor's Preface
Caryl Emerson

Bakhtin's book on Dostoevsky has a curious history. The text translated here (*Problemy poetiki Dostoevskogo*, Moscow, 1963) is the much-expanded second edition of a book by Bakhtin which appeared more than thirty years earlier under the title *Problems of Dostoevsky's Art* (*Problemy tvorchestva Dostoevskogo*, Leningrad, 1929). From Bakhtin's personal correspondence we know that he had been at work on a study of Dostoevsky since at least 1921;[1] in 1922, a Petrograd journal carried the notice that a monograph by Bakhtin on Dostoevsky was being prepared for publication.[2] Publication came only seven years later, however, in 1929. The book caused considerable stir in literary circles, occasioning a long and positive review by the high-ranking Bolshevik intellectual Anatoly Lunacharsky, then Minister of Education.[3] But 1929 was a threshold time for Soviet politics and for the politicization of Russian life in general. The very year the book appeared, Bakhtin was arrested, probably in connection with his activity as a member of the underground church. He escaped assignment to a death camp on the plea of poor health (a chronic bone disease that eventually led to the amputation of a leg), and was sentenced instead to exile in distant Kazakhstan.

For thirty years Bakhtin lived and worked in relative obscurity, first in Kazakhstan and then in Saransk and Moscow. In the 1950s, on the other side of the Stalinist night, Bakhtin's 1929 Dostoevsky book was rediscovered by a group of young literary scholars in Moscow. They also discovered, to their astonishment, that its author was still alive, teaching and chairing the Department of Russian and World Literature at the University of Saransk. They begged Bakhtin to rework the book for a second edition. Bakhtin, always magnificently cavalier with respect to his manuscripts, was not especially interested; only the insistent pressure of this new and devoted Bakhtin Circle finally persuaded him to take up the task. In 1961, Bakhtin made some provocative notes in preparation for the revision; these survived, were published in 1977, and are translated in an Appendix to this volume. In 1963, after some ominous delays in publishing houses, the second edition appeared, and Bakhtin was back in print in the Soviet Union. The publication of other long-delayed manuscripts followed.

At the time of writing, *Problemy poetiki Dostoevskogo* is in its fourth Soviet edition (1979). These subsequent reissuings of the text are essentially unchanged.

Bakhtin confronts the translator of his work with many intriguing questions, and some of these are relevant to readers of Bakhtin as well. What sort of prose is written by a man who for many years could hope to publish at best only a fraction of his work? What type of book is produced by a writer who gave away his manuscripts to his friends, lost track of his notebooks—by a writer, in short, for whom "being an author" meant something quite different than it means to most? Bakhtin's very themes generate a whole series of self-conscious and self-reflexive questions. How should we understand an author whose key ideas concern the nature of understanding? What kind of dialogue do we establish with a writer whose key idea is dialogue? And finally, how does a translator find equivalences for an author who believes that two utterances can never be, and must never be, equivalent? This Preface discusses possible approaches to these questions—although, indeed, raising such questions is perhaps as valuable as answering them. One place to start would be a consideration of the genre in which Bakhtin worked.

This question of genre has special relevance for English-speaking audiences. There is a widespread feeling that Bakhtin—like the baggy-monster novelists he so admires—is indifferent to form, that he is a thinker whose greatness is in the *idea* and most definitely not in the exposition of the idea. But the idea and its exposition are not easily separated in Bakhtin. Much of the compelling quality of his voice has to do with the peculiar organizing principles of his prose, and these are perhaps best approached through a disclaimer: Bakhtin did not write "essays." The formal structure and streamlining of the critical essay, at least as we know it in the English-speaking world, is simply not his mode. He is often at his most provocative in the tiny fragment, in his jottings for future projects not yet worked out or beyond hope of publication; on the other hand, his longer worked-out pieces seem loosely structured, even luxuriously inefficient. Available evidence suggests[4] that Bakhtin did not conceive even his published books as concise, self-sufficient theoretical statements. He thought, read, wrote down what he thought, and moved on; he was not in the habit of reworking his prose, because the important ideas always came around again in new contexts. Manuscripts themselves (this is by now legendary) were left to rot in damp cellars or were smoked away when cigarette papers ran out. Bakhtin could be so careless with the individual inscription of an idea because he seems to have reprocessed the same body of questions all his life. His works in print can in fact be seen as ripped-out segments of one vast philosophical project, begun in 1920, on the nature of language, literature, and moral responsibility. That huge text was written at various times, and in the various languages of the time; literary, philosophical, Marxist, even, when necessary, in the Stalinist rhetoric of the First Five-Year Plan.[5] It constituted a basically religious quest into the nature of the Word. How that word was made flesh brings us to another general comment bearing on Bakhtin's prose: his understanding of dialogue, and in particular that category of dialogue called translation.

It must be said at the outset that nowhere does Bakhtin offer us a theory of translation. Theory, in the quantitative sense of a "technology," is not to be found in his work. But what can be said with certainty is that for Bakhtin, to translate was never to betray; on the contrary, translation, broadly conceived, was for him the essence of all human communication. Crossing language boundaries was perhaps the most fundamental of human acts. Bakhtin's writing is permeated by awe at the multiplicity of languages he hears. These are not just the bluntly distinct national languages—Russian, English, French—that exist as the normative material of dictionaries and grammars, but also the scores of different "languages" that exist simultaneously within a single culture and a single speaking community. In fact, Bakhtin viewed the boundaries between national languages as only one extreme on a continuum; at the other extreme, translation processes were required for one social group to understand another in the same city, for children to understand parents in the same family, for one day to understand the next.[6] These stratifications of language, Bakhtin argued, do not exclude one another; they intersect and overlap, pulling words into various gravitational fields and casting specific light and shadow. Living discourse, unlike a dictionary, is always in flux and in rebellion against its own rules. Bakhtin delighted in the fact that procedures for conveying meaning were forever multiplying —and that the nonreducible individual had such a unique "speech energy."[7] "It might even seem that the very word 'language' loses all meaning in this process," he writes, "for apparently there is no single plane on which all these 'languages' might be juxtaposed to one another."[8] Each language embodies its own specific worldview, its own system of values. And this means that every speaking subject speaks something of a foreign language to everyone else. It also means that every speaking subject has more than one native language at his disposal. To understand another person at any given moment, therefore, is to come to terms with meaning on the boundary between one's own and another's language: to translate.

What happens in translation, therefore, is not an exception to our everyday practice of communication through direct and indirect discourse; it could even be seen as a dramatic illustration of these processes. This celebration of difference in language is a bit awkward for a translator—who inevitably must, at some level, be concerned with equivalence. That very concept is somehow incompatible with Bakhtin's insights into language.

One of Bakhtin's major premises, in fact, might be called the vitality of nonequivalence. Multilingual environments, he argued, liberate man by opening up a gap between things and their labels;[9] analogously, the novel is more free than the epic because novelistic heroes are never equivalent to their plots.[10] Nonequivalence is not a matter for despair but is rather the impulse to life. In fact, the interaction of two different, discrete systems is the only way a true *event* ever comes to pass.[11] Bakhtin was not sympathetic to the ultimate fusion or erasing of differences. He had little use for grand nineteenth-century schemes of philosophical evolution toward a disembodied truth. For it must be remembered that for Bakhtin "dialogic" does not mean "dialectic"; his universe owes much more to Kant than to Hegel.[12] Consider, for example, this note jotted down in 1970-71:

Dialogue and dialectics. Take a dialogue and remove the voices . . . remove the intonations . . . carve out abstract concepts and judgments from living words and responses, cram everything into one abstract consciousness—and that's how you get dialectics.[13]

In place of the comfortable patterns of synthesis and *Aufhebung*, Bakhtin posits a dualistic universe of *permanent* dialogue. Life in language is in fact dependent upon the preservation of a gap. Two speakers must not, and never do, completely understand each other; they must remain only partially satisfied with each other's replies, because the continuation of dialogue is in large part dependent on neither party knowing exactly what the other means. Thus true communication never makes languages sound the same, never erases boundaries, never pretends to a perfect fit. In a fragment written near the end of his life, Bakhtin in fact compared understanding itself to a sort of obligatorily imperfect translation:

> Understanding cannot be understood as emotional empathy, or as the placing of oneself in another's place (the loss of one's own place). This is required only for the peripheral aspects of understanding. Understanding cannot be understood as translation from someone else's language into one's own language.[14]

The ideal here is contiguity without fusion. Equivalence, too, is a threshold phenomenon.

Thus are all students of Bakhtin sensitized to the peculiar challenges confronting his translators. Where should the necessary strangeness or otherness of the translated text be reflected? Translation always involves creating a hierarchy of fidelities. To what does one wish to be faithful? What are the operative constraints, what can in fact be preserved in a given transfer, and what should be not so much preserved as reinterpreted? It is important to bear in mind that translation is not merely a matter of moving one text into another text, that is, it is not a language shift along one plane; it is rather a triangular activity, always performed for and in the light of a third party, the intended audience. I suspect that the audience Bakhtin had in mind was more a listening than a reading public. His works seem designed less to be read than to be overheard, in a sort of transcribed speech. And one is in fact surprised to discover how comfortably Bakhtin can be read aloud. He has that generous inefficiency characteristic of certain oral genres. Like an epic singer, he presents his concepts in formulaic groupings of words; by italicizing key phrases he seems to emphasize an almost spoken accent. His prose is sprinkled with conversational markers, and he is at times capricious with punctuation. Sentences of enormous and undifferentiated length pile up. These labyrinthine sentences are, however, built out of a rather small lexicon. Ideas (words, phrases, whole sentences) seem to recur in patterns at astonishingly short intervals. And yet one seeks in vain for the conventional "technical term." At one pole Bakhtin invests everyday words (such as *vstrecha* [meeting], or *doroga* [road]) with an italicized and almost metaphysical significance; at the other pole he exploits the rich capacity of Russian to build abstract nouns by coining, or calquing from the German or the Greek, ingenious but almost untranslatable neologisms. Among the more notorious are *raznorechie* [heteroglossia], *vnenakhodimost'* [the condition of being located external to], *inojazychie* [other-languagedness], *raznomirnost'* [the condition of containing many separate and different worlds]. This has led some translators, in desperation and in desire to pin down the term, simply to embed the poorly translated Russian original within the English text inside apologetic parentheses, thus turning the translation into a sort of hybrid where the implied readers are bilingual, competent to understand the translation only if they do not need to use it.

Such wordplay and burdened syntax is in part the stylistic influence of German post-Kantian philosophy, especially noticeable in Bakhtin's prose of his earliest and latest periods. But there are other reasons as well. It seems, first, that Bakhtin modeled his syntax on the utterance and not the sentence. The distinction is his own: a sentence is a unit of language, while an utterance is a unit of communication.[15] Sentences are relatively complete thoughts existing within a single speaker's speech, and the pauses between them are "grammatical," matters of punctuation. Utterances, on the other hand, are impulses, and cannot be so normatively transcribed; their boundaries are marked only by a change of speech subject. Bakhtin never really made a distinction between casual and formally inscribed utterances, nor—more importantly—between speaking and writing.[16] Syntax and punctuation within the utterance can be complex and whimsical; periods and commas serve more to mark intonation than to rank components of a sentence hierarchically or to signify completion. Bakhtin's sentences, in fact, have that congenial shapelessness of a voice expecting at any moment to be interrupted.[17]

This is not the sort of critical prose that finds a ready-made vehicle in English. Readers, and translators, are therefore apt to treat it carelessly, perhaps even to recommend that Bakhtin's texts be edited, simplified, or condensed.[18] Such an approach to prose (both artistic and nonartistic) is in fact rather common, and has to do, of course, with the general difficulty of defining "prose equivalents." The translator of poetry can work with lines, verses, stanzas, rhymes, but workers in prose have no such easily discernible translation units. A paraphrase, in prose, of a poetic text is not usually considered adequate; but a paraphrase of a prose text is often considered a good (that is, a readable) translation. As one theorist has put it, it is "easier for the (careless) prose translator to consider content as *separable* from form."[19]

With Bakhtin the matter is even more complicated, for he writes not just *in* words but *about* the word. He places high value on the irreplaceable specificity of the utterance—including, one may presume, his own. Language, Bakhtin insists, is not a product or detachable attribute of a person; it is an energy negotiating between a person's inner consciousness and the outer world.[20] How we talk, or write, is a trace not only of how we think but of how we interact. It is of some importance, then, to take Bakhtin's style seriously. And with that purpose in mind we might consider the possible functions of repetition and neologism in his voice.

On the issue of repetition, Bakhtin is his own best counsel. His entire understanding of the word, and of the specificity of the utterance, invalidates the very concept of repetition.[21] Nothing "recurs"; the same word over again might accumulate, reinforce, perhaps parody what came before it, but it cannot be the same word if it is in a different place. Repetitiveness is not repetitiousness. The phenomenon is perhaps better understood in the linguistic category of "redundancy," that is, as the surplus necessary for a certain mode, or force, of communication.[22] Bakhtin's nonessayistic style makes use of repetition almost as music makes use of the refrain, to bind the work together, provide tonal background, produce a cumulative effect. The benefits are less strictly semantic than auditory. "How often," Bakhtin writes, "we use words we do not need for their meaning, or repeat one and the same word or phrase, only to have a material carrier for some necessary intonation . . ."[23]

Bakhtin's new coinages serve another but related purpose. If they at times seem ponderous, this could be because ordinary language does not offer Bakhtin the categories of discourse he seeks. Thus he creates new words, and impresses old words into new service. These new categories must somehow be brought to saturate the text, to become a generic norm for him and a sort of background signal for his audience. Bakhtin's peculiar redundancy provides that neutral conceptual surface against which he makes some of his most stunning stylistic moves. Against a sea of abstract nouns and oft-repeated categories, Bakhtin will suddenly cast a single palpable image—driving-shaft, clamp, suck out, wedge in, swallow up—a graphic illustration of the sensuous body of language.[24] The ratio between this sudden vibrant image and the background sea, with its peculiar density, is crucial to Bakhtin's intonation.

In this translation I have tried to re-speak both redundancy and neologisms, with the same alternating effects of slackness and sudden tension that characterize the original. This principle established itself only gradually in my "hierarchy of fidelities." My first drafts were in fact quite free with such surface features as punctuation, word order, excessive reiteration of terms. But it became quickly clear that these were not surface features at all. Bakhtin is a passionately contiguous writer, one for whom the "linkage obligation" is extremely strong. New ideas are introduced slowly, their territory unhurriedly filled in, and the message seems to be relayed along the outer edges of these interlocking words. I thus strove to retain wherever possible his linear sequence of ideas. Where that was not possible, I retained at least his distinction between inner and outer in a sentence, between words at the beginnings/ends of a phrase and those in the middle. To reproduce in English the shape of Bakhtin's sentences is a delicate task, since English word-order options are rather limited in comparison with the highly inflected and more flexible Russian. Thus the "lexical equivalents" of words came to be chosen in a special way: out of the many dictionary possibilities, the correct meaning was one that permitted the basic order and density of Bakhtin's phrases to be preserved.

Why, we might ask, should these external features of punctuation, sentence length, and sequence of images be so critical in a piece of expository prose? There is the argument recently made popular by Stanley Fish, that sentences are events that unfold in the reader and therefore the *order* of impressions, the linear processing of information within it, is crucial to understanding.[25] In Bakhtin's case, however, there are deeper and more energetic structures at work that shape his utterance. Above all else, Bakhtin is sensitive to authority in discourse: who is speaking, when, how, to whom, through how many intermediaries—and how these levels of authority are represented in hybrid constructions. His own prose, I should add, is often a fabric of such hybrids. In one sentence he will represent direct speech, indirect speech, quasi-direct speech, his own voice interwoven with the voices and arguments of his opponents and fellow-travelers. Bakhtin's own term for this is "voice interference." And this has some relevance for translators. If—to take a simple example—a long sentence is broken up in translation, it becomes less relativized by its surrounding clauses and rings more authoritatively in the text. Ironies do not carry so well across periods as across commas. Alter punctuation, eliminate repetitions, radically adjust the sequence of phrases, and the dialogue is scrambled, the balance and juxtaposition of authorities within it is undone. In dialogic writing, ideas grow out of contexts; the shape of a sentence can govern the shape of the response.

This is "shape" in the most physical sense. Bakhtin *visualizes* voices, he senses their proximity and interaction as bodies. A voice, Bakhtin everywhere tells us, is not just words or ideas strung together: it is a "semantic position," a point of view on the world, it is one personality orienting itself among other personalities within a limited field. Hence Bakhtin's partiality to spatial markers and metaphors: situation, positioning, orientation [*ustanovka*], point of view, field of vision. How a voice sounds is a function of where it is and what it can "see"; its orientation is measured by the field of responses it evokes. This understanding of voice lies at the base of Bakhtin's non-referential—that is, *responsive*—theory of language. An utterance responds both to others without, and others embedded within itself.

This sensitivity to balancing authorities or voices in a text is developed in Bakhtin to an excruciating degree. It is connected, certainly, with his larger concepts of polyphony and heteroglossia, and is at the core of his dialogism. We might explore this aspect of Bakhtin's prose through his comments on rhetoric—more precisely, in a note on the role of rhetoric in literature that is itself probably a hidden polemic with the Russian Formalist critic Viktor Vinogradov:

In rhetoric there are the unconditionally right and the unconditionally guilty; there is total victory, and annihilation of the opponent. In dialogue, annihilation of the opponent also annihilates the very dialogic sphere in which discourse lives. . . . This sphere is very fragile and easily destroyed (the slightest violence is sufficient, the slightest reference to authority, etc.).[26]

Bakhtin's own "references to authority" in the texts signed by him are very instructive. He does not invest the dialogic sphere of his own work with authoritative presences. When he cites other critics—as, say, in the first chapter of *Problems of Dostoevsky's Poetics*—he does so at length, and lets each voice sound fully. He understands that the frame is always in the power of the framer, and that there is an outrageous privilege in the power to cite others.[27] Thus Bakhtin's footnotes rarely serve to narrow down debate by discrediting totally, or (on the other hand) by conferring exclusive authority. They might identify, expand, illustrate, but they do not pull rank on the body of the text—and are thus more in the nature of a marginal gloss than an authoritative footnote.[28] Bakhtin's impulse to keep his texts open had its effect on the packaging of the text as well. He explicitly opened an early article (1924) on the disclaimer that "we have freed our work from the superfluous ballast of quotations and footnotes," as they had "no direct methodological significance" for his project and "were not needed by the competent reader."[29]

In a climate that would soon require, in the most innocuous publication, an obligatory reference to the authority of Lenin or Stalin, such a disclaimer was welcome indeed. What does it mean to be a "competent reader" of Bakhtin? Surely it means to hear a dialogue, perhaps even to recognize the major voices embedded in it, but it must be a dialogue where no voice is done the "slightest violence." At first this might seem paradoxical, given Bakhtin's fondness for military metaphors. In his texts words are always competing, doing battle, winning and losing territory. Such imagery in part reflects the Soviet Marxist rhetoric of the Stalin years, resurrecting (as it were) class struggle in the realm of discourse itself; it also reflects the reality of Soviet life, so permeated by aggression both domestic and foreign. But this "violence" among languages—although deadly serious—is ultimately a *happy* war. Here Bakhtin resembles his beloved Rabelais:

when Friar John lops off heads in the monastery vineyard, we see all the bloody parts but no one seems hurt. Bakhtin's language-violence is carnivalized. So while voices "do battle" they do not die out—that is, no authority is established once and for all. Bakhtin's prose style, I suggest, is subtly tied to this sensitivity toward coexisting authorities in the written word, and to his insistence on the inadequacy of any final hierarchy or resolution.

This leads us to the more general issue of Bakhtin's relationship to the authors and texts he explores, which might serve as a summary of the translation issues raised in this Preface. How Bakhtin read Dostoevsky and Rabelais gives us a clue for our own reading of Bakhtin, and an insight into the sort of coherence Bakhtin valued in a literary text. For there is indeed some similarity between the style and structure of Bakhtin's writing, and his perception of the style of his favorite novelists. Bakhtin, the great singer of the novel, does not do the traditional "close reading" of novels as texts. He does not analyze individual novels as finished wholes; in fact, the larger the work, the more fragmented Bakhtin's treatment of it.[30] Many have noted this, most recently Donald Fanger:

Nowhere [Fanger writes] does he analyze a single novel thoroughly, or seek to account either for all it contains or for the sense of its shape. He refers frequently to the fates of individual characters, yet seems to deny these any controlling meaning . . . Thus, though he posits a formal unity in Dostoevsky's practice, he defines it only negatively and approximately.[31]

Closural principles, tending as they do toward the monologic, seem to elude Bakhtin; the occasional reading that disappoints us usually rests on the way he reads *ends.*[32] Openings, closings, the specific organization of parts and their necessary presence as part of a whole are all of secondary interest to Bakhtin. When he does do "close readings," of *Eugene Onegin, Little Dorrit, Virgin Soil,*[33] he focuses on the subtle shifts of meaning or intonation within a single line or paragraph. What he notices are the smaller shapes: voice zones, shifts in speakers, the overlapping boundaries between various characters' fields of vision. The larger shape might be absent, but the smaller shape is crucial.

This mode of critical reading has relevance, I suggest, for Bakhtin's own compositions. In 1961 he made a number of notes for his reworking of the Dostoevsky book. He summed up the novelist's major discoveries in the realm of the word, of which one was "the *depiction* (or rather the re-creation) of the *self-developing* idea (inseparable from personality)."[34] Ten years later, commenting on the forthcoming 1975 publication of his essays, he applied the same phrase to his own creative work, in a rather rare self-reflexive moment.

The proposed collection of my articles is unified by one theme in various stages of its development.

The unity of the becoming (developing) idea. This is the source of a certain internal *open-endedness* in many of my thoughts. But I do not want to turn a shortcoming into a virtue: in these pieces there is much external open-endedness, an open-endedness not of the thought itself but of its expression and exposition. It is sometimes difficult to separate one open-endedness from another. . . .[35]

Bakhtin overlaps his own themes here in a curious way. Internal open-endedness is part of his theme and external open-endedness a feature of its exposition. He is hard put to separate them, and this is significant. It has something to do with his understanding of wholeness. Bakhtin's very interesting ideas on the nature of unity and closure lie outside the scope of this essay,[36] but suffice it to say that for Bakhtin "the whole" is not a finished entity; it is always a *relationship*. An aesthetic object—or for that matter, any aspect of life—acquires wholeness only when an individual assumes a concrete attitude toward it.[37] Thus, the whole can never be finalized and set aside; when a whole is realized, it is by definition already open to change. Bakhtin has this in mind when, in *Problems of Dostoevsky's Poetics*, he juxtaposes Dostoevskian and Aristotelian catharsis. The catharsis finalizing Dostoevsky's novels consists in the realization that

. . . nothing conclusive has yet taken place in the world, the ultimate word of the world and about the world has not yet been spoken, the world is open and free, everything is still in the future and will always be in the future (p. 166).

That one aspect of Bakhtin's style most inseparable from his personality is the *developing idea*. Its subtle shifts, redundancies, self-quotations—ultimately, its open-endedness—is the genre in which, and with which, he worked. To translate Bakhtin, I suggest, is therefore not only to translate the ideas (they can be paraphrased) but also to reproduce the sound of the open-ended, self-developing idea. This would be his "conversation in progress," his dialogue about dialogue, his interlocution with readers who have still to respond.

NOTES

1. In a letter to Matvey Kagan (18 January 1922) Bakhtin writes: "I am now writing a work on Dostoevsky, which I hope to finish very soon . . ." See "M. M. Bakhtin i M. I. Kagan (po materialam semeinogo arkhiva): publikatsija K. Nevel'skoi" ([M. M. Bakhtin and M. I. Kagan (materials from a family archive): a publication of K. Nevelskaya], in *Pamiat'* No. 4 (Paris: YMCA, 1979-81), p. 263.

2. Ibid., p. 279, fn. 37. The notice appeared in *Zhizn' iskusstva* [The Life of Art], Petrograd, November 1922. This 1922 manuscript has not survived, so we do not know its relationship to the 1929 published text.

3. Lunacharsky's 1929 review, "O 'mnogogolosnosti' Dostoevskogo" [On Dostoevsky's

'Multi-voicedness'] was later widely anthologized. The review is itself reviewed by Bakhtin in chapter 1 of the revised edition of the Dostoevsky book (see this volume, pp. 32-36).

4. I am indebted to Michael Holquist and Katerina Clark for sharing their ideas and early drafts of several chapters from their forthcoming *Life and Works of Mikhail Bakhtin*. The "vast philosophical project," which Holquist suggests entitling "The Architectonics of Answerability," was begun during the Nevel period (1918-20). It was to contain four parts, of which only portions of the first and second have survived: a preface on the nature of moral responsibility, and a discussion of the relationship between authors and the characters they create. These texts, "Iskusstvo i otvetstvennost'" [Art and Answerability] and "Avtor i geroi v esteticheskoi deiatel'nosti" [Author and Hero in Aesthetic Activity] were published posthumously in M. M. Bakhtin, *Estetika slovesnogo tvorchestva* (Moscow: Iskusstvo, 1979), and a translation is forthcoming from The University of Texas Press. In English until then, see the fine discussion by Michael Holquist, "The Politics of Representation," in *Allegory and Representation: Selected Papers from the English Institute, 1979-80*, ed. Stephen J. Greenblatt (Baltimore: The Johns Hopkins Press, 1981), pp. 163-183.

5. Writing one's "word" in various different languages—in order to pass the censor, avoid arrest, or simply be paid for one's work so one can live—is of course commonplace for authors in unfree societies. For the first half of his life Bakhtin was desperately poor, and hoped for a position in a scholarly institution that would permit him to support and establish himself. He sought acceptable packaging for his ideas in all the discourses and genres of his (increasingly restrictive) epoch. A good example of Bakhtin in the mode of Stalinist rhetoric are his prefaces to two volumes of a 1929 edition of Tolstoy's Collected Works (volume #11 on the plays, and #13 on *Resurrection*). Bakhtin seems to have absorbed almost instantaneously the language of his time, already making reference (possibly doublevoiced) to the "kulak nature of Tolstoyanism" (M. Bakhtin, "Predislovie," in L. Tolstoy, *Polnoe sobranie khudozhestvennykh proizvedenii*, ed. Khalabaev and Eikhenbaum [Moscow-Leningrad, 1929], vol. #11, p. x).

6. See his essay "Discourse in the Novel," in M. M. Bakhtin, *The Dialogic Imagination*, ed. Michael Holquist, trans. Caryl Emerson and Michael Holquist (Austin: The University of Texas Press, 1981), pp. 288-93.

7. Bakhtin's delight, even awe, at the nonreducible individual and his utterance had nothing mystical about it, however. Throughout his life he sought material and even physiological explanations for the uniquely human phenomenon of verbal communication. For a discussion of Bakhtin's connection with the well-known biologists and physiologists of his day, Ivan Kanaev and Aleksei Ukhtomsky, see Michael Holquist, "Answering as Authoring: Bakhtin's Translinguistics," *Critical Inquiry*, December, 1983, vol. 10, no. 2.

8. "Discourse in the Novel," p. 291.

9. The case is made in "From the Prehistory of Novelistic Discourse," in *The Dialogic Imagination*, pp. 51-83.

10. This is Bakhtin's answer to Lukács in "Epic and Novel," in *The Dialogic Imagination*, pp. 31-40.

11. For a discussion of the Russian word *sobytie* [event] in Bakhtin's peculiar use of it, see this volume, p. 6, fn. a.

12. For Bakhtin, the Dostoevskian novel was a profoundly non-Hegelian entity. An eloquent development of this position is found in chapter 1, during Bakhtin's critique of Engelhardt's dialectical approach [p. 26]: "Each novel presents an opposition, which is never canceled out dialectically, of many consciousnesses, and they do not merge in the unity of an evolving spirit . . . Within the limits of the novel the heroes' worlds interact by means of the event, but these interrelationships . . . are the last thing that can be reduced to thesis, antithesis, and synthesis." Somewhat later Bakhtin elaborates [p. 26]: "The unified, dialectically evolving spirit, understood in Hegelian terms, can give rise to nothing but a philosophical monologue."

13. "Iz zapisei 1970-1971 godov" (From Jottings of 1970-1971], in M. M. Bakhtin, *Estetika slovesnogo tvorchestva*, p. 352.

14. Ibid., p. 346.

15. See "Problemy rechevykh zhanrov" [The Problem of Speech Genres], in *Estetika*, pp. 251-52.

16. Bakhtin often modifies the phrase "speaking subject" with the phrase "writing subject" in parentheses, and he writes (or speaks) not of periods after statements, but of *pauses*. See, for example, in "Problemy rechevykh zhanrov," pp. 251 and 275.

17. This should not surprise us. Orality is of necessity a present-tense experience in time, and presumes a high degree of shared context with one's audience. In Bakhtin's world the speaking voice is inevitably dialogic; it calls up a response and creates an immediate community. Anything else is a performance, a recitation, what Bakhtin calls "footlights."

18. See, for example, Gary Saul Morson's early review (still among the best) of the 1975 Russian edition of Bakhtin's essays: "The Heresiarch of Meta," *PTL*, vol. 3, No. 3, October 1978: 407-27. ". . . Baxtin . . . resembles the early Formalists in playfulness and inconsistency. Ideas are often toys for him; he is extravagant in his expression of them, and he could have used a good editor" [p. 409].

19. From the excellent discussion of this problem in Susan Bassnett-McGuire, *Translation Studies* (New York: Methuen, 1980), pp. 109-20. The quotation occurs on p. 110.

20. See V. N. Vološinov, *Marxism and the Philosophy of Language*, trans. Ladislav Matejka and I. R. Titunik (New York: Seminar Press, 1973), p. 81: "People do not 'accept' their native language; it is in their native language that they first reach awareness."

21. During a discussion of the problem of the text, Bakhtin makes a distinction between what he calls a "natural singularity" (say, a fingerprint, which is unique but which can be mechanically reproduced indefinitely), and the semiotic unrepeatability of a text. A text, too, can be mechanically reproduced (for example, reprinted), but "a reproduction of the text by the subject (a return to him, a repeat reading, a new performance, quotation) is a new, unrepeatable event in the life of the text, a new link in the historical chain of speech communion." See "Problema teksta v lingvistike, filologii i drugikh gumanitarnykh naukakh"/ The Problem of the Text in Linguistics, Philology and other Humanities Studies/, in *Estetika*, p. 284. Further along in the essay Bakhtin is even more explicit (287): "Within one and the same utterance, a sentence may be repeated (a repetition, a self-quotation, or even accidentally), but each time this is a new part of the utterance, since its place and function in the utterance as a whole is changed."

For an (unreliable) translation of this essay, see M. Bakhtin, "The Problem of the Text," *Soviet Studies in Literature*, Winter 1977-78/vol. XIV, #1: 3-33.

22. See the good discussion by Susan Rubin Suleiman, "Redundancy and the 'Readable' Text," *Poetics Today*, vol. 1:3 (1980): 119-21. In ordinary and literary language, she points out, redundancy has a negative connotation: it means something superfluous, excessive, better done without. For linguists and information theorists, however, redundancy is a positive term; all language is necessarily redundant because communication never takes place under optimal conditions. To this I would add that each voice has its own pattern of redundancy; to discover that pattern is one of the first tasks of a translator.

23. "K metodologii gumanitarnikh nauk" [Toward a Methodology for the Humanities], in *Estetika*, p. 369.

24. An example occurs early in *Problems of Dostoevsky's Poetics* [p. 7], the sudden insertion of *skrepa* [clamp] into a paragraph of otherwise abstract nouns: "It follows that ordinary pragmatic links at the level of the plot (whether of an objective or psychological order) are insufficient in Dostoevsky's world: such links presuppose, after all, that characters have become objects, fixed elements in the author's design; such links bind and combine finalized images of people in the unity of a monologically perceived and understood world; there is no presumption of a plurality of equally valid consciousnesses, each with its own

world. In Dostoevsky's novels, the ordinary pragmatics of the plot play a secondary role and perform special and unusual functions. The ultimate clamps that hold his novelistic world together are of a different sort entirely . . ."

25. See his "Literature in the Reader: Affective Stylistics" [1970], reprinted in Stanley Fish, *Is There a Text in This Class?* (Cambridge, MA: Harvard University Press, 1980), pp. 21-67. Translators are inevitably disadvantaged here, of course, for the syntactic conventions of a target language might not be remotely compatible with those of a source language. When such conventions do overlap (as is the case with Russian and English), they should be a factor in seeking prose equivalence.

26. "Iz zapisei 1970-1971 godov," in *Estetika*, p. 355.

27. As Nina Perlina has pointed out, "Bakhtin did not trust the validity of an isolated quotation, cut off from the original and then re-accented and structurally transformed under the pressure of a new nonhomogeneous context." See her "Bakhtin-Medvedev-Voloshinov: An Apple of Discourse," *University of Ottawa Quarterly*, January-March 1983, vol. 53, no. 1.

28. For a fine discussion of textual apparatus in terms of authority, see Lawrence Lipking, "The Marginal Gloss," *Critical Inquiry* 3, No. 4 (Summer 1977):609-55. According to Lipking, the gloss originally reaffirmed the relation of the part to the whole in a world perceived as One Text, and testified to "an unfolding of parallel, equally-authoritative meanings into infinity" (p. 622). By the end of the seventeenth century, the gloss had lost its integrative authority. As texts disintegrated into many equally valid readings, glosses were in effect secularized; so-called "facts" were relegated to footnotes, which then became gestures of submission by the author to pre-established authorities.

Bakhtin's ideal "apparatus" would in fact probably be the gloss. Scholarly footnotes, by contrast, bolster a text by invoking a higher authority, and are intended to provide an authoritative frame or scaffolding upon which one's own word rests. Such a frame is quite alien to Bakhtin's intonation.

29. In the introductory paragraphs of "Problema soderzhaniia, materiala i formy v slovesnom khudozhestvennom tvorchestve" [The Problem of Content, Material and Form in Verbal Art], in M. M. Bakhtin, *Voprosy literatury i estetiki* (Moscow: Khudozhestvennaia literatura, 1975), pp. 6-7.

30. Tiny "Bobok," as a carnivalized menippea, is exhaustively analyzed, but *The Brothers Karamazov* and *The Idiot* are dealt with only episodically and in passing. Nowhere are the great authoritative presences—Father Zosima, Myshkin—given the comprehensive integration they require. For some reasons why this might be so, see Nina Perlina, "Bakhtin and Buber: The Concept of Dialogic Discourse," forthcoming in *Studies in Twentieth Century Literature*, vol. IX, no. 1, 1984.

31. Donald Fanger, "Dostoevsky as Contemporary," paper delivered in Venice, 26-28 October 1981 and published in the proceedings of the Fondazione Cini.

It should be pointed out that Bakhtin does not conceal his reluctance to address this issue in the Dostoevsky book. He closes his note "From the Author" with the words: "Even in this new edition, the book cannot pretend to a complete analysis of the questions it raises, especially questions as complex as that of *the whole* in a polyphonic novel] " [p. 4].

32. See, for example, Bakhtin's unimaginative interpretation of the Epilogue to *Crime and Punishment*, which he calls a "conventionally monologic ending" [this volume, p. 39].

33. These readings can be found in the following essays, translated in *The Dialogic Imagination*: of Pushkin's *Eugene Onegin*, in "From the Prehistory of Novelistic Discourse," pp. 43-49; of Dickens' *Little Dorrit*, in "Discourse in the Novel," pp. 302-08; of Turgenev's *Virgin Soil*, ibid., pp. 317-20.

34. "Toward a Reworking of the Dostoevsky Book," Appendix II in this volume, p. 284.

35. "Iz zapisei 1970-1971 godov," in *Estetika*, p. 360.

36. In chapter 3 of the Dostoevsky book ("The Idea in Dostoevsky") Bakhtin gives a critique of monologism, and through it we can glimpse his complicated attitude toward unity

and closure. The search for a unified truth, he insists, need not be carried on under repressive monologic conditions. "It is quite possible," Bakhtin writes, "to imagine and postulate a unified truth that requires a plurality of consciousnesses, one that cannot in principle be fitted into the bounds of a single consciousness, one that is, so to speak, by its very nature *full of event potential* and is born at a point of contact among various consciousnesses" [p. 81]. This might even be seen as Bakhtin's ultimate task: to make a unified truth compatible with *multiple* consciousnesses.

37. See, for example, "Avtor i geroi v esteticheskoi deiatel'nosti" [Author and Hero in Aesthetic Activity], in *Estetika*, p. 8: "All true relationships are, as a rule, creative and productive. That which in life, in cognition, in deed we call a specific object acquires its specificity, its profile only in our relationship to it; our relationship defines the object and its structure, but not the reverse; only where the relationship becomes random from our side, as it were capricious, only when we retreat from our authentic relationship to things and to the world, does the specificity of the object confront us as something alien and independent; it begins to decompose, and we ourselves succumb to the power of the random, we lose ourselves, and we lose as well the stable definitiveness of the world."

Problems of Dostoevsky's Poetics

From the Author

The present book is devoted to problems of Dostoevsky's *poetics*,[1] and surveys his work from that viewpoint *only*.

We consider Dostoevsky one of the greatest innovators in the realm of artistic form. He created, in our opinion, a completely new type of artistic thinking, which we have provisionally called *polyphonic*. This type of artistic thinking found its expression in Dostoevsky's novels, but its significance extends far beyond the limits of the novel alone and touches upon several basic principles of European aesthetics. It could even be said that Dostoevsky created something like a new artistic model of the world, one in which many basic aspects of old artistic form were subjected to a radical restructuring. The present work aims at bringing out, through theoretical literary analysis, this *fundamental* innovation of Dostoevsky.

In the voluminous literature on Dostoevsky, the chief distinctive features of his poetics could not, of course, have gone unnoticed (the first chapter of this work surveys the most important contributions in this area), but the fundamental innovation that this poetics represents, its organic unity within the whole of Dostoevsky's work, has received far too little elucidation in the scholarship. Literature on Dostoevsky has focused primarily on the ideological problems raised by his work. The topical acuteness of those problems has overshadowed the deeper and more permanent structural elements in his mode

3

of artistic visualization. Critics are apt to forget that Dostoevsky is first and foremost an *artist* (of a special type, to be sure) and not a philosopher or a publicist.

The specialized study of Dostoevsky's poetics remains an urgent task of literary scholarship.

For this second edition, our book, which appeared originally in 1929 under the title *Problems of Dostoevsky's Art [Problemy tvorchestva Dostoevskogo]*, has been considerably revised and expanded. But of course even in this new edition the book cannot pretend to a complete analysis of the questions it raises, especially questions as complex as that of *the whole* in a polyphonic novel.

NOTE

1. Bakhtin's emphasis is indicated by italics; the emphasis of the authors he quotes, by boldface.

Chapter One
Dostoevsky's Polyphonic Novel
and Its Treatment
in Critical Literature

Any acquaintance with the voluminous literature on Dostoevsky leaves the impression that one is dealing not with a *single* author-artist who wrote novels and stories, but with a number of philosophical statements by *several* author-thinkers—Raskolnikov, Myshkin, Stavrogin, Ivan Karamazov, the Grand Inquisitor, and others. For the purposes of critical thought, Dostoevsky's work has been broken down into a series of disparate, contradictory philosophical stances, each defended by one or another character. Among these also figure, but in far from first place, the philosophical views of the author himself. For some scholars Dostoevsky's voice merges with the voices of one or another of his characters; for others, it is a peculiar synthesis of all these ideological voices; for yet others, Dostoevsky's voice is simply drowned out by all those other voices. Characters are polemicized with, learned from; attempts are made to develop their views into finished systems. The character is treated as ideologically authoritative and independent; he is perceived as the author of a fully weighted ideological conception of his own, and not as the object of Dostoevsky's finalizing artistic vision. In the consciousness of the critics, the direct and fully weighted signifying power of the characters' words destroys the monologic plane of the novel and calls forth an unmediated response—as if the character were not an object of authorial discourse, but rather a fully valid, autonomous carrier of his own individual word.

5

B. M. Engelhardt has been quite correct in noting this peculiarity of the literature on Dostoevsky. "A survey of Russian critical literature on Dostoevsky's works," he writes, "shows at once that with very few exceptions it does not rise above the spiritual level of Dostoevsky's favorite characters. It does not dominate the material at hand; the material dominates it completely. It is still learning from Ivan Karamazov and Raskolnikov, from Stavrogin and the Grand Inquisitor, entangling itself in the same contradictions that entangled them, stopping in bewilderment before the problems that they failed to solve and bowing respectfully before their complex and tormenting experiences."[1]

J. Meier-Gräfe has made a similar observation. "Would it ever occur to anyone to participate in any of the numerous conversations in *L'Education sentimentale*? But we do enter into discussions with Raskolnikov, and not only with him, but with every bit-player as well."[2]

This peculiar feature of the critical literature on Dostoevsky cannot, of course, be explained solely by the methodological helplessness of critical thought, nor should it be viewed as a complete violation of the author's artistic intent. No, such an approach on the part of the critics, similar to the uninstructed perception of readers who are continually arguing with Dostoevsky's *characters*, does in fact correspond to a basic structural feature of Dostoevsky's works. Dostoevsky, like Goethe's Prometheus, creates not voiceless slaves (as does Zeus), but *free* people, capable of standing *alongside* their creator, capable of not agreeing with him and even of rebelling against him.

A plurality of independent and unmerged voices and consciousnesses, a genuine polyphony of fully valid voices is in fact the chief characteristic of Dostoevsky's novels. What unfolds in his works is not a multitude of characters and fates in a single objective world, illuminated by a single authorial consciousness; rather a *plurality of consciousnesses, with equal rights and each with its own world*, combine but are not merged in the unity of the event.[a] Dostoevsky's

---

[a]*Sobytie* (event) and its adjective *sobytiinyi* (full of event potential) are crucial terms in Bakhtin. At their root lies the Russian word for "existence" or "being" (*bytie*), and—although the etymology here can be disputed—*so-bytie* can be read both in its ordinary meaning of "event," and in a more literal rendering as "co-existing, co-being, shared existence or being *with* another." An event can occur only among interacting consciousnesses; there can be no isolated or solipsistic events. See the long discussion of Bakhtin's use of *sobytie* by S. S. Averintsev and S. G. Bocharov, editors of the posthumous volume of Bakhtin's essays and fragments, M. M. Bakhtin, *Estetika slovesnogo tvorchestva* (Moscow, 1979), pp. 384-85. In English, see Michael Holquist, "The Politics of Representation," in *Allegory and Representation: Selected Papers from the English Institute, 1979-1980* [New Series, no. 5], ed. Stephen J. Greenblatt (Baltimore: The Johns Hopkins Press, 1981), pp. 172-73.

major heroes are, by the very nature of his creative design, *not only objects of authorial discourse but also subjects of their own directly signifying discourse*. In no way, then, can a character's discourse be exhausted by the usual functions of characterization and plot development,[3] nor does it serve as a vehicle for the author's own ideological position (as with Byron, for instance). The consciousness of a character is given as *someone else's* consciousness, another consciousness, yet at the same time it is not turned into an object, is not closed, does not become a simple object of the author's consciousness. In this sense the image of a character in Dostoevsky is not the usual objectified image of a hero in the traditional novel.

Dostoevsky is the creator of the polyphonic novel. He created a fundamentally new novelistic genre. Therefore his work does not fit any of the preconceived frameworks or historico-literary schemes that we usually apply to various species of the European novel. In his works a hero appears whose voice is constructed exactly like the voice of the author himself in a novel of the usual type. A character's word about himself and his world is just as fully weighted as the author's word usually is; it is not subordinated to the character's objectified image as merely one of his characteristics, nor does it serve as a mouthpiece for the author's voice. It possesses extraordinary independence in the structure of the work; it sounds, as it were, *alongside* the author's word and in a special way combines both with it and with the full and equally valid voices of other characters.

It follows that ordinary pragmatic links at the level of the plot (whether of an objective of psychological order) are insufficient in Dostoevsky's world: such links presuppose, after all, that characters have become objects, fixed elements in the author's design; such links bind and combine finalized images of people in the unity of a monologically perceived and understood world; there is no presumption of a plurality of equally-valid consciousnesses, each with its own world. In Dostoevsky's novels, the ordinary pragmatics of the plot play a secondary role and perform special and unusual functions. The ultimate clamps that hold his novelistic world together are a different sort entirely; the fundamental event revealed through his novel does not lend itself to an ordinary pragmatic interpretation at the level of the plot.

Furthermore, the very orientation of the narrative—and this is equally true of narration by the author, by a narrator, or by one of the characters—must necessarily be quite different than in novels of the monologic type. The position from which a story is told, a portrayal built, or information provided must be oriented in a new way to this new world—a world of autonomous subjects, not objects.

Skaz,[b] representational, and informational discourses must develop some new attitude toward their object.

Thus, all the elements of novelistic structure in Dostoevsky are profoundly original; all are determined by that new artistic task that only he could pose and solve with the requisite scope and depth: the task of constructing a polyphonic world and destroying the established forms of the fundamentally *monologic* (homophonic) European novel.[4]

From the viewpoint of a consistently monologic visualization and understanding of the represented world, from the viewpoint of some monologic canon for the proper construction of novels, Dostoevsky's world may seem a chaos, and the construction of his novels some sort of conglomerate of disparate materials and incompatible principles for shaping them. Only in the light of Dostoevsky's fundamental artistic task, which we will formulate here, can one begin to understand the profound organic cohesion, consistency and wholeness of Dostoevsky's poetics.

Such is our thesis. Before developing it with material from Dostoevsky's works, we shall examine how this fundamental characteristic of his art has been interpreted in the critical literature. We do not intend to give here an even remotely complete outline of the literature on Dostoevsky. Of the twentieth-century works about him we will pause on only a few, namely on those that, first, concern themselves with questions of Dostoevsky's *poetics*, and second, come closest to dealing with the basic distinguishing features of this poetics, as we understand them. The selection, therefore, is made with our thesis as vantage point, and is consequently subjective. But in this case a subjective selection is both unavoidable and fully justified: we are not, after all, providing an historical outline here, or even a survey. For us it is important only to orient our thesis, our point of view among already existing points of view on Dostoevsky's poetics in the literature. In the process of orientation, we will clarify specific aspects of our thesis.

Critical literature on Dostoevsky has been, until very recently, too direct an ideological echoing of the voices of his heroes—and has therefore been unable to perceive objectively the distinctive artistic features of Dostoevsky's new novelistic structure. Moreover, in its attempt to get its theoretical bearings in this new multivoiced world, the critical literature has found no other course than to monologize this world as if it were a world of the usual type, that is, to perceive the product of an essentially new artistic intention from the vantage point of the old and ordinary intention. Some critics, enslaved by the

---

[b]*Skaz* has no precise equivalent in English, and will be retained as a Russian term throughout. It refers to a technique or mode of narration that imitates the oral speech of an individualized narrator.

content of individual heroes' ideological views, have attempted to reduce these views to a systemically monologic whole, thus ignoring
the fundamental plurality of unmerged consciousnesses which is part
and parcel of the artist's design. Other critics, having resisted the charm
of unmediated ideology, transformed the fully valid consciousnesses
of the heroes into objectified psyches, psyches perceived as "things,"
and took Dostoevsky's world as the ordinary world of the socio-psychological European novel. And what resulted, instead of an event of
interaction between fully valid consciousnesses, was in the first instance a philosophical monologue, and in the second instance a monologically understood, objectified world, a world corresponding to a
single and unified authorial consciousness.

Both approaches—a passionate philosophizing with the characters,
and a dispassionate psychological or psychopathological analysis of
them as objects—are equally incapable of penetrating the special artistic architectonics of Dostoevsky's works. The enthusiasm of the
one is incapable of visualizing, in an objective and authentically
realistic way, a world of other people's consciousnesses; the realism
of the other "swims in too shallow waters." In both cases it is quite
obvious that artistic problems as such are either avoided entirely, or
are treated superficially, almost by accident.

The path of philosophical monologization has been the fundamental path followed by critical literature on Dostoevsky. It was the path
taken by Rozanov,* Volynsky,* Merezhkovsky,* Shestov,* and many
others. In their attempt to squeeze the artist's demonstrated plurality
of consciousnesses into the systemically monologic framework of a
single worldview, these researchers were forced to resort either to
antinomy or to dialectics. Out of the concrete and integral consciousnesses of the characters (and of the author himself) they surgically
removed ideological theses, which they either arranged in a dynamic
dialectical series or juxtaposed to one another as absolute and irreducible antinomies. The interaction of several unmerged consciousnesses was replaced by an interrelationship of ideas, thoughts, and attitudes gravitating toward a single consciousness.

Both dialectics and antinomy are in fact present in Dostoevsky's
world. The thinking of his characters is indeed sometimes dialectic or
antinomic. But all *logical* links remain within the limits of individual
consciousnesses, and do not govern the event-interrelationships among
them. Dostoevsky's world is profoundly personalized. He perceives
and represents every thought as the position of a personality. Therefore even within the limits of individual consciousnesses, a dialectic
or antinomic series can be no more than an abstract element, indissolubly interwoven with other elements of an integral and concrete
consciousness. Through this concrete consciousness, embodied in *the*

living voice of an integral person, the logical relation becomes part of the unity of a represented event. Thought, drawn into an event, becomes itself part of the event and takes on that special quality of an "idea-feeling," an "idea-force," which is responsible for the unique peculiarity of the "idea" in Dostoevsky's creative world. Extracted from this interrelationship of consciousnesses in the event, forced into a systemically monologic context (even the most dialectic), the idea inevitably loses its uniqueness and is transformed into a poor philosophical assertion. This is why all the major monographs on Dostoevsky—products of this philosophical monologization of his work—contribute so little toward understanding what we formulate here as the defining structural feature of his artistic world. To be sure, this feature did give rise to all those scholarly works—but it has been the feature least acknowledged in them.

Acknowledgment can begin only when attempts are made at a more objective approach to Dostoevsky's work—not only to the ideas in and of themselves, but also to the works as artistic entities.

The first to grope his way toward this basic structural feature of Dostoevsky's artistic world was Vyacheslav Ivanov*—and, to be sure, he only groped.[5] He defined Dostoevsky's realism as a realism based not on cognition (objectified cognition), but on "penetration." To affirm someone else's "I" not as an object but as another subject—this is the principle governing Dostoevsky's worldview. To affirm someone else's "I"—"thou art"—is a task that, according to Ivanov, Dostoevsky's characters must successfully accomplish if they are to overcome their ethical solipsism, their disunited "idealistic" consciousness, and transform the other person from a shadow into an authentic reality. At the heart of the tragic catastrophe in Dostoevsky's work there always lies the solipsistic separation of a character's consciousness from the whole, his incarceration in his own private world.[6]

Thus the affirmation of someone else's consciousness—as an autonomous subject and not as an object—is the ethico-religious postulate determining the *content* of the novel (the catastrophe of a disunited consciousness). It is a principle of the author's worldview, and from that vantage point the author understands the world of his characters. Ivanov subsequently shows how this principle is refracted, solely and entirely on the thematic plane, in the content of the novel —a refraction which is, it turns out, predominantly negative: the heroes suffer destruction because they cannot wholeheartedly affirm the other, "thou art." Affirmation (and nonaffirmation) of someone else's "I" by the hero—this is the theme of Dostoevsky's work.

But this theme is altogether possible in a novel of the purely monologic type as well, and is in fact often found in that sort of novel. As the ethico-religious postulate of an author or as an important theme in a work, the affirmation of someone else's consciousness does not in itself create a new form or a new type of novelistic construction.

Vyacheslav Ivanov did not show how this principle of Dostoevsky's worldview becomes the principle behind Dostoevsky's *artistic* visualization of the world, the principle behind his artistic structuring of a *verbal* whole, the novel. But it is only in this form, as a principle governing concrete literary construction and not as the ethico-religious principle behind an abstract worldview, that it is essential for the literary scholar. And only in this form can it be objectively dissected, using empirical material from concrete literary works.

But this Vyacheslav Ivanov did not do. In the chapter devoted to the "principle of form," despite a series of highly valuable observations, he insists nevertheless on locating the Dostoevskian novel inside the bounds of the monologic type of novel. The radical artistic revolution brought about by Dostoevsky was not in essence understood. The basic definition Ivanov gave to Dostoevsky's novel, "novel-tragedy," seems to us incorrect.[7] Such a definition is characteristic of attempts to reduce a new artistic form to an already familiar artistic intention. As a result, Dostoevsky's novel ends up as a sort of artistic hybrid.

Thus Vyacheslav Ivanov, having arrived at a profound and correct definition of Dostoevsky's fundamental principle—the affirmation of someone else's "I" not as an object but as another subject—proceeded to monologize this principle, that is, he incorporated it into a monologically formulated authorial worldview and perceived it as merely one of the interesting themes in a world represented from the point of view of a monologic authorial consciousness.[8] And in addition, he linked this thought with a whole series of direct metaphysical and ethical assertions which are not subject to any objective verification from actual material in Dostoevsky's works.[9] The artistic task of constructing a polyphonic novel, a task Dostoevsky was the first to resolve, had yet to be discovered.

Sergei Askoldov* defines Dostoevsky's chief characteristic feature in much the same way that Ivanov does.[10] But Askoldov, too, remains within the limits of Dostoevsky's monologic religious-ethical worldview, within the limits of the monologically perceived content of his works.

"Dostoevsky's first ethical thesis," Askoldov says, "is something that appears at first glance to be of a highly formal nature, yet is, in a certain sense, the most important thing. In all his evaluations and sympathies he tells us, 'Be a personality.'"[11] Personality, according to Askoldov, differs from character, type, and temperament—which ordinarily serve as the object of representation in literature—because

of its extraordinary internal freedom and its utter independence from
the external environment.

Such, apparently, is the principle behind the author's ethical worldview. From this worldview Askoldov passes directly to the content of
Dostoevsky's works, showing how and for what reasons Dostoevsky's
characters become personalities *in life*, how they show themselves
for what they are. Thus personality inevitably comes into collision
with the external environment—and this is above all an external collision with accepted convention of any kind. Thus "scandal"—that
first and most external instance of the pathos of the personality—
plays so huge a role in Dostoevsky's work.[12] An even more profound
instance of the pathos of the personality in life can be found, according to Askoldov, in crime. "Crime in Dostoevsky's novels," he says,
"is life's way of posing the religious and ethical problem. Punishment
is the form of its resolution. Thus both together constitute the fundamental theme of Dostoevsky's art . . ."[13]

At issue, therefore, is always the means for revealing personality in
actual life—not the means for artistically visualizing and representing
personality under the conditions of a specific artistic construction,
the novel. Moreover, the very interrelationship between an author's
worldview and the characters' world is portrayed incorrectly. From
the pathos of personality in the worldview of the author, a direct
transition to the real-life pathos of the characters, and from there back
again for a monologic conclusion by the author: this is the typical
path taken by a monologic novel of the romantic type. But it is not
Dostoevsky's path.

"Dostoevsky," Askoldov says, "in all his artistic sympathies and
evaluations, proclaims one exceedingly important proposition: the
villain, the saint, the ordinary sinner, if they carry their personal essence to its furthest extreme, are all somehow of equal value precisely in their capacity as personalities, opposing the murky currents of
the all-leveling 'environment.'"[14]

Proclamations of this sort are characteristic of the Romantic novel,
which knew consciousness and ideology solely as the pathos of an
author or as the deduction of an author—and which knew the hero
solely as an implementer of authorial pathos or as an object of authorial deduction. It is precisely the Romantics who in the very reality they depict give direct expression to their own artistic sympathies
and evaluations, all the while objectifying and turning into a material
thing all they cannot mark with the accent of their own voice.

The uniqueness of Dostoevsky lies not in the fact that he monologically proclaimed the value of personality (others had done that
before him); it lies in the fact that he was able, in an objective and artistic way, to visualize and portray personality as another, as someone

else's personality, without making it lyrical or merging it with his own voice—and at the same time without reducing it to a materialized psychic reality. Dostoevsky's worldview was not the first to place high value on personality, but the artistic image of someone else's personality (to use Askoldov's term), the image of many unmerged personalities joined together in the unity of some spiritual event, was fully realized for the first time in his novels.

This astonishing internal independence of Dostoevsky's characters, which Askoldov correctly notes, is achieved by specific artistic means. It is above all due to the freedom and independence characters possess, in the very structure of the novel, vis-à-vis the author—or, more accurately, their freedom vis-à-vis the usual externalizing and finalizing authorial definitions. This does not mean, of course, that a character simply falls out of the author's design. No, this independence and freedom of a character is precisely what is incorporated into the author's design. This design, as it were, predestines the character for freedom (a relative freedom, of course), and incorporates him as such into the strict and carefully calculated plan of the whole.

This relative freedom of a hero does not violate the strict specificity of the construction, just as the specificity of a mathematical formula is not violated by the presence of irrational or transfinite quantities. This new placement of the hero is achieved not through the choice of some abstractly formulated theme (although, of course, the theme is of some significance), but is achieved rather through an entire accumulation of special artistic devices for constructing a novel—devices Dostoevsky was the first to introduce.

So Askoldov, too, monologizes Dostoevsky's artistic world, shifting the *dominant*[c] of that world to a monological sermon and thereby reducing characters to the status of simple illustrations to that sermon. Askoldov correctly perceived that a completely new way of visualizing and representing the inner man was fundamental to Dostoevsky, and, consequently, so was the event that bound inner men to one another. But he transferred his explanation onto the plane of the author's worldview and the plane of the characters' psychology.

A later article of Askoldov's—"The Psychology of Characters in Dostoevsky"[15]—is likewise limited to an analysis of the purely characterological peculiarities of his heroes and does not uncover any principles behind their visualization and representation in art. What distinguishes personality from character, type, and temperament is

---

[c]By "dominant" Bakhtin has in mind the Formalist concept of the *dominanta*, the "leading value" in the hierarchical system of values inherent in any work of art. See Roman Jakobson, "The Dominant," in *Readings in Russian Poetics: Formalist and Structuralist Views*, ed. L. Matejka and K. Pomorska (Cambridge, MA: MIT Press, 1971), p. 82:"The dominant may be defined as the focusing component of a work of art: it rules, determines, and transforms the remaining components. It is the dominant which guarantees the integrity of the structure."

dealt with, as before, on the psychological plane only. In this article, however, Askoldov adheres much more closely to concrete material from the novels, and it is therefore full of highly valuable observations on specific features of Dostoevsky's art. But Askoldov's conception of the problem goes no further than isolated observations.

It must be said that Vyacheslav Ivanov's formula—to affirm someone else's "I" not as an object, but as another subject, "thou art"—is, despite its philosophical abstractness, a good deal more appropriate than Askoldov's formula "Be a personality." Ivanov's formula shifts the dominant to someone else's personality, and in addition corresponds more closely to Dostoevsky's *internally dialogic* approach to the represented consciousness of a character; Askoldov's formula, meanwhile, is more monologic and shifts the center of gravity to a realization of one's own private personality. If, in the realm of artistic creation, Dostoevsky had ever really postulated such a thing, it would have led to a subjective romantic type of novelistic construction.

Another approach to this same fundamental characteristic of Dostoevsky's novels is taken by Leonid Grossman*; he approaches it from the viewpoint of artistic construction itself. For Grossman, Dostoevsky is above all the creator of a new and utterly original species of novel. "It would seem," he states, "that upon surveying Dostoevsky's vast creative activity and all the varied strivings of his spirit, one must admit that his major significance is to be found not so much in philosophy, psychology or mysticism as in the creation of a new and authentically brilliant page in the history of the European novel."[16]

We must recognize Grossman as the pioneer, in our literary scholarship, of objective and consistent research into Dostoevsky's *poetics*.

Grossman sees the distinguishing trait of Dostoevsky's poetics in his violation of that organic unity of material required by the usual canon, his joining together of the most varied and incompatible elements in the unity of novelistic construction, and in his destruction of the unified and integral fabric of narration.

Such [he says] is the basic principle of his novelistic composition: to subordinate polar-opposite narrative elements to the unity of a philosophical design and to the whirlwind movement of events. To link together in one artistic creation philosophical confessions and criminal adventures, to incorporate religious drama into the story-line of a boulevard novel, to lead the reader through all the peripeteia of an adventure narrative only to arrive at the revelation of a new mystery—such are the artistic tasks Dostoevsky set for himself, and which inspired him to such complex creative work. Contrary to the time-honored traditions of that aesthetic which requires a correspondence between material and its treatment—an aesthetic presupposing the unity or at least the homogeneity and the interconnectedness of constructive elements in a given work of art—Dostoevsky merges opposites. He issues a decisive challenge to the fundamental canon of the theory of art. His task: to overcome the greatest difficulty that an artist can face, to create out of heterogeneous and profoundly disparate materials of varying worth a unified and integral artistic creation. Thus the Book of Job, the Revelation of St. John, the Gospel texts, the discourses of St. Simeon the New Theologian,* everything that feeds the pages of his novels and contributes tone to one or another of his chapters, is combined here in a most original way with the newspaper, the anecdote, the parody, the street scene, with the grotesque, even with the pamphlet. He boldly casts into his crucibles ever newer elements, knowing and believing that in the blaze of his creative work these raw chunks of everyday life, the sensations of boulevard novels and the divinely inspired pages of Holy Writ, will melt down and fuse in a new compound, and take on the deep imprint of his personal style and tone.[17]

This is a splendid descriptive characterization of the generic and compositional features of Dostoevsky's novels. Almost nothing can be added to it. But the explanation which Grossman gives seem to us insufficient.

In actual fact a whirlwind movement of events, however powerful, and the unity of a philosophical design, however profound, are hardly sufficient to solve that highly complex and contradictory compositional task which was formulated so precisely and graphically by Leonid Grossman. As far as whirlwind movement is concerned, the most banal contemporary film-romance can outdo Dostoevsky. And the unity of a philosophical design cannot, in and of itself, serve as the ultimate basis of artistic unity.

In our opinion Grossman is also incorrect in his claim that all of Dostoevsky's highly heterogeneous material takes on "the deep imprint of his personal style and tone." If that were so, how would Dostoevsky's novel differ from the ordinary type of novel, from that "epopee of the Flaubert school, cut from a single piece, polished and monolithic"? A novel such as *Bouvard et Pécuchet**, for example, unites material of the most heterogeneous content, but this heterogeneity does not function in the structure of the novel itself and cannot so function in any well-defined way — because it is subordinated to the unity of a personal style and tone permeating it through and through, the unity of a single world and a single consciousness. The unity of a Dostoevskian novel, however, is *above* personal style and *above* personal tone — as these were understood in the pre-Dostoevskian novel.

If viewed from a monologic understanding of the unity of style (and so far that is the only understanding that exists), Dostoevsky's novel is *multi-styled* or styleless; if viewed from a monologic understanding of tone, Dostoevsky's novel is *multi-accented* and contradictory in its values; contradictory accents clash in every word of his creations. If Dostoevsky's highly heterogeneous material had been

developed within a unified world corresponding to the unified monologic consciousness of the author, then the task of joining together
the incompatible would not have been accomplished, and Dostoevsky
would be a poor artist, with no style at all; such a monologic world
"fatally disintegrates into its component parts, dissimilar and alien to
one another; there would spread out before us motionlessly, helplessly, absurdly, a page from the Bible alongside a note from a travel
diary, a lackey's ditty alongside Schiller's dithyramb of joy."[18]

In actual fact, the utterly incompatible elements comprising
Dostoevsky's material are distributed among several worlds and several autonomous consciousnesses; they are presented not within a
single field of vision but within several fields of vision, each full and
of equal worth; and it is not the material directly but these worlds,
their consciousnesses with their individual fields of vision that combine in a higher unity, a unity, so to speak, of the second order, the
unity of a polyphonic novel. The world of the ditty combines with
the world of the Schillerian dithyramb, Smerdyakov's field of vision
combines with Dmitry's and Ivan's. Thanks to these *various worlds*
the material can develop to the furthest extent what is most original
and peculiar in it, without disturbing the unity of the whole and
without mechanizing it. It is as if varying systems of calculation were
united here in the complex unity of an Einsteinian universe (although
the juxtaposition of Dostoevsky's world with Einstein's world is, of
course, only an artistic comparison and not a scientific analogy).

In another work, Grossman more closely approaches precisely this
multi-voicedness of the Dostoevskian novel. In his book *Dostoevsky's
Path* he emphasizes the exceptional importance of dialogue in
Dostoevsky's work. "The form of a conversation or quarrel," he says
here, "where various points of view can dominate in turn and reflect
the diverse nuances of contradictory creeds, is especially appropriate
for embodying this philosophy, forever being shaped and yet never
congealing. To such an artist and observer of images as Dostoevsky,
there must have occurred in a moment of profound contemplation
on the meaning of phenomena and the secret of the world, this particular form of philosophical conceptualization, in which every
opinion becomes a living creature and is expounded by an impassioned
human voice."[19]

Grossman is inclined to explain this dialogism as a contradiction,
never quite overcome, in Dostoevsky's worldview. Two powerful
forces—humanistic skepticism and faith—collided early in his consciousness, and they wage an uninterrupted struggle for predominance
in his worldview.[20]

One can disagree with this explanation, which certainly exceeds
the bounds of objectively available material, but Grossman does

correctly point out the very fact of a plurality (in this case a duality) of unmerged consciousnesses. He also notes correctly the highly personalized manner in which the concept of an idea is perceived in Dostoevsky. In Dostoevsky's work each opinion really does become a living thing and is inseparable from an embodied human voice. If incorporated into an abstract, systemically monological context, it ceases to be what it is.

Had Grossman linked Dostoevsky's compositional principle—the unification of highly heterogeneous and incompatible material—with the plurality of consciousness-centers not reduced to a single ideological common denominator, then he would have arrived in earnest at the artistic key to Dostoevsky's novels: polyphony.

It is characteristic that Grossman understands dialogue in Dostoevsky as a dramatic form, and every dialogization as necessarily a dramatization. Literature of recent times knows only the dramatic dialogue and to some extent the philosophical dialogue, weakened into a mere form of exposition, a pedagogical device. And in any case, the dramatic dialogue in drama and the dramatized dialogue in the narrative forms are always encased in a firm and stable monologic framework. In drama, of course, this monologic framework does not find direct verbal expression, but precisely in drama is it especially monolithic. The rejoinders in a dramatic dialogue do not rip apart the represented world, do not make it multi-leveled; on the contrary, if they are to be authentically dramatic, these rejoinders necessitate the utmost monolithic unity of that world. In drama the world must be made from a single piece. Any weakening of this monolithic quality leads to a weakening of dramatic effect. The characters come together dialogically in the unified field of vision of author, director, and audience, against the clearly defined background of a single-tiered world.[21] The whole concept of a dramatic action, as that which resolves all dialogic oppositions, is purely monologic. A true multiplicity of levels would destroy drama, because dramatic action, relying as it does upon the unity of the world, could not link those levels together or resolve them. In drama, it is impossible to combine several integral fields of vision in a unity that encompasses and stands above them all, because the structure of drama offers no support for such a unity. For this reason, authentically dramatic dialogue can play only a very secondary role in Dostoevsky's polyphonic novel.[22]

More substantial is Grossman's claim that the novels of Dostoevsky's later years are in fact mystery plays.[23] The mystery play is truly multi-leveled, and to a certain extent polyphonic. But the multi-leveled and polyphonic quality of the mystery play is purely formal, and in fact the very construction of a mystery play, the nature of its content, does not permit the development of a plurality of consciousnesses and their worlds. From the very beginning everything is predetermined, closed-off and finalized—although not, it is true, finalized on a single plane.[24]

In Dostoevsky's polyphonic novel we are dealing not with ordinary dialogic form, that is, with an unfolding of material within the framework of its own monologic understanding and against the firm background of a unified world of objects. No, here we are dealing with an ultimate dialogicality, that is, a dialogicality of the ultimate whole. The dramatic whole is, as we have pointed out, in this respect monologic; Dostoevsky's novel is dialogic. It is constructed not as the whole of a single consciousness, absorbing other consciousnesses as objects into itself, but as a whole formed by the interaction of several consciousnesses, none of which entirely becomes an object for the other; this interaction provides no support for the viewer who would objectify an entire event according to some ordinary monologic category (thematically, lyrically or cognitively)—and this consequently makes the viewer also a participant. Not only does the novel give no firm support outside the rupture-prone world of dialogue for a third, monologically all-encompassing consciousness—but on the contrary, everything in the novel is structured to make dialogic opposition inescapable.[25] Not a single element of the work is structured from the point of view of a nonparticipating "third person." In the novel itself, nonparticipating "third persons" are not represented in any way. There is no place for them, compositionally or in the larger meaning of the work. And this is not a weakness of the author but his greatest strength. By this means a new authorial position is won and conquered, one located above the monologic position.

This plurality of equally authoritative ideological positions and an extreme heterogeneity of material has also been singled out as a primary characteristic of Dostoevsky's work by Otto Kaus,* in his book *Dostojewski und sein Schicksal*. No author, according to Kaus, concentrated in himself so many utterly contradictory and mutually exclusive concepts, judgments, and evaluations as did Dostoevsky—but most astonishing is the fact that Dostoevsky's works justify as it were all these contradictory points of view: every one of them really does find support for itself in Dostoevsky's novels.

Here is how Kaus characterizes this extraordinary multi-sided and multi-leveled quality of Dostoevsky:

Dostoevsky is like a host who gets on marvelously with the most motley guests, who is able to command the attention of the most ill-assorted company and can hold all in an equal state of suspense. An old-fashioned realist can with full justification admire the descriptions of forced labor, of the streets and squares of Petersburg, of the arbitrary will of the autocracy; but a mystic can with no less justification be enthusiastic about coming into contact with Alyosha, with Prince Myshkin, with Ivan Karamazov who is visited by the devil. Utopians of all persuasions will take delight in the dreams of the "Ridiculous Man," or the dreams of Versilov or Stavrogin, and religious people can fortify their spirit by that struggle for God waged in these novels by saints and sinners alike. Health and strength, radical pessimism and an ardent faith in redemption, a thirst for life and a longing for death — here all these things wage a struggle that is never to be resolved. Violence and goodness, proud arrogance and sacrificial humility — all the immense fullness of life is embodied in the most vivid form in every particle of his work. Even being as strict and as critically conscientious as possible, each reader can interpret Dostoevsky's ultimate word in his own way. Dostoevsky is many-sided and unpredictable in all the movements of his artistic thought; his works are saturated with forces and intentions which seem to be separated from one another by insurmountable chasms.[26]

How does Kaus explain this peculiar characteristic of Dostoevsky? Kaus claims that Dostoevsky's world is the purest and most authentic expression of the spirit of capitalism. At some earlier time those worlds, those planes — social, cultural, and ideological — which collide in Dostoevsky's work were each self-sufficient, organically sealed, and stable; each made sense internally as an isolated unit. There was no real-life, material plane of essential contact or interpenetration with one another. Capitalism destroyed the isolation of these worlds, broke down the seclusion and inner ideological self-sufficiency of these social spheres. In its tendency to level everything, to leave intact no divisions except the division between proletariat and capitalist, capitalism jolted these worlds and wove them into its own contradictory evolving unity. These worlds had not yet lost their own individual profile, worked out over centuries, but they had ceased to be self-sufficient. Their blind co-existence and their peaceful and trusting ideological ignorance of one another came to an end; their mutual contradictoriness and at the same time their interconnectedness was revealed with the utmost clarity. Every atom of life trembled with this contradictory unity of the capitalist world and capitalist consciousness, permitting nothing to rest easily in isolation, but at the same time resolving nothing. The spirit of this world-in-the-state-of-becoming found its fullest expression in the works of Dostoevsky. "Dostoevsky's powerful influence in our time, and all that is unclear and undefined in this influence, finds its explanation and sole justification in the fundamental trait of his nature: Dostoevsky is the most decisive, consistent, and implacable singer of capitalist man. His art is not the funeral dirge but the cradle song of our contemporary world, a world born out of the fiery breath of capitalism."[27]

The explanations Kaus offers are in many respects correct. The polyphonic novel could indeed have been realized only in the capitalist era. The most favorable soil for it was moreover precisely in Russia, where capitalism set in almost catastrophically, and where it came upon an untouched multitude of diverse worlds and social groups which had not been weakened in their individual isolation, as in the West, by the gradual encroachment of capitalism. Here in Russia the contradictory nature of evolving social life, not fitting within the framework of a confident and calmly meditative monologic consciousness, was bound to appear particularly abrupt, and at the same time the individuality of those worlds, worlds thrown off their ideological balance and colliding with one another, was bound to be particularly full and vivid. In this way the objective preconditions were created for the multi-leveledness and multi-voicedness of the polyphonic novel.

But Kaus's explanations fail to clarify the very fact he sets out to explain. The "spirit of capitalism" is, after all, present here in the language of art, and specifically in the language of a particular variety of novel. The first priority must be to explore the structural peculiarities of this multi-leveled novel, a novel denied the usual monologic unity. This task Kaus does not take on. He correctly points out the fact of multi-leveledness and semantic multi-voicedness, but then transfers his explanations directly from the plane of the novel to the plane of reality. It is to Kaus's credit that he refrains from monologizing this world, and refrains from any attempt to unite and reconcile the contradictions it contains; he accepts its multi-leveledness and contradictoriness as an essential aspect of its very construction and creative design.

Another aspect of this same basic characteristic of Dostoevsky's is dealt with by V. Komarovich* in his article "Dostoevsky's Novel *The Adolescent* as an Artistic Unity." In his analysis of the novel, he uncovers five distinct thematic plots, linked together only very superficially by the story-line. This forces him to presume some other sort of bond beyond the realm of pragmatic plot considerations. "Snatching . . . chunks of reality, extending 'empiricism' to its utmost extreme, Dostoevsky does not for a single moment permit us to lose ourselves in joyous recognition of that reality (as Flaubert does, or Leo Tolstoy); instead he frightens us, and this is precisely because he snatches and rips everything out of the normal and predictable chain of the real; in transferring these chunks to *himself*, Dostoevsky does not transfer along with them the predictable links familiar to us from our experience: the Dostoevskian novel is bound up in an organic unity that has nothing to do with the plot."[28]

Indeed, the monologic unity of the world is destroyed in a Dostoevskian novel, but those ripped-off pieces of reality are in no sense directly combined in the unity of the novel: each of these pieces gravitates toward the integral field of vision of a specific character; each makes sense only at the level of a specific consciousness. If these chunks of reality, deprived of any pragmatic links, were combined directly as things emotionally, lyrically, or symbolically harmonious in the unity of a single and monologic field of vision, then before us would be the world of the Romantic, the world of Hoffmann, for example, but in no way could it be Dostoevsky's world.

The ultimate "extra-plot" unity of the Dostoevskian novel is interpreted by Komarovich in a monologic, even exclusively monologic way, although he does introduce an analogy with polyphony and with the contrapuntal combination of voices in a fugue. Under the influence of Broder Christiansen's* monologic aesthetics, Komarovich understands this extra-plot, extra-pragmatic unity of the novel as the dynamic unity of an act of the will:

Thus the teleological coordination of elements (that is, plots) which are, from a pragmatic viewpoint, disunified parts, is the source of artistic unity in a Dostoevskian novel. And in this sense it can be compared to the artistic whole in polyphonic music: the five voices of a fugue, entering one by one and developing in contrapuntal harmony, remind one of the 'harmonization of voices' in a Dostoevskian novel. Such a similarity—if it is correct—leads to a more generalized definition of the very source of the unity. In music as in the Dostoevskian novel there is realized that same law of unity we embody in ourselves, in the human 'I': the law of purposeful activity. In the novel *The Adolescent*, for example, this principle of unity is absolutely appropriate to that which is symbolically represented in the novel: the 'love-hate' of Versilov for Akhmakova is a symbol of the tragic outbursts of the individual will toward the supra-personal; the entire novel is correspondingly constructed on this model of the individual act of will.[29]

Komarovich's basic error, it seems to us, lies in the fact that he seeks a *direct* combination of separate elements of reality or separate plot lines, while in fact the issue here is the combination of fully valid consciousnesses, together with their worlds. In place of the unity of an event, in which there are several autonomous participants, one ends up instead with the empty unity of an individual act of will. And in this sense polyphony is interpreted by Komarovich in a completely incorrect way. The essence of polyphony lies precisely in the fact that the voices remain independent and, as such, are combined in a unity of a higher order than in homophony. If one is to talk about individual will, then it is precisely in polyphony that a combination of several individual wills takes place, that the boundaries of the individual will can be in principle exceeded. One could put it this way: the artistic will of polyphony is a will to combine many wills, a will to the event.

The unity of Dostoevsky's world cannot under any condition be reduced to the unity of an individual and emotionally accented will, any more than musical polyphony can be so reduced. After such a reduction, the novel *The Adolescent* becomes, in Komarovich's treatment, some sort of lyrical unity of the simplified monologic type, for its thematic unities are combined according to their emotional and volitional accents; that is, combined according to the lyric principle.

It must be noted that the comparison we draw between Dostoevsky's novel and polyphony is meant as a graphic analogy, nothing more. The image of polyphony and counterpoint only points out those new problems which arise when a novel is constructed beyond the boundaries of ordinary monologic unity, just as in music new problems arose when the boundaries of a single voice were exceeded. But the material of music and of the novel are too dissimilar for there to be anything more between them than a graphic analogy, a simple metaphor. We are transforming this metaphor into the term "polyphonic novel," since we have not found a more appropriate label. It should not be forgotten, however, that the term has its origin in metaphor.

The fundamental characteristic of Dostoevsky's art was, we think, very profoundly understood by B. M. Engelhardt in his essay "Dostoevsky's Ideological Novel."

Engelhardt begins with a sociological and cultural-historical definition of the Dostoevskian hero. Dostoevsky's hero is a déclassé member of the intelligentsia, cut off from cultural tradition, from the soil and the earth, a representative of an "accidental tribe." Such a person enters into special relations with the idea: he is defenseless before it and its power, for he is not rooted in objective reality and is deprived of any cultural tradition. He becomes a "person of the idea," a person possessed by an idea. An idea becomes for him an idea-force, omnipotently defining and distorting his consciousness and his life. The idea leads an independent life in the hero's consciousness: in fact it is not he but the idea that lives, and the novelist describes not the life of the hero but the life of the idea in him; the historian of the "accidental tribe" becomes "the historiographer of the idea." The dominant of a hero's represented image is therefore the idea which possesses him, rather than a biographical dominant of the usual type (as in Tolstoy or Turgenev, for example). This is the origin of that generic definition of the Dostoevskian novel as an "ideological novel." But this is not an ordinary novel of ideas, or novel with an idea.

"Dostoevsky," Engelhardt says, "portrayed the life of an idea in individual and social consciousness, because he considered it to be the determining factor of educated society. But this need not be understood to mean that Dostoevsky wrote of ideas, stories with a didactic purpose, and was therefore a tendentious artist, more a philosopher than a poet. What he wrote were not novels with an idea, not philosophical novels in the style of the eighteenth century, but *novels about the idea*. And just as the central object for other novelists might be adventure, anecdote, psychological type, a scene from everyday life or from history, for him the central object was the 'idea.' He cultivated and raised to extraordinary heights an utterly special type of novel that, in contrast to the adventure, sentimental, psychological, or historical novel, might be called *ideological*. In this sense his creative work—despite its inherent polemicism—concedes nothing in objectivity to the works of the other great artists of the word: Dostoevsky was himself such an artist, and what he posed and resolved in his novels were purely artistic problems above all. Only the material was highly original: his hero was the idea."[30]

The idea, as an object of representation and as the dominant in structuring the images of characters, leads to a disintegration of the novelistic world into the worlds of its characters, organized and shaped by the ideas that possess them. Engelhardt gets to the heart of the multi-leveledness in Dostoevsky's novels when he writes: "The particular form of a hero's **ideological relationship to the world** becomes the principle behind a purely artistic **orientation of the hero to his surroundings.** Just as the complex of idea-forces ruling the hero serves as the dominant in an artistic representation of him, so the point of view from which the hero observes the world serves as the dominant in the representation of surrounding reality. The world is present to each character in a particular aspect—and in keeping with that aspect its representation is contructed. It is impossible to find in Dostoevsky a so-called objective description of the external world; strictly speaking his novels contain no everyday life, no city-life or country-life, no nature. What can be found is environment, soil, and earth, depending upon the plane in which all these are observed by his characters. This gives rise to that multi-leveledness of reality in an artistic work—which in Dostoevsky's successors often leads to that peculiar disintegration of everyday life—so that the action of the novel flows simultaneously or consecutively in completely different ontological spheres."[31]

Depending on the nature of the idea governing the consciousness and life of the character, Engelhardt distinguishes three planes in which the action of the novel can unfold. The first plane is the "environment." Here, mechanical necessity reigns; here there is no freedom; every act of the will in life is the natural product of external conditions. The second plane is the "soil." This is the organic system of the ever-evolving spirit of the people. And finally, the third plane is the "earth."

"The third concept, **earth**, is one of the most profound which we find in Dostoevsky," says Engelhardt of this plane. "It is the earth that is not distinguished from children, the earth that Alyosha Karamazov kissed, weeping, sobbing, watering with his tears, and that he ecstatically swore to love; it is everything—all of nature, and man, and beasts, and birds—that wonderful garden planted by the Lord, who took seeds from other worlds and sowed them on this earth.

"It is both the highest degree of reality, and at the same time that world where the earthly life of the spirit unfolds, having achieved true freedom . . . It is the third kingdom, the kingdom of love, and therefore also the kingdom of complete freedom, the kingdom of eternal joy and gaiety."[32]

Such, according to Engelhardt, are the planes of the novel. Every element of reality (of the external world), every experience and every action invariably fits into one of these three planes. Engelhardt also distributes the basic themes of Dostoevsky's novels along these planes.[33]

How, then, are these planes linked together in the unity of the novel? What principles govern their combining with one another?

These three planes and their corresponding themes, considered in relationship to one another, represent in Engelhardt's view separate *stages in the dialectical development of the spirit*. "In this sense," he says, "they form a **unified path** along which, amid great sufferings and dangers, the seeker passes in his striving toward an unconditional affirmation of existence. And one can easily uncover the subjective significance of this path for Dostoevsky himself."[34]

Such is Engelhardt's interpretation. It casts much light on the most essential structural features of Dostoevsky's works, and in his perception and evaluation of these traits he consistently tries to avoid any one-sidedness or abstract playing with ideas. However, not everything in his interpretation seems to us correct. And we consider totally incorrect those conclusions he draws at the end of his essay on Dostoevsky's work as a whole.

Engelhardt was the first to define correctly the place occupied by the idea in the Dostoevskian novel. An idea here is indeed neither a *principle of representation* (as in any ordinary novel), nor the leitmotif of representation, nor a conclusion drawn from it (as in a novel of ideas, or a philosophical novel); it is, rather, the *object of representation*. As a principle for visualizing and understanding the world, for shaping the world in the perspective of a given idea, the idea is present only for the characters,[35] and not for Dostoevsky himself as the author. The characters' worlds are constructed according to the ordinary monologic-ideational principle, constructed as it were by the characters themselves. The "earth" is also present as only one of the worlds incorporated into the unity of the novel, as only one of its planes. Even if it receives a definite, hierarchically higher emphasis than does "soil" or "environment," nevertheless "earth" is merely the idea-perspective of certain characters such as Sonya Marmeladova, the Elder Zosima, Alyosha.

The heroes' ideas lying at the base of this plane in the novel are as much the subject of representation, as much "idea-heroes," as the ideas of Raskolnikov, Ivan Karamazov, or any of the others. In no way do they become principles of representation or construction for the entire novel as a whole, that is, principles of the author himself as the artist. If that were the case we would have an ordinary philosophical novel of ideas. The hierarchical emphasis or accent given to some of these ideas does not transform the Dostoevskian novel into an ordinary monologic novel, which always and ultimately contains at heart only a single accent. From the viewpoint of the novel's artistic construction, these ideas are merely full and equal participants in an action, along with the ideas of Raskolnikov, Ivan Karamazov, and the others. What is more, the tone for the construction of the novel as a whole is set precisely by such characters as Raskolnikov and Ivan Karamazov; this is why the hagiographic overtones in the speeches of the lame woman[d], in the stories and speeches of the pilgrim Makar Dolgoruky, in the "Life of Zosima" stand out so sharply in Dostoevsky's novels. If the authorial world coincided with the plane "earth," then the novels would have been constructed in the hagiographic style corresponding to that plane.

Thus not a single one of the ideas of the heroes—neither of "negative" nor "positive" heroes—becomes a principle of authorial representation, and none constitute the novelistic world in its entirety. And this raises the question: how are the heroes' worlds, and the ideas that lie at their base, united with the world of the author, that is, with the world of the novel? To this question Engelhardt gives an incorrect answer; or more precisely, he avoids it and in fact answers an entirely different question.

Actually, the interrelationships of worlds and planes in the novel—in Engelhardt's terms, "environment," "soil," "earth"—are in no sense present in the novel as links in a unified dialectical sequence, as stages along the path in the evolution of a unified spirit. For if the ideas contained in each separate novel—the planes of the novel being determined by the ideas lying at their base—were in fact arranged as links of a unified dialectical sequence, then each novel would form a completed philosophical whole, structured according to the dialectical

[d]*Khromonozhka*: Marya Lebyadkina, Stavrogin's half-mad crippled wife in *The Possessed*.

method. We would have in the best instance a philosophical novel, a novel with an idea (albeit a dialectical idea); in the worst instance we would have philosophy in the form of a novel. The ultimate link in the dialectical sequence would inevitably turn out to be the author's synthesis—which would then cancel out all preceding links as abstract and totally superseded.

This is not in fact what happens. In none of Dostoevsky's novels is there any evolution of a unified spirit; in fact there is no evolution, no growth in general, precisely to the degree that there is none in tragedy (in this sense the analogy between Dostoevsky's novels and tragedy is correct).[36] Each novel presents an opposition, which is never canceled out dialectically, of many consciousnesses, and they do not merge in the unity of an evolving spirit, just as souls and spirits do not merge in the formally polyphonic world of Dante. At best each could form, as in Dante's world, a static figure, one that did not lose its individuality and that linked together rather than merged with other figures—but this static figure would resemble a congealed event, similar to Dante's image of the cross (the souls of the crusaders), the eagle (the souls of the emperors), or the mystical rose (the souls of the blessed). Likewise the author's spirit does not develop or evolve within the limits of the novel itself, but, as in Dante's world, this spirit is either a spectator, or becomes one of the participants. Within the limits of the novel the heroes' worlds interact by means of the event, but these interrelationships, as we have said before, are the last thing that can be reduced to thesis, antithesis, and synthesis.

But even Dostoevsky's work as a whole must not be understood as the dialectical evolution of the spirit. For the path taken by his creative work is the artistic evolution of his novel—linked, to be sure, with an evolution of ideas, but not dissolved in it. About the dialectical evolution of the spirit, its passing through stages of "environment," "soil," and "earth," one can only conjecture from beyond the boundaries of Dostoevsky's artistic work. His novels, as artistic unities, do not represent or express the dialectical evolution of spirit.

In the final analysis, Engelhardt, just like his predecessors, monologizes Dostoevsky's world, reduces it to a philosophical monologue unfolding dialectically. The unified, dialectically evolving spirit, understood in Hegelian terms, can give rise to nothing but a philosophical monologue. And the soil of monistic idealism is the least likely place for a plurality of unmerged consciousnesses to blossom. In this sense the unified evolving spirit, even as an image, is organically alien to Dostoevsky. Dostoevsky's world is profoundly *pluralistic*. If we were to seek an image toward which this whole world gravitates, an image in the spirit of Dostoevsky's own worldview, then it would be the church as a communion of unmerged souls, where sinners and righteous men come together; or perhaps it would be the image of Dante's world, where multi-leveledness is extended into eternity, where there are the penitent and the unrepentant, the damned and the saved. Such an image would be in the style of Dostoevsky himself, or, more precisely, in the style of his ideology, while the image of a unified spirit is deeply alien to him.

But even the image of the church remains only an image, explaining nothing of the structure of the novel itself. The artistic task resolved by the novel is in essence independent of that secondhand ideological refraction which perhaps occasionally accompanied it in Dostoevsky's consciousness. The concrete artistic links between the various planes of the novel, their combination in the unity of the work, must be explained and demonstrated by the material of the novel itself, and both "Hegelian spirit" and "church" distract equally from this immediate task.

If we were to raise the question of those extra-artistic reasons and factors that made possible the construction of the polyphonic novel, then here, too, the least appropriate approach would be to resort to subjective facts, however profound they may be. If multi-leveledness and contradictoriness were present to Dostoevsky or perceived by him solely as a fact of his personal life, as the multi-leveledness and contradictoriness of the spirit—his own and others—then Dostoevsky would be a Romantic, and he would have created a monologic novel about the contradictory evolution of the human spirit, very much in keeping with the Hegelian idea. But in fact Dostoevsky found and was capable of perceiving multi-leveledness and contradictoriness not in the spirit, but in the objective social world. In this social world, planes were not stages but *opposing camps*, and the contradictory relationships among them were not the rising or descending course of an individual personality, but the *condition of society*. The multi-leveledness and contradictoriness of social reality was present as an objective fact of the epoch.

The epoch itself made the polyphonic novel possible. *Subjectively* Dostoevsky participated in the contradictory multi-leveledness of his own time: he changed camps, moved from one to another, and in this respect the planes existing in objective social life were for him stages along the path of his own life, stages of his own spiritual evolution. This personal experience was profound, but Dostoevsky did not give it a direct monologic expression in his work. This experience only helped him to understand more deeply the extensive and well-developed contradictions which coexisted among people—among people, not among ideas in a single consciousness. Thus the objective contradictions of the epoch did determine Dostoevsky's creative work—although not at the level of some personal surmounting of contradictions in the history of his own spirit, but rather at the level of an objective visualization of contradictions as forces coexisting simultaneously (to be sure, this vision was deepened by personal experience).

We approach here one very important characteristic of Dostoevsky's creative vision, one which has either not been understood at all or underestimated in the literature on him. Underestimating this characteristic was what led Engelhardt to his false conclusions. The fundamental category in Dostoevsky's mode of artistic visualizing was not evolution, but *coexistence* and *interaction*. He saw and conceived his world primarily in terms of space, not time. Hence his deep affinity for the dramatic form.[37] Dostoevsky strives to organize all available meaningful material, all material of reality, in one time-frame, in the form of a dramatic juxtaposition, and he strives to develop it extensively. An artist such as Goethe, for example, gravitates organically toward an evolving sequence. He strives to perceive all existing contradictions as various stages of some unified development; in every manifestation of the present he strives to glimpse a trace of the past, a peak of the present-day, or a tendency of the future; and as a consequence, nothing for him is arranged along a single extensive plane. Such in any case was the basic tendency of his mode for viewing and understanding the world.[38]

In contrast to Goethe, Dostoevsky attempted to perceive the very stages themselves in their *simultaneity*, to *juxtapose* and *counterpose* them dramatically, and not stretch them out into an evolving sequence. For him, to get one's bearings on the world meant to conceive all its contents as simultaneous, and *to guess at their interrelationships in the cross-section of a single moment.*

This stubborn urge to see everything as coexisting, to perceive and show all things side by side and simultaneous, as if they existed in space and not in time, leads Dostoevsky to dramatize, in space, even internal contradictions and internal stages in the development of a single person—forcing a character to converse with his own double, with the devil, with his alter ego, with his own caricature (Ivan and the Devil, Ivan and Smerdyakov, Raskolnikov and Svidrigailov, and so forth). This characteristic explains the frequent occurrence of paired characters in Dostoevsky's work. One could say, in fact, that out of every contradiction within a single person Dostoevsky tries to create two persons, in order to dramatize the contradiction and develop it extensively. This trait finds its external expression in Dostoevsky's passion for mass scenes, his impulse to concentrate, often at the expense of credibility, as many persons and themes as possible in one place at one time, that is, his impulse to concentrate in a single moment the greatest possible qualitative diversity. Hence also Dostoevsky's urge to observe in a novel the dramatic principle of unity of time. And hence the catastrophic swiftness of action, the "whirlwind motion," the dynamics of Dostoevsky. Dynamics and speed here (as, incidentally, everywhere) represent not only the triumph of time, but also the triumph over time, for speed is the single means for overcoming time in time.

The possibility of simultaneous coexistence, the possibility of being side by side or one against the other, is for Dostoevsky almost a criterion for distinguishing the essential from the nonessential. Only such things as can conceivably be linked together at a single point in time are essential and are incorporated into Dostoevsky's world; such things can be carried over into eternity, for in eternity, according to Dostoevsky, all is simultaneous, everything coexists. That which has meaning only as "earlier" or "later," which is sufficient only unto its own moment, which is valid only as past, or as future, or as present in relation to past or future, is for him nonessential and is not incorporated into his world. That is why his characters remember nothing, they have no biography in the sense of something past and fully experienced. They remember from their own past only that which has not ceased to be present for them, that which is still experienced by them as the present: an unexpiated sin, a crime, an unforgiven insult. Dostoevsky incorporates into the framework of his novels only facts such as these from his heroes' biographies, for they are in keeping with his principle of simultaneity.[39] Thus there is no causality in Dostoevsky's novels, no genesis, no explanations based on the past, on the influences of the environment or of upbringing, and so forth. Every act a character commits is in the present, and in this sense is not predetermined; it is conceived of and represented by the author as free.

The characteristic of Dostoevsky we offer here is not, of course, a trait of his worldview in the ordinary sense of the word. It is a trait of his artistic perception of the world: only in the category of coexistence could he see and represent the world. But of course this trait was necessarily reflected in his abstract worldview as well. And we can observe in this worldview analogous phenomena: in Dostoevsky's thinking as a whole, there are no genetic or causal categories. He constantly polemicizes, and with a sort of organic hostility, against the theory of environmental causality, in whatever form it appears (as in, for example, lawyers' appeals to the environment to justify a crime); he almost never appeals to history as such, and treats every social and political question on the plane of the present-day—and this is explained not only by his position as a journalist, which required that everything be treated in the context of the present. We would suggest, on the contrary, that Dostoevsky's passion for journalism and his love of the newspaper, his deep and subtle understanding of the newspaper page as a living reflection of the contradictions of contemporary society in the cross-section of a single day, where the most diverse and contradictory material is laid out, extensively, side by side and one side against the other—all this is explained precisely by the above characteristic of Dostoevsky's artistic vision.[40] And finally, on the level of abstract worldview, this trait expressed itself in Dostoevsky's eschatology, both political and religious, and in his tendency to bring the "ends" closer, to feel them out while still in the present, to guess at the future as if it were already at hand in the struggle of coexisting forces.

Dostoevsky's extraordinary artistic capacity for seeing everything in coexistence and interaction is his greatest strength, but his greatest weakness as well. It made him deaf and dumb to a great many essential things; many aspects of reality could not enter his artistic field of vision. But on the other hand this capacity sharpened, and to an extreme degree, his perception in the cross-section of a given moment, and permitted him to see many and varied things where others saw one and the same thing. Where others saw a single thought, he was able to find and feel out two thoughts, a bifurcation; where others saw a single quality, he discovered in it the presence of a second and contradictory quality. Everything that seemed simple became, in his world, complex and multi-structured. In every voice he could hear two contending voices, in every expression a crack, and the readiness to go over immediately to another contradictory expression; in every gesture he detected confidence and lack of confidence simultaneously; he perceived the profound ambiguity, even multiple ambiguity, of every phenomenon. But none of these contradictions and bifurcations ever became dialectical, they were never set in motion along a temporal path or in an evolving sequence: they were, rather, spread out in one plane, as standing alongside or opposite one another, as consonant but not merging or as hopelessly contradictory, as an eternal harmony of unmerged voices or as their unceasing and irreconcilable quarrel. Dostoevsky's visualizing power was locked in place at the moment diversity revealed itself—and remained there, organizing and shaping this diversity in the cross-section of a given moment.

Dostoevsky's particular gift for hearing and understanding all voices immediately and simultaneously, a gift whose equal we find only in Dante, also permitted him to create the polyphonic novel. The objective complexity, contradictoriness and multi-voicedness of Dostoevsky's epoch, the position of the déclassé intellectual and the social wanderer, his deep biographical and inner participation in the objective multi-leveledness of life and finally his gift for seeing the world in terms of interaction and coexistence—all this prepared the soil in which Dostoevsky's polyphonic novel was to grow.

These characteristics of Dostoevsky's mode of visualization, his special artistic conception of space and time, found additional support (as we shall show in detail below, in the fourth chapter) in the literary tradition with which Dostoevsky was organically connected.

Thus Dostoevsky's world is the artistically organized coexistence and interaction of spiritual diversity, not stages in the evolution of a unified spirit. And thus, despite their different hierarchical emphasis, the worlds of the heroes and the planes of the novel, by virtue of the novel's very structure, lie side by side on a plane of coexistence (as do Dante's worlds) and of interaction (not present in Dante's formal polyphony); they are not placed one after the other, as stages of evolution. But this does not mean, of course, that Dostoevsky's world is ruled by some logical vicious circle, by the inability to think a thought through, by an ill-tempered *subjective* contradictoriness. No, Dostoevsky's world is in its own way just as finalized and well-rounded as Dante's world. But it is futile to seek in it a *systemically monologic*, even if dialectical, *philosophical* finalization—and not because the author has failed in his attempts to achieve it, but because it did not enter into his design.

What induced Engelhardt to seek in Dostoevsky's work "the individual links of a complex philosophical construction expressing the history of the gradual evolution of the human spirit,"[41] that is, to enter upon the well-traveled path of a philosophical monologization of Dostoevsky's work?

It seems to us that Engelhardt made his basic mistake at the beginning of the path, with his definition of Dostoevsky's "ideological novel." The idea as the subject of representation does indeed occupy an enormous place in Dostoevsky's work, but it is nevertheless not the hero of his novels. His hero was a man, and in the final analysis he represented not the idea in man, but (to use his own words) the "man in man." The idea for him was either a touchstone for testing the man in man, or a form for revealing it, or—and this is the last and most important—a "medium," an environment in which human consciousness could be revealed in its deepest essence. Engelhardt underestimates Dostoevsky's profound personalism. Dostoevsky neither knows, nor perceives, nor represents the "idea in itself" in the Platonic sense, nor "ideal existence" as phenomenologists understand it. For Dostoevsky there are no ideas, no thoughts, no positions which belong to no one, which exist "in themselves." Even "truth in itself" he presents in the spirit of Christian ideology, as incarnated in Christ;

that is, he presents it as a personality entering into relationships with other personalities.

Thus Dostoevsky portrayed not the life of an idea in an isolated consciousness, and not the interrelationship of ideas, but the interaction of consciousnesses in the sphere of ideas (but not of ideas only). And since a consciousness in Dostoevsky's world is presented not on the path of its own evolution and growth, that is, not historically, but rather *alongside* other consciousnesses, it cannot concentrate on itself and its own idea, on the immanent logical development of that idea; instead, it is pulled into interaction with other consciousnesses. In Dostoevsky, consciousness never gravitates toward itself but is always found in intense relationship with another consciousness. Every experience, every thought of a character is internally dialogic, adorned with polemic, filled with struggle, or is on the contrary open to inspiration from outside itself—but it is not in any case concentrated simply on its own object; it is accompanied by a continual sideways glance at another person. It could be said that Dostoevsky offers, in artistic form, something like a sociology of consciousnesses —to be sure, only on the level of coexistence. But even so, Dostoevsky as an artist does arrive at an *objective* mode for visualizing the life of consciousnesses and the forms of their living coexistence, and thus offers material that is valuable for the sociologist as well.

Every thought of Dostoevsky's heroes (the Underground Man, Raskolnikov, Ivan, and others) senses itself to be from the very beginning a *rejoinder* in an unfinalized dialogue. Such thought is not impelled toward a well-rounded, finalized, systemically monologic whole. It lives a tense life on the borders of someone else's thought, someone else's consciousness. It is oriented toward an event in its own special way and is inseparable from a person.

The term "ideological novel" therefore seems to us inadequate, for it distracts from Dostoevsky's authentic artistic task.

So Engelhardt too failed to divine the full extent of Dostoevsky's artistic intention. He noted several of its essential aspects, but then interpreted this intention in its totality as philosophically monologic —transforming the polyphony of coexisting consciousnesses into the homophonic evolution of a single consciousness.

The problem of polyphony was posed very concisely and thoroughly by A. V. Lunacharsky* in his article "On Dostoevsky's 'Multivoicedness'."[42]

For the most part Lunacharsky shares our thesis on Dostoevsky's polyphonic novel. "Thus," he says, "I concede that Bakhtin has succeeded not only in establishing more clearly than anyone had before him the enormous significance of the multi-voicedness in the Dostoevskian novel, its role as the most essential characteristic feature of his novels, but also in correctly defining that extraordinary (and in the works of the vast majority of other writers, unthinkable) autonomy and full validity of each 'voice,' which is developed to such a staggering degree in Dostoevsky" (p. 405).

At a later point Lunacharsky emphasizes, and correctly, that

all the voices playing a truly essential role in the novel are actually "convictions" or "points of view on the world."

Dostoevsky's novels are in fact brilliantly staged dialogues.

Under these conditions the profound independence of the individual 'voices' takes on, as it were, a special poignancy. One must assume that there was in Dostoevsky this impulse to put different vital problems up for discussion by these highly individual "voices," trembling with passion, ablaze with the fire of fanaticism — while he himself, as it were, is merely a witness to these convulsive disputes and looks on with curiosity to see how all of it will end, what turn the matter will take. To a great extent this is a true picture (p. 406).

Further on, Lunacharsky poses the question of Dostoevsky's predecessors in the realm of polyphony. Two such predecessors, in his opinion, are Shakespeare and Balzac.

Here is what he says on the polyphonic essence of Shakespeare.

Being untendentious (or so, at least, it was long assumed about him), Shakespeare is polyphonic to the extreme. We could cite a long list of judgments on Shakespeare from the most distinguished scholars, and from his imitators and admirers, all enraptured by precisely Shakespeare's ability to create persons independent from himself, and moreover to create an unbelievably great variety of them, while observing an incredible inner logic in the convictions and acts of each personality in this endless procession . . .

It cannot be said of Shakespeare that his plays sought to prove some thesis, or that the "voices" incorporated into the great polyphony of the Shakespearean dramatic world sacrificed their full and valid status for the sake of the dramatic design, or for the sake of construction as such (p. 410).

In Lunacharsky's opinion, even the social conditions of Shakespeare's epoch are analogous to those of Dostoevsky's.

What were the social factors reflected in Shakespearean polyphonism? In the final analysis, of course, essentially the same ones we have in Dostoevsky. That gaudily colored Renaissance broken up into a myriad of glittering splinters, that Renaissance which gave birth to Shakespeare and to the other playwrights of his time, was of course also the result of a stormy invasion of capitalism into relatively peaceful medieval England. And likewise there, too, a gigantic breakdown began, gigantic shifts and unexpected collisions occurred between social structures and systems of consciousness that had never before come into contact with one another (p. 411).

In our opinion, Lunacharsky is correct in the sense that certain elements, embryonic rudiments, early buddings of polyphony can indeed be detected in the dramas of Shakespeare. Shakespeare, along with

Rabelais, Cervantes, Grimmelshausen* and others, belongs to that line of development in European literature in which the early buds of polyphony ripened, and whose great culminator, in this respect, Dostoevsky was to become. But to speak of a fully formed and deliberate polyphonic quality in Shakespeare's dramas is in our opinion simply impossible, and for the following reasons.

First, drama is by its very nature alien to genuine polyphony; drama may be multi-leveled, but it cannot contain *multiple worlds*; it permits only one, and not several, systems of measurement.

Secondly, if one can speak at all of a plurality of fully valid voices in Shakespeare, then it would only apply to the entire body of his work and not to individual plays. In essence each play contains only one fully valid voice, the voice of the hero, while polyphony presumes a plurality of fully valid voices within the limits of a single work—for only then may polyphonic principles be applied to the construction of the whole.

Thirdly, the voices in Shakespeare are not points of view on the world to the degree they are in Dostoevsky; Shakespearean characters are not ideologists in the full sense of the word.

One may also speak of elements of polyphony in Balzac's work—but only of elements. Balzac belongs to the same line of development in the European novel as Dostoevsky, and is one of his direct and most immediate predecessors. Points in common between Balzac and Dostoevsky have been frequently noted (especially well and thoroughly by Leonid Grossman[e]), and there is no need to return to them here. But Balzac did not transcend the object-ness of his characters, nor the monologic finalization of his world.

In our opinion Dostoevsky alone can be considered the creator of genuine polyphony.

Lunacharsky devotes most of his attention to an explanation of the social and historical reasons for Dostoevsky's multivoicedness.

Agreeing with Kaus, Lunacharsky exposes even more boldly the exceptionally acute contradictory nature of Dostoevsky's epoch, the epoch of young Russian capitalism, and he also exposes the contradictory nature and *duality* of Dostoevsky's own social personality, his oscillations between a revolutionary materialistic socialism and a conservative religious worldview—oscillations that never led to any decisive resolution. We cite here the concluding passage of Lunacharsky's historical and genetic analysis.

> Only the internal splintering of Dostoevsky's consciousness, together with the splintering of young Russian capitalist society, awoke in Dostoevsky the need to hear again and again the trial of socialist principles and socialist reality—but meanwhile the author heard these trials under conditions as unfavorable as possible to materialistic socialism (p. 427).

---

[e]See, in English, Leonid Grossman, *Balzac and Dostoevsky*, trans. Lena Karpov (Ardis, 1973).

And somewhat further:

And that unheard-of freedom of 'voices' in Dostoevsky's polyphony, which so strikes the reader, is in fact an immediate result of the limitations of Dostoevsky's power over the spirits he has called into being . . .

If Dostoevsky is master in his own home as a writer, is he his own master as a man?

No, Dostoevsky the man is not master in his own home, and the disintegration of his personality, its splintering—the fact that he would have liked to believe something which did not inspire in him true faith, the fact that he would have liked to refute something which constantly and repeatedly filled him with doubt—this is what makes him subjectively qualified to be the tormented and necessary reflector of the confusion of his epoch (p. 428).

The genetic analysis of Dostoevsky's polyphony which Lunacharsky offers us is, without question, profound, and as long as it remains within the limits of historical-genetic analysis does not raise any serious doubts. But doubts begin at that point where Lunacharsky draws from his analysis direct and immediate conclusions about the artistic value and historical progressiveness (as regards art) of the new type of polyphonic novel Dostoevsky had created. The exceptionally acute contradictions of early Russian capitalism and the duality of Dostoevsky as a social personality, his personal inability to take a definite ideological stand, are, if taken by themselves, something negative and historically transitory, but they proved to be the optimal conditions for creating the polyphonic novel, "that unheard-of freedom of voices in Dostoevsky's polyphony," and this was without question a step forward in the development of the Russian and European novel. Both Dostoevsky's epoch, with its concrete contradictions, and Dostoevsky's biological and social personality, with its epilepsy and ideological duality, have long since faded into the past— but the new structural principle of polyphony, *discovered* under these conditions, retains and will continue to retain its artistic significance under the completely different conditions of subsequent epochs. Great discoveries of human genius are made possible by the specific conditions of specific epochs, but they never die or lose their value along with the epochs that gave them birth.

No clearly incorrect conclusions on the dying-out of the polyphonic novel are drawn by Lunacharsky from his genetic analysis. But the final words of his article might give grounds for such an interpretation. Here are those words:

"Dostoevsky has not yet died, neither here nor in the West, because capitalism has not yet died, and even less the vestiges of capitalism. . . . Hence the importance of devoting careful study to all the problems of this tragic 'Dostoevskyism'[f]" (p. 429).

---

[f]*Dostoevshchina*. The *shchina* suffix in Russian is more explicitly derogatory than our neutral "ism." When attached to a proper name, it means the excesses or bad times associated with that personality. Maxim Gorky (1868-1936), in a famous article of 1913 "On Karamazovism" [O Karamazovshchine], set the tone for later Soviet attacks on Dostoevsky.

We cannot consider this formulation of the problem successful. Dostoevsky's discovery of the polyphonic novel will outlive capitalism.

"Dostoevskyism," against which Lunacharsky (following Gorky) rightly calls us to battle, must not, of course, be equated with polyphony. "Dostoevskyism" is a reactionary, *purely monologic* extract from Dostoevsky's polyphony. It is locked forever within the limits of a single consciousness, rummages around in it, and creates a cult of the duality of the *isolated* personality. The imporant thing in Dostoevsky's polyphony is precisely what happens *between various consciousnesses*, that is, their interaction and interdependence.

One should learn not from Raskolnikov or Sonya, not from Ivan Karamazov or Zosima, ripping their voices out of the polyphonic whole of the novels (and by that act alone distorting them)—one should learn from Dostoevsky himself as the creator of the polyphonic novel.

In his historical-genetic analysis Lunacharsky investigates only the contradictions of Dostoevsky's epoch and Dostoevsky's own personal duality. But before these important factors could become a new mode of artistic visualization, before they could give birth to the new structure of the polyphonic novel, a lengthy preparation was necessary in general aesthetic and literary traditions. New forms of artistic visualization prepare themselves slowly, over centuries; a given epoch can do no more than create optimal conditions for the final ripening and realization of a new form. To investigate this process of artistic preparation for the polyphonic novel is the task of an historical poetics. A poetics cannot, of course, be divorced from social and historical analyses, but neither can it be dissolved in them.

In the following two decades, that is, in the 1930s and '40s, problems of Dostoevsky's poetics retreated into the background before other important tasks in the study of his work. Work on the texts continued, there were valuable publications of the manuscripts and notebooks to individual novels, progress was made on the four-volume collection of his letters, the history of the writing of individual novels was studied.[43] But specific theoretical works on Dostoevsky's poetics, works which would have been of interest from the point of view of our thesis (the polyphonic novel), did not appear in that period.

From that vantage point several observations by V. Kirpotin* in his brief work *F. M. Dostoevsky* merit attention.

In contrast to very many scholars who see in all of Dostoevsky's works a single soul—the soul of the author himself—Kirpotin emphasizes Dostoevsky's special ability to *see* precisely the soul of *others*.

"Dostoevsky had the seeming capacity to *visualize directly someone else's psyche*. He looked into someone else's soul as if equipped with a magnifying glass that permitted him to detect the subtlest nuances, to follow the most inconspicuous modulations and transitions in the inner life of a man. Dostoevsky, as if *passing over the external barriers*, observes directly the psychological processes taking place in a man, and fixes them on paper . . .

"There was nothing *a priori* in Dostoevsky's gift for seeing into someone else's psyche, someone else's soul. To be sure, in him this gift grew to extraordinary proportions; but it relied on introspection as well, on observation of other people, on a diligent study of man in the works of Russian and world literature, that is, it relied on internal and external experience and therefore had *objective significance*."[44]

Refuting incorrect ideas about the subjectivism and individualism of Dostoevsky's "psychologism," Kirpotin emphasizes the writer's *realistic* and *social* character.

"In contrast to the degenerate decadent psychologism of Proust or Joyce, signaling the decline and fall of bourgeois literature, *Dostoevsky's psychologism* in his affirmative works is not *subjective*, but *realistic*. His psychologism is a special artistic method for penetrating the objective essence of the *contradictory human collective*, for penetrating into the very heart of the *social relationships* which so agitated him, and a special artistic method for reproducing them in the art of the word. . . . Dostoevsky thought in psychologically wrought images, but he thought *socially*."[45]

This correct understanding of Dostoevsky's "psychologism," as a mode for visualizing, objectively and realistically, a contradictory collective of other people's psyches, also leads Kirpotin to a correct understanding of Dostoevsky's *polyphony*—although he himself does not use the term.

"The history of each individual 'soul' is presented . . . in Dostoevsky not in isolation, but together with a description of the psychological tribulations of many other individuals. Whether the Dostoevskian narrative is conducted in the first person, or in the form of a confession, or in the person of a narrator-author—in all cases we see that the writer proceeds from an assumption of *equal rights* for simultaneously existing, experiencing persons. His world is the world of a multitude of objectively existing and interacting psychologies, and this excludes from his treatment of psychological processes the subjectivism and solipsism so characteristic of bourgeois decadence."[46]

Such are the conclusions of Kirpotin, who, following his own special path, arrived at positions quite similar to our own.

In the last decade, literature on Dostoevsky has been enriched by a number of valuable synthesizing works (books and articles), covering all aspects of his creative work (studies by V. Ermilov,* V. Kirpotin, G. Fridlender,* A. Belkin,* F. Evnin,* and Ya. Bilinkis,* among others). But all these studies are dominated by historico-literary and historico-sociological analyses of Dostoevsky's work and the social reality reflected in it. Problems relating strictly to poetics are as a rule treated only in passing (although several of these studies contain valuable, if somewhat random, observations on individual aspects of Dostoevsky's artistic form).

Particularly interesting from the point of view of our thesis is Shklovsky's* book *Pro and Contra. Remarks on Dostoevsky.*[47]

Shklovsky proceeds from the assumption, first advanced by Grossman, that precisely *conflict*, the struggle of ideological voices, lies at the very heart of artistic *form* in Dostoevsky's works, at the very heart of his *style*. But Shklovsky is interested not so much in Dostoevsky's polyphonic form as in the historical (epochal) and real-life biographical sources of the ideological conflict that gave rise to the form. In his own polemical remarks "Contra" he himself defines the essence of his book in this way:

"What distinguishes my study is not an emphasis on those stylistic characteristics which I consider self-evident—Dostoevsky himself emphasized them in *The Brothers Karamazov*, when he titled one of the books of the novel 'Pro and Contra.' In my book I attempt to explain something different: what is the source of that conflict whose trace in fact constitutes Dostoevsky's literary form, and, simultaneously, what accounts for the universality of Dostoevsky's novels, that is, who today would be interested in that conflict?"[48]

Drawing on large amounts of the most varied historical, historico-literary and biographical material, Shklovsky brings to light, in that lively and witty way characteristic of him, the conflict of historical forces and voices of the epoch—social, political, ideological; it is a conflict running through all stages of Dostoevsky's life and creative activity, permeating all events of his life and organizing both the form and the content of all his works. This conflict remained open-ended both for Dostoevsky's epoch, and for Dostoevsky himself. "Thus Dostoevsky died, having resolved nothing, avoiding dénouements and not reconciling himself to the wall."[49]

With all this one can agree (although it is possible to take issue with some of Shklovsky's positions). But we must emphasize here that if Dostoevsky died "having resolved nothing" of the ideological problems posed by his epoch, then nevertheless he died having created a new form of artistic visualization, the polyphonic novel—and it will retain its artistic significance when the epoch, with all its contradictions, has faded into the past.

Shklovsky's book contains valuable observations that touch on questions of Dostoevsky's poetics as well. From the point of view of our thesis, two of his observations are especially interesting.

The first concerns certain characteristics of Dostoevsky's creative process, and the plans in his notebooks.

"Fyodor Mikhailovich loved to jot down plans for things; he loved even more to develop, mull over, and complicate his plans; he did not like to finish up a manuscript . . .

"This was not, of course, because he was 'in too great a hurry,' since Dostoevsky worked with numerous drafts, "becoming inspired by it [by the scene. —V. Sh.] several times over' (1858, in a letter to M. Dostoevsky [31 May 1858, Pis'ma I, p. 236]). But Dostoevsky's plans contain by their very nature an open-endedness which in effect refutes them as plans.

"I assume that Dostoevsky had too little time not because he signed too many contracts or because he himself procrastinated with his works. *As long as a work remained multi-leveled and multi-voiced, as long as the people in it were still arguing, then despair over the absence of a solution would not set in.* The end of a novel signified for Dostoevsky the fall of a new Tower of Babylon."[50]

This is a very true observation. In Dostoevsky's rough drafts the polyphonic nature of his work, the fundamental open-endedness of his dialogues, is revealed in raw and naked form. In general, Dostoevsky's creative process, as reflected in rough drafts, differs sharply from that of other writers (Leo Tolstoy, for example). Dostoevsky does not labor over objectified images of people, he seeks no objectified speech for *personages* (characteristic and typical), he does not seek expressive, graphic, finalizing authorial words—what he seeks above all are words *for the hero*, maximally full of meaning and seemingly independent of the author, words that express not the hero's character (or his typicality) and not his position under given real-life circumstances, but rather his ultimate semantic (ideological) position in the world, his point of view on the world; *for the author and as the author*, Dostoevsky seeks words and plot situations that provoke, tease, extort, dialogize. In this lies the profound originality of Dostoevsky's creative process.[51] The study of his manuscript materials from this angle is an interesting and important task.

In the passage quoted above, Shklovsky raises the complex question of the fundamental open-endedness of the polyphonic novel. We do in fact observe in Dostoevsky's novels a unique conflict between the internal open-endedness of the characters and dialogue, and the *external* (in most cases compositional and thematic) *completedness* of every individual novel. We cannot go deeply into this difficult problem here. We will say only that almost all of Dostoevsky's novels have a *conventionally literary, conventionally monologic* ending (especially characteristic in this respect is *Crime and Punishment*)[g] In essence only *The Brothers Karamazov* has a completely polyphonic ending, but precisely for that reason, from the ordinary (that is, the monologic) point of view, the novel remained uncompleted.

Shklovsky's second observation is equally interesting. It concerns the dialogic nature of all elements in Dostoevsky's novelistic structure.

"It is not only the heroes who quarrel in Dostoevsky, but separate elements in the development of the plot seem to contradict one another: facts are decoded in different ways, the psychology of the characters is self-contradictory; the form is a result of the essence."[52]

Indeed, the essential dialogicality of Dostoevsky is in no way exhausted by the external, compositionally expressed dialogues carried on by the characters. *The polyphonic novel is dialogic through and through*. Dialogic relationships exist among all elements of novelistic structure; that is, they are juxtaposed contrapuntally. And this is so because dialogic relationships are a much broader phenomenon than mere rejoinders in a dialogue, laid out compositionally in the text; they are an almost universal phenomenon, permeating all human speech and all relationships and manifestations of human life—in general, everything that has meaning and significance.

Dostoevsky could hear dialogic relationships everywhere, in all manifestations of conscious and intelligent human life; where consciousness began, there dialogue began for him as well. Only purely mechanistic relationships are not dialogic, and Dostoevsky categorically denied their importance for understanding and interpreting life and the acts of man (his struggle against mechanistic materialism, fashionable "physiologism," Claude Bernard, the theory of environmental causality, etc.). Thus all relationships among external and internal parts and elements of his novel are dialogic in character, and he structured the novel as a whole as a *"great dialogue."* Within this "great dialogue" could be heard, illuminating it and thickening its texture, the compositionally expressed dialogues of the heroes; ultimately, dialogue penetrates within, into every word of the novel, making it double-voiced, into every gesture, every mimic movement on the hero's face, making it convulsive and anguished; this is already the *"microdialogue"* that determines the peculiar character of Dostoevsky's verbal style.

The final work from the critical literature that we will consider in the present survey is an anthology of essays published in 1959, by

[g]For a refutation of this claim that *Crime and Punishment* has a "conventionally monologic ending"—a refutation that uses Bakhtin to undo Bakhtin—see Michael Holquist, *Dostoevsky and the Novel* (Princeton: Princeton University Press, 1977), ch. 3, "Puzzle and Mystery, the Narrative Poles of Knowing: Crime and Punishment," pp. 75-101.

the Institute for World Literature of the Academy of Sciences of the USSR, entitled *The Art of F. M. Dostoevsky.*[h]

In almost all the works of Soviet literary scholars included in this volume, there are many valuable individual observations and also broader theoretical generalizations on questions of Dostoevsky's poetics.[53] But for us, from the point of view of our thesis, the most interesting is L. P. Grossman's large-scale work "Dostoevsky the Artist," and within that work its second chapter, "Laws of Composition."

In this new work Grossman expands, deepens, and enriches with new insights those concepts which he had been developing in the 1920s and which were analyzed by us above.

The composition of every Dostoevskian novel, according to Grossman, is based on "the principle of two or several converging tales," which reinforce one another by means of contrast and are linked by the musical principle of polyphony.

Following Vogüé* and Vyacheslav Ivanov, whom he cites sympathetically, Grossman emphasizes the musical character of Dostoevsky's composition.

We shall quote those of Grossman's observations and conclusions most interesting for us.

Dostoevsky himself pointed out this compositional vehicle [of a musical type —M. B.] and once drew an analogy between his structural system and the musical theory of 'modulations' or counter-positions. He was writing at the time a short novel of three chapters, each with a different content, but internally unified. The first chapter was a monologue, polemical and philosophical; the second was a dramatic episode, which prepared the way for the catastrophic dénouement in the third chapter. Could these chapters be published separately? asks the author. After all, they echo one another internally, in them different but inseparable motifs sound, and while this does permit an organic shift of tonalities it does not permit a mechanistic severing of one from the other. This makes it possible to decode the brief but highly significant reference Dostoevsky made in a letter to his brother on the subject of the forthcoming publication of "Notes from Underground" in the Journal *Time*: "The tale is divided into three chapters . . . The first chapter is perhaps one-and-a-half printer's sheets in length . . . Is it really possible to print it separately? People will laugh at it, and all the more so since without the two remaining (main) chapters it loses all its juice. You know what a *modulation* is in music. It's exactly the same thing here. The first chapter is apparently idle chatter; but suddenly this chatter is resolved, in the last two

[h]*Tvorchestvo F. M. Dostoevskogo*, ed. N. L. Stepanov et al (Moscow: Izd AN SSSR, 1959). This is apparently one of the major anthologies Bakhtin has in mind on p. 37, when he mentions the "valuable synthesizing works" of the 1950s. It contains important articles by Ermilov, Fridlender (on *The Idiot*), Belkin (on *The Karamazovs* and on Dostoevsky's realism), Evnin (on *Crime and Punishment* and *The Possessed*), and Grossman's major work on Dostoevsky the artist.

chapters, by an unexpected catastrophe." [Letter to Michael Dostoevsky, 13 April 1864; *Pis'ma*, I, p. 365]

Here Dostoevsky, with great subtlety, transfers onto the plane of literary composition the law of musical modulation from one tonality to another. The tale is built on the principle of artistic counterpoint. The psychological torment of the fallen girl in the second chapter corresponds to the insult received by her tormentor in the first, but at the same time, because of its meekness, its refusal to answer back in kind, her torment contradicts his feeling of wounded and embittered self-love. This is indeed point versus point (punctum contra punctum). *These are different voices singing variously on a single theme.* This is indeed "multivoicedness," exposing the diversity of life and the great complexity of human experience. '*Everything in life is counterpoint, that is, opposition,*' said one of Dostoevsky's favorite composers, Mikhail Glinka, in his *Notes*.[54]

Grossman's observations on the musical nature of Dostoevsky's compositions are very true and subtle. Transposing Glinka's statement that "everything in life is counterpoint" from the language of musical theory to the language of poetics, one could say that for Dostoevsky *everything in life was dialogue, that is, dialogic opposition.* And indeed, from the point of view of philosophical aesthetics, contrapuntal relationships in music are only a musical variety of the more broadly understood concept of *dialogic relationships.*

Grossman sums up the above observations in this way:

This was in fact a realization of the law, uncovered by the novelist, that some other story," tragic and terrible, always forces its way into a dry, factual description of real life. In keeping with Dostoevsky's poetics, these two stories might be augmented with new plots and other stories, which account for that frequent and familiar multi-leveledness in Dostoevsky's novels. But a two-sided illumination of the main theme remains the dominant principle. It is linked with the often-studied phenomenon of "doubles" in Dostoevsky, who fulfill in his conceptual world a function important not only in terms of ideas and psychologies, but in terms of composition as well.[55]

Such are Grossman's valuable observations. For us they are especially interesting because Grossman, in contrast to other scholars, approaches Dostoevsky's polyphony from the standpoint of composition. What interests him is not so much the *ideological* multivoicedness of Dostoevsky's novels as the specifically compositional application of counterpoint, linking together the various tales incorporated into the novel, the various stories, the various planes.

Such is the interpretation of Dostoevsky's polyphonic novel in that portion of the critical literature that concerned itself at all with questions of his poetics. To this day, the majority of critical and historico-literary studies on him still ignore the uniqueness of his artistic form and seek this uniqueness in his content—in themes, ideas, individual images extracted from the novels and evaluated solely from the point of view of real-life content. But in so doing the content itself is inevitably impoverished—it loses the most essential thing, the *new thing* that Dostoevsky had glimpsed. Without understanding this new form of visualization, one cannot correctly understand that which was seen and unveiled in life for the first time with the help of that form. Artistic form, correctly understood, does not shape already prepared and found content, but rather permits content to be found and seen for the first time.

That which in the European and pre-Dostoevskian Russian novel constituted the ultimate whole—the unified, monologic world of the author's consciousness—becomes in Dostoevsky's novel a part, an element of the whole; that which had been all of reality here becomes only one of the aspects of reality; that which bound together the whole—the pragmatic progression of the plot and a personal style and tone—here becomes only one subordinated element. New principles appear for an artistic combination of elements and for the construction of the whole; what appears—metaphorically speaking—is novelistic counterpoint.

But the consciousness of critics and scholars has up to now been enslaved by the ideology of Dostoevsky's heroes. Dostoevsky's artistic intention has not yet won clear theoretical recognition. It seems that each person who enters the labyrinth of the polyphonic novel somehow loses his way in it and fails to hear the whole behind the individual voices. It often happens that even the dim outlines of the whole are not grasped; the artistic principles governing the combination of voices cannot be detected by the ear. Everyone interprets in his own way Dostoevsky's ultimate word, but all equally interpret it as a *single* word, a *single* voice, a *single* accent, and therein lies their fundamental mistake. The unity of the polyphonic novel—a unity standing above the word, above the voice, above the accent—has yet to be discovered.

NOTES

1. B. M. Engel'gardt, *Ideologicheskii roman Dostoevskogo* [Dostoevsky's Ideological Novel], in F. M. Dostoevskii, *Stat'i i materialy*, II, ed. A. S. Dolinin (Moscow-Leningrad: "Myal'," 1924), p. 71 [on book cover, 1925].

2. Julius Meier-Gräfe, *Dostojewski der Dichter* (Berlin, 1926), p. 189. I quote from the reliable work by T. L. Motyleva, "Dostoevskii i mirovaia literatura (k postanovke voprosa)" [Dostoevsky and World Literature (Toward a Formulation of the Question)], published in *Tvorchestvo F. M. Dostoevskogo* (Moscow: Academy of Sciences of the USSR, 1959). [Meier-Gräfe's book has been translated into English by Herbert H. Marks as *Dostoevsky: The Man and His Work* (New York: Harcourt, Brace & Co., 1928); the passage Bakhtin cites appears on p. 141, during a discussion of character development in *Crime and Punishment*.]

3. That is, by practical everyday motivations.

4. This does not mean, of course, that Dostoevsky is an isolated instance in the history of the novel, nor does it mean that the polyphonic novel which he created was without predecessors. But we must refrain here from historical questions. In order properly to localize Dostoevsky in history, to disclose the *essential* links between him and his predecessors and contemporaries, we must first discover what is unique to him alone, we must show the Dostoevsky in Dostoevsky—even though such a definition of his uniqueness will only be a preliminary one, for the purposes of orientation, until more thorough historical investigations are undertaken. Without such a preliminary orientation, historical research degenerates into a disconnected series of chance contrasts. It is only in the fourth chapter of our book that we will consider the question of Dostoevsky's generic traditions, that is, the question of *historical* poetics.

5. See his work "Dostoevskii i roman-tragediia" [Dostoevsky and the novel-tragedy] in the book *Borozdi i mezhi* [Furrows and Boundaries] (Moscow: "Musaget," 1916). ["Dostoevsky and the novel-tragedy" has appeared in English, in slightly expanded form, as *Freedom and the Tragic Life: A Study of Dostoevsky*, trans. Norman Cameron and ed. S. Konovalov (New York: Noonday Press, 1952). Page numbers to this English translation are appended in brackets to Bakhtin's references.]

6. See *Borozdi i mezhi*, pp. 33-34 [*Freedom*, pp. 26-27].

7. At a later point we shall give a critical analysis of Vyacheslav Ivanov's definition.

8. Here Vyacheslav Ivanov commits a typical methodological error: he moves directly from the author's worldview to the content of the author's works, passing over the form. In other instances Ivanov more correctly understands the interrelationshiop between worldview and form.

9. Such, for example, is Ivanov's assertion that Dostoevsky's heroes are multiplied doubles of the author himself, who has been reborn and who has, as it were, cast off his earthly shell while still in this life (See *Borozdi i mezhi*, pp. 39-40 [*Freedom*, pp. 34-36]).

10. See Askol'dov's article "Religiozno-eticheskoe znachenie Dostoevskogo" [The Religious and Ethical Significance of Dostoevsky] in the book *F. M. Dostoevskii. Stat'i i materialy I*, ed. A. S. Dolinin (Moscow-Leningrad: "Mysl'," 1922).

11. Ibid., p. 2.

12. Ibid., p. 5.

13. Ibid., p. 10.

14. Ibid., p. 9.

15. "Psikhologiia kharakterov u Dostoevskogo," in *F. M. Dostoevskii. Stat'i i materialy II*, ed. A. S. Dolinin, 1924/5.

16. Leonid Grossman, *Poetika Dostoevskogo* [Dostoevsky's Poetics] (Moscow: GAKhN, 1925), p. 165.

17. Ibid., pp. 174-75.

18. Ibid., p. 178.

19. Leonid Grossman, *Put' Dostoevskogo* (Leningrad: Brokgauz-Efron, 1924), pp. 9-10.

20. Ibid., p. 17.

21. The heterogeneity of material mentioned by Grossman is simply inconceivable in drama.

22. This is another reason why Vyacheslav Ivanov's formula—"novel-tragedy"—is incorrect.

23. See Leonid Grossman, *Put' Dostoevskogo*, p. 10.

24. We shall return to the mystery play, and to the Platonic philosophical dialogue as well, in connection with the question of Dostoevsky's generic traditions (see chapter 4).

25. We are not, of course, talking here of antinomy or the juxtaposition of abstract ideas, but of the juxtaposition of whole personalities in concrete events.

26. Otto Kaus, *Dostojewski und sein Schicksal* [Dostoevsky and his Fate] (Berlin: E. Laub'sche, 1923), p. 36. [While certainly true to the spirit of the German, Bakhtin's translation of this passage takes some liberties: the original reads "in the dreams of 'Ridiculous

Men," and in the final sentence there is an accent on *is* ("Dostoevsky *is* many-sided . . .").
Bezdna (abyss, chasm) is a rather exotic rendering of the final word *Gegensatz* (contrast, opposition).]

27. Ibid., p. 63.

28. V. Komarovich, "Roman Dostoevskogo *Podrostok*, kak khudozhestvennoe edinstvo," in *F. M. Dostoevskii. Stat'i i materialy*, II, ed. A. S. Dolinin, p. 48.

29. Ibid., p. 67-68.

30. B. M. Engel'gardt, "Ideologicheskii roman Dostoevskogo" [Dostoevsky's Ideological Novel], in *F. M. Dostoevskii. Stat'i i materialy*, II, ed. A. S. Dolinin, p. 90.

31. Ibid., p. 93.

32. Ibid.

33. Themes of the first plane are as follows: (1) the Russian superman (*Crime and Punishment*), (2) the Russian Faust (Ivan Karamazov), and so on. Themes of the second plane: (1) *The Idiot*, (2) passion in thrall to the sensual "I" (Stavrogin), and so on. The theme of the third plane: the Russian map of righteousness (Zosima, Alyosha). See the Engel'gardt, p. 98 ff.

34. B. M. Engel'gardt, op. cit., p. 96.

35. For Ivan Karamazov, as author of "A Philosophical Poem," the idea is also a principle for representing the world, but then every one of Dostoevsky's heroes is a potential author.

36. Dostoevsky's only design for a biographical novel — *The Life of a Great Sinner*, intended as the history of the evolution of a consciousness — was never realized. Or more precisely, in the process of its realization it disintegrated into a series of polyphonic novels. See V. Komarovich, "Nenapisannaia poema Dostoevskogo" [Dostoevsky's Unwritten Poem], in *F. M. Dostoevskii. Stat'i i materialy*, I, ed. A. S. Dolinin.

37. But, as we have said, without the dramatic prerequisite of a unified monologic world.

38. On this characteristic of Goethe, see the book by G. Simmel, *Goethe* (Leipzig, 1913; Russian translation, GAKhN, 1928), and by F. Gundolf, *Goethe* (1916).

39. Pictures of the past occur only in Dostoevsky's early works (for example, the childhood of Varenka Dobroselova [in *Poor Folk*, 1845]).

40. In Dostoevsky's passion for the newspaper, Grossman puts it well: "Dostoevsky never experienced that aversion to the newspaper page, that contemptuous disgust for the daily press so characteristic of men of his intellectual set and so openly expressed by Hoffmann, Schopenhauer, and Flaubert. In contrast to them, Dostoevsky loved to immerse himself in newspaper articles, condemned his contemporary writers for their indifference to these 'most real and oddest of facts,' and with the intuition of a true journalist he was able to re-create an integral profile of the current historical moment out of the fragmentary trivia of a past day [. . .] 'Do you get any newspapers?' Dostoevsky asked one of his female correspondents in 1867. 'For God's sake, read them, one can't do otherwise nowadays — and this is not to be fashionable, but so that the visible connection between all things public and private might be stronger and more obvious . . .'" (Leonid Grossman, *Poetika Dostoevskogo* [Dostoevsky's Poetics], Moscow: GAKhN, 1925, p. 176).

41. Engel'gardt, op. cit., p. 105.

42. "O 'mnogogolosnosti' Dostoevskogo." Lunacharsky's article was originally published in the journal *Novyi mir*, 1929, No. 10. It has been reprinted several times. We shall quote the article as it appears in the anthology *F. M. Dostoevskii v russkoi kritike* (Moscow: GIKhL, 1956), pp. 403-29. Lunacharsky's article was written apropos of the first edition of our book on Dostoevsky (M. M. Bakhtin, *Problemy tvorchestva Dostoevskogo* [Leningrad: "Priboi," 1929]). [For a translation of the essay (as "Dostoevsky's 'Plurality of Voices'"), see A. Lunacharsky, *On Literature and Art* (Moscow: Progress Publishers, 1973), pp. 79-106.]

43. See, for example, A. S. Dolinin's* very valuable work *V tvorcheskoi laboratorii Dostoevskogo (istoriia sozdaniia roman "Podrostok")* [In Dostoevsky's Creative Laboratory

(The History of the Creation of the Novel *The Adolescent*) (Moscow: Sovetskii pisatel', 1947)].

44. V. Kirpotin, *F. M. Dostevskii: tvorcheskii put'* (Moscow: "Sovetskii pisatel'," 1947), pp. 63-64.

45. Ibid., pp. 64-65.

46. Ibid., pp. 66-67.

47. Viktor Shklovskii, *Za i protiv. Zametki o Dostoevskom* [Pro and Contra. Remarks on Dostoevsky] (Moscow: "Sovetskii pisatel'," 1957).

48. *Voprosy literatury* [Questions of Literature], 1960, No. 4, p. 98. [In the section of the journal entitled "Rejoinders and Remarks," Shklovsky responds to a review by Roman Jakobson of his *Pro and Contra*, which had appeared in a Western journal. Shklovsky summarizes the essence of his book before proceeding to criticize Jakobson's application of ideas in *Pro and Contra* to the works of Mayakovsky.]

49. Viktor Shklovskii, *Za i protiv*, p. 258.

50. Ibid., pp. 171-72.

51. Lunacharsky offers an analogous characterization of Dostoevsky's creative process: ". . . Dostoevsky—if not in the final execution of the novel, then certainly *during its original planning stage and gradual evolution*—was not in the habit of working from a preconceived structural plan . . . we have here instead a true polyphonism of the type that links together and interweaves *absolutely free personalities*. Dostoevsky himself was perhaps interested, extremely and intensely interested, to discover the ultimate outcome of this ideological and ethical conflict between the imaginary persons he had created (or, more precisely, who had created themselves in him)." (*F. M. Dostoevskii v russkoi kritike*, p. 405; "Dostoevsky's 'Plurality of Voices,'" p. 81)

52. Viktor Shklovskii, *Za i protiv*, p. 223.

53. The majority of the authors in the anthology do not endorse the concept of the polyphonic novel.

54. Leonid Grossman, "Dostoevskii-khudozhnik," in *Tvorchestvo F. M. Dostoevskogo*, pp. 341-42.

55. Ibid., p. 342.

Chapter Two
The Hero, and the Position of the Author with Regard to the Hero, in Dostoevsky's Art

We have advanced a thesis, and in the light of this thesis provided a somewhat monologic survey of the more substantial attempts to define the basic characteristic of Dostoevsky's art. In the process of this critical analysis, we have made our own point of view clearer. Now we must move on to a more detailed and documented development of this position, based on the material of Dostoevsky's works.

We will pause, in turn, on three aspects of our thesis: on the relative freedom and independence enjoyed by the hero and his voice under the conditions of polyphonic design; on the special placement of the idea in such a design; and, finally, on those new principles of linkage shaping the novel into a whole. The present chapter is devoted to the hero.

The hero interests Dostoevsky not as some manifestation of reality that possesses fixed and specific socially typical or individually characteristic traits, nor as a specific profile assembled out of unambiguous and objective features which, taken together, answer the question "Who is he?" No, the hero interests Dostoevsky as a *particular point of view on the world and on oneself*, as the position enabling a person to interpret and evaluate his own self and his surrounding reality. What is important to Dostoevsky is not how his hero appears in the world but first and foremost how the world appears to his hero, and how the hero appears to himself.

This is a very important and fundamental feature of the way a fictional character is perceived. The hero as a point of view, as an opinion on the world and on himself, requires utterly special methods of discovery and artistic characterization. And this is so because what must be discovered and characterized here is not the specific existence of the hero, not his fixed image, but the *sum total of his consciousness and self-consciousness*, ultimately *the hero's final word on himself and on his world.*

Consequently those elements out of which the hero's image is composed are not features of reality—features of the hero himself or of his everyday surroundings—but rather the *significance* of these features for the *hero himself*, for his self-consciousness. All the stable and objective qualities of a hero—his social position, the degree to which he is sociologically or characterologically typical, his habitus, his spiritual profile and even his very physical appearance—that is, everything that usually serves an author in creating a fixed and stable image of the hero, "who he is," becomes in Dostoevsky the object of the hero's own introspection, the subject of his self-consciousness; and the subject of the author's visualization and representation turns out to be in fact a *function* of this self-consciousness. At a time when the self-consciousness of a character was usually seen merely as an element of his reality, as merely one of the features of his integrated image, here, on the contrary, all of reality becomes an element of the character's self-consciousness. The author retains for himself, that is, for his exclusive field of vision, not a single essential definition, not a single trait, not the smallest feature of the hero: he enters it all into the field of vision of the hero himself, he casts it all into the crucible of the hero's own self-consciousness. In the author's field of vision, as an object of his visualization and representation, there remains only pure self-consciousness in its totality.

Even in the earliest "Gogolian period" of his literary career, Dostoevsky is already depicting not the "poor government clerk" but the *self-consciousness* of the poor clerk (Devushkin, Golyadkin, even Prokharchin). That which was presented in Gogol's field of vision as an aggregate of objective features, coalescing in a firm socio-characterological profile of the hero, is introduced by Dostoevsky into the field of vision of the hero himself and there becomes the object of his agonizing self-awareness; even the very physical appearance of the "poor clerk," described by Gogol, Dostoevsky forces his hero to contemplate in the mirror.[1] And thanks to this fact all the concrete features of the hero, while remaining fundamentally unchanged in content, are transferred from one plane of representation to another, and thus acquire a completely different artistic significance: they can no longer finalize and close off a character, can no longer construct an integral image of him or provide an artistic answer to the question, "Who is he?" We see not who he is, but *how* he is conscious of himself; our act of artistic visualization occurs not before the reality of the hero, but before a pure function of his awareness of that reality. In this way the Gogolian hero becomes Dostoevsky's hero.[2]

One might offer the following, and somewhat simplified, formula for the revolution that the young Dostoevsky brought about in Gogol's world: he transferred the author and the narrator, with all their accumulated points of view and with the descriptions, characterizations, and definitions of the hero provided by them, into the field of vision of the hero himself, thus transforming the finalized and integral reality of the hero into the material of the hero's own self-consciousness. Not without reason does Dostoevsky force Makar Devushkin to read Gogol's "Overcoat" and to take it as a story about himself, as "slander" against himself; this is how Dostoevsky literally introduces the author into the hero's field of vision.

Dostoevsky carried out, as it were, a small-scale Copernican revolution when he took what had been a firm and finalizing authorial definition and turned it into an aspect of the hero's self-definition. The content of Gogol's world, the world of "The Overcoat," "The Nose," "Nevsky Prospect," and "Notes of a Madman," remained quite unchanged in Dostoevsky's earliest works, *Poor Folk* and *The Double*. But in Dostoevsky the distribution of this identical material among the structural elements of the work is completely different. What the author used to do is now done by the hero, who illuminates himself from all possible points of view; the author no longer illuminates the hero's reality but the hero's self-consciousness, as a reality of the second order. The dominant governing the entire act of artistic visualization and construction had been shifted, and the whole world took on a new look—although in essence almost no new non-Gogolian material had been introduced by Dostoevsky.[3]

Not only the reality of the hero himself, but even the external world and the everyday life surrounding him are drawn into the process of self-awareness, are transferred from the author's to the hero's field of vision. They no longer lie in a single plane with the hero, alongside him and external to him in the unified world of the author —and for this reason they cannot serve as causal or genetic factors determining the hero, they cannot fulfill in the work any explanatory function. Alongside and on the same plane with the self-consciousness of the hero, which has absorbed into itself the entire world of objects, there can be only another consciousness; alongside its field of vision, another field of vision; alongside its point of view on the world, another point of view on the world. *To the all-devouring consciousness of the hero the author can juxtapose only a single objective world—a world of other consciousnesses with rights equal to those of the hero.*

One must not interpret the self-consciousness of a hero on the socio-characterological plane and see it merely as a new trait of the character—that is, see in Devushkin or Golyadkin a Gogolian hero plus self-consciousness. That is exactly how Devushkin was understood by Belinsky.*[a] He cites the passage with the mirror and the torn-off button, a passage which struck him especially, but he does not grasp its formal artistic significance: for him, self-consciousness merely enriches the image of the "poor clerk" in a humanistic direction, arranging itself alongside other features in a fixed image of the character constructed within the usual authorial field of vision. Perhaps this is what prevented Belinsky from correctly assessing *The Double* as well.

Self-consciousness, as the *artistic dominant* governing the construction of a character, cannot lie alongside other features of his image; it absorbs these other features into itself as its own material and deprives them of any power to define and finalize the hero.

Self-consciousness can be made the dominant in the representation of any person. But not all persons are equally favorable material for such a representation. The Gogolian clerk in this respect offered too narrow a potential. Dostoevsky sought a hero who would be occupied primarily with the task of becoming conscious, the sort of hero whose life would be concentrated on the pure function of gaining consciousness of himself and the world. And at this point in his work there begin to appear the "dreamer" and the "underground man." Both "dreamer-ness" and "underground-ness" are socio-characterological features of people, but here they also answer to Dostoevsky's artistic dominant. The consciousness of a dreamer or an underground man—who are not personified, and cannot be personified—is most favorable soil for Dostoevsky's creative purposes, for it allows him to fuse the artistic dominant of the representation with the real-life and characterological dominant of the represented person.

Oh, if I had done nothing simply out of laziness! Heavens, how I would have respected myself then. I would have respected myself because I would at least have been capable of being lazy; there would at least have been in me one positive quality, as it were, in which I could have believed myself. Question: Who is he? Answer: A loafer. After all, it would have been pleasant to hear that about oneself! It would mean that I was positively defined, it would mean that there was something to be said about me. "Loafer"—why, after all, it is a calling and

[a]On Belinsky's enthusiastic reception of *Poor Folk*, see Dostoevsky's own reminiscence of the event 32 years later, in *The Diary of a Writer*, January 1877, chapter II, 3 (pp. 584-87). Belinsky's review of *Poor Folk* can be found in V. G. Belinskii, *Sobranie sochinenii* (Moscow: OGIz, 1948), III, pp. 61-86 ("Peterburgskii sbornik").

an appointment, it is a career, gentlemen. [*SS* IV, 147; "Notes from Underground," Part One, VI]

The Underground Man not only dissolves in himself all possible fixed features of his person, making them all the object of his own introspection, but in fact he no longer has any such traits at all, no fixed definitions, there is nothing to say about him, he figures not as a person taken from life but rather as the subject of consciousness and dream. And for the author as well he is not a carrier of traits and qualities that could have been neutral toward his self-consciousness and could have finalized him; no, what the author visualizes is precisely the hero's self-consciousness and the inescapable open-endedness, the vicious circle of that self-consciousness. Thus the real-life characterological definition of the Underground Man and the artistic dominant of his image are fused into one.

Only among the classicists, only in Racine is it possible to find so deep and complete a concurrence between the form of the hero and the form of the man, between the dominant by which the image is constructed and the dominant of the hero's character. This comparison of Dostoevsky with Racine sounds like a paradox, for the material out of which each realizes a whole and adequate art is indeed far too diverse. Racine's hero is all objective existence, stable and fixed, like plastic sculpture. Dostoevsky's hero is all self-consciousness. Racine's hero is an immobile and finite substance; Dostoevsky's hero is infinite function. Racine's hero is equal to himself; Dostoevsky's hero never for an instant coincides with himself. But artistically, Dostoevsky's hero is just as precise as Racine's.

Self-consciousness, as the artistic dominant in the construction of the hero's image, is by itself sufficient to break down the monologic unity of an artistic world—but only on condition that the hero, as self-consciousness, is really represented and not merely expressed, that is, does not fuse with the author, does not become the mouthpiece for his voice; only on condition, consequently, that accents of the hero's self-consciousness are really objectified and that the work itself observes a distance between the hero and the author. If the umbilical cord uniting the hero to his creator is not cut, then what we have is not a work of art but a personal document.

Dostoevsky's works are in this sense profoundly objective—because the hero's self-consciousness, once it becomes the dominant, breaks down the monologic unity of the work (without, of course, violating artistic unity of a new and nonmonologic type). The hero becomes relatively free and independent, because everything in the author's design that had defined him and, as it were, sentenced him, everything that had qualified him to be once and for all a completed image of reality, now no longer functions as a form for finalizing him, but as the material of his self-consciousness.

In a monologic design, the hero is closed and his semantic boundaries strictly defined: he acts, experiences, thinks, and is conscious within the limits of what he is, that is, within the limits of his image defined as reality; he cannot cease to be himself, that is, he cannot exceed the limits of his own character, typicality or temperament without violating the author's monologic design concerning him. Such an image is constructed in the objective authorial world, objective in relation to the hero's consciousness; the construction of that authorial world with its points of view and finalizing definitions presupposes a fixed external position, a fixed authorial field of vision. The self-consciousness of the hero is inserted into this rigid framework, to which the hero has no access from within and which is part of the authorial consciousness defining and representing him—and is presented against the firm background of the external world.

Dostoevsky renounces all these monologic premises. Everything that the author-monologist kept for himself, using it to create the ultimate unity of a work and the world portrayed in it, Dostoevsky turns over to his hero, transforming all of it into an aspect of the hero's self-consciousness.

There is literally nothing we can say about the hero of "Notes from Underground" that he does not already know himself: his typicality for his time and social group, the sober psychological or even psychopathological delineation of his internal profile, the category of character to which his consciousness belongs, his comic as well as his tragic side, all possible moral definitions of his personality, and so on—all of this, in keeping with Dostoevsky's design, the hero knows perfectly well himself, and he stubbornly and agonizingly soaks up all these definitions from within. Any point of view from without is rendered powerless in advance and denied the finalizing word.

Because the dominant of representation in this literary work coincides maximally with the dominant of that which is represented, the formal task of the author can be very clearly expressed in the content. What the Underground Man thinks about most of all is what others think or might think about him; he tries to keep one step ahead of every other consciousness, every other thought about him, every other point of view on him. At all the critical moments of his confession he tries to anticipate the possible definition or evaluation others might make of him, to guess the sense and tone of that evaluation, and tries painstakingly to formulate these possible words about himself by others, interrupting his own speech with the imagined rejoinders of others.

"Isn't that shameful, isn't that humiliating?" you will say, perhaps, shaking your heads contemptuously. "You long for life and try to settle the problems of life by a logical tangle. . . . You may be truthful in what you have said but you have no modesty; out of the pettiest vanity you bring your truth to public exposure, to the market place, to ignominy. You doubtlessly mean to say something, but hide your real meaning for fear, because you lack the resolution to say it, and only have a cowardly impudence. You boast of consciousness, but you are unsure of your ground, for though your mind works, yet your heart is corrupted by depravity, and you cannot have a full, genuine consciousness without a pure heart. And how tiresome you are, how you thrust yourself on people and grimace! Lies, lies, lies!"

Of course I myself have made up just now all the things you say. That, too, is from underground. *For forty years I have been listening to your words there through a crack under the floor. I have invented them myself. After all, there was nothing else I could invent.* It is no wonder that I have learned them by heart and that it has taken a literary form. [*SS* IV, 164-65; "Notes from Underground," Part One, XI]

The hero from the underground eavesdrops on every word someone else says about him, he looks at himself, as it were, in all the mirrors of other people's consciousnesses, he knows all the possible refractions of his image in those mirrors. And he also knows his own objective definition, neutral both to the other's consciousness and to his own self-consciousness, and he takes into account the point of view of a "third person." But he also knows that all these definitions, prejudiced as well as objective, rest in his hands and he cannot finalize them precisely because he himself perceives them; he can go beyond their limits and can thus make them inadequate. He knows that he has the *final word*, and he seeks at whatever cost to retain for himself this final word about himself, the word of his self-consciousness, in order to become in it that which he is not. His consciousness of self lives by its unfinalizability, by its unclosedness and its indeterminancy.

And this is not merely a character trait of the Underground Man's self-consciousness, it is also the dominant governing the author's construction of his image. The author does indeed leave the final word to his hero. And precisely that final word—or, more accurately, the tendency toward it—is necessary to the author's design. The author constructs the hero not out of words foreign to the hero, not out of neutral definitions; he constructs not a character, nor a type, nor a temperament, in fact he constructs no objectified image of the hero at all, but rather the hero's *discourse* about himself and his world.

Dostoevsky's hero is not an objectified image but an autonomous discourse, *pure voice*; we do not see him, we hear him; everything that we see and know apart from his discourse is nonessential and is swallowed up by discourse as its raw material, or else remains outside it as something that stimulates and provokes. We will demonstrate below that the entire artistic construction of a Dostoevskian novel is directed toward discovering and clarifying the hero's discourse, and performs provoking and directing functions in relation to that discourse. The epithet "a cruel talent," applied to Dostoevsky by N. K. Mikhailovsky,* has some justification, although not as simple a one as it seemed at the time. The special sort of moral torture that Dostoevsky inflicts upon his heroes, in order to force out of them that ultimate word of a self-consciousness pushed to its extreme limits, permits him to take all that is merely material, merely an object, all that is fixed and unchanging, all that is external and neutral in the representation of a person, and dissolve it in the realm of the hero's self-consciousness and self-utterance.

To convince ourselves of the artistic depth and subtlety of these provocative artistic devices of Dostoevsky, it is enough to compare him with recent enthusiastic imitators of this "cruel talent"—the German Expressionists Kornfeld,* Werfel,* and others. In most cases these writers cannot get beyond provocations of hysteria and various hysterical frenzies, because they are incapable of creating around the hero that extremely complex and subtle atmosphere that would force him to reveal and explain himself dialogically, to catch aspects of himself in others' consciousnesses, to build loopholes for himself, prolonging and thereby laying bare his own final word as it interacts intensely with other consciousnesses. Those who are artistically the most restrained, such as Werfel, create a symbolic setting for the hero's self-revelation. Such, for example, is the court scene from Werfel's "Spiegelmensch," in which the hero passes judgment on himself and the judge takes minutes and summons witnesses.

This dominant of self-consciousness in the construction of the hero is correctly grasped by the Expressionists, but they are incapable of compelling self-consciousness to reveal itself spontaneously and in an artistically convincing way. What results is either a crude and deliberate experiment on the hero, or a symbolic action.

The self-clarification, self-revelation of the hero, his discourse about himself not predetermined (as the ultimate goal of his construction) by some neutral image of him, does indeed sometimes make the author's setting "fantastic," even for Dostoevsky. For Dostoevsky the verisimilitude of a character is verisimilitude of the character's own internal discourse about himself in all its purity—but, in order to hear and display that discourse, in order to incorporate it into the field of vision of another person, the laws of that other field must be violated, for the normal field can find a place for the object-image of another person but not for another field of vision in its entirety. Some fantastical viewpoint must be sought for the author outside ordinary fields of vision.

Here is what Dostoevsky says in the author's foreword to "A Meek One":

Now for the story itself. I have called it a fantastic story, whereas I personally consider it highly realistic. There is, however, a fantastic element in it, that is, in the very composition of the story, and this, I think, needs to be explained beforehand.

The fact is that this is neither a narrative nor a collection of notes. Imagine to yourself a husband whose wife has committed suicide only a few hours ago by jumping out of the window. Her body is laid out on the table. He is confused and has not arranged his thoughts. He is pacing his rooms, trying to take in what has happened, and "bring his thoughts to a focus." The man, it must be said, is an inveterate hypochondriac, one of those who talk to themselves. And so he is talking to himself, going over what has happened and trying to take it all in. Despite his seeming coherence he often contradicts himself both in his logic and his feelings. He both justifies himself and accuses her, then goes into irrelevant explanations: coarseness of heart and mind is mingled with depth of feeling. By degrees he does take it all in and "focuses his thoughts." A train of memories he has called up bring him at last irresistibly to the *truth*, and truth irresistibly ennobles his heart and mind. Towards the end the very tone of his narrative becomes different from its incoherent beginning. The truth is revealed to the poor man quite clearly and definitely, sufficiently for himself to see at least.

So much for the theme. The telling of the story, of course, takes a few hours in breaks and snatches; it is disconnected in form, for he either argues with himself or addresses some unseen listener, a judge as it were. However, it is always like that in real life. If a stenographer could have listened to him and taken it all down, it would have sounded rather less smooth and finished than my account, but I do believe that the psychological sequence would have probably been the same. Now this hypothetical stenographer (whose notes I have given shape to) is what I call "fantastic" in my story. However, something of the sort has been allowed in literature before: Victor Hugo, for instance, in his masterpiece *Le Dernier Jour d'un Condamné* [The Last Day of a Man Condemned] resorted to almost the same medium; and though he portrayed no stenographer he made it even less credible by assuming that a man sentenced to death was able (and had sufficient time) to make notes not only of his last day on earth, but also of his last hour and, actually, his last minute. Were it not for this fantastic situation, however, the work itself would not have been written—the most realistic and the most truthful of all his books. [*SS* X, 378-79]

We have quoted this foreword almost in its entirety because the statements expressed there are of extraordinary importance for understanding Dostoevsky's creative method: the "*truth*" at which the hero must and indeed ultimately does arrive through clarifying the events to himself, can essentially be for Dostoevsky only *the truth of the hero's own consciousness*. It cannot be neutral toward his self-consciousness. In the mouth of another person, a word or a definition identical in content would take on another meaning and tone, and would no longer be the truth. Only in the form of a confessional self-utterance, Dostoevsky maintained, could the final word about a person be given, a word truly adequate to him.

But how can this word be introduced into the story without destroying the individuality of the word, and at the same time without destroying the fabric of the story, without reducing the story to a simple motivating device for the introduction of the confession? The fantastical form of "A Meek One" is only one possible solution to this problem, and it is limited by the scope of a novella. But what artistic effort was required of Dostoevsky to replace the functions of a fantastic stenographer throughout an entire multi-voiced novel!

The issue here is not, of course, pragmatic difficulties or external compositional devices. Tolstoy, for example, calmly introduces the final thoughts of his dying hero, the final flicker of consciousness with its final word, directly into the fabric of the story and straight from the author (as early as the "Sevastopol Stories," but it is especially evident in the later works, "The Death of Ivan Ilych," "Master and Man"). For Tolstoy the very problem does not even arise; he has no need to stipulate the fantastic nature of his device. Tolstoy's world is monolithically monologic; the hero's discourse is confined in the fixed framework of the author's discourse about him. Even the hero's final word is given in the shell of someone else's (the author's) word; the hero's self-consciousness is only one aspect of his fixed image and is in fact predetermined by that image, even where thematically consciousness undergoes a crisis and the most radical inner revolution (as in "Master and Man"). In Tolstoy, self-consciousness and spiritual rebirth remain entirely in the realm of content and have no form-shaping significance; the ethical unfinalizability of a man before his death does not become the structural and artistic unfinalizability of the hero. The artistic structure of Brekhunov's or Ivan Ilych's image differs in no way from that of the old prince Bolkonsky or Natasha Rostova. For all their thematic importance in Tolstoy's work, a character's self-consciousness and discourse never become the dominant by which he is constructed. A second autonomous voice (alongside the author's voice) does not appear in Tolstoy's world; for that reason there is no problem of linking voices, and no problem of a special positioning for the author's point of view. Tolstoy's discourse and his monologically naive point of view permeate everywhere, into all corners of the world and the soul, subjugating everything to its unity.

In Dostoevsky, the author's word stands opposite the fully valid and pure unalloyed word of the hero. Therefore a problem does arise with the positioning of authorial discourse, the problem of its formal and artistic position with regard to the hero's discourse. This problem lies deeper than the question of authorial discourse on the superficial level of composition, and deeper than any superficially compositional device for eliminating authorial discourse by means of the *Ich-Erzählung* form (first-person narration), or by the introduction of a narrator, or by constructing the novel in scenes and thus reducing authorial discourse to the status of a stage direction. All these compositional devices for eliminating or weakening authorial discourse at the level of composition do not in themselves tackle the essence of the problem; their underlying artistic meaning can be profoundly different, depending on the different artistic tasks they perform. The *Ich-Erzählung* form of "The Captain's Daughter" [by Alexander Pushkin, 1836] is infinitely far removed from the *Ich-Erzählung* form of "Notes from Underground," even if we abstractly think away the content that fills these forms. Grinev's story is constructed by Pushkin in a fixed monologic field of vision, even though this field is not represented externally in the composition because there is no direct authorial discourse. But it is precisely that field of vision that determines the entire construction. As a result *the fixed image of Grinev* is an image, and not a discourse; Grinev's discourse is an element of his image, that is, it is fully exhausted by functions of characterization and pragmatic development of the plot. Grinev's point of view on the world and its events is likewise only a component of his image: he is presented as a *characteristic reality*, and not as a directly signifying, fully weighted *semantic position*. The direct and unmediated power to mean belongs only to the authorial point of view lying at the base of the construction; everything else is merely its object. The introduction of a narrator may in fact not weaken the monologism of the author's position at all, which would continue to see and know all things only in one way; and it need not strengthen at all the semantic weight and independence of the hero's discourse. Of such a sort, for example, is Pushkin's narrator Belkin.[b]

Thus all these compositional devices are in themselves still incapable of destroying the monologism of an artistic world. But in Dostoevsky they do in fact perform this function, becoming a tool in the realization of his polyphonic artistic design. We will see below how and by what means they perform this function. But for our present purposes only the artistic design itself is important, and not the means for concretely realizing it.

Self-consciousness, as the artistic dominant in the structure of a character's image, presupposes a radically new *authorial position* with regard to the represented person. We repeat: what is at issue here is not the discovery of new features or new types of man, for those could be discovered, glimpsed, and portrayed in art through an

---

[b]Pushkin twice used the garrulous provincial squire Ivan Petrovich Belkin as his narrator: in the five *Tales of Belkin* (1830) and in the *History of the Village of Goryukhino* (1830).

ordinary monologic approach to the person, that is, without any radical change in the author's position. No, at issue here is precisely the discovery of a *new integral view on the person*—the discovery of "personality" (Askoldov) or "the man in man" (Dostoevsky)—possible only by approaching the person from a correspondingly new and *integral* authorial position.

We will try to clarify in somewhat greater detail this integral position, this fundamentally new *form* for visualizing a human being in art.

In Dostoevsky's earliest literary work one can already see something like a revolt of the hero against literature's secondhand, externalizing and finalizing approach to the "little man." As we noted above, Makar Devushkin read Gogol's "Overcoat" and was deeply offended by it *personally*. He recognized himself in Akaky Akakievich and was outraged that his poverty had been *spied upon*, that his entire life had been analyzed and described, that he had been defined once and for all, that he had been left with no other prospects.

One hides oneself sometimes, one hides oneself, one tries to conceal one's weak points, one's afraid to show one's nose at times anywhere because one is afraid of tittle-tattle, because they can work up a tale against you about anything in the world—anything. And here now all one's private and public life is being dragged into literature, it is all printed, read, laughed and gossiped about! [*SS* I, 146; *Poor Folk*, Letter of July 8]

Devushkin was especially outraged that Akaky Akakievich had died unchanged, just the same as he had always been.

Devushkin had glimpsed himself in the image of the hero of "The Overcoat," which is to say, as something totally quantified, measured, and defined to the last detail: all of you is here, there is nothing more in you, and nothing more to be said about you. He felt himself to be hopelessly predetermined and finished off, as if he were already quite dead, yet at the same time he sensed the falseness of such an approach. This peculiar "revolt" of the hero against his literary finalization is presented by Dostoevsky in the consistent, primitive forms of Devushkin's consciousness and speech.

The serious and deeper meaning of this revolt might be expressed this way: a living human being cannot be turned into the voiceless object of some secondhand, finalizing cognitive process. *In a human being there is always something that only he himself can reveal, in a free act of self-consciousness and discourse, something that does not submit to an externalizing secondhand definition.* In *Poor Folk* Dostoevsky made his first attempt to show—although still incompletely and unclearly—*that internally unfinalizable something in man*, the thing that Gogol and the other authors of "tales about poor government clerks" could not show from their monologic positions. Thus in his first work Dostoevsky is already beginning to grope his way toward his future radically new position with regard to the hero.

In Dostoevsky's subsequent works, the characters no longer carry on a *literary* polemic with finalizing secondhand definitions of man (although the author himself sometimes does this for them, in very subtle ironic-parodic form), but they all do furious battle with such definitions of their personality in the mouths of other people. They all acutely sense their own inner unfinalizability, their capacity to outgrow, as it were, from within and to render *untrue* any externalizing and finalizing definition of them. As long as a person is alive he lives by the fact that he is not yet finalized, that he has not yet uttered his ultimate word. We have already noted how agonizingly the Underground Man eavesdrops on all actual and potential words others say of him, and how he tries to outguess and outwit all possible definitions of his personality others might offer. The hero of "Notes from Underground" is the first hero-ideologist in Dostoevsky's work. One of his basic ideas, which he advances in his polemic with the socialists, is precisely the idea that man is not a final and defined quantity upon which firm calculations can be made; man is free, and can therefore violate any regulating norms which might be thrust upon him.

Dostoevsky's hero always seeks to destroy that framework of *other people's* words about him that might finalize and deaden him. Sometimes this struggle becomes an important tragic motif in the character's life (as, for example, with Nastasya Filippovna).

In the major heroes, in such protagonists of the great dialogue as Raskolnikov, Sonya, Myshkin, Stavrogin, Ivan and Dmitry Karamazov, the profound consciousness of their own unfinalizability and indeterminacy is realized in very complex ways, by ideological thought, crime, or heroic deed.[4]

A man never coincides with himself. One cannot apply to him the formula of identity A ≡ A. In Dostoevsky's artistic thinking, the genuine life of the personality takes place at the point of non-coincidence between a man and himself, at his point of departure beyond the limits of all that he is as a material being, a being that can be spied on, defined, predicted apart from its own will, "at second hand." The genuine life of the personality is made available only through a *dialogic* penetration of that personality, during which it freely and reciprocally reveals itself.

The truth about a man in the mouths of others, not directed to him dialogically and therefore a *secondhand* truth, becomes a *lie* degrading and deadening him, if it touches upon his "holy of holies," that is, "the man in man."

We will cite several statements by Dostoevsky's heroes that express the same thought about *secondhand analyses* of the human soul.

In *The Idiot*, Myshkin and Aglaya are discussing Ippolit's unsuccessful attempted suicide. Myshkin gives an analysis of the deeper motives behind the act. Aglaya says to him:

I find all this very mean on your part, for it's very *brutal* to *look on* and *judge a man's soul*, as you judge Ippolit. You have no tenderness, *nothing but truth, and so you judge unjustly.* [SS VI, 484; *The Idiot*, Part III, ch. 8]

Truth is unjust when it concerns the depths of *someone else's* personality.

The same motif sounds even more clearly, if in somewhat more complex form, in *The Brothers Karamazov*, in Alyosha's conversation with Liza about Captain Snegirev, who had trampled underfoot the money offered him. Having told the story, Alyosha analyzes Snegirev's emotional state and, as it were, *predetermines* his further behavior by *predicting* that next time he would *without fail* take the money. To this Liza replies:

. . . Listen, Alexey Fyodorovich. Isn't there in all our analysis—I mean *your* analysis . . . no, better call it ours—aren't we showing *contempt* for him, for that poor man—*in analyzing his soul like this*, as it were, *from above*, eh? In deciding so *certainly* that he will take the money? [SS IX, 271-72; *The Brothers Karamazov*, Book Five, I]

An analogous motif, that of the impermissability of some *other outside person* penetrating the depths of a personality, is heard in Stavrogin's angry words uttered in Tikhon's cell, where he had come with his "Confession":

"Listen, I don't like *spies* and *psychologists*, at least those who poke into my soul."[5]

It must be pointed out that in the given instance Stavrogin is utterly wrong in his attitude toward Tikhon: Tikhon approaches him in a profoundly *dialogic* manner, and understands fully the unfinalizability of his inner personality.

At the very end of his creative career, Dostoevsky defined in his notebook the distnguishing features of his realism in this way:

"With utter realism *to find the man in man* . . . They call me a *psychologist; this is not true.* I am merely a realist *in the higher sense*, that is, I portray all the *depths of the human soul*."[6]

We will have occasion to return more than once to this remarkable formula. But at this point it is important to emphasize three of its aspects.

First, Dostoevsky considers himself a realist, but not a subjective romantic trapped in the world of his own consciousness. He solves his *new* task—"portraying all the depths of the human soul"—with "utter realism," that is, he sees these depths *outside* himself, in the souls of *others*.

Second, Dostoevsky believes that this *new* task cannot be adequately performed by realism in the usual sense, that is, by what is in our terminology *monologic* realism; what is needed here is a special approach to the "man in man," that is, a "realism in the higher sense."

Third, *Dostoevsky categorically denies that he is a psychologist.*

We must examine this third aspect in somewhat more detail. Toward the psychology of his day—as it was expressed in scientific and artistic literature, and as it was practiced in the law courts—Dostoevsky had no sympathy at all. He saw in it a degrading *reification* of a person's soul, a discounting of its freedom and its unfinalizability, and of that peculiar indeterminacy and indefiniteness which in Dostoevsky constitute the main object of representation: for in fact Dostoevsky always represents a person *on the threshold* of a final decision, at a moment of *crisis*, at an unfinalizable—and *unpredeterminable*—turning point for his soul.

Dostoevsky constantly and severely criticized mechanistic psychology, both its pragmatic lines based on the concepts of *natural law* and *utility*, and even more its physiological line, which reduced psychology to physiology. He ridicules it in his novels as well. It is enough to remember the "tubercles on the brain" in Lebezyatnikov's explanation of Katerina Ivanovna's spiritual crisis (*Crime and Punishment*)[c], or the transformation of Claude Bernard's name into a pejorative symbol of man's liberation from responsibility—the "Bernards" of Mitenka Karamazov (*The Brothers Karamazov*).[d]

But particularly revealing for an understanding of Dostoevsky's artistic position is his criticism of legal investigative psychology, which is at best a "double-edged sword," that is, something that permits mutually exclusive solutions to be accepted with an equal probability of being true, and at worst simply a lie degrading the individual.

In *Crime and Punishment* the remarkable court investigator Porfiry Petrovich—it was he who called psychology a "double-edged sword"—is governed not by it, that is not by legal investigative psychology, but by a special *dialogic intuition* that allows him to penetrate the unfinalized and unresolved soul of Raskolnikov. The three meetings of Porfiry with Raskolnikov are in no sense ordinary investigative interrogations; but this is not only because they do not "follow the proper form" (a point Porfiry continually emphasizes), but because

---

[c]*Crime and Punishment*, Part V, ch. 5
[d]*The Brothers Karamazov*, Book Twelve, IX ("Psychology at Full Steam")

they violate the very basis of the traditional psychological relationship between investigator and criminal (this Dostoevsky emphasizes). All three of Porfiry's meetings with Raskolnikov are authentic and remarkable polyphonic dialogues.

The most profound picture of false psychology in practice is provided by the scenes of Dmitry's preliminary investigation and trial in *The Brothers Karamazov*. The investigator, judges, prosecutor, defense attorney, and commission of experts are all equally incapable of approaching the unfinalized and undecided core of Dmitry's personality, for he is a man who stands, in essence throughout his entire life, on the threshold of great internal decisions and crises. In place of this living core, bursting with new life, they substitute a sort of *ready-made definitiveness*, "naturally" and "normally" *predetermined* in all its words and acts by "psychological laws." All who judge Dmitry are devoid of a genuinely dialogic approach to him, a dialogic penetration into the unfinalized core of his personality. They seek and see in him only the factual, *palpable definitiveness* of experiences and actions, and subordinate them to already defined concepts and schemes. The authentic Dmitry remains outside their judgment (he will pass judgment on himself).

This is why Dostoevsky did not consider himself a psychologist in any sense of the term. What is important for us, of course, is not the philosophical and theoretical side of his criticism in and of itself; it cannot satisfy us and in any case suffers from a misunderstanding of the dialectics of freedom and necessity in the acts and consciousness of a man.[7] What is important for us here is the striving of Dostoevsky's *artistic* energies and the new *form* of his artistic visualization of the inner man.

It is appropriate here to emphasize that the major emotional thrust of all Dostoevsky's work, in its form as well as its *content*, is the struggle against a *reification* of man, of human relations, of all human values under the conditions of capitalism. Dostoevsky did not, to be sure, completely understand the deep economic roots of reification; nowhere, as far as we know, did he use the actual term "reification," but it is this term precisely that best expresses the deeper sense of his struggle on behalf of man. With great insight Dostoevsky was able to see how this *reifying devaluation* of man had permeated into all the pores of contemporary life, and even into the very foundations of human thinking. In his criticism of this reifying mode of thought he sometimes "addresses the wrong social party," as Ermilov expressed it[8]; he accused all the representatives of the revolutionary democratic movement and Western socialism, considering them outgrowths of the capitalist spirit. But, we repeat, what is important for us is not the abstractly theoretical and not the journalistic side of his criticism, but rather the *larger sense of his artistic form*, which liberates and de-reifies the human being.

Thus the new artistic position of the author with regard to the hero in Dostoevsky's polyphonic novel is a *fully realized and thoroughly consistent dialogic position*, one that affirms the independence, internal freedom, unfinalizability, and indeterminacy of the hero. For the author the hero is not "he" and not "I" but a fully valid "thou," that is, another and other autonomous "I" ("thou art"). The hero is the subject of a deeply serious, *real* dialogic mode of address, not the subject of a rhetorically *performed* or *conventionally* literary one. And this dialogue—the "great dialogue" of the novel as a whole —takes place not in the past, but right now, that is, in the *real present* of the creative process.[9] This is no stenographer's report of a *finished* dialogue, from which the author has already withdrawn and *over* which he is now located as if in some higher decision-making position: that would have turned an authentic and unfinished dialogue into an objectivized and finalized *image of a dialogue*, of the sort usual for every monologic novel. The great dialogue in Dostoevsky is organized as an *unclosed whole* of life itself, life poised *on the threshold*.

Dostoevsky realizes a dialogic relationship toward his characters at every moment of the creative process and at the moment of its completion; this is part of his general design, and thus remains in even the most finished novel as an indispensable element for shaping form.

In Dostoevsky's novels, the author's discourse about a character is organized as discourse about *someone actually present*, someone who hears him (the author) and is *capable of answering him*. Such organization of authorial discourse in Dostoevsky's works is no conventional device, but rather the unconditional *ultimate* position of the author.[e] In the fifth chapter of our work we will try to show that the distinctiveness of Dostoevsky's verbal style is due to the overriding importance of precisely such dialogically oriented discourse, and to the negligible role played by monologically closed-off discourse, by words that expect no answer.

In Dostoevsky's larger design, the character is a carrier of a fully valid word and not the mute, voiceless object of the author's words. The author's design for a character is a *design for discourse*. Thus the author's discourse about a character is discourse about discourse. It is oriented toward the hero as if toward a discourse, and is therefore dialogically *addressed* to him. By the very construction of the novel, the author speaks not *about* a character, but *with* him. And it

---

[e]"Conventional" and "conditional" are rendered by the same word [*uslovnyi*] in Russian; in English, the parallelism of this sentence is lost.

cannot be otherwise: only a dialogic and participatory orientation takes another person's discourse seriously, and is capable of approaching it both as a semantic position and as another point of view. Only through such an inner dialogic orientation can my discourse find itself in intimate contact with someone else's discourse, and yet at the same time not fuse with it, not swallow it up, not dissolve in itself the other's power to mean; that is, only thus can it retain fully its independence as a discourse. To preserve distance in the presence of an intense semantic bond is no simple matter. But distance is an integral part of the author's design, for it alone guarantees genuine objectivity in the representation of a character.

Self-consciousness as the dominant in the construction of a character's image requires the creation of an artistic atmosphere that would permit his discourse to reveal and illuminate itself. Not a single element in this atmosphere can be neutral: everything must touch the *character* to the quick, provoke him, interrogate him, even polemicize with him and taunt him; everything must be directed toward the hero himself, turned toward him, everything must make itself felt as *discourse about someone actually present*, as the word of a "second" and not of a "third" person. The semantic point of view of a "third person," on whose territory a stable image of the hero is constructed, would destroy this atmosphere, and therefore such a point of view does not enter into Dostoevsky's creative world; and this is not because such a viewpoint is unavailable (due to the characters' autobiographical origins, or to Dostoevsky's extreme polemicism), but because it does not enter into Dostoevsky's creative design. This design requires a thorough dialogization of all elements in the construction. Here is the source of that apparent nervousness, that extreme overstrain and agitation of the atmosphere in Dostoevsky's novels that superficially conceal the most subtle artistic calculations, the balance and necessity of each tone, each accent, each unexpected turn of events, each scandal, each eccentricity. Only in the light of this artistic project can one understand the authentic function of such compositional elements as the narrator and his tone, the compositionally expressed dialogue, and the peculiarities of narration direct from the author (in those places where it exists).

Such is the relative independence of characters within the limits of Dostoevsky's creative design. Here we must warn against one possible misunderstanding. It might seem that the independence of a character contradicts the fact that he exists, entirely and solely, as an aspect of a work of art, and consequently is wholly created from beginning to end by the author. In fact there is no such contradiction. The characters' freedom we speak of here exists within the limits of the artistic design, and in that sense is just as much a created thing as is the unfreedom of the objectivized hero. But to create does not mean to invent. Every creative act is bound by its own special laws, as well as by the laws of the material with which it works. Every creative act is determined by its object and by the structure of its object, and therefore permits no arbitrariness; in essence it invents nothing, but only reveals what is already present in the object itself. It is possible to arrive at a correct thought, but this thought has its own logic and therefore cannot be invented, that is, it cannot be fabricated from beginning to end. Likewise an artistic image, of whatever sort, cannot be invented, since it has its own artistic logic, its own norm-generating order. Having set a specific task for himself, the creator must subordinate himself to this order.

Dostoevsky's hero is likewise not invented, just as the hero of the ordinary realistic novel, and the romantic hero, and the hero of the classicists are not invented. But each has his own order, his own logic, which enters into the realm of the author's artistic intention but is not infringed upon by the author's whim. Once he has chosen a hero and the dominant of his hero's representation, the author is already bound by the inner logic of what he has chosen, and he must reveal it in his representation. The logic of self-consciousness permits only certain artistic means for revealing and representing itself. Self-consciousness can be interrogated and provoked into revealing and representing itself, but not by giving it a predetermined or finalizing image. Such an objectified image is precisely what is inadequate to the very thing that the author has selected as his subject.

Thus the freedom of a character is an aspect of the author's design. A character's discourse is created by the author, but created in such a way that it can develop to the full its inner logic and independence as *someone else's discourse*, the word of the *character himself*. As a result it does not fall out of the author's design, but only out of a monologic authorial field of vision. And the destruction of this field of vision is precisely a part of Dostoevsky's design.

In his book *On the Language of Artistic Literature* V. V. Vinogradov* refers to a very interesting, almost *polyphonic* plan for an unfinished novel by N. G. Chernyshevsky.* He cites it as an example of the impulse toward a maximally objective construction of the *author's image*. Chernyshevsky's novel in manuscript had several titles, one of which was *The Pearl of Creation*. In his foreword to the novel Chernyshevsky reveals the essence of his design in this way:

To write a novel without love—without a single female character—is a very difficult thing. But I felt the need to try my strength at a task even more difficult: *to write a purely objective novel, in which there would be no trace not only of my personal attitudes, but also of my personal sympathies. In Russian literature there is not a single such novel. Onegin* and *A Hero of Our Time* are unabashedly subjective things; *Dead Souls* contains no portrait of the author nor portraits of his acquaintances, but the personal sympathies of the author have certainly been incorporated; they are in fact the source of that strong impression the novel produces. It seems that for me, a man of strong and fixed convictions, the most difficult thing would be to write as Shakespeare wrote: *he portrays people and life without saying what he himself thinks on the questions that are resolved by his characters in a way appropriate for each.* Othello says "yes," Iago says "no," Shakespeare says nothing, he has no desire to state his love or lack of love for a "yes" or a "no." It is understood that I am speaking of the manner, and not of the strength, of the talent . . . *Try to discover whom I sympathize with and whom I don't . . . You won't find out . . .* In *The Pearl of Creation* each poetic position is examined from all four sides—try to discover which opinion I sympathize with, which I do not. *Try to discover how one point of view passes over into another completely incompatible with it.* This is the true meaning of the title "The Pearl of Creation"—here, as in mother-of-pearl, are all the shades of colors in the rainbow. But as in mother-of-pearl all these shades slide by one another, and play against a background of snowy whiteness. It is thus to my novel that the lines of verse in the epigraph refer:

> Wie Schnee, so weiss,
> Und Kalt, wie Eis,

The second line refers to me.

There is "whiteness, like the whiteness of snow" in my novel, "but coldness, like the coldness of ice" in its author . . . to be cold, like ice, this was difficult for me, for a person who loves ardently what he loves. But I succeeded. Thus I see that I have the necessary power of artistic creativity to become a novelist . . . *My characters are very diverse in the expressions their faces must assume . . .* Think of each what you will: *each says for himself: "The full right is on my side"—you be the judge of these conflicting claims. I do not judge.* These characters praise one another, condemn one another—all that is none of my business.[10]

Such is Chernyshevsky's intention (insofar, naturally, as we can judge from his foreword). We see that Chernyshevsky was groping here toward the essentially new structural form of an "objective novel," as he calls it. Chernyshevsky himself emphasizes the utter novelty of the form ("In all of Russian literature there is not a single such novel") and contrasts it to the ordinary "subjective" novel (we would have said "monologic").

What, according to Chernyshevsky, is the essence of this new novelistic structure? The subjective point of view of the author must not be represented in it; neither must the author's sympathies and antipathies, his agreement or disagreement with the individual characters, nor his personal ideological position ("without saying what he himself thinks on the questions that are resolved by his characters . . .").

This does not mean, of course, that Chernyshevsky had in mind a novel without an authorial position. Such a novel is in general impossible. Vinogradov is absolutely correct when he writes: "The tendency toward 'objectifying' the artistic reproduction and the various devices for 'objective' construction are all merely special, but correlative, principles for constructing an *image of the author*."[11] The issue here is not an absence of, but a *radical change in, the author's position*, and Chernyshevsky himself emphasizes that this new position is considerably more difficult than the ordinary position and presupposes an enormous "power of poetic creativity."

This new "objective" authorial position (whose realization Chernyshevsky finds only in Shakespeare) permits the characters' points of view to unfold to their maximal fullness and independence. Each character *freely* (without the author's interference) reveals and substantiates the rightness of his own position: "each says *for himself*: 'the full right is on my side'—you judge these conflicting claims. I do not judge."

Precisely in this *freedom for others' points of view to reveal themselves* without any finalizing evaluations from the author does Chernyshevsky see the chief advantage of the new "objective" form of novel. We emphasize that Chernyshevsky saw in this no betrayal of "his strong and fixed convictions." Thus we can say that Chernyshevsky came very close indeed to the idea of polyphony.

What is more, Chernyshevsky also comes close here to the concepts of counterpoint and the "image of an idea." "*Try to discover*," he says, "*how one point of view passes over into another completely incompatible with it*. This is the true meaning of the title 'The Pearl of Creation'—*here, as in mother-of-pearl, are all the shades of colors in the rainbow*." This is in fact a splendid graphic definition of counterpoint in literature.

Such is the interesting conception of new novelistic structure by one of Dostoevsky's contemporaries, who keenly sensed, as Dostoevsky himself did, the extraordinary multi-voicedness of his epoch. True, this conception cannot be called polyphonic in the full sense of the word. The new authorial position in it is characterized as something essentially negative, as an absence of the usual authorial subjectivity. There is no mention of the author's dialogic activity, without which a new authorial position cannot be realized. But nevertheless Chernyshevsky clearly felt the need to go beyond the limits of the prevailing monologic form of the novel.

Here it is again appropriate to emphasize the *positive and active quality* of the new authorial position in a polyphonic novel. It would be absurd to think that the author's consciousness is nowhere expressed in Dostoevsky's novels. The consciousness of the creator of a polyphonic novel is constantly and everywhere present in the novel, and is active in it to the highest degree. But the function of this consciousness and the forms of its activity are different than in the monologic novel: the author's consciousness does not transform others' consciousnesses (that is, the consciousnesses of the characters) into objects, and does not give them secondhand and finalizing definitions. Alongside and in front of itself it senses others' equally valid consciousnesses, just as infinite and open-ended as itself. It reflects and re-creates not a world of objects, but precisely these other consciousnesses with their worlds, re-creates them in their authentic *unfinalizability* (which is, after all, their essence).

The consciousnesses of other people cannot be perceived, analyzed, defined as objects or as things—one can only *relate to them dialogically*. To think about them means to *talk with them; otherwise they immediately turn to us their objectivized side*: they fall silent, close up, and congeal into finished, objectivized images. An enormous and intense dialogic activity is demanded of the author of a polyphonic novel: as soon as this activity slackens, the characters begin to congeal, they become mere things, and monologically formed chunks of life appear in the novel. Such chunks, which fall out of the polyphonic design, can be found in all of Dostoevsky's novels, but they do not of course determine the nature of the whole.

The author of a polyphonic novel is not required to renounce himself or his own consciousness, but he must to an extraordinary extent broaden, deepen and rearrange this consciousness (to be sure, in a specific direction) in order to accommodate the autonomous consciousnesses of others. This was a very difficult and unprecedented project (something Chernyshevsky apparently understood very well when he devised his plan for the "objective novel"). But it was essential if the polyphonic nature of life itself was to be artistically recreated.

Every *true* reader of Dostoevsky, who perceives his novels not in the monologic mode and who is capable of rising to Dostoevsky's new authorial position, can sense this peculiar *active broadening* of his consciousness, not solely in the sense of an assimilation of new objects (human types, character, natural and social phenomena), but primarily in the sense of a special dialogic mode of communication with the autonomous consciousnesses of others, something never before experienced, an active dialogic penetration into the unfinalizable depths of man.

The finalizing activity of the author of a monologic novel is, indeed, especially evident in the fact that such authors cast a mantle of objectivity over every point of view they do not share, turning it, to one degree or another, into a thing. In contrast to this, Dostoevsky's authorial activity is evident in his extension of every contending point of view to its maximal force and depth, to the outside limits of plausibility. He strives to expose and develop all the semantic possibilities embedded in a given point of view (Chernyshevsky, as we have seen, strove for the same thing in his *Pearl of Creation*). This Dostoevsky knew how to do with extraordinary power. And this activity, the intensifying of someone else's thought, is possible only on the basis of a dialogic relationship to that other consciousness, that other point of view.

We see no special need to point out that the polyphonic approach has nothing in common with relativism (or with dogmatism). But it should be noted that both relativism and dogmatism equally exclude all argumentation, all authentic dialogue, by making it either unnecessary (relativism) or impossible (dogmatism). Polyphony as an *artistic* method lies in an entirely different plane.

The new position of the author in the polyphonic novel can be made clearer if we juxtapose it concretely with a distinctly expressed monologic position in a specific work.

We shall therefore analyze briefly, from the vantage point most relevant to us, Leo Tolstoy's short story "Three Deaths" [1858]. This work, not large in size but nevertheless tri-leveled, is very characteristic of Tolstoy's monologic manner.

Three deaths are portrayed in the story—the deaths of a rich noblewoman, a coachman, and a tree. But in this work Tolstoy presents death as a stage of life, as a stage illuminating that life, as the optimal point for understanding and evaluating that life in its entirety. Thus one could say that this story in fact portrays three lives totally finalized in their meaning and in their value. And in Tolstoy's story all three lives, and the levels defined by them, are *internally self-enclosed and do not know one another*. There is no more than a purely external pragmatic connection between them, necessary for the compositional and thematic unity of the story: the coachman Seryoga, transporting the ailing noblewoman, removes the boots from a coachman who is dying in a roadside station (the dying man no longer has any need for boots) and then, after the death of the coachman, cuts down a tree in the forest to make a cross for the man's grave. In this way three lives and three deaths come to be externally connected.

But an internal connection, *a connection between consciousnesses,* is not present here. The dying noblewoman knows nothing of the life and death of the coachman or the tree, they do not enter into her field of vision or her consciousness. And neither the noblewoman nor the tree enter the consciousness of the dying coachman. The lives and deaths of all three characters, together with their worlds, lie side by side in a unified objective world and are even *externally* contiguous, but they know nothing of one another and are not reflected in one another. They are self-enclosed and deaf; they do not hear and do not answer one another. There are not and cannot be any dialogic relationships among them. They neither argue nor agree.

But all three personages, with their self-enclosed worlds, are united, juxtaposed and made meaningful to one another in the *author's* unified field of vision and consciousness that encompasses them. He, the author, knows everything about them, he juxtaposes, contrasts, and evaluates all three lives and all three deaths. All three lives and deaths illuminate one another, but only for the author, who is located *outside* them and takes advantage of his *external position* to give them a definitive meaning, to finalize them. The all-encompassing field of vision of the author enjoys an enormous and fundamental "surplus" in comparison with the fields of vision of the characters. The noblewoman sees and understands only her own little world, her own life and her own death; she does not even suspect the possibility of the sort of life and death experienced by the coachman or the tree. Therefore she cannot herself understand and evaluate the *lie* of her own life and death; she does not have the dialogizing background for it. And the coachman is not able to understand and evaluate the wisdom and truth of his life and death. All this is revealed only in the author's field of vision, with its "surplus." The tree, of course, is by its very nature incapable of understanding the wisdom and beauty of its death—the author does that for it.

Thus the total finalizing meaning of the life and death of each character is revealed only in the author's field of vision, and thanks solely to the advantageous "surplus" which that field enjoys over every character, that is, thanks to that which the character cannot himself see or understand. This is the finalizing, monologic function of the author's "surplus" field of vision.

As we have seen, there are no dialogic relationships between characters and their worlds. But the author does not relate to them dialogically either. A dialogic position with regard to his characters is quite foreign to Tolstoy. He does not extend his own point of view on a character to the character's own consciousness (and in principle he could not); likewise the character is not able to respond to the author's point of view. In a monologic work the ultimate and finalizing authorial evaluation of a character is, by its very nature, a *second-hand evaluation*, one that does not presuppose or take into account any potential *response* to this evaluation on the part of the character himself. The hero is not given the last word. He cannot break out of the fixed framework of the author's secondhand evaluation finalizing him. The author's attitude encounters no internal dialogic resistance on the part of the character.

The words and consciousness of the author, Leo Tolstoy, are nowhere addressed to the hero, do not question him, and expect no response from him. The author neither argues with his hero nor agrees with him. He speaks not with him, but about him. The final word belongs to the author, and that word—based on something the hero does not see and does not understand, on something located outside the hero's consciousness—can never encounter the hero's words on a single dialogic plane.

That external world in which the characters of the story live and die is the *author's world*, an objective world vis-à-vis the consciousnesses of the characters. Everything within it is seen and portrayed in the author's all-encompassing and omniscient field of vision. Even the noblewoman's world—her apartment, its furnishings, the people close to her and their experiences, the doctors, and so forth—is portrayed from the author's point of view, and not as the noblewoman herself sees and experiences that world (although while reading the story we are also fully aware of her *subjective* perception of that world). And the world of the coachman (the hut, the stove, the cook, etc.) and of the tree (nature, the forest)—all these things are, as is the noblewoman's world, parts of one and the same objective world, seen and portrayed from *one and the same authorial position*. The author's field of vision nowhere intersects or collides dialogically with the characters' fields of vision or attitudes, nowhere does the word of the author encounter resistance from the hero's potential word, a word that might illuminate the same object differently, in its own way—that is, from the vantage point of its own *truth*. The author's point of view cannot encounter the hero's point of view on one plane, on one level. The point of view of the hero (in those places where the author lets it be seen) always remains an object of the author's point of view.

Thus, despite the multiple levels in Tolstoy's story, it contains neither polyphony nor (in our sense) counterpoint. It contains only *one cognitive subject*, all else being merely *objects* of its cognition. Here a dialogic relationship of the author to his heroes is impossible, and thus there is no *"great dialogue"* in which characters and author might participate with equal rights; there are only the objectivized dialogues of characters, compositionally expressed within the author's field of vision.

In the above story Tolstoy's monologic position comes to the fore very distinctly and with *great external visibility*. That is the reason we chose this story. In Tolstoy's novels and in his longer stories, the issue is, of course, considerably more complex.

In the novels, the major characters and their worlds are not self-enclosed and deaf to one another; they intersect and are interwoven in a multitude of ways. The characters do know about each other, they exchange their individual "truths," they argue or agree, they carry on dialogues with one another (including dialogues on ultimate questions of worldview). Such characters as Andrei Bolkonsky, Pierre Bezukhov, Levin, and Nekhlyudov have their own well-developed fields of vision, sometimes *almost* coinciding with the author's (that is, the author sometimes sees the world as if through their eyes), their voices sometimes *almost* merge with the author's voice. But not a single one ends up on the same plane with the author's word and the author's truth, and with none of them does the author enter into dialogic relations. All of them, with their fields of vision, with their quests and their controversies, are inscribed into the *monolithically monologic whole* of the novel that finalizes them all and that is never, in Tolstoy, the kind of "great dialogue" that we find in Dostoevsky. All the clamps and finalizing moments of this monologic whole lie in the zone of authorial "surplus," a zone that is fundamentally inaccessible to the consciousnesses of the characters.

Let us return to Dostoevsky. How would "Three Deaths" look if (and let us permit ourselves for a moment this strange assumption) Dostoevsky had written them, that is, if they had been structured in a polyphonic manner?

First of all, Dostoevsky would have forced these three planes to be reflected in one another, he would have bound them together with dialogic relationships. He would have introduced the life and death of the coachman and the tree into the field of vision and consciousness of the noblewoman, and the noblewoman's life into the field of vision and consciousness of the coachman. He would have forced his characters to see and know all those essential things that he himself — the author — sees and knows. He would not have retained for himself any *essential* authorial "surplus" (essential, that is, from the point of view of the desired truth). He would have arranged a face-to-face confrontation between the truth of the noblewoman and the truth of the coachman, and he would have forced them to come into dialogic contact (although not necessarily in direct compositionally expressed dialogues, of course), and he would himself have assumed, in relation to them, a dialogic position with equal rights. The entire work would have been constructed by him as a great dialogue, but one where the author acts as organizer and participant in the dialogue without retaining for himself the final word; that is, he would have reflected in his work in the dialogic nature of human life and human thought itself. And in the words of the story not only the pure *intonations of the author* would be heard, but also the intonations of the noblewoman and the coachman; that is, words would be double-voiced, in each word an argument (a microdialogue) would ring out, and there could be heard echoes of the great dialogue.

Of course Dostoevsky would never have depicted three *deaths*: in his world, where self-consciousness is the dominant of a person's image and where the interaction of full and autonomous consciousnesses is the fundamental event, death cannot function as something that finalizes and elucidates life. Death in the Tolstoyan interpretation of it is totally absent from Dostoevsky's world.[12] Dostoevsky would have not depicted the deaths of his heroes, but the *crises* and *turning points* in their lives; that is, he would have depicted their lives *on the threshold*. And his heroes would have remained internally *unfinalized* (for self-consciousness cannot be finalized *from within*). Such would have been a polyphonic treatment of the story.

Dostoevsky never left anything of any real consequence outside the realm of his major heroes' consciousness (that is, outside the consciousness of those heroes who participate as equals in the great dialogues of his novels); he brings them into dialogic contact with everything essential that enters the world of his novels. Whenever someone else's "truth" is presented in a given novel, it is introduced without fail into the *dialogic field of vision* of all the other major heroes of the novel. Ivan Karamazov, for example, knows and understands Zosima's truth, as well as Dmitry's truth, and Alyosha's truth, and the "truth" of that old sensualist, his father Fyodor Pavlovich. Dmitry understands all these truths as well; Alyosha, too, understands them perfectly. In *The Possessed*, there is not a single idea that fails to find a dialogic response in Stavrogin's consciousness.

For himself Dostoevsky never retains any essential "surplus" of *meaning*, but only that indispensable minimum of pragmatic, purely *information-bearing* "surplus" necessary to carry forward the story. For if any essential surplus of meaning were available to the author, it would transform the great dialogue of the novel into a finalized and objectivized dialogue, or into a dialogue rhetorically performed.

We shall cite some excerpts from Raskolnikov's first great interior monologue (at the beginning of *Crime and Punishment*); the issue is Dunechka's decision to marry Luzhin:

It's clear that Rodion Romanovich Raskolnikov is the central figure in the business, and no one else. Oh yes, she can ensure his happiness, keep him in the university, make him a partner in the office, make his whole future secure; perhaps he may even be a rich man later on, prosperous, respected, and may even end his life a famous man! But my mother? It's all Rodya, precious Rodya, her firstborn! For such a son who would not sacrifice such a daughter! Oh, loving, over-partial hearts! Why, for his sake we would not shrink even from Sonya's fate. Sonya, Sonya Marmeladova, the eternal victim so long as the world lasts. Have you taken the measure of your sacrifice, both of you? Is it right? Can you bear it? Is it any use? Is there sense in it? And let me tell you, Dounia, Sonya's life is no worse than life with Mr. Luzhin. 'There can be no question of love,' mother writes. And what if there can be no respect either, if on the contrary there is aversion, contempt, repulsion, what then? So you will have to 'keep up your appearance,' too. Is not that so? Do you understand what that smartness means? Do you understand that the Luzhin smartness is just the same thing as Sonya's and may be worse, viler, baser, because in your case, Dounia, it's a bargain for luxuries, after all, but with Sonya it's simply a question of starvation. It has to be paid for, it has to be paid for, Dounia, this smartness. And what if it's more than you can bear afterwards, if you regret it? The bitterness, the misery, the curses, the tears hidden from all the world, for you are not a Marfa Petrovna. And how will your mother feel then? Even now she is uneasy, she is worried, but then, when she sees it all clearly? And I? Yes, indeed, what have you taken me for? I won't have your sacrifice, Dounia, I won't have it, mother! It shall not be, so long as I am alive, shall not, it shall not! I won't accept it!" [. . .]

"Or throw up life altogether!" he cried suddenly, in a frenzy—"accept one's lot humbly as it is, once for all and stifle everything in oneself, giving up all claim to activity, life and love!"

"Do you understand, sir, do you understand what it means when you have absolutely nowhere to turn?" Marmeladov's question came suddenly into his mind, "for every man must have somewhere to turn." . . . [*SS* V, 49-51; *Crime and Punishment*, Part I, ch. 4]

This interior dialogue, as we have said, takes place at the very beginning, on the second day of the novel's action, before the final decision to murder the old woman has been made. Raskolnikov has just received his mother's detailed letter with the history of Dounia and Svidrigailov and the news about the engagement to Luzhin. The evening before, Raskolnikov had met Marmeladov and had learned from him the whole history of Sonya. And all these future major characters of the novel are already reflected here in Raskolnikov's consciousness, they have entered into a thoroughly dialogized interior monologue, entered with their own "truths," with their own positions in life, and Raskolnikov has entered into a fundamental and intense interior dialogue with them, a dialogue of ultimate questions and ultimate life decisions. From the very beginning he already knows everything, takes everything into account, anticipates everything. He has already entered into dialogic contact with the whole of life surrounding him.

The excerpt we cited from Raskolnikov's dialogized interior monologue is a splendid model of the microdialogue; all words in it are double-voiced, and in each of them a conflict of voices takes place. In the beginning of the passage Raskolnikov actually re-creates

Dounia's words with her evaluating and persuading intonations, and over her intonations he layers his own—ironic, indignant, precautionary; that is, in these words two voices are sounding simultaneously—Raskolnikov's and Dounia's. In the subsequent words "It's all Rodya, precious Rodya, her firstborn!" etc.) one can already hear the mother's voice with her intonations of love and tenderness, and at the same time there is Raskolnikov's voice with its intonations of bitter irony, indignation (at the gesture of sacrifice), and sorrowful reciprocal love. Further we hear in Raskolnikov's words both Sonya's voice and Marmeladov's voice. Dialogue has penetrated inside every word, provoking in it a battle and the interruption of one voice by another. This is microdialogue.

Thus, at the very beginning of the novel the leading voices in the great dialogue have already begun to sound. These voices are not self-enclosed or deaf to one another. They hear each other constantly, call back and forth to each other, and are reflected in one another (especially in the microdialogues). And outside this dialogue of "conflicting truths" not a single essential act is realized, nor a single essential thought of the major characters.

In the subsequent course of the novel, nothing incorporated into its content—people, ideas, things—remains external to Raskolnikov's consciousness; everything is projected against him and dialogically reflected in him. All possible evaluations and points of view on his personality, his character, his idea, his acts are extended to his own consciousness and addressed to him in dialogues with Porfiry, Sonya, Svidrigailov, Dounia, and others. All others' perception of the world intersects with his perception. Everything that he sees and observes—both Petersburg slums and monumental Petersburg, all his chance encounters and trivial happenings—everything is drawn into dialogue, responds to his questions and puts new questions to him, provokes him, argues with him, or reinforces his own thoughts. The author retains for himself no essential "surplus" of meaning and enters on an equal footing with Raskolnikov into the great dialogue of the novel as a whole.

This is the new position of the author with regard to the hero in Dostoevsky's polyphonic novel.

NOTES

1. Devushkin, on his way to the General, sees himself in a mirror:

I was so flustered that my lips were trembling, my legs were trembling. And I had reason to be, my dear girl! To begin with, I was ashamed; I glanced into the looking-glass on the right hand and what I saw there was enough to send one out of one's mind. . . . I remembered what I had seen in the looking-glass: I flew to catch the button! (*SS* I, 186; *Poor Folk*, Letter of Sept. 9)

Devushkin sees in the mirror exactly what Gogol, when he described the coat and appearance of Akaky Akakievich, had depicted, but Devushkin sees what Akaky Akakievich himself could not see or become aware of; the constant agonizing reflection of the heroes on their external appearance is the function, for them, of the mirror; for Golyadkin, it is his double.

2. Dostoevsky often gives external portraits of his heroes, directly from the author, or from the narrator, or through other characters. But in Dostoevsky these external portraits do not perform the function of finalizing the hero; they do not create a fixed and predetermining image. The functions of one or another of a character's traits do not, of course, depend solely upon the elementary artistic methods used to reveal this trait (self-characterization by the hero, or directly from the author, or by some indirect route, etc.).

3. "Prokharchin" also remained within the boundaries of this same Gogolian material, and also the piece "The Shaved-off Sideburns" [Sbritye bakenbardy], which Dostoevsky destroyed. But here Dostoevsky began to sense that his new principle applied to the same Gogolian material was already becoming a repetition, and that it was imperative to tackle material essentially new in content. In 1846 he wrote to his brother: "I'm not writing 'The Shaved-off Sideburns' either. I threw everything out. Because all of it is nothing but a repeat of the old things I finished saying long ago. Now brighter, more original and alive thoughts are begging me to put them down on paper. As soon as I had finished writing 'Shaved-off Sideburns' this all came to me spontaneously. In my position, monotony is ruin." [Letter to Mikhail Dostoevsky, end of October 1846; Pis'ma, 1, p. 100.] Then he began work on Netochka Nezvanova and "The Landlady"; that is, he sought to apply his new principle to another area of the same Gogolian world ("The Portrait," and somewhat in "The Terrible Vengeance").

4. This inner unfinalizability of Dostoevsky's characters was correctly understood and identified by Oscar Wilde as their single most important feature. In her work Dostoevskii i mirovaia literatura [Dostoevsky and World Literature] T. L. Motyleva says of Wilde: "Wilde saw the greatest merit in Dostoevsky the artist in the fact that he 'never completely explains his characters.' Dostoevsky's heroes, in Wilde's words, 'always astound us by what they say and do, and preserve within themselves to the end of the eternal secret of existence." [In Tvorchestvo F. M. Dostoevskogo (Moscow: AN SSSR, 1959), p. 32].

5. Dokumenty po istorii literatury i obshchestvennosti [Documents on the History of Literature and Society], Issue I: "F. M. Dostoevskii" [Moscow: Izd Tsentrarkhiv RSFSR, 1922], p. 13. [This chapter, known as "At Tikhon's: Stavrogin's Confession," was intended by Dostoevsky as Chapter 9 of Part Two of The Possessed. It was not included in the first serialized appearance of the novel, ostensibly because of the editor's objections, and Dostoevsky did not include it in any edition of the novel published during his lifetime. The English version used here (and elsewhere) is by F. D. Reeve, and appears as an appendix to the Garnett translation.]

6. Biografiia, pis'ma i zametki iz zapisnoi knigi F. M. Dostoevskogo [Biography, Letters and Notes from the Notebook of F. M. Dostoevsky] (St. Petersburg, 1883), p. 373.

7. In his "Diary of a Writer" for 1877 Dostoevsky says this apropos of Anna Karenina: "It is clear and evident to the point of being obvious that evil lurks deeper in mankind than the socialist-healers suppose, that no matter how you arrange society you will not avoid evil, that the human soul will remain the same, that abnormality and sin originate in the soul itself, and that, finally, the laws of the spirit are still so unfamiliar, so unknown to science, so undefined and so mysterious, that there is not and cannot yet be any healers, or even any definitive judges, but there is one who says: 'Vengeance is mine, I will repay.'" [PS IX, 210]; The Diary of a Writer, July-August 1877, ch. 11, 3 ("Anna Karenina as a Fact of Special Significance"), p. 787.

8. See V. Ermilov, F. M. Dostoevskii (Moscow: Goslitizdat, 1956). [See the English version, V. Yermilov, F. M. Dostoyevsky, trans. J. Katzer (Moscow: Foreign Languages Publishing House, 1957), p. 13.]

9. Because meaning "lives" not in that type of time that has a "yesterday," a "today,"

and a "tomorrow," that is, not in that time in which the heroes "lived" and in which the biographical life of the author unfolds.

10. Cited from V. V. Vinogradov, *O jazyke khudozhestvennoi literatury* [On the Language of Artistic Literature] (Moscow: Goslitizdat, 1959), pp. 141-42.

11. V. V. Vinogradov, *ibid*., p. 140.

12. Characteristic for Dostoevsky's world are murders (portrayed from within the murderer's field of vision), suicides, and insanity. Normal deaths are rare in his work, and he usually notes them only in passing. [See the eloquent expansion of this idea in Bakhtin's notes for the 1963 edition, "Toward a Reworking of the Dostoevsky Book," Appendix II, pp. 289-91, 300.]

Chapter Three
The Idea in Dostoevsky

Let us now move on to the next aspect of our thesis—the positioning of the idea in Dostoevsky's artistic world. The polyphonic project is incompatible with a mono-ideational framework of the ordinary sort. In the positioning of the idea, Dostoevsky's originality emerges with special force and clarity. In our analysis we shall avoid matters of content in the ideas introduced by Dostoevsky—what is important for us here is their artistic function in the work.

Dostoevsky's hero is not only a discourse about himself and his immediate environment, but also a discourse about the world; he is not only cognizant, but an ideologist as well.

The "Underground Man" is already an ideologist. But the ideological creativity of Dostoevsky's characters reaches full significance only in the novels; there, the idea really does become almost the hero of the work. Even there, however, the dominant of the hero's representation remains what it had been earlier: self-consciousness.

Thus discourse about the world merges with confessional discourse about oneself. The truth about the world, according to Dostoevsky, is inseparable from the truth of the personality. The categories of self-consciousness that were already determining the life of Devushkin and even more so of Golyadkin—acceptance or nonacceptance, rebellion or reconciliation—now become the basic categories for thinking about the world. Thus the loftiest principles of a worldview are the same principles that govern the most concrete personal experiences. And the result is an artistic fusion, so characteristic for Dostoevsky, of personal life with worldview, of the most intimate experiences with the idea. Personal life becomes uniquely unselfish and principled, and lofty ideological thinking becomes passionate and intimately linked with personality.

This merging of the hero's discourse about himself with his ideological discourse about the world greatly increases the direct signifying power of a self-utterance, strengthens its internal resistance to all sorts of external finalization. The idea helps self-consciousness assert its sovereignty in Dostoevsky's artistic world, and helps it triumph over all fixed, stable, neutral images.

But on the other hand, the idea itself can preserve its power to mean, its full integrity as an idea, only when self-consciousness is the dominant in the artistic representation of the hero. In a monologic artistic world, the idea, once placed in the mouth of a hero who is portrayed as a fixed and finalized image of reality, inevitably loses its direct power to mean, becoming a mere aspect of reality, one more of reality's predetermined features, indistinguishable from any other manifestation of the hero. An idea of this sort might be characteristic of a social type or an individual, or it might ultimately be a simple intellectual gesture on the part of the hero, an intellectual expression of his spiritual face. The idea ceases to be an idea and becomes a simple artistic characterizing feature. As such, as a characteristic, it is combined with the hero's image.

If, in a monologic world, an idea retains its power to signify as an idea, then it is inevitably separated from the fixed image of the hero and is no longer artistically combined with this image: the idea is merely placed in his mouth, but it could with equal success be placed in the mouth of any other character. For the author it is important only that a given true idea be uttered somewhere in the context of a given work; who utters it, and when, is determined by considerations of composition, by what is convenient or appropriate, or by purely negative criteria: it must not jeopardize the verisimilitude of the image of him who utters it. Such an idea, in itself, belongs to *no one*. The hero is merely the carrier of an independently valid idea; as a true signifying idea it gravitates toward some impersonal, systemically monologic context; in other words, it gravitates toward the systemically monologic worldview of the author himself.

A monologic artistic world does not recognize someone else's thought, someone else's idea, as an object of representation. In such a world everything ideological falls into two categories. Certain thoughts—true, signifying thoughts—gravitate toward the author's consciousness, and strive to shape themselves in the purely semantic unity of a worldview; such a thought is not represented, it is affirmed; its affirmation finds objective expression in a special accent of its own, in its special position within the work as a whole, in the very verbal and stylistic form of its utterance and in a whole series of other infinitely varied means for advancing a thought as a signifying, affirmed thought. We can always hear them in the context of the work; an affirmed thought always sounds different from an unaffirmed one. Other thoughts and ideas—untrue or indifferent from the author's point of view, not fitting into his worldview—are not affirmed; they are either polemically repudiated, or else they lose their power to signify directly and become simple elements of characterization, the mental gestures of the hero or his more stable mental qualities.

In the monologic world, *tertium non datur*: a thought is either affirmed or repudiated; otherwise it simply ceases to be a fully valid thought. An unaffirmed thought, if it is to enter into the artistic structure, must be deprived in general of its power to mean, must become a psychical fact. And as for polemically repudiated thoughts, they also are not represented, because denial, whatever form it takes, excludes the possibility of any genuine representation of the idea. Someone else's repudiated thought cannot break out of a monologic context; on the contrary, it is confined all the more harshly and implacably within its own boundaries. Another's repudiated thought is not capable of creating alongside one consciousness another autonomous consciousness, if repudiation remains a purely theoretical repudiation of the thought as such.

The artistic representation of an idea is possible only when the idea is posed in terms beyond affirmation and repudiation, but at the same time not reduced to simple psychical experience deprived of any direct power to signify. In a monologic world, such a status for the idea is impossible: it contradicts the most basic principles of that world. These basic principles go far beyond the boundaries of artistic creativity alone; they are the principles behind the entire ideological culture of recent times. What are these principles?

Ideological monologism found its clearest and theoretically most precise expression in idealistic philosophy. The monistic principle, that is, the affirmation of the unity of *existence*, is, in idealism, transformed into the unity of the *consciousness*.

For us, of course, the important thing is not the philosophical side of the question, but rather something characteristic of ideology in general, something also present here in this idealistic transformation of the monism of existence into the monologism of consciousness. And even this general characteristic of ideology is important to us only from the point of view of its further application in art.

The unity of consciousness, replacing the unity of existence, is inevitably transformed into the unity of a *single* consciousness; when this occurs it makes absolutely no difference what metaphysical form the unity takes: "consciousness in general" ("*Bewusstsein überhaupt*"), "the absolute *I*," "the absolute spirit," "the normative consciousness," and so forth. Alongside this unified and inevitably *single* consciousness can be found a multitude of empirical human consciousnesses. From the point of view of "consciousness in general" this plurality of consciousnesses is accidental and, so to speak, superfluous. Everything in them that is essential and true is incorporated into the unified context of "consciousness in general" and deprived of its individuality. That which is individual, that which distinguishes one consciousness from another and from others, is cognitively not essential and belongs to the realm of an individual human being's psychical organization and limitations. From the point of view of truth, there are no individual consciousnesses. Idealism recognizes only one principle of cognitive individualization: *error*. True judgments are not attached to a personality, but correspond to some unified, systemically monologic context. Only error individualizes. Everything that is true finds a place for itself within the boundaries of a single consciousness, and if it does not actually find for itself such a place, this is so for reasons incidental and extraneous to the truth itself. In the ideal a single consciousness and a single mouth are absolutely sufficient for maximally full cognition; there is no need for a multitude of consciousnesses, and no basis for it.

It should be pointed out that the single and unified consciousness is by no means an inevitable consequence of the concept of a unified truth. It is quite possible to imagine and postulate a unified truth that requires a plurality of consciousnesses, one that cannot in principle be fitted into the bounds of a single consciousness, one that is, so to speak, by its very nature *full of event potential* and is born at a point of contact among various consciousnesses. The monologic way of perceiving cognition and truth is only one of the possible ways. It arises only where consciousness is placed above existence, and where the unity of existence is transformed into the unity of consciousness.

In an environment of philosophical monologism the genuine interaction of consciousnesses is impossible, and thus genuine dialogue is impossible as well. In essence idealism knows only a single mode of cognitive interaction among consciousnesses: someone who knows and possesses the truth instructs someone who is ignorant of it and in error; that is, it is the interaction of a teacher and a pupil, which, it follows, can be only a pedagogical dialogue.[1]

A monologic perception of consciousness holds sway in other spheres of ideological creativity as well. All that has the power to mean, all that has value, is everywhere concentrated around one center—the carrier. All ideological creative acts are conceived and perceived as possible expressions of a single consciousness, a single spirit. Even when one is dealing with a collective, with a multiplicity of creating forces, unity is nevertheless illustrated through the image of a single consciousness: the spirit of a nation, the spirit of a people, the spirit of history, and so forth. Everything capable of meaning can be gathered together in one consciousness and subordinated to a unified accent; whatever does not submit to such a reduction is accidental and unessential. The consolidation of monologism and its permeation into all spheres and ideological life was promoted in modern times by European rationalism, with its cult of a unified and exclusive reason, and especially by the Enlightenment, during which time the basic generic forms of European artistic prose took shape. All of European utopianism was likewise built on this monologic principle. Here too belongs utopian socialism, with its faith in the omnipotence of the conviction. Semantic unity of any sort is everywhere represented by a single consciousness and a single point of view.

This faith in the self-sufficiency of a single consciousness in all spheres of ideological life is not a theory created by some specific thinker; no, it is a profound structural characteristic of the creative ideological activity of modern times, determining all its external and internal forms. We are interested only in its manifestations in literary art.

In literature, as we have seen, the statement of an idea is usually thoroughly monologistic. An idea is either confirmed or repudiated. All confirmed ideas are merged in the unity of the author's seeing and representing consciousness; the unconfirmed ideas are distributed among the heroes, no longer as signifying ideas, but rather as socially typical or individually characteristic manifestations of thought. The one who knows, understands, and sees is in the first instance the author himself. He alone is an ideologist. The author's ideas are marked with the stamp of his individuality. Thus the author *combines in his person a direct and fully competent ideological power to mean* with *individuality*, in such a way that *they do not weaken one another*. But this occurs in his person alone. In the characters, individuality kills the signifying power of their ideas, or, if these ideas retain their power to mean, then they are detached from the individuality of the character and are merged with that of the author. Hence the *single ideational accent of the work*; the appearance of a second accent would inevitably be perceived as a crude contradiction within the author's worldview.

In a work of the monologic type, a confirmed and fully valid authorial idea can perform a triple function: first, it is the *principle for visualizing and representing the world*, the principle behind the *choice* and unification of material, the principle behind the *ideological single-toned quality* of all the elements of the work; second, the idea can be presented as a more or less distinct or conscious deduction drawn from the represented material; third and finally, an authorial idea can receive direct expression in the *ideological position of the main hero.*

The idea, as a principle of representation, merges with the form. It determines all formal accents, all those ideological evaluations that constitute the formal unity of an artistic style and the unified tone of the work.

The deeper layers of this form-shaping ideology, which determine the basic generic characteristics of artistic works, are traditional; they take shape and develop over the course of centuries. To these deeper layers of form also belongs the very concept we are analyzing here, artistic monologism.

In the presence of the monologic principle, ideology — as a deduction, as a semantic summation of representation — inevitably transforms the represented world into a *voiceless object of that deduction.* The forms of this ideological deduction can themselves be most varied. Depending on these forms, the positioning of represented material changes: it can be a simple illustration to an idea, a simple example, it can be material for ideological generalization (as in the experimental novel), or it can exist in more complex relationship to the final result. Where the representation is oriented entirely toward ideological deduction, we have an ideational philosophical novel (Voltaire's *Candide*, for example) or — in the worst instance — simply a crudely tendentious novel. And even if this direct, straightforward orientation is absent, an element of ideological deduction is nevertheless present in every representation, however modest or concealed the formal functions of that deduction might be. The accents of ideological deduction must not contradict the form-shaping accents of the representation itself. If such a contradiction exists it is felt to be a flaw, for within the limits of a monologic world contradictory accents collide within a single voice. A unity of viewpoint must weld into one both the most formal elements of style and the most abstract philosophical deductions.

In one plane together with form-shaping ideology and ultimate ideological deduction can also be found the semantic position of the hero. The point of view of the hero can be transferred from the objectivized sphere into the sphere of principle. In that case the ideological principles which underlie the construction no longer merely represent the hero, defining the author's point of view toward him, but are expressed by the hero himself, defining his own personal point of view on the world. Such a hero is formally very different from heroes of the ordinary type. There is no need to go beyond the bounds of a given work to seek other documents that attest to a concurrence of the author's ideology with the ideology of the hero. Such a concurrence in matters of content, moreover, established elsewhere than in the work, does not in itself have any persuasive power. Any unity between an author's ideological principles of representation and the hero's ideological position must be revealed in the work itself, *as a single accent common both to the authorial representation and to the speech and experiences of the hero*, and not as some concurrence in the content of the hero's thoughts with the author's ideological views, uttered in some other place. The very discourse of a hero and his experiences are presented differently: they are not turned into objects, but rather they characterize the object toward which they are directed and not only the speaker himself. The discourse of such a hero lies in a single plane with the discourse of the author.

The absence of any distance between the author's position and the hero's position is also manifested in a whole series of other formal characteristics. The hero, for example, is not closed and not internally finalized, like the author himself, and for that reason he does not fit wholly into the procrustean bed of the plot, which is in any case conceived as only one of many possible plots and is consequently in the final analysis merely accidental for a given hero. This open-ended hero is characteristic for Romanticism, for Byron, Chateaubriand; Lermontov's Pechorin[a] is in some ways this sort of hero.

Finally, the ideas of the author can be scattered sporadically throughout the whole work. They can appear in authorial speech as isolated sayings, as maxims, as whole arguments, or they can be placed in the mouth of one or another character — often in quite large and compact chunks — without, however, merging with the character's individual personality (Turgenev's Potugin,[b] for example).

This whole mass of ideology, both organized and unorganized, from the form-shaping principles to the random and removable maxims of the author, must be subordinated to a single accent and must express a single and unified point of view. All else is merely the object of this point of view, "sub-accentual material." Only that idea which has fallen into the rut of the author's point of view can retain its significance without destroying the single-accented unity of the work. Whatever these authorial ideas, whatever function they fulfill, they are *not represented*: they either represent and internally govern a representation, or they shed light on some other represented thing, or, finally, they accompany the representation as a detachable semantic ornament. *They are expressed directly, without distance.* And

---

[a]Hero of Mikhail Lermontov's novel *A Hero of Our Time* (1840).
[b]Character in Ivan Turgenev's novel *Smoke* (1867).

within the bounds of that monologic world shaped by them, someone else's idea cannot be represented. It is either assimilated, or polemically repudiated, or ceases to be an idea.

*

Dostoevsky was capable of *representing someone else's idea*, preserving its full capacity to signify as an idea, while at the same time also preserving a distance, neither confirming the idea nor merging it with his own expressed ideology. The idea, in his work, becomes the *subject of artistic representation*, and Dostoevsky himself became a great *artist of the idea*.

It comes as no surprise that the image of an "artist of the idea" had already occurred to Dostoevsky in 1846-47, that is, at the very beginning of his career as a writer. We have in mind the image of Ordynov, the hero in "The Landlady." He is a lonely young scholar. He has his own creative system, his own unusual approach to the scientific idea;

He was creating a system for himself, it was being evolved in him over the years; and the dim, vague, but marvellously soothing *image of an idea*, embodied in a *new, clarified form*, was gradually emerging in his soul. And this form craved expression, fretting his soul; he was still timidly aware of its originality, its *truth*, its independence: creative genius was already showing, it was gathering strength and taking shape. [SS I, 425; "The Landlady," Part I, 1]

And further, at the end of the story:

Possibly a complete, original, independent idea really did exist within him, Perhaps he had been destined to be *the artist in science*. [SS I, 498; "The Landlady," Part II, 3]

Dostoevsky was also destined to become just such an artist of the idea, not in science, but in literature.

What are the conditions that make possible in Dostoevsky the artistic expression of an idea?

We must remember first of all that the image of an idea is inseparable from the image of a person, the carrier of that idea. It is not the idea in itself that is the "hero of Dostoevsky's works," as Engelhardt has claimed, but rather the *person born of that idea*. It again must be emphasized that the hero in Dostoevsky is a man of the idea; this is not a character, not a temperament, not a social or psychological type; such externalized and finalized images of persons cannot of course be combined with the image of a *fully valid* idea. It would be absurd, for example, even to attempt to combine Raskolnikov's idea, which we understand and *feel* (according to Dostoevsky an idea can and must not only be understood, but also "felt") with his finalized character or his social typicality as a déclassé intellectual of the '60s:

Raskolnikov's idea would immediately lose its direct power to signify as a fully valid idea, and would withdraw from the quarrel where it had *lived* in uninterrupted dialogic interaction with other fully valid ideas—the ideas of Sonya, Porfiry, Svidrigailov, and others. The carrier of a fully valid idea must be the "man in man" about which we spoke in the preceding chapter, with its free unfinalized nature and its indeterminacy. It is precisely to this unfinalized inner core of Raskolnikov's personality that Sonya, Porfiry and the others address themselves dialogically. And the author himself dialogically addresses this same unfinalized core of Raskolnikov's personality, as evidenced by the entire structure of his novel about him.

It follows that only the unfinalized and inexhaustible "man in man" can become a man of the idea, whose image is combined with the image of a fully valid idea. This is the first condition for representing an idea in Dostoevsky.

But this condition has, as it were, retroactive force. We could say that in Dostoevsky man transcends his "thingness" and becomes the "man in man" only by entering the pure and unfinalized realm of the idea, that is, only after he has become an unselfish man of the idea. Such are all the major heroes in Dostoevsky—that is, those who participate in the great dialogue.

In this respect one might apply to all these characters the same definition that Zosima offered of Ivan Karamazov's personality. He offered it, of course, in his own churchly language, that is, within the realm of that Christian idea where he, Zosima, lived. We shall quote the appropriate passage from what is for Dostoevsky a very characteristic *penetrative* dialogue between the Elder Zosima and Ivan Karamazov.

"Is that really your conviction as to the consequences of the disappearance of the faith in immortality?" the elder asked Ivan Fyodorovich suddenly.

"Yes. That was my contention. There is no virtue if there is no immortality."

"You are blessed in believing that, or else most unhappy."

"Why unhappy?" Ivan Fyodorovich asked smiling.

"Because, in all probability you don't believe yourself in the immortality of your soul, nor in what you have written yourself in your article on Church jurisdiction."

"Perhaps you are right! . . . But I wasn't altogether joking," Ivan Fyodorovich suddenly and strangely confessed, flushing quickly.

"You were not altogether joking. That's true. The question is still fretting your heart, and not answered. But the martyr likes sometimes to divert himself with his despair, as it were driven to it by despair itself. Meanwhile, in your despair, you, too, divert yourself with magazine articles, and discussions in society, though you don't believe your own arguments, and with an aching heart mock at them inwardly. . . . That question you have not answered, and it is your great grief, for it clamors for an answer."

"But can it be answered by me? Answered in the affirmative?" Ivan Fyodorovich went on asking strangely, still looking at the elder with the same inexplicable smile.

"If it can't be decided in the affirmative, it will never be decided in the negative. You know that that is the peculiarity of your heart, and all its suffering is due to it. But thank the Creator who has given you a lofty heart capable of such suffering; of thinking and seeking higher things, for our dwelling is in the heavens. God grant that your heart will attain the answer on earth, and may God bless your path." [*SS* IX, 91-92; *The Brothers Karamazov*, Book Two, ch. 6]

Alyosha, in his conversation with Rakitin, gives an analogous definition of Ivan but in more secular language:

"Oh, Misha, his soul [Ivan's—M. B.] is a stormy one. His mind is a prisoner of it. *There is a great and unresolved thought in him. He is one of those who don't need millions, they just need to get a thought straight.*" [*SS* IX, 105; *The Brothers Karamazov*, Book Two, ch. 7]

It is given to all of Dostoevsky's characters to "think and seek higher things"; in each of them there is a "great and unresolved thought"; all of them must, before all else, "get a thought straight." And in this resolution of a thought (an idea) lies their entire real life and their own personal unfinalizability. If one were to think away the idea in which they live, their image would be totally destroyed. In other words, the image of the hero is inseparably linked with the image of an idea and cannot be detached from it. We *see* the hero in the idea and through the idea, and we *see* the idea in him and through him.

All of Dostoevsky's major characters, as people of an idea, are absolutely unselfish, insofar as the idea has really taken control of the deepest core of their personality. This unselfishness is neither a trait of their objectivized character nor an external definition of their acts—unselfishness expresses their real life in the realm of the idea (they "don't need millions, they just need to get a thought straight"); idea-ness and unselfishness are, as it were, synonyms. In this sense even Raskolnikov, who killed and robbed the old pawnbroker, is absolutely unselfish, as is the prostitute Sonya, as is Ivan the accomplice in his father's murder; absolutely unselfish also is the *idea* of the Adolescent to become a Rothschild. We repeat again: what is important is not the ordinary qualifications of a person's character or actions, but rather the index of a person's devotion to an idea in the deepest recesses of his personality.

The second condition for creating an image of the idea in Dostoevsky is his profound understanding of the dialogic nature of human thought, the dialogic nature of the idea. Dostoevsky knew how to reveal, to see, to show the true realm of the life of an idea. The idea *lives* not in one person's *isolated* individual consciousness—if it remains there only, it degenerates and dies. The idea begins to live, that is, to take shape, to develop, to find and renew its verbal expression, to give birth to new ideas, only when it enters into genuine dialogic relationships with other ideas, with the ideas of *others*. Human thought becomes genuine thought, that is, an idea, only under conditions of living contact with another and alien thought, a thought embodied in someone else's voice, that is, in someone else's consciousness expressed in discourse. At that point of contact between voice-consciousnesses the idea is born and lives.

The idea—as it was *seen* by Dostoevsky the artist—is not a subjective individual-psychological formation with "permanent resident rights" in a person's head; no, the idea is inter-individual and inter-subjective—the realm of its existence is not individual consciousness but dialogic communion *between* consciousnesses. The idea is a *live event*, played out at the point of dialogic meeting between two or several consciousnesses. In this sense the idea is similar to the *word*, with which it is dialogically united. Like the word, the idea wants to be heard, understood, and "answered" by other voices from other positions. Like the word, the idea is by nature dialogic, and monologue is merely the conventional compositional form of its expression, a form that emerged out of the ideological monologism of modern times characterized by us above.

It is precisely as such a live event, playing itself out between consciousness-voices, that Dostoevsky saw and artistically represented the *idea*. It is this artistic discovery of the dialogic nature of the idea of consciousness, of every human life illuminated by consciousness (and therefore to some minimal degree concerned with ideas) that made Dostoevsky a great artist of the idea.

Dostoevsky never expounds prepared ideas in monologic form, but neither does he show their *psychological* evolution within a *single* individual consciousness. In either case, ideas would cease to be living images.

We remember, for example, Raskolnikov's first interior monologue, portions of which we quoted in the preceding chapter. That was not a psychological evolution of an idea within a single self-enclosed consciousness. On the contrary, the consciousness of the solitary Raskolnikov becomes a field of battle for others' voices; the events of recent days (his mother's letter, the meeting with Marmeladov), reflected in his consciousness, take on the form of a most intense dialogue with absentee participants (his sister, his mother, Sonya, and others), and in this dialogue he tries to "get his thoughts straight."

Before the action of the novel begins, Raskolnikov has published a newspaper article expounding the theoretical bases of his idea. Nowhere does Dostoevsky give us this article in its monologic form. We first become acquainted with its content and consequently with Raskolnikov's basic idea in the intense and, for Raskolnikov, terrible dialogue with Porfiry (Razumikhin and Zametov participate in this dialogue as well). Porfiry is the first to give an account of the article, and he does so in a deliberately exaggerated and provocative form. This internally dialogized account is constantly interrupted by questions addressed to Raskolnikov, and by the latter's replies. Then Raskolnikov himself gives an account of the article, and he is constantly interrupted by Porfiry's provocative questions and comments. And Raskolnikov's account is itself shot through with interior polemic, from the point of view of Porfiry and his like. Razumikhin too puts in his replies. As a result, Raskolnikov's idea appears before us in an inter-individual zone of intense struggle among several individual consciousnesses, while the theoretical side of the idea is inseparably linked with the ultimate positions on life taken by the participants in the dialogue.

In the course of this dialogue Raskolnikov's idea reveals its various facets, nuances, possibilities, it enters into various relationships with other life-positions. As it loses its monologic, abstractly theoretical finalized quality, a quality sufficient to a *single* consciousness, it acquires the contradictory complexity and living multi-facedness of an idea-force, being born, living and acting in the great dialogue of the epoch and calling back and forth to kindred ideas of other epochs. Before us rises up an *image of the idea.*

Raskolnikov's very same idea appears before us again in his dialogues with Sonya, no less intense; here it already sounds in a different tonality, it enters into dialogic contact with another very strong and integral life-position, Sonya's, and thus reveals new facets and possibilities inherent in it. Next we hear this idea in Svidrigailov's dialogized exposition of it in his dialogue with Dounia. But here, in the voice of Svidrigailov, who is one of Raskolnikov's parodic doubles, the idea has a completely different sound and turns toward us another of its sides. And finally, Raskolnikov's idea comes into contact with various manifestations of life throughout the entire novel; it is tested, verified, confirmed or repudiated by them. Of this we have already spoken in the preceding chapter.

Let us again recall Ivan Karamazov's idea that "everything is permitted" if there is no immortality for the soul. What an intense dialogic life that idea leads throughout the whole of *The Brothers Karamazov*, what heterogeneous voices relay it along, into what unexpected dialogic contacts it enters!

On both of these ideas (Raskolnikov's and Ivan Karamazov's) the reflections of other ideas fall, similar to what happens in painting when a distinct tone, thanks to the reflections of surrounding tones, loses its abstract purity, and only then begins to live an authentic "painterly" life. If one were to extract these ideas from the dialogic realm of their life and give them a monologically finished theoretical form, what withered and easily refuted ideological constructs would result!

As an artist, Dostoevsky did not create his ideas in the same way philosophers or scholars create theirs—he created images of ideas found, heard, sometimes divined by him *in reality itself*, that is, ideas already living or entering life as idea-forces. Dostoevsky possessed an extraordinary gift for hearing the dialogue of his epoch, or, more precisely, for hearing his epoch as a great dialogue, for detecting in it not only individual voices, but precisely and predominantly the *dialogic relationship* among voices, their dialogic *interaction*. He heard both the loud, recognized, reigning voices of the epoch, that is, the reigning dominant ideas (official and unofficial), as well as voices still weak, ideas not yet fully emerged, latent ideas heard as yet by no one but himself, and ideas that were just beginning to ripen, embryos of future worldviews. "Reality in its entirety," Dostoevsky himself wrote, "is not to be exhausted by what is immediately at hand, for an overwhelming part of this reality is contained in the form of a still *latent, unuttered future Word*."[2]

In the dialogue of his time Dostoevsky also heard resonances of the voice-ideas of the past—both the most recent past (the '30s and '40s) and the more remote. Also, as we have just said, he attempted to hear the voice-ideas of the future, trying to divine them, so to speak, from the place prepared for them in the dialogue of the present, just as it is possible to divine a future, as yet unuttered response in an already unfolded dialogue. Thus on the plane of the present there came together and quarreled past, present, and future.

We repeat: Dostoevsky never created his idea-images out of nothing, he never "made them up" any more than a visual artist makes up the people he represents—he was able to hear or divine them in the reality at hand. And thus for the idea-images in Dostoevsky's novels, as well as for the images of his heroes, it is possible to locate and indicate specific *prototypes*. Thus the prototypes for Raskolnikov's ideas, for example, were the ideas of Max Stirner* as expounded by him in his treatise *Der Einzige und sein Eigentum*, and the ideas of Napoleon III as developed by him in *Histoire de Jules César* (1865);[3] one of the prototypes for Pyotr Verkhovensky's ideas was *The Catechism of a Revolutionary*;[4] the prototypes of Versilov's ideas (*The Adolescent*) were the ideas of Chaadaev* and Herzen.*[5] By no means have all prototypes for Dostoevsky's idea-images been discovered and clarified. We must emphasize that we are not talking of Dostoevsky's "sources" (that term would be inappropriate here), but precisely about the *prototypes* for his idea-images.

Dostoevsky neither copied nor expounded these prototypes in any way; rather he freely and creatively reworked them into living artistic images of ideas, exactly as an artist approaches his human prototypes. Above all he destroyed the self-enclosed monologic form of idea-prototypes and incorporated them into the great dialogue of his novels, where they began living a new and eventful artistic life.

As an artist, Dostoevsky uncovered in the image of a given idea not only the historically actual features available in the prototype (in Napoleon III's *Histoire de Jules César*, for example), but also its *potentialities*, and precisely this potential is of the utmost importance for the artistic image. As an artist Dostoevsky often divined how a given idea would develop and function under certain changed conditions, what unexpected directions it would take in its further development and transformation. To this end, Dostoevsky placed the idea on the borderline of dialogically intersecting consciousnesses. He brought together ideas and worldviews, which in real life were absolutely estranged and deaf to one another, and forced them to quarrel. He extended, as it were, these distantly separated ideas by means of a dotted line to the point of their dialogic intersection. In so doing he anticipated future dialogic encounters between ideas which in his time were still dissociated. He foresaw new linkages of ideas, the emergence of new voice-ideas and changes in the arrangement of all the voice-ideas in the worldwide dialogue. And thus the Russian, and worldwide, dialogue that resounds in Dostoevsky's novels with voice-ideas already living and just being born, voice-ideas open-ended and fraught with new possibilities, continues to draw into its lofty and tragic game the minds and voices of Dostoevsky's readers, up to the present day.

In such a way, without losing any of their full and essential semantic validity, the idea-prototypes used in Dostoevsky's novels change the form of their existence: they become thoroughly dialogized images of ideas not finalized monologically; that is, they enter into what is for them a new realm of existence, *artistic* existence.

Dostoevsky was not only an artist who wrote novels and stories; he was also a journalist and a thinker who published articles in *Time, Epoch, The Citizen*, and *Diary of a Writer*. In these articles he expressed definite philosophical, religious-philosophical, and socio-political *ideas*; he expressed them there (that is, in the articles) as *his own confirmed* ideas in a *systemically monologic* or rhetorically monologic (*in fact, journalistic*) form. These same ideas were sometimes expressed by him in letters to various correspondents. What we have in the articles and letters are not, of course, images of ideas, but straightforward monologically confirmed ideas.

But we also meet these "Dostoevskian ideas" in his novels. How should we regard them there, that is, in the artistic context of his creative work?

In exactly the same way we regard the ideas of Napoleon III in *Crime and Punishment* (ideas with which Dostoevsky the thinker was in total disagreement), or the ideas of Chaadaev and Herzen in *The Adolescent* (ideas with which Dostoevsky the thinker was in partial agreement): that is, we should regard the ideas of Dostoevsky the thinker as the *idea-prototypes* for certain ideas in his novels (the idea-images of Sonya, Myshkin, Alyosha Karamazov, Zosima).

In fact, the ideas of Dostoevsky the thinker, upon entering his polyphonic novel, change the very form of their existence, they are transformed into artistic images of ideas: they are combined in an indissoluble unity with images of people (Sonya, Myshkin, Zosima), they are liberated from their monologic isolation and finalization, they become thoroughly dialogized and enter the great dialogue of the novel on *completely equal terms* with other idea-images (the ideas of Raskolnikov, Ivan Karamazov, and others). It is absolutely impermissible to ascribe to these ideas the finalizing function of authorial ideas in a monologic novel. Here they fulfill no such function, for they are all equally privileged participants in the great dialogue. If a certain partiality on the part of Dostoevsky the journalist for specific ideas and images is sometimes sensed in his novels, then it is evident only in superficial aspects (for example, in the conventionally monologic epilogue to *Crime and Punishment*) and is not capable of destroying the powerful artistic logic of the polyphonic novel. Dostoevsky the artist always triumphs over Dostoevsky the journalist.

Thus the ideas of Dostoevsky himself, uttered by him in monologic form outside the artistic context of his work (in articles, letters, oral conversations) are merely the prototypes for several of the idea-images in his novels. For this reason it is absolutely impermissible to substitute a critique of these monologic idea-prototypes for genuine analysis of Dostoevsky's polyphonic artistic thought. It is important to investigate the *function* of ideas in Dostoevsky's polyphonic world, and not only their *monologic substance*.

For a correct understanding of the way an idea is represented in Dostoevsky, one must take into consideration one more trait of its form-shaping ideology. We have in mind primarily the ideology that served Dostoevsky as his principle for seeing and representing the world, precisely a form-shaping ideology, for upon it ultimately depend the functions of abstract ideas and thoughts in the work.

Dostoevsky's form-shaping ideology lacks those two basic elements upon which any ideology is built: *the separate thought*, and a unified world of objects giving rise to a *system* of thoughts. In the usual ideological approach, there exist separate thoughts, assertions, propositions that can by themselves be true or untrue, depending on their relationship to the subject and independent of the carrier to whom they belong. These "no-man's" thoughts, faithful to the referential world, are united in a systemic unity of a referential order. In this systemic unity, thought comes into contact with thought and one thought is bound up with another on referential grounds. A thought gravitates toward system as toward an ultimate whole; the system is put together out of separate thoughts, as out of elements.

Dostoevsky's ideology knows neither the separate thought nor systemic unity in this sense. For him the ultimate indivisible unit is not the separate referentially bounded thought, not the proposition, not the assertion, but rather the integral point of view, the integral position of a personality. For him, referential meaning is indissolubly fused with the position of a personality. In every thought the personality is given, as it were, in its totality. And thus the linking-up of thoughts is the linking-up of integral positions, the linking-up of personalities.

Dostoevsky—to speak paradoxically—thought not in thoughts but in points of view, consciousnesses, voices. He tried to perceive and formulate each thought in such a way that a whole person was expressed and began to sound in it; this, in condensed form, is his entire worldview, from alpha to omega. Only that idea which compressed in itself an entire spiritual orientation could Dostoevsky accept as an element of his artistic worldview; for him it was an indivisible unit; out of such units emerged not a system, united through a world of objects, but a concrete event made up of organized human orientations and voices. In Dostoevsky, two thoughts are already two people, for there are no thoughts belonging to no one and every thought represents an entire person.

This striving of Dostoevsky to perceive each thought as an integrated personal position, to think in voices, is clearly evidenced even in the compositional structure of his journalistic articles. His manner of developing a thought is everywhere the same: he develops it dialogically, not in a dry logical dialogue but by juxtaposing whole, profoundly individualized voices. Even in his polemical articles he does not really persuade but rather organizes voices, yokes together semantic orientations, most often in the form of some imagined dialogue.

Here is the typical structure of one of Dostoevsky's journalistic articles.

In his article "The Environment," Dostoevsky begins by making a series of observations in the form of questions and presuppositions about the psychological condition and attitudes of jury members, as always interrupting and illustrating his thoughts with the voices and semi-voices of various people; for example:

> It seems that the one feeling common to all jurors throughout the world, and to our jurors in particular (aside, of course, from other emotions), must be the feeling of authority, or, to express it better, absolute power. This is a miserable feeling, that is, when it prevails over all others. . . .
>
> In my fancies I was dreaming of court sessions made up, for instance, almost exclusively of peasants, serfs of yesterday. The district attorney and the lawyers would address them, seeking their favors, while our good peasants would be sitting and silently pondering in their heads: "See how things have shaped themselves: now if it pleases me, I'll acquit; if it pleases me, I'll send him away to Siberia!" . . .
>
> "Simply, it is a pity to ruin somebody else's fate: they are human beings too. The Russian people are compassionate." — Such is the opinion of others, as this has sometimes been expressed.

Further on, Dostoevsky directly proceeds to orchestrate his theme with the help of an imaginary dialogue.

> "Even though it be presumed" — I can hear a voice — "that your solid (that is, Christian) foundations are the same and that, in truth, one has to be, above all, a citizen, and, well, that one must hold the banner, etc., as you insisted — even if this be presumed for the time being, without challenge — think, where shall we find citizens? Consider only what we had yesterday! Now, you know that civil rights (and what rights!) rolled down upon him as from a hill. They crushed him and, as yet, they are to him but a burden — indeed, a burden!"
>
> "Of course, there is truth in your observation," I answer the voice, slightly downcast — "nevertheless, the Russian people . . ."
>
> "The Russian people? — Let me tell you!" — I hear another voice — "Here, we are told that the gifts rolled down from a hill and crushed the people. But, perhaps, they feel that that much they have received as a gift; and, on top of this, they realize that they have received these gifts gratis; and that as yet they, the people, are not worthy of them . . . [This viewpoint is then developed further.]
>
> "This, in a way, is a Slavophile voice" — I say to myself. "The thought is, indeed, encouraging, while my conjecture concerning popular humility before the power, received gratuitously, and bestowed upon the still 'unworthy,' is certainly smarter than the suggestion of a desire 'to tease the district attorney,' . . . [Development of the answer.]
>
> "However," I can hear a sarcastic voice — "it seems that it is you who are pressing on the people the latest environmental philosophy, for whence did it come to them? Since these twelve jurors — at times, all of them peasants — sit there, and each one of them considers it a mortal sin to eat forbidden food in Lent, you should have accused them point-blank of social tendencies."
>
> "Of course, of course, why should they be worrying about the 'environment.'

I mean, they as a body—I began to ponder—yet, the ideas are soaring in the air; there is something penetrating in an idea. . . ."

"There you are!"—laughs the caustic voice.

"And what if our people are particularly inclined toward the environmental doctrine—by their very nature, by their, let us say, Slav propensities? What if they—our people—are the best material in Europe for certain propagandists?"

The sarcastic voice laughs still louder, but somewhat artificially.[6]

The further development of the theme is built on semi-voices and on the material of concrete, everyday scenes and situations, ultimately having as its final goal the characterization of some human orientation: that of a criminal, a lawyer, a juror, and so forth.

Many of Dostoevsky's journalistic articles are constructed in this way. Everywhere his thought makes its way through a labyrinth of voices, semi-voices, other people's words, other people's gestures. He never proves his own positions on the basis of other abstract positions, he does not link thoughts together according to some referential principle, but juxtaposes orientations and amid them constructs his own orientation.

Of course, in the journalistic articles this form-shaping characteristic of Dostoevsky's ideology cannot manifest itself in any particular depth. There it is simply the form of the exposition. The monologic mode of thinking is not, of course, overcome. Journalistic writing creates the least favorable conditions for overcoming monologism. But nevertheless even there Dostoevsky cannot and does not want to separate the thought from the person, from a living mouth, in order to bind it to another thought on a purely referential and impersonal plane. While the ordinary ideological orientation sees in a thought its referential meaning, its objective "crests," Dostoevsky sees first and foremost its "roots" in the human being; for him a thought is two-sided, and these two sides, according to Dostoevsky, are even as an abstraction inseparable from one another. His entire material unfolds before him as a series of human orientations. His path leads not from idea to idea, but from orientation to orientation. To think, for him, means to question and to listen, to try out orientations, to combine some and expose others. For it must be emphasized that in Dostoevsky's world even *agreement* retains its *dialogic* character, that is, it never leads to a *merging* of voices and truths in a single *impersonal* truth, as occurs in the monologic world.

It is characteristic that in Dostoevsky's works there are absolutely no *separate* thoughts, propositions or formulations such as maxims, sayings, aphorisms which, when removed from their context and detached from their voice, would retain their semantic meaning in an impersonal form. But how many such separate and true thoughts can be isolated (and in fact commonly are isolated) from the novels of

Leo Tolstoy, Turgenev, Balzac, and others; these thoughts are scattered throughout the characters' speech and in the author's speech; separated from a voice, they still retain their full power to mean as impersonal aphorisms.

In the literature of classicism and the Enlightenment a special type of aphoristic thinking was developed, that is, thinking in separate rounded-off and self-sufficient thoughts which were purposely meant to stand independent of their context. Still another type of aphoristic thinking was developed by the Romantics.

Dostoevsky found these types of thinking particularly alien and antagonistic. His form-shaping worldview does not know an *impersonal truth*, and in his works there are no detached, impersonal verities. There are only integral and indivisible voice-ideas, voice-viewpoints, but they too cannot be detached from the dialogic fabric of the work without distorting their nature.

To be sure, there are among Dostoevsky's characters representatives of an epigonic, worldly line of aphoristic thinking—or more precisely, of aphoristic babbling—who spout banal witticisms and aphorisms, as does, for example, old Prince Sokolsky (*The Adolescent*). To this group Versilov also belongs, but only in part, only because of a peripheral side of his personality. These worldly aphorisms are, of course, objectified. But there is in Dostoevsky a hero of a special type, Stepan Trofimovich Verkhovensky. He is an epigone of the loftier lines of aphoristic thinking—of the Enlightenment and Romanticism. He spouts his "verities" precisely because he has no "dominating idea" that determines the core of his personality, he has no truth *of his own*, but only those separate impersonal verities which for that reason cease to be ultimately true. On his deathbed he himself defines his relationship to the truth:

> "My friend, I've been telling lies all my life. Even when I told the truth I never spoke for the sake of the truth, but always for my own sake. I knew it before, but I only see it now . . ." [SS, VII, 678; *The Possessed*, Part III, ch. 7, 2]

None of Stepan Trofimovich's aphorisms retain their full significance out of context; they are all to some extent objectified, and the author's ironic stamp lies on them all (that is, they are double-voiced).

In the compositionally expressed dialogues of Dostoevsky's characters there are also no separate thoughts or positions. They never argue over *separate points*, but always over *whole points of view*, inserting themselves and their entire idea into even the briefest exchange. They almost never dismember or analyze their integral ideational position.

And in the great dialogue of the novel as a whole, separate voices and their worlds are juxtaposed to one another as inseparable wholes, and not dismembered, not compared point by point or separate position by separate position.

In one of his letters to Pobedonostsev* on *The Brothers Karamazov*, Dostoevsky characterizes very aptly his method of integral dialogic juxtapositions:

"As an answer to all this *negative side*, I am offering this sixth book, *A Russian Monk*, which will appear on August 31. And therefore I tremble for it, and in this sense: will it be a *sufficient* answer? All the more so because *the answer here is not a direct one, it is not a point-by-point response to any previously expressed positions* (in the Grand Inquisitor or earlier) but only an oblique response. What is presented here is something directly [and inversely] opposite to the worldview expressed above — but it is presented, again, not point by point but, so to speak, in an *artistic picture*." [*Pis'ma*, IV, p. 109; 24 Aug./13 Sept. 1879]

These features of Dostoevsky's form-shaping ideology, outlined by us above, determine all aspects of his polyphonic creative activity.

As a result of such an ideological approach, what unfolds before Dostoevsky is not a world of objects, illuminated and ordered by his monologic thought, but a world of consciousnesses mutually illuminating one another, a world of yoked-together semantic human orientations. Among them Dostoevsky seeks the highest and most authoritative orientation, and he perceives it not as his own true thought, but as another authentic human being and his discourse. The image of the ideal human being or the image of Christ represents for him the resolution of ideological quests. This image or this highest voice must crown the world of voices, must organize and subdue it. Precisely the image of a human being and his voice, a voice not the author's own, was the ultimate artistic criterion for Dostoevsky: not fidelity to his own convictions and not fidelity to convictions themselves taken abstractly, but precisely a fidelity to the authoritative image of a human being.[7]

In answer to Kavelin Dostoevsky jotted down in his notebook:

It is not enough to define morality as fidelity to one's own convictions. One must continually pose oneself the question: are my convictions true? Only one verification of them exists — Christ. But this is no longer philosophy, it is faith, and faith is a red color . . .

I cannot recognize one who burns heretics as a moral man, because I do not accept your thesis that morality is an agreement with internal convictions. That is merely **honesty** (the Russian language is rich), but not morality. I have a moral model and an ideal, Christ. I ask: would he have burned heretics? — no. That means the burning of heretics is an immoral act . . .

Christ was mistaken — it's been proved! A scorching feeling tells me: better that I remain with a mistake, with Christ, than with you . . .

Living life has fled you, only the formulas and categories remain, and that, it seems, makes you happy. You say there's more peace and quiet (laziness) that way . . .

You say that to be moral one need only act according to conviction. But where do you get your convictions? I simply do not believe you and say that on the contrary it is immoral to act according to one's convictions. And you, of course, cannot find a way to prove me wrong.[8]

In these thoughts the important thing for us is not Dostoevsky's Christian declaration of faith in itself, but those living *forms* of his artistic and ideological thinking that are here so lucidly realized and expressed. Formulas and categories are foreign to his thinking. He prefers to remain with the mistake but with Christ, that is, without truth in the theoretical sense of the word, without truth-as-formula, truth-as-proposition. It is extremely characteristic of Dostoevsky that *a question is put* to the ideal image (how would Christ have acted?), that is, there is an internal dialogic orientation with regard to it, not a fusion with it but a following of it.

A distrust of convictions and their usual monologic function, a quest for truth not as the deduction of one's own consciousness, in fact not in the monologic context of an individual consciousness at all, but rather in the ideal authoritative image of another human being, an orientation toward the other's voice, the other's word: all this is characteristic of Dostoevsky's form-shaping ideology. An authorial idea or thought must not perform in the work the function of totally illuminating the represented world, but must rather enter into that world as an image of a human being, as one orientation among other orientations, as one word among many words. This ideal orientation (the true word) and its potential must never be lost sight of, but it must not color the work with the personal ideological tone of the author.

In the plan for *The Life of a Great Sinner* there is the following very revealing section:

1. OPENING PAGES. 1) Tone, 2) compress the thoughts artistically and concisely.

First NB is **tone** (the story is a **Life**—that is, although it is told from the author, it is told concisely, not skimping on explanations, but even presenting scenes. Harmony is necessary here). *The dryness of the story sometimes borders on* Gil Blas. In the especially effective and dramatic places—as if there were nothing of any special value.

But the *dominating idea* of the Life must be visible—that is, although *the entire dominating idea will not be explained in words* and will always remain a puzzle, the reader must nevertheless always be aware that the idea is a devout one, that the Life was so important that it was worth beginning with the childhood years. Also, through the choice of **story**, and all the facts in it, it is as if **(some special thing)** is constantly being put forth and *the man of the future is constantly before our eyes and placed on a pedestal* . . .[9]

A "dominating idea" was mentioned in the plan of every one of Dostoevsky's novels. In his letters he often emphasized the extraordinary importance he attached to the basic idea. On *The Idiot* he says in a letter to Strakhov: "Much in the novel was written hurriedly, much is too diffuse and did not turn out well, but some of it did turn out well. I do not stand behind the novel, but I do stand behind the idea."[10] Of *The Possessed* he writes to Maikov' "The *idea* seduced me and I've fallen terribly in love with it, but can I manage it without ruining the whole novel—that's the trouble!"[11] But the function of the dominating idea, even in the plans, is somewhat special. It does not extend beyond the limits of the great dialogue and does not finalize it. It must exercise leadership only in the choice and arrangement of material ("through the choice of story"), and that material is other people's voices, other people's points of view, and among them "the man of the future is constantly placed on a pedestal."[12]

We have already said that the idea functions only for the characters as an ordinary monologic principle for seeing and understanding the world. Everything in the work that might serve as direct expression and support for the idea is distributed among them. The author stands before the hero, before the pure voice of the hero. In Dostoevsky there is no objective representation of the environment, of everyday life, of nature, of objects, that is, no representation of all those things that could become a support for the author. Upon entering Dostoevsky's novel, the enormously diverse world of things and relationships among things is presented as the characters understand it, in their spirit and in their tone. The author as carrier of his own idea does not come into direct contact with a single thing; he comes into contact only with people. It comes as no surprise that both the ideological motif, and the ideological deduction transforming its material into an object, are quite impossible in this world of subjects.

In 1878 Dostoevsky wrote to one of his correspondents: "Add to this, on top of all this [the topic is man's nonsubmission to the general law of nature—M. B.] my I, which perceived everything. If it really has perceived everything, that is, the whole earth and its axiom [the law of self-preservation—M. B.], then of necessity my I is higher than all this, or at least does not fit into this but stands as it were off to one side, above all this, judging and perceiving it . . . But in that case this I is not only not subject to the earthly axiom, the earthly law, but goes beyond them, has its own law higher than them."[13]

In his work Dostoevsky did not, however, make monologic use of such a basically idealistic evaluation of consciousness. The cognizant and judging "I," and the world as its object, are present there not in the singular but in the plural. Dostoevsky overcame solipsism. He reserved idealistic consciousness not for himself but for his characters, and not only for one of them but for them all. At the center of

Dostoevsky's creative work there stands, in place of the relationship of a single cognizant and judging "I" to the world, the problem of the interrelationship of all these cognizant and judging "I's" to one another.

NOTES

1. The idealism of Plato is not purely monologic. It becomes purely monologic only in a neo-Kantian interpretation. Nor is Platonic dialogue of the pedagogical type, although there is a strong element of monologism in it. We shall discuss the Platonic dialogues in greater detail below, in connection with the generic traditions of Dostoevsky (see chapter 4).

2. *Zapisnye tetradi F. M. Dostoevskogo* (The Notebooks of F. M. Dostoevsky), Moscow-Leningrad, "Academia," 1935, p. 179. L. P. Grossman speaks to this point well, using Dostoevsky's own words: "The artist 'hears, has presentiments, even sees' that 'new elements, thirsting for a new word, are rising up and going forward,' Dostoevsky wrote much later; those elements must be captured and expressed." (L. P. Grossman, "Dostoevskii-khudozhnik" [Dostoevsky the Artist], in *Tvorchestvo F. M. Dostoevskogo* (Moscow: Akademiia nauk SSSR, 1959) p. 366. [The context of Dostoevsky's note is interesting. It is on Shakespeare, and the paragraph continues: "From time to time prophets appear who divine and utter this integral word. Shakespeare was a prophet sent by God to proclaim to us the mysteries of man and the human soul."]

3. This book, published while Dostoevsky was working on *Crime and Punishment*, found great resonance in Russia. See F. I. Evnin, "Roman *Prestuplenie i nakazanie*," in *Tvorchestvo F. M. Dostoevskogo*, ibid., pp. 153-57.

4. On this, see F. I. Evnin, "Roman *Besy*," ibid., pp. 228-29.

5. On this, see the book by A. S. Dolinin, *V tvorcheskoi laboratorii Dostoevskogo* [In Dostoevsky's Creative Laboratory] (Moscow, Sovetskii pisatel', 1947).

6. *PS* XI, pp. 11-15; *The Diary of a Writer*, 1873, "The Milieu," pp. 9-14.

7. We have in mind here, of course, not a finalized and closed image of reality (a type, a character, a temperament), but an open image-discourse. Such an ideal authoritative image, one not contemplated but followed, was only envisioned by Dostoevsky as the ultimate limit of his artistic project; this image was never realized in his work.

8. *Biografiia, pis'ma i zametki iz zapisnoi knizhki F. M. Dostoevskogo* [Biography, Letters and Notes from F. M. Dostoevsky's Notebook] (St. Petersburg, 1883), pp. 371-73, 374.

9. *Dokumenty po istorii literatury i obshchestvennosti*, Issue I: "F. M. Dostoevskii" (Moscow: Tsentrarkhiv RSFSR, 1922), pp. 71-72. [An English version of the plan and discussion of it can be found in Konstantin Mochulsky, *Dostoevsky: His Life and Work*, trans. Michael A. Minihan (Princeton, 1967), pp. 398-403.]

10. *Pis'ma*, II, p. 170. [Dostoevsky to N. N. Strakhov from Florence, 26 Feb./10 March, 1869.]

11. *Pis'ma*, II, p. 333. [Dostoevsky to A. N. Maikov from Dresden, 2/14 March, 1871.]

12. In a letter to Maikov Dostoevsky says: "In the second story I want to put forth as the main figure Tikhon Zadonsky, of course under another name, but he also will live peacefully in a monastery as a high-ranking member of the clergy . . . Perhaps I shall make of him a majestic, *positive* holy figure. He is not a Kostanzhoglo, not the German (I've forgotten his name) in Oblomov . . . and not a Lopukhov nor a Rakhmetov. *To tell the truth, I won't create a thing.* I'll simply put forth the real Tikhon, whom I have long ago taken joyously into my heart." (*Pis'ma*, II, p. 264) [Dostoevsky to A. N. Maikov, from Dresden, 25 March/6 April, 1870.) A larger chunk of this letter to Maikov is translated in Mochulsky, op. cit., pp. 396-98.]

13. F. M. Dostoevskii, *Pis'ma*, IV, p. 5. [Dostoevsky to N. L. Ozmidov, February 1878.]

Chapter Four
Characteristics of Genre
and Plot Composition
in Dostoevsky's Works

Those characteristics of Dostoevsky's poetics investigated by us in the preceding chapters presuppose, of course, a completely new treatment in his work of generic and plot-compositional elements. Neither the hero, nor the idea, nor the very polyphonic principle for structuring a whole can be fitted into the generic and plot-compositional forms of a biographical novel, a socio-psychological novel, a novel of everyday life or a family novel, that is, into the forms dominant in the literature of Dostoevsky's time and developed by such of his contemporaries as Turgenev, Goncharov, and Leo Tolstoy. In comparison with those writers Dostoevsky's work clearly belongs to a completely different generic type, one quite foreign to them.

The plot of the biographical novel is not adequate to Dostoevsky's hero, for such a plot relies wholly on the social and characterological definitiveness of the hero, on his full embodiment in life. Between the character of the hero and the plot of his life there must be a deep and organic unity. The biographical novel is built on it. The hero and the objective world surrounding him must be made of one piece. But Dostoevsky's hero in this sense is not embodied and cannot be embodied. He cannot have a normal biographical plot. The heroes themselves, it turns out, fervently dream of being embodied, they long to attach themselves to one of life's normal plots. The longing for embodiment by the "dreamer," born of the idea of the "underground man'' and the ''hero of an accidental family,'' is one of Dostoevsky's important themes.

Dostoevsky's polyphonic novel is constructed on another plot-compositional base, and is connected with other generic traditions in the development of European artistic prose.

In the literature on Dostoevsky, very often the characteristics of his work are linked with the traditions of the European adventure novel. And there is a certain measure of truth in this.

Between the adventure hero and the Dostoevskian hero there is one formal similarity, very fundamental to the structure of the novel. As regards the adventure hero also, it is impossible to say who he is. He has no firm socially typical or individually characterological qualities out of which a stable image of his character, type, or temperament might be composed. Such a definitive image would weigh down the adventure plot, limit the adventure possibilities. To the adventure hero anything can happen, he can become anything. He too is not a substance, but a pure function of adventures and escapades. The adventure hero is, to the same degree as Dostoevsky's hero, not finalized and not predetermined by his image.

To be sure, this is a very external and very crude similarity. But it is sufficient to make Dostoevsky's heroes potential carriers of an adventure plot. The circle of connections that heroes can establish, the circle of events in which they participate, is not predetermined and not limited by their character, nor by any social world in which they might actually have been embodied. Therefore Dostoevsky could calmly make use of the most extreme and consistent devices not only of the respectable adventure novel, but even of the boulevard novel. His hero excludes nothing from his life except one thing—the social respectability of a fully embodied hero of the family or biographical novel.

Thus Dostoevsky would be the least likely to follow, or find any significant kinship with, Turgenev, Tolstoy, or the Western European representatives of the biographical novel. On the other hand, the adventure novel, in all its many guises, left a deep mark on his work. As Grossman says:

His most important contribution was to reproduce—and this is the single instance of it in the entire history of the classic Russian novel—the typical story lines of adventure literature. The traditional patterns of the European novel of adventure often served Dostoevsky as models for the construction of his intrigues.

He even made use of the clichés of that literary genre. In the heat of hurried work he was seduced by the types of adventure stories then current, which were grist for boulevard novelists and writers of feuilletons . . .

It seems there is not a single attribute of the old novel of adventure that Dostoevsky failed to use. Alongside secret crimes and mass catastrophes, titled personages and unexpected fortunes, we find that feature most typical of melodrama—aristocrats who wander through slums and fraternize with the dregs of society. Stavrogin is not the only one of Dostoevsky's heroes with this trait. It is equally characteristic of Prince Valkovsky, Prince Sokolsky, and even in part Prince Myshkin.[1]

But what need did Dostoevsky have for the adventure world? What functions does it fulfill in the whole of his artistic design?

In answering that question, Leonid Grossman points to three basic functions of the adventure plot. The introduction of an adventure world, first of all, guaranteed narrative interest, thus facilitating the reader's difficult journey through the labyrinth of philosophical theories, images, and human relationships all packed into a single novel. Secondly, Dostoevsky found in the novel-feuilleton[a] "a spark of sympathy for the insulted and the injured, which is felt behind all the adventures of beggars-made-happy and redeemed outcasts." Finally, the adventure world gave expression to a "primordial trait" of Dostoevsky's art: "the impulse to introduce the extraordinary into the very thick of the commonplace, to fuse into one, according to Romantic principles, the sublime with the grotesque, and by an imperceptible process of conversion to push images and phenomena of everyday reality to the limits of the fantastic."[2]

One cannot help agreeing with Grossman that all the functions he has pointed out are indeed essential to adventure material in the Dostoevskian novel. But these functions, it seems to us, far from exhaust the matter. For Dostoevsky, entertainment was never a goal in itself, nor did he ever set for himself as an artistic goal the Romantic principle of interweaving the sublime with the grotesque, the extraordinary with the commonplace. Even if the authors of adventure novels had indeed paved the way for the social novel by introducing slums, forced labor, and hospitals, Dostoevsky nevertheless had before him examples of the genuine social novel—the social-psychological, everyday, and biographical novel—which, however, he scarcely heeded at all. Grigorovich and others who began with Dostoevsky arrived at the same world of the insulted and injured, following completely different models.

The functions Grossman has pointed out are peripheral ones. What is most fundamental and important is not contained in them.

In a social-psychological novel, a novel of everyday life, a family

---

[a]The *feuilleton* was that section of a French newspaper, usually detachable, devoted to serials, light literature, and criticism. The *roman-feuilleton* or serialized novel was, in its heyday (1830-50), a major genre of such authors as Sue, Soulié, Balzac, and George Sand.

For an excellent discussion of Dostoevsky and the *feuilleton*, see Gary Saul Morson, *The Boundaries of Genre: Dostoevsky's Diary of a Writer and the Traditions of Literary Utopia* (Austin: U. of Texas Press, 1981), pp. 14-30.

or biographical novel, the modes for plotting the story link one character to another not as one person to another person but as father to son, husband to wife, rival to rival, lover to beloved, or as landlord to peasant, property-owner to proletarian, well-to-do-bourgeois to déclassé tramp, and so forth. Relationships of family, of life-story and biography, of social status and social class are the stable all-determining basis for all plot connections; contingency has no place here. The hero is assigned to a plot as someone fully embodied and strictly localized in life, as someone dressed in the concrete and impenetrable garb of his class or social station, his family position, his age, his life and biographical goals. His *humanness* is to such an extent made concrete and specific by his place in life that it is in itself denied any decisive influence on plot relationships. It can be revealed only within the strict framework of those relationships.

Characters are distributed according to plot, and they can interact with one another in a meaningful way only on this well-defined and concrete ground. Their interrelationships are created by the plot and by that same plot are finalized. Their self-consciousnesses and consciousnesses as persons cannot establish any connections of even the slightest significance exterior to the plot. The plot here can never become simple material for "extra-plot" communication among consciousnesses, because the hero and the plot are made of a single piece. Heroes as heroes are born of the plot itself. The plot is not merely their clothing, it is their body and their soul. And conversely: their body and soul can be revealed and finalized in essence only within the plot.

The adventure plot, on the contrary, is precisely clothing draped over the hero, clothing which he can change as often as he pleases. The adventure plot relies not on what the hero is, not on the place he occupies in life, but more often on what he is not, on what (from the vantage point of the reality at hand) is unexpected and not predetermined. The adventure plot does not rely on already available and stable positions—family, social, biographical; it develops in spite of them. The adventure position is a position in which any person may appear as a person. What is more, the adventure plot uses any stable social localization not as a finalizing real-life form but precisely as a "position." Thus, a boulevard-novel aristocrat has nothing in common with an aristocrat of a social-family novel. Being an aristocrat in a boulevard novel is simply a position in which a person finds himself. The person functions, in the clothing of an aristocrat, as a person: he shoots, commits crimes, flees from enemies, overcomes obstacles, and so forth. All social and cultural institutions, establishments, social states and classes, family relationships are no more than positions in which a person can be eternally equal to himself. Problems dictated by his eternal human nature — self-preservation, the thirst for victory and triumph, the thirst for dominance or for sensual love — determine the adventure plot.

True, this eternal man of the adventure plot is (so to speak) a corporeal and corporeal-spiritual man. Outside the plot he is therefore quite empty, and consequently he can establish no extra-plot connections with any other characters. The adventure plot cannot therefore be the ultimate binding force in Dostoevsky's world, but as a plot it offers favorable material for the realization of Dostoevsky's artistic design.

In Dostoevsky, the adventure plot is combined with the posing of profound and acute problems; and it is, in addition, placed wholly at the service of the idea. It places a person in extraordinary positions that expose and provoke him, it connects him and makes him collide with other people under unusual and unexpected conditions precisely for the purpose of *testing* the idea and the man of the idea, that is, for testing the "man in man." And this permits the adventure story to be combined with other genres that are, it would seem, quite foreign to it, such as the confession and the saint's Life.

Such a combination of adventurism (often of the boulevard-novel sort) with the idea, with the problematic dialogue, with the Life and the confession, seemed, from the vantage point of these concepts about genre dominant in the nineteenth century, something quite out of the ordinary; it was perceived as a crude and absolutely unjustified violation of the "aesthetics of genre." And indeed, in the nineteenth century these genres and generic elements were sharply delimited and presented as alien and unrelated to one another. We recall the excellent characterization of this "foreignness" given by Grossman (see chapter 1, pp. 14-15). We have tried to show that this generic and stylistic foreignness is made meaningful and even surmounted in Dostoevsky, through the consistent polyphonism of his work. But the time has now come to consider this question from the viewpoint of a *history* of genres, that is, to shift the question onto the plane of *historical poetics*.

The fact is that a combination of adventurism with the posing of acute problematic questions, with a dialogic approach, with the confession, with the Life and the sermon was by no means something absolutely new and never before existing. The only new thing was Dostoevsky's polyphonic use and interpretation of generic combinations. Its roots reach back into the most remote antiquity. The adventure novel of the nineteenth century is only one of the branches — and a rather impoverished and deformed branch at that — of a powerful and multi-branched generic tradition, reaching, as we have said, into the depths of the past, to the very sources of European literature. We consider it essential to trace back this tradition precisely to its sources. One must not limit oneself to an analysis of the generic phenomena closest to Dostoevsky. We even intend to concentrate our main attention precisely on the sources. Therefore we must take leave of Dostoevsky for a time and leaf through some ancient pages, as yet almost totally unexamined in our scholarship, in the history of genres. This historical digression will help us to understand, in a deeper and truer way, the generic and plot-compositional characteristics of Dostoevsky's works which to this day remain essentially unexplored in the literature on him. In addition, we believe this question has broader significance for the theory and history of literary genres.

A literary genre, by its very nature, reflects the most stable, "eternal" tendencies in literature's development. Always preserved in a genre are undying elements of the *archaic*. True, these archaic elements are preserved in it only thanks to their constant *renewal*, which is to say, their contemporization. A genre is always the same and yet not the same, always old and new simultaneously. Genre is reborn and renewed at every new stage in the development of literature and in every individual work of a given genre. This constitutes the life of the genre. Therefore even the archaic elements preserved in a genre are not dead but eternally alive; that is, archaic elements are capable of renewing themselves. A genre lives in the present, but always *remembers* its past, its beginning. Genre is a representative of creative memory in the process of literary development. Precisely for this reason genre is capable of guaranteeing the *unity* and *uninterrupted continuity* of this development.

For the correct understanding of a genre, therefore, it is necessary to return to its sources.

*

At the close of classical antiquity, and again in the epoch of Hellenism, a number of genres coalesced and developed, fairly diverse externally but bound together by an inner kinship and therefore constituting a special realm of literature, which the ancients themselves very expressively called σπουδογέλοιον, that is, the realm of the serio-comical.[b] Here the ancients assigned the mimes of Sophron*,

[b]For a summary of Bakhtin's position on the *spoudogeloios* ("serious-smiling") genres, see Philip Holland, "Robert Burton's *Anatomy of Melancholy* and Menippean Satire, Humanist and English," Ph.D. dissertation, University of London, 1979, pp. 36-37:

". . . the seriocomic genres are united not only from within but from without, through their common opposition to the serious genres. . . . The serious genres, in Bakhtin's terms, are monological, i.e. they presuppose (or impose) an integrated and stable universe of discourse. The seriocomic genres, by contrast, are dialogical; they deny the possibility, or more precisely, the experience of such integration. As tragedy and epic enclose, Menippean forms the "Socratic dialogue" (as a special genre), the voluminous literature of the Symposiasts* (also a special genre), early memoir literature (Ion of Chios,* Critias*), pamphlets, the whole of bucolic poetry, "Menippean satire"* (as a special genre) and several other genres as well. Precise and stable boundaries within the realm of the serio-comical are almost impossible for us to distinguish. But the ancients themselves distinctly sensed its fundamental uniqueness and counterposed it to the serious genres—the epic, the tragedy, the history, classical rhetoric, and the like. And in fact the differences between this realm and the rest of the literature of classical antiquity are very substantial.

What are the distinguishing characteristics of the genres of the serio-comical?

For all their motley external diversity, they are united by their deep bond with *carnivalistic folklore*. They are all—to a greater or lesser degree—saturated with a specific *carnival sense of the world*, and several of them are direct literary variants of oral carnival-folkloric genres. The carnival sense of the world, permeating these genres from top to bottom, determines their basic features and places image and word in them in a special relationship to reality. In all genres of the serio-comical, to be sure, there is a strong rhetorical element, but in the atmosphere of *joyful relativity* characteristic of a carnival sense of the world this element is fundamentally changed: there is a weakening of its one-sided rhetorical seriousness, its rationality, its singular meaning, its dogmatism.

This carnival sense of the world possesses a mighty life-creating and transforming power, an indestructible vitality. Thus even in our time those genres that have a connection, however remote, with the traditions of the serio-comical preserve in themselves the carnivalistic leaven (ferment), and this sharply distinguishes them from the medium of other genres. These genres always bear a special stamp by which we can recognize them. The sensitive ear will always catch even the most distant echoes of a carnival sense of the world.

Literature that was influenced—directly and without mediation, or indirectly, through a series of intermediate links—by one or another variant of carnivalistic folklore (ancient or medieval) we shall call *carnivalized literature*. The entire realm of the serio-comical constitutes the first example of such literature. In our opinion the problem of carnivalized literature is one of the very important problems in historical poetics, and in particular of the poetics of genre.

---

open up, anatomize. The serious forms comprehend man; the Menippean forms are based on man's inability to know and contain his fate. To any vision of a completed system of truth, the menippea suggests some element outside the system. Seriocomic forms present a challenge, open or covert, to literary and intellectual orthodoxy, a challenge that is reflected not only in their philosophic content but also in their structure and language."

However, the problem of carnivalization itself we shall address somewhat later (after an analysis of carnival and the carnivalistic sense of the world). Here we shall pause on several external generic features of the serio-comical realm which are in fact already a result of the transforming influence of a carnival sense of the world.

The first characteristic of all genres of the serio-comical is their new relationship to reality: their subject, or—what is more important—their starting point for understanding, evaluating, and shaping reality, is the living *present*, often even the very day. For the first time in ancient literature the subject of *serious* (to be sure, at the same time comical) representation is presented without any epic or tragic distance, presented not in the absolute past of myth and legend but on the plane of the present day, in a zone of immediate and even crudely familiar contact with living contemporaries. In these genres, the heroes of myth and the historical figures of the past are deliberately and emphatically contemporized; they act and speak in a zone of familiar contact with the open-ended present. In the realm of the serio-comical, consequently, a radical change takes place in that time-and-value zone where the artistic image is constructed. Such is its first characteristic.

The second characteristic is inseparably bound up with the first: the genres of the serio-comical do not rely on *legend* and do not sanctify themselves through it, they *consciously* rely on *experience* (to be sure, as yet insufficiently mature) and on *free invention*; their relationship to legend is in most cases deeply critical, and at times even resembles a cynical exposé. Here, consequently, there appears for the first time an image almost completely liberated from legend, one which relies instead on experience and free invention. This is a complete revolution in the history of the literary image.

A third characteristic is the deliberate multi-styled and hetero-voiced nature of all these genres. They reject the stylistic unity (or better, the single-styled nature) of the epic, the tragedy, high rhetoric, the lyric. Characteristic of these genres are a multi-toned narration, the mixing of high and low, serious and comic; they make wide use of inserted genres—letters, found manuscripts, retold dialogues, parodies on the high genres, parodically reinterpreted citations; in some of them we observe a mixing of prosaic and poetic speech, living dialects and jargons (and in the Roman stage, direct bilingualism as well) are introduced, and various authorial masks make their appearance. Alongside the representing word there appears the *represented* word; in certain genres a leading role is played by the double-voiced word. And what appears here, as a result, is a radically new relationship to the word as the material of literature.

These are the three basic characteristics common to all genres that enter the realm of the serio-comical. From this it is already clear what enormous significance this realm of ancient literature has for the development of the future European novel, and for that branch of artistic prose gravitating toward the novel and developing under its influence.

Speaking somewhat too simplistically and schematically, one could say that the novelistic genre has three fundamental roots: the *epic*, the *rhetorical*, and the *carnivalistic* (with, of course, many transitional forms in between). It is in the realm of the serio-comical that one must seek the starting points of development for the diverse varieties of the third, that is the carnivalistic, line of the novel, including that variety which leads to Dostoevsky.

In shaping that variety in the development of the novel, and in shaping that artistic prose which we will provisionally call "dialogic" and which, as we have said, leads to Dostoevsky, two genres from the realm of the serio-comical have definitive significance: the *Socratic dialogue* and *Menippean satire*. They must be treated in somewhat greater detail.

The Socratic dialogue was a special and, in its time, very widespread genre. Socratic dialogues were written by Plato, Xenophon,* Antisthenes,* Aeschines,* Phaedo,* Euclid,* Alexamenos,* Glaucon,* Simias,* Crito,* and others. Only the dialogues of Plato and Xenophon have survived; of the others we have only reports and a few fragments. But on the basis of all this we can create for ourselves some idea of the character of this genre.

The Socratic dialogue is not a rhetorical genre. It grows out of a folk-carnivalistic base and is thoroughly saturated with a carnival sense of the world, especially, of course, in the *oral* Socratic stage of its development. But to the carnivalistic base of this genre we will return below.

Originally the genre of the Socratic dialogue—already at the literary stage of its development—was almost a memoir genre: it consisted of reminiscences of actual conversations that Socrates had conducted, transcriptions of remembered conversations framed by a brief story. But very soon a freely creative attitude toward the material liberated the genre almost completely from the limitations of history and memoir, and retained in it only the Socratic method of dialogically revealing the truth and the external form of a dialogue written down and framed by a story. The Socratic dialogues of Plato are of just such a freely creative sort, as are, to a lesser extent, the dialogues of Xenophon and those of Antisthenes, known to us only through fragments.

We shall pause on those aspects of the genre of Socratic dialogue that have special significance for our understanding of the genre.

*Anacrisis → provocation of
the word by the word*

1. At the base of the genre lies the Socratic notion of the dialogic nature of truth, and the dialogic nature of human thinking about truth. The dialogic means of seeking truth is counterposed to *official* monologism, which pretends to *possess a ready-made truth*, and it is also counterposed to the naive self-confidence of those people who think that they know something, that is, who think that they possess certain truths. Truth is not born nor is it to be found inside the head of an individual person, it is born *between people* collectively searching for truth, in the process of their dialogic interaction. Socrates called himself a "pander": he brought people together and made them collide in a quarrel, and as a result truth was born; with respect to this emerging truth Socrates called himself a "midwife," since he assisted at the birth. For this reason also he called his method "obstetric." But Socrates never called himself the exclusive possessor of a ready-made truth. We emphasize that Socratic notions of the dialogic nature of truth lay at the folk-carnivalistic base of the genre of Socratic dialogue, determining its *form*, but they did not by any means always find expression in the actual content of the individual dialogues. The content often assumed a monologic character that contradicted the form-shaping idea of the genre. In Plato's dialogues of his first and second periods, the dialogic nature of truth is still recognized in the philosophical worldview itself, although in weakened form. Thus the dialogue of these early periods has not yet been transformed into a simple means for expounding ready-made ideas (for pedagogical purposes) and Socrates has not yet been transformed into a "teacher." But in the final period of Plato's work that has already taken place: the monologism of the content begins to destroy the form of the Socratic dialogue. Consequently, when the genre of the Socratic dialogue entered the service of the established, dogmatic worldviews of various philosophical schools and religious doctrines, it lost all connection with a carnival sense of the world and was transformed into a simple form for expounding already found, ready-made irrefutable truth; ultimately, it degenerated completely into a question-and-answer form for training neophytes (catechism).

2. The two basic devices of the Socratic dialogue were the syncrisis (σύγκρισις) and the anacrisis (ἀνάκρισις). Syncrisis was understood as the juxtaposition of various points of view on a specific object. The technique of juxtaposing various discourse-opinions on an object was accorded very great importance in the Socratic dialogue; this derived from the very nature of the genre. Anacrisis was understood as a means for eliciting and provoking the words of one's interlocutor, forcing him to express his opinion and express it thoroughly. Socrates was a great master of the anacrisis: he knew how to force people to *speak*, to clothe in discourse their dim but stubbornly preconceived

opinions, to illuminate them by the word and in this way to expose their falseness or incompleteness; he knew how to drag the going truths out into the light of day. Anacrisis is the provocation of the word by the word (and not by means of plot situation, as in Menippean satire, of which more below). Syncrisis and anacrisis dialogize thought, they carry it into the open, turn it into a *rejoinder*, attach it to dialogic intercourse among people. Both of these devices have their origin in the notion of the dialogic nature of truth, which lies at the base of the Socratic dialogue. On the territory of this carnivalized genre, syncrisis and anacrisis lose their narrow, abstractly rhetorical character.

3. The heroes of the Socratic dialogue are *ideologists*. The prime ideologist is Socrates himself, but everyone he converses with is an ideologist as well—his pupils, the Sophists, the simple people whom he draws into dialogue and makes ideologists against their will. And the very event that is accomplished in a Socratic dialogue (or, more precisely, that is reproduced in it) is the purely ideological event of seeking and *testing* truth. This event sometimes unfolds with genuine (but peculiar) dramatic effect, for example the peripetations of the idea of the immortality of the soul in Plato's *Phaedo*. The Socratic dialogue was thus the first to introduce into the history of European literature the hero-ideologist.

4. In the Socratic dialogue, the plot situation of the dialogue is sometimes utilized alongside anacrisis, or the provocation of the word by the word, for the same purpose. In Plato's *Apology* the situation of the trial and expected death sentence determines the special character of Socrates' mode of speaking; it is the summing-up and confession of a man standing *on the threshold*. In *Phaedo* the discussion of the immortality of the soul, with all its internal and external peripetations, is determined directly by the situation of impending death. In both of these situations there is a tendency to create the *extraordinary* situation, one which would cleanse the word of all of life's automatism and object-ness, which would force a person to reveal the deepest layers of his personality and thought. Of course, the freedom to create extraordinary situations, situations provoking a profound word, are very limited in the Socratic dialogue, due to the historical and memoirist nature of the genre (in its literary stage). Nevertheless we can already speak of the birth, even on this soil, of a special type of "dialogue on the threshold" (*Schwellendialog*), which became very widespread in Hellenistic and Roman literature and, ultimately, in the literature of the Renaissance and the Reformation.

5. In the Socratic dialogue the idea is organically combined with the image of a person, its carrier (Socrates and other essential participants in the dialogue). The dialogic testing of the idea is simultaneously

also the testing of the person who represents it. We may therefore speak here of an embryonic *image of an idea*. We should also note that this image is treated freely and creatively. The ideas of Socrates, of the leading Sophists and other historical figures are not quoted here, not paraphrased, but are presented in their free and creative development against a dialogizing background of other ideas. As the historical and memoir basis of the genre is weakened, the ideas of others become more and more plastic; people and ideas which in historical reality never entered into real dialogic contact (but could have done so) begin to come together in dialogues. This is only one step away from the future "Dialogue of the Dead," in which people and ideas separated by centuries collide with one another on the dialogic plane. But the Socratic dialogue did not take that step. To be sure, in the *Apology* Socrates seems almost to predict that future dialogic genre when, in a premonition of his death sentence, he speaks of those dialogues he will conduct in the nether world with the shades of the past, as he had conducted them here on earth. It must be emphasized, however, that in contrast to the *image of an idea* in Dostoevsky, the image of an idea in the Socratic dialogue is of a *syncretic* sort: in the epoch of the Socratic dialogue, the process of differentiation between the abstractly scientific or philosophical *concept* and the artistic *image* had not yet been completed. The Socratic dialogue remained a syncretic philosophical-artistic genre.

Such are the basic characteristics of the Socratic dialogue. They justify our considering this genre one of the starting points for that line of development in European artistic prose and the novel that leads to the work of Dostoevsky.

As a well-defined genre the Socratic dialogue did not exist for long, but in the process of its disintegration other dialogic genres were formed, including Menippean satire. But Menippean satire cannot of course be considered a pure product of the decomposition of the Socratic dialogue (as is sometimes done), since its roots reach *directly* back into carnivalized folklore, whose decisive influence is here even more significant than it is in the Socratic dialogue.

Before analyzing Menippean satire in its essence, we offer here some details of a purely informational sort.[c]

The genre took its name from the philosopher Menippus of Gadara* (third century B.C.) who fashioned it into its classical form[3], although the term itself as signifying a specific genre was first introduced by the Roman scholar Varro* (first century B.C.), who called his satires

---

[c]For a good discussion of Menippean satire – its motives, history, and generic vigor – see Eugene P. Kirk's Introduction to his *Menippean Satire: An Annotated Catalogue of Texts and Criticism* (New York: Garland Publishing, 1980). Information on many of the texts cited by Bakhtin can be found conveniently in this catalogue.

"saturae menippeae." But the genre itself arose considerably earlier: its first representative was perhaps Antisthenes, a pupil of Socrates and one of the authors of Socratic dialogues. Menippean satires were also written by Aristotle's contemporary Heraclides Ponticus,* who, according to Cicero, was also the creator of a kindred genre, the logistoricus (a combination of the Socratic dialogue with fantastic histories). We already have an indisputable representative of Menippean satire in Bion Borysthenes,* that is, "the man from the banks of the Dniepr" (third century B.C.). Then came Menippus, who gave the genre more definitive form, and then Varro, of whose satires numerous fragments have survived. A classical Menippean satire is the *Apocolocyntosis*, that is, the "Pumpkinification," of Seneca.* The *Satyricon* of Petronius* is nothing other than a Menippean satire extended to the limits of a novel. The fullest picture of the genre is of course provided by the Menippean satires of Lucian,* which have come down to us intact (although not representing all varieties of the genre). The *Metamorphoses* (*The Golden Ass*) of Apuleius* (and also its Greek source, known to us through Lucian's brief summary) is a full-blown Menippean satire. A very interesting example of Menippean satire is the so-called "Hippocratic Novel"* (the first European epistolary novel). The development of Menippean satire in its ancient phase culminates in *De Consolatione Philosophiae* of Boethius.* We find elements of Menippean satire in several varieties of the "Greek novel," in the ancient utopian novel, and in Roman satire (Lucilius and Horace). Within the orbit of Menippean satire various kindred genres developed, genetically linked with the Socratic dialogue: the diatribe, the above-mentioned genre of the logistoricus, the soliloquy, aretalogical genres,[d] and others.

Menippean satire exercised a very great influence on old Christian literature (of the ancient period) and on Byzantine literature (and through it, on ancient Russian writing as well). In diverse variants and under diverse generic labels it also continued its development into the post-classical epochs: into the Middle Ages, the Renaissance and Reformation, and modern times; in fact it continues to develop even now (both with and without a clear-cut awareness of itself as a genre). This carnivalized genre, extraordinarily flexible and as changeable as Proteus, capable of penetrating other genres, has had an enormous and as yet insufficiently appreciated importance for the development of European literatures. Menippean satire became one of the main carriers and channels for the carnival sense of the world in literature, and remains so to the present day. We shall return to its importance below.

Now after our brief (and of course far from complete) survey of

---

[d]Aretalogical genres: narratives about the miraculous deeds of gods or heroes.

the ancient Menippean satires, we must examine the basic character-istics of this genre as they were defined in the epoch of antiquity. From now on we shall call the "menippean satire" simply the *me-nippea*.

1. As compared with the Socratic dialogue, the specific weight of the comic element is generally increased in the menippea, although this vacillates significantly in the diverse varieties of this flexible genre: the comic element is very great in Varro, for example, but it disappears, or rather is reduced,[4] in Boethius. The specifically *carni-val* nature (in the broad sense of the word) of the comic element we shall deal with in more detail below.

2. The menippea is fully liberated from those limitations of his-tory and memoir that were so characteristic of the Socratic dialogue (although externally the memoir form is sometimes preserved); it is free of legend and not fettered by any demands for an external veri-similitude to life. The menippea is characterized by an *extraordinary freedom of plot and philosophical invention*. The fact that the lead-ing heroes of the menippea are historical and legendary figures (Diogenes, Menippus and others) presents no obstacle. Indeed, in all of world literature we could not find a genre more free than the menippea in its invention and use of the fantastic.

3. The most important characteristic of the menippea as a genre is the fact that its bold and unrestrained use of the fantastic and ad-venture is internally motivated, justified by and devoted to a purely ideational and philosophical end: the creation of *extraordinary situa-tions* for the provoking and testing of a philosophical idea, a dis-course, a *truth*, embodied in the image of a wise man, the seeker of this truth. We emphasize that the fantastic here serves not for the positive *embodiment* of truth, but as a mode for searching after truth, provoking it, and, most important, *testing* it. To this end the heroes of Menippean satire ascend into heaven, descend into the nether world, wander through unknown and fantastic lands, are placed in extraordinary life situations (Diogenes, for example, sells himself in-to slavery in the marketplace, Peregrinus* triumphantly immolates himself at the Olympic Games, Lucius the Ass finds himself constant-ly in extraordinary situations). Very often the fantastic takes on the character of an adventure story; sometimes it assumes a symbolic or even mystical-religious character (as in Apuleius). But in all these instances the fantastic is subordinated to the purely ideational func-tion of provoking and testing a truth. The most unrestrained and fantastic adventures are present here in organic and indissoluble ar-tistic unity with the philosophical idea. And it is essential to empha-size once again that the issue is precisely the testing of an *idea*, of a *truth*, and not the testing of a particular human character, whether

an individual or a social type. The testing of a wise man is a test of his philosophical position in the world, not a test of any other features of his character independent of that position. In this sense one can say that the content of the menippea is the adventures of an *idea* or a *truth* in the world: either on earth, in the nether regions, or on Olympus.

4. A very important characteristic of the menippea is the organic combination within it of the free fantastic, the symbolic, at times even a mystical-religious element with an extreme and (from our point of view) crude *slum naturalism*. The adventures of truth on earth take place on the high road, in brothels, in the dens of thieves, in taverns, marketplaces, prisons, in the erotic orgies of secret cults, and so forth. The idea here fears no slum, is not afraid of any of life's filth. The man of the idea — the wise man — collides with worldly evil, depravity, baseness, and vulgarity in their most extreme expression. This slum naturalism is apparently already present in the earliest menippea. Of Bion Borysthenes the ancients were already saying that he "was the first to deck out philosophy in the motley dress of a hetaera." There is a great deal of slum naturalism in Varro and Lucian. But slum naturalism could develop to its broadest and fullest extent only in the menippea of Petronius and Apuleius, menippea expanded into novels. The organic combination of philosophical dialogue, lofty symbol-systems, the adventure-fantastic, and slum naturalism is the outstanding characteristic of the menippea, and it is preserved in all subsequent stages in the development of the dialogic line of novelistic prose right up to Dostoevsky.

5. Boldness of invention and the fantastic element are combined in the menippea with an extraordinary philosophical universalism and a capacity to contemplate the world on the broadest possible scale. The menippea is a genre of "ultimate questions." In it ultimate philosophical positions are put to the test. The menippea strives to provide, as it were, the ultimate and decisive words and acts of a person, each of which contains the whole man, the whole of his life in its entirety. This feature of the genre was apparently especially prominent in the early menippea (in Heraclides Ponticus, Bion, Teles,* and Menippus), but it has been preserved, although sometimes in weakened form, as the characteristic feature in all varieties of the genre. Under menippean conditions the very nature and process of posing philosophical problems, as compared with the Socratic dialogue, had to change abruptly: all problems that were in the least "academic" (gnoseological and aesthetic) fell by the wayside, complex and extensive modes of argumentation also fell away, and there remained essentially only naked "ultimate questions" with an ethical and practical bias. Typical for the menippea is syncrisis (that is,

juxtaposition) of precisely such stripped-down "ultimate positions in the world." Take, for example, the carnivalistic-satirical representation of the "Vitarum auctio," that is, the sale of ultimate life positions, in Lucian, the fantastic sailings over ideological seas in Varro (*Sesculixes* [A Ulysses and a Half]), travels through all the philosophical schools (apparently already in Bion), and so forth. Everywhere one meets the stripped-down *pro et contra* of life's ultimate questions.

6. In connection with the philosophical universalism of the menippea, a three-planed construction makes its appearance: action and dialogic syncrisis are transferred from earth to Olympus and to the nether world. This three-planed construction is present with great external visibility in, for example, Seneca's *Apocolocyntosis*; here also "dialogues of the threshold" are presented with great external clarity: at the gates of Olympus (where Claudius was not admitted) and on the threshold of the underworld. The three-planed construction of the menippea exercised a decisive influence on the corresponding structure of the medieval mystery play and mystery scene. The genre of the "threshold dialogue" was also extremely widespread in the Middle Ages, in the serious as well as the comic genres (the famous fabliau of the peasant arguing at the gates of heaven, for example), and is especially well represented in the literature of the Reformation — the so-called "literature of the heavenly gates" (*Himmelspforten-Literatur*). The menippea accorded great importance to the *nether world*: here was born that special genre of "dialogues of the dead," widespread in European literature of the Renaissance, and in the seventeenth and eighteenth centuries.

7. In the menippea a special type of *experimental fantasticality* makes its appearance, completely foreign to ancient epic and tragedy: observation from some unusual point of view, from on high, for example, which results in a radical change in the scale of the observed phenomena of life; Lucian's *Icaromenippus*, for example, or Varro's *Endymiones* (observations of the life of a city from a great height). This line of experimental fantasticality continues, under the defining influence of the menippea, into the subsequent epochs as well — in Rabelais, Swift, Voltaire (*Micromégas*) and others.

8. In the menippea there appears for the first time what might be called moral-psychological experimentation: a representation of the unusual, abnormal moral and psychic states of man — insanity of all sorts (the theme of the maniac), split personality, unrestrained daydreaming, unusual dreams, passions bordering on madness,[5] suicides, and so forth. These phenomena do not function narrowly in the menippea as mere themes, but have a formal generic significance. Dreams, daydreams, insanity destroy the epic and tragic wholeness of a person and his fate: the possibilities of another person and

another life are revealed in him, he loses his finalized quality and ceases to mean only one thing; he ceases to coincide with himself. Dreams are common in the epic as well, but there they are prophetic, motivating, cautionary—they do not take the person beyond the bounds of his fate and his character, they do not violate his integrity. Of course, this unfinalizability of a man, his noncoincidence with himself, are still rather elementary and embryonic in the menippea, but they are openly there and permit us to look at a person in a new way. This destruction of the wholeness and finalized quality of a man is facilitated by the appearance, in the menippea, of a dialogic relationship to one's own self (fraught with the possibility of split personality). Very interesting in this respect is Varro's menippea *Bimarcus*, that is, *The Double Marcus*.[e] As in all the menippea of Varro, the comic element here is very strong. Marcus had promised to write a work on tropes and figures, but he does not keep his promise. The Second Marcus—that is, his conscience, his double—constantly reminds him of it, gives him no peace. The First Marcus tries to fulfill the promise but cannot concentrate: he distracts himself by reading Homer, he begins to write poems himself, and so on. This dialogue between the two Marcuses, that is between a person and his conscience, is in Varro presented comically, but nevertheless as a sort of artistic discovery it exercised crucial influence on the *Soliloquia* of Augustine. We should mention in passing that Dostoevsky too, when representing the phenomenon of the double, always preserved alongside the tragic element an element of the *comic* as well (in *The Double*, and in Ivan Karamazov's conversation with the devil).

9. Very characteristic for the menippea are scandal scenes, eccentric behavior, inappropriate speeches and performances, that is, all sorts of violations of the generally accepted and customary course of events and the established norms of behavior and etiquette, including manners of speech. These scandals are sharply distinguished by their artistic structure from epic events and tragic catastrophes. They are also different in essence from comic brawls and exposés. One could say that in the menippea new artistic categories of the scandalous and the eccentric emerge which are completely foreign to the classical epic and to the dramatic genres (on the carnivalistic character of these categories we shall speak in more detail below). Scandals and eccentricities destroy the epic and tragic wholeness of the world, they make a breach in the stable, normal ("seemly") course of human affairs and events, they free human behavior from the norms and motivations that predetermine it. Scandals and eccentric scenes fill the meetings of the gods on Olympus (in Lucian, Seneca, Julian the Apostate,* and others) as well as scenes on earth (in

---

[e]Also known in English as "The Double Varro" and "Varro Split."

Petronius, for example, the scandals on the public square, in the hotel, in the bath). The "inappropriate word"—inappropriate because of its cynical frankness, or because it profanely unmasks a holy thing, or because it crudely violates etiquette—is also very characteristic for the menippea.

10. The menippea is full of sharp contrasts and oxymoronic combinations: the virtuous hetaera, the true freedom of the wise man and his servile position, the emperor who becomes a slave, moral downfalls and purifications, luxury and poverty, the noble bandit, and so forth. The menippea loves to play with abrupt transitions and shifts, ups and downs, rises and falls, unexpected comings together of distant and disunited things, mésalliances of all sorts.

11. The menippea often includes elements of *social utopia* which are incorporated in the form of dreams or journeys to unknown lands; sometimes the menippea grows outright into a utopian novel (*Abaris* by Heraclides Ponticus). This utopian element is organically combined with all the other elements of the genre.

12. Characteristic for the menippea is a wide use of inserted genres: novellas, letters, oratorical speeches, symposia, and so on; also characteristic is a mixing of prose and poetic speech. The inserted genres are presented at various distances from the ultimate authorial position, that is, with varying degrees of parodying and objectification. Verse portions are almost always given with a certain degree of parodying.

13. The presence of inserted genres reinforces the multi-styled and multi-toned nature of the menippea; what is coalescing here is a new relationship to the word as the material of literature, a relationship characteristic for the entire dialogic line of development in artistic prose.

14. Finally, the last characteristic of the menippea: its concern with current and topical issues. This is, in its own way, the "journalistic" genre of antiquity, acutely echoing the ideological issues of the day. The satires of Lucian, taken as a group, are an entire encyclopedia of his times: they are full of overt and hidden polemics with various philosophical, religious, ideological and scientific schools, and with the tendencies and currents of his time; they are full of the images of contemporary or recently deceased public figures, "masters of thought" in all spheres of societal and ideological life (under their own names, or disguised); they are full of allusions to the great and small events of the epoch; they feel out new directions in the development of everyday life; they show newly emerging types in all layers of society, and so on. They are a sort of *Diary of a Writer*, seeking to unravel and evaluate the general spirit and direction of evolving contemporary life. Just such a *Diary of a Writer* (with,

however, a sharp preponderance of the carnivalistic-comic element) are the satires of Varro, taken in their entirety. We find the same characteristic in Petronius, in Apuleius and others. A journalistic quality, the spirit of publicistic writing or of the feuilleton, a pointed interest in the topics of the day are characteristic to a greater or lesser extent of all representatives of the menippea. And this final characteristic is organically combined with all the other traits of the genre.

Such are the basic generic characteristics of the menippea. We must again emphasize the organic unity of all these seemingly very heterogeneous features, the deep internal integrity of this genre. It was formed in an epoch when national legend was already in decay, amid the destruction of those ethical norms that constituted the ancient idea of "seemliness" ("beauty," "nobility"), in an epoch of intense struggle among numerous and heterogeneous religious and philosophical schools and movements, when disputes over "ultimate questions" of worldview had become an everyday mass phenomenon among all strata of the population and took place whenever and wherever people came together—in marketplaces, on the streets and highroads, in taverns, in bathhouses, on the decks of ships; when the figure of the philosopher, the wise man (the cynic, the stoic, the epicurean) or of the prophet or wonder-worker became typical and were encountered more often than one met the figure of the monk in the Middle Ages during the greatest flowering of the monastic orders. It was the epoch of preparation and formation of a new world religion: Christianity.

The other side of this epoch was a devaluation of all external positions that a person might hold in life, their transformation into *roles* played out on the stageboards of the theater of the world in accordance with the wishes of blind fate (there is a profound philosophical awareness of this in Epictetus* and Marcus Aurelius, and on the literary plane in Lucian and Apuleius). This led to the destruction of the epic and tragic wholeness of a man and his fate.

Thus the genre of the menippea is perhaps the most adequate expression of the characteristics of the epoch. Here, the content of life was poured into a stable form that possessed an *inner logic*, insuring the indissoluble linking up of all its elements. Thanks to this, the genre of the menippea was able to wield such immense influence—to this day almost entirely unappreciated in scholarship—in the history of the development of European novelistic prose.

While possessing an inner integrity, the genre of the menippea simultaneously possesses great external plasticity and a remarkable capacity to absorb into itself kindred small genres, and to penetrate as a component element into other large genres.

Thus the menippea absorbs into itself such kindred genres as the diatribe, the soliloquy, the symposium. These genres are all akin to one another in the external and *internal dialogicality* of their approach to human life and human thought.

The diatribe is an internally dialogized rhetorical genre, usually structured in the form of a conversation with an absent interlocutor —and resulting in a dialogization of the very process of speech and thought. The founder of the diatribe was considered by the ancients to be that same Bion Borysthenes who was also a founder of the menippea. It should be noted that it was precisely the diatribe, and not classical rhetoric, that exercised a defining influence on the generic characteristics of the ancient Christian sermon.

A dialogic relationship to one's own self defines the genre of the soliloquy. It is a discussion with oneself. Already Antisthenes (a pupil of Socrates and perhaps already a writer of menippea) considered the greatest achievement of his philosophy "the ability to communicate dialogically with one's self."[f] Epictetus, Marcus Aurelius, and Augustine were remarkable masters of this genre. At the heart of the genre lies the discovery of the *inner man*—"one's own self," accessible not to passive self-observation but only through an *active dialogic approach to one's own self*, destroying that naive wholeness of one's notions about the self that lies at the heart of the lyric, epic, and tragic image of man. A dialogic approach to oneself breaks down the outer shell of the self's image, that shell which exists for other people, determining the external assessment of a person (in the eyes of others) and dimming the purity of self-consciousness.

Both genres—the diatribe and the soliloquy—developed within the orbit of the menippea, were interwoven with it and permeated it (especially on Roman and early Christian soil).

The symposium is a banquet dialogue, already in existence during the epoch of the Socratic dialogue (there are examples of it in Plato and Xenophon), but receiving its full and diverse development only in subsequent epochs. Dialogic banquet discourse possessed special privileges (originally of a cultic sort): the right to a certain license, ease and familiarity, to a certain frankness, to eccentricity, ambivalence; that is, the combination in one discourse of praise and abuse, of the serious and the comic. The symposium is by nature a purely carnivalistic genre. Menippea were sometimes formulated directly as symposia (apparently as early as Menippus; three of Varro's satires are formulated as symposia, and there are elements of the symposium in Lucian and Petronius).

The menippea, as we have said, was capable of infiltrating the large

---

[f]From Diogenes Laertius, *Lives of the Eminent Philosophers*, VI. 6-8 Antisthenes. The R. D. Hicks translation (Loeb, vol. II) renders this Greek phrase as "the ability to hold converse with myself," but the verb can also mean to consort with, associate with, join battle with, and be a disciple of.

genres, subjecting them to a certain transformation. Thus elements of the menippea can be detected in the "Greek novels." Certain images and episodes from the *Ephesian Tales* of Xenophon of Ephesus,* for example, have the distinct scent of the menippea about them. The dregs of society are represented in the spirit of slum naturalism: prisons, slaves, thieves, fishermen, and so forth. Other novels are characterized by an internal dialogicality, by elements of parody and reduced laughter. Elements of the menippea also penetrate the utopian works of antiquity, as well as works belonging to the aretalogical genre (*The Life of Apollonius of Tyana* by Philostratus,* for example). The menippea's transforming power to penetrate other genres has great significance for the narrative genres of ancient Christian literature as well.

Our descriptive characterization of the generic features of the menippea, and of kindred genres connected with it, is extraordinarily close to the characterization one might give of the generic features of Dostoevsky's work (see, for example, that given by Grossman, cited by us on pp. 14-15). Essentially all of the defining features of the menippea (with, of course, the appropriate modifications and complications) we will find also in Dostoevsky. This is in fact one and the same generic world, although present in the menippea at the *beginning* of its development, in Dostoevsky at its very *peak*. But we know that the beginning, that is the archaic stage of a genre, is preserved in renewed form at the highest stages of the genre's development. Moreover, the higher a genre develops and the more complex its form, the better and more fully it remembers its past.

Does this mean that Dostoevsky proceeded *directly* and *consciously* from the ancient menippea? Of course not. In no sense was he a *stylizer* of ancient genres. Dostoevsky linked up with the chain of a given generic tradition at that point where it passed through his own time, although the past links in this chain, including the ancient link, were to a greater or lesser degree familiar and close to him (we shall return later to the question of Dostoevsky's generic sources). Speaking somewhat paradoxically, one could say that it was not Dostoevsky's subjective memory, but the objective memory of the very genre in which he worked, that preserved the peculiar features of the ancient menippea.

The generic characteristics of the menippea were not simply reborn, but also *renewed*, in Dostoevsky's work. In his creative utilization of this generic potential, Dostoevsky departed widely from the authors of the ancient menippea. In its posing of philosophical and social problems, in its artistic qualities, the ancient menippea seems in comparison with Dostoevsky primitive and pale. And the most important difference is that the ancient menippea does not yet know *polyphony*. The menippea, like the Socratic dialogue, could only prepare certain generic conditions necessary for polyphony's emergence.

We must now move on to the problem of carnival and the carnivalization of literature, already mentioned by us earlier.

The problem of *carnival* (in the sense of the sum total of all diverse festivities, rituals and forms of a carnival type)—its essence, its deep roots in the primordial order and the primordial thinking of man, its development under conditions of class society, its extraordinary life force and its undying fascination—is one of the most complex and most interesting problems in the history of culture. We cannot, of course, do justice to it here. What interests us here is essentially only the problem of carnivalization, that is, the determining influence of carnival on literature and more precisely on literary genre.

Carnival itself (we repeat: in the sense of a sum total of all diverse festivities of the carnival type) is not, of course, a literary phenomenon. It is *syncretic pageantry* of a ritualistic sort. As a form it is very complex and varied, giving rise, on a general carnivalistic base, to diverse variants and nuances depending upon the epoch, the people, the individual festivity. Carnival has worked out an entire language of symbolic concretely sensuous forms—from large and complex mass actions to individual carnivalistic gestures. This language, in a differentiated and even (as in any language) articulate way, gave expression to a unified (but complex) carnival sense of the world, permeating all its forms. This language cannot be translated in any full or adequate way into a verbal language, and much less into a language of abstract concepts, but it is amenable to a certain transposition into a language of artistic images that has something in common with its concretely sensuous nature; that is, it can be transposed into the language of literature. We are calling this transposition of carnival into the language of literature the carnivalization of literature. From the vantage point of this transposition, we will isolate and examine individual aspects and characteristic features of carnival.

Carnival is a pageant without footlights and without a division into performers and spectators. In carnival everyone is an active participant, everyone communes in the carnival act. Carnival is not contemplated and, strictly speaking, not even performed; its participants *live* in it, they live by its laws as long as those laws are in effect; that is, they live a *carnivalistic life*. Because carnivalistic life is life drawn out of its *usual* rut, it is to some extent "life turned inside out," "the reverse side of the world" ("*monde à l'envers*").

The laws, prohibitions, and restrictions that determine the structure and order of ordinary, that is noncarnival, life are suspended during

Carnival suspended.

carnival: what is suspended first of all is hierarchical structure and all the forms of terror, reverence, piety, and etiquette connected with it—that is, everything resulting from socio-hierarchical inequality or any other form of inequality among people (including age). All *distance* between people is suspended, and a special carnival category goes into effect: *free and familiar contact among people*. This is a very important aspect of a carnival sense of the world. People who in life are separated by impenetrable hierarchical barriers enter into free familiar contact on the carnival square. The category of familiar contact is also responsible for the special way mass actions are organized, and for free carnival gesticulation, and for the outspoken carnivalistic word.

Carnival is the place for working out, in a concretely sensuous, half-real and half-play-acted form, a *new mode of interrelationship between individuals*, counterposed to the all-powerful socio-hierarchical relationships of noncarnival life. The behavior, gesture, and discourse of a person are freed from the authority of all hierarchical positions (social estate, rank, age, property) defining them totally in noncarnival life, and thus from the vantage point of noncarnival life become eccentric and inappropriate. *Eccentricity* is a special category of the carnival sense of the world, organically connected with the category of familiar contact; it permits—in concretely sensuous form—the latent sides of human nature to reveal and express themselves.

Linked with familiarization is a third category of the carnival sense of the world: *carnivalistic mésalliances*. A free and familiar attitude spreads over everything: over all values, thoughts, phenomena, and things. All things that were once self-enclosed, disunified, distanced from one another by a noncarnivalistic hierarchical worldview are drawn into carnivalistic contacts and combinations. Carnival brings together, unifies, weds, and combines the sacred with the profane, the lofty with the low, the great with the insignificant, the wise with the stupid.

Connected with this is yet a fourth carnivalistic category, *profanation*: carnivalistic blasphemies, a whole system of carnivalistic debasings and bringings down to earth, carnivalistic obscenities linked with the reproductive power of the earth and the body, carnivalistic parodies on sacred texts and sayings, etc.

These carnivalistic categories are not *abstract thoughts* about equality and freedom, the interrelatedness of all things or the unity of opposites. No, these are concretely sensuous ritual-pageant "thoughts" experienced and played out in the form of life itself, "thoughts" that had coalesced and survived for thousands of years among the broadest masses of European mankind. This is why they were able to exercise such an immense *formal, genre-shaping* influence on literature.

These carnival categories, and above all the category of free familiarization of man and the world, were over thousands of years transposed into literature, particularly into the dialogic line of development in novelistic prose. Familiarization facilitated the destruction of epic and tragic distance and the transfer of all represented material to a zone of familiar contact; it was reflected significantly in the organization of plot and plot situations, it determined that special familiarity of the author's position with regard to his characters (impossible in the higher genres); it introduced the logic of mésalliances and profanatory debasings; finally, it exercised a powerful transforming influence on the very verbal style of literature. All this already shows up quite clearly in the menippea. We shall return to this later, but first we must touch upon several other aspects of carnival, most importantly *carnivalistic acts*.

The primary carnivalistic act is the *mock crowning and subsequent decrowning of the carnival king*. This ritual is encountered in one form or another in all festivities of the carnival type: in the most elaborately worked out forms—the saturnalia, the European carnival and festival of fools (in the latter, mock priests, bishops or popes, depending on the rank of the church, were chosen in place of a king); in a less elaborated form, all other festivities of this type, right down to festival banquets with their election of short-lived kings and queens of the festival.

Under this ritual act of decrowning a king lies the very core of the carnival sense of the world—*the pathos of shifts and changes, of death and renewal*. Carnival is the festival of all-annihilating and all-renewing time. Thus might one express the basic concept of carnival. But we emphasize again: this is not an abstract thought but a living sense of the world, expressed in the concretely sensuous forms (either experienced or play-acted) of the ritual act.

Crowning/decrowning is a dualistic ambivalent ritual, expressing the inevitability and at the same time the creative power of the shift-and-renewal, the *joyful relativity* of all structure and order, of all authority and all (hierarchical) position. Crowning already contains the idea of immanent decrowning: it is ambivalent from the very start. And he who is crowned is the antipode of a real king, a slave or a jester; this act, as it were, opens and sanctifies the inside-out world of carnival. In the ritual of crowning all aspects of the actual ceremony—the symbols of authority that are handed over to the newly crowned king and the clothing in which he is dressed—all become ambivalent and acquire a veneer of joyful relativity; they become almost stage props (although these are ritual stage props); their symbolic meaning becomes two-leveled (as real symbols of power, that is in the noncarnival world, they are single-leveled, absolute, heavy, and monolithically serious). From the very beginning, a decrowning glimmers through the crowning. And all carnivalistic symbols are of such a sort: they always include within themselves a perspective of negation (death) or vice versa. Birth is fraught with death, and death with new birth.

The ritual of decrowning completes, as it were, the coronation and is inseparable from it (I repeat: this is a dualistic ritual). And through it, a new crowning already glimmers. Carnival celebrates the shift itself, the very process of replaceability, and not the precise item that is replaced. Carnival is, so to speak, functional and not substantive. It absolutizes nothing, but rather proclaims the joyful relativity of everything. The ceremonial of the ritual of decrowning is counterposed to the ritual of crowning: regal vestments are stripped off the decrowned king, his crown is removed, the other symbols of authority are taken away, he is ridiculed and beaten. All the symbolic aspects of this ceremonial of decrowning acquire a second and positive level of meaning—it is not naked, absolute negation and destruction (absolute negation, like absolute affirmation, is unknown to carnival). Moreover, precisely in this ritual of decrowning does there emerge with special clarity the carnival pathos of shifts and renewals, the image of constructive death. Thus the ritual of decrowning has been the ritual most often transposed into literature. But, we repeat, crowning and decrowning are inseparable, they are dualistic and pass one into the other; in any absolute dissociation they would completely lose their carnivalistic sense.

The carnivalistic act of crowning/decrowning is, of course, permeated with carnival categories (with the logic of the carnival world): free and familiar contact (this is very clearly manifest in decrowning), carnivalistic mésalliances (slave-king), profanation (playing with the symbols of higher authority), and so on.

We shall not dwell here on the details of the crowning-decrowning ritual (although they are very interesting), nor on its diverse variations from epoch to epoch and in the various festivities of the carnival type. Nor shall we analyze the various accessory rituals of carnival, for example, disguise—that is, carnivalistic shifts of clothing and of positions and destinies in life; nor carnival mystifications, bloodless carnival wars, verbal agons[g] and cursing matches, exchanges of gifts (abundance as an aspect of carnivalistic utopia), and so on. These rituals too were transposed into literature, imparting symbolic depth and ambivalence to the corresponding plots and plot situations, imparting a joyful relativity, carnival levity and rapidity of change.

But of course an extraordinarily great influence on literary-artistic

---

[g]*Agon*: in Greek, "contest." An agon is that part of a Greek drama in which two protagonists, each aided by half of the chorus, engage in verbal conflict.

thinking was exercised by the ritual of crowning/decrowning. This ritual determined a special *decrowning type* of structure for artistic images and whole works, one in which the decrowning was essentially ambivalent and two-leveled. If carnivalistic ambivalence should happen to be extinguished in these images of decrowning, they degenerated into a purely negative *exposé* of a moral or socio-political sort, they became single-leveled, lost their artistic character, and were transformed into naked journalism.

We must consider again in more detail the ambivalent nature of carnival images. All the images of carnival are dualistic; they unite within themselves both poles of change and crisis: birth and death (the image of pregnant death), blessing and curse (benedictory carnival curses which call simultaneously for death and rebirth), praise and abuse, youth and old age, top and bottom, face and backside, stupidity and wisdom. Very characteristic for carnival thinking is paired images, chosen for their contrast (high/low, fat/thin, etc.) or for their similarity (doubles/twins). Also characteristic is the utilization of things in reverse: putting clothes on inside out (or wrong side out), trousers on the head, dishes in place of headgear, the use of household utensils as weapons, and so forth. This is a special instance of the carnival category of *eccentricity*, the violation of the usual and the generally accepted, life drawn out of its usual rut.

Deeply ambivalent also is the image of *fire* in carnival. It is a fire that simultaneously destroys and renews the world. In European carnivals there was almost always a special structure (usually a vehicle adorned with all possible sorts of gaudy carnival trash) called "hell," and at the close of carnival this "hell" was triumphantly set on fire (sometimes this carnival "hell" was ambivalently linked with a horn of plenty). Characteristic is the ritual of "moccoli" in Roman carnival: each participant in the carnival carried a lighted candle ("a candle stub"), and each tried to put out another's candle with the cry "Sia ammazzato!" ("Death to thee!"). In his famous description of Roman carnival (in *Italienische Reise*)[h] Goethe, striving to uncover the deeper meaning behind carnival images, relates a profoundly symbolic little scene: during "moccoli" a boy puts out his father's candle with the cheerful carnival cry: "Sia ammazzato il Signore Padre!" [that is, "death to thee, Signor Father!"]

Deeply ambivalent also is carnival *laughter* itself. Genetically it is linked with the most ancient forms of ritual laughter. Ritual laughter was always directed toward something higher: the sun (the highest god), other gods, the highest earthly authority were put to shame

[h]J. W. Goethe, *Italian Journey*, trans. W. H. Auden and Elizabeth Mayer (London: Collins, 1962). See Part Three (January 1788), "The Roman Carnival," and especially the section "Moccoli," pp. 467-69.

and ridiculed to force them to *renew themselves*. All forms of ritual laughter were linked with death and rebirth, with the reproductive act, with symbols of the reproductive force. Ritual laughter was a reaction to *crises* in the life of the sun (solstices), crises in the life of a deity, in the life of the world and of man (funeral laughter). In it, ridicule was fused with rejoicing.

This ancient ritualistic practice of directing laughter toward something higher (a deity or authority) defined the privileges of laughter in antiquity and in the Middle Ages. Much was permitted in the form of laughter that was impermissible in serious form. In the Middle Ages, under cover of the legitimized license of laughter, "parodia sacra" became possible—that is, parody of sacred texts and rituals.

Carnivalistic laughter likewise is directed toward something higher —toward a shift of authorities and truths, a shift of world orders. Laughter embraces both poles of change, it deals with the very process of change, with *crisis* itself. Combined in the act of carnival laughter are death and rebirth, negation (a smirk) and affirmation (rejoicing laughter). This is a profoundly universal laughter, a laughter that contains a whole outlook on the world. Such is the specific quality of ambivalent carnival laughter.

In connection with laughter we shall touch upon one more question—the carnivalistic nature of *parody*. Parody, as we have already noted, is an integral element in Menippean satire and in all carnivalized genres in general. To the pure genres (epic, tragedy) parody is organically alien; to the carnivalized genres it is, on the contrary, organically inherent. In antiquity, parody was inseparably linked to a carnival sense of the world. Parodying is the creation of a *decrowning double*; it is that same "world turned inside out." For this reason parody is ambivalent. Antiquity parodied essentially everything: the satyr drama, for example, was originally the parodic and laughing aspect of the tragic trilogy that preceded it. Parody here was not, of course, a naked rejection of the parodied object. Everything has its parody, that is, its laughing aspect, for everything is reborn and renewed through death. In Rome, parody was an obligatory aspect of funeral as well as of triumphant laughter (both were of course rituals of the carnivalistic type). In carnival, parodying was employed very widely, in diverse forms and degrees: various images (for example, carnival pairs of various sorts) parodied one another variously and from various points of view; it was like an entire system of crooked mirrors, elongating, diminishing, distorting in various directions and to various degrees.

Parodying doubles have become a rather common phenomenon in carnivalized literature. They find especially vivid expression in Dostoevsky—almost every one of the leading heroes of his novels has several doubles who parody him in various ways: for Raskolnikov there are Svidrigailov, Luzhin, and Lebeziatnikov; for Stavrogin— Peter Verkhovensky, Shatov, and Kirillov; for Ivan Karamazov— Smerdyakov, the devil, Rakitin. In each of them (that is, in each of the doubles) the hero dies (that is, is negated) in order to be renewed (that is, in order to be purified and to rise above himself).

In the narrowly formal literary parody of modern times, the connection with a carnival sense of the world is almost entirely broken. But in the parodies of the Renaissance (in Erasmus, Rabelais, and others) the carnival fire still burned: parody was ambivalent and sensed its bond with death/renewal. Thus could be born in the bosom of parody one of the greatest and at the same time most carnivalistic novels of world literature: Cervantes' *Don Quixote*. Here is how Dostoevsky assessed that novel: "There is nothing in the world more profound and powerful than this work. It is the ultimate and greatest word yet uttered by human thought, it is the most bitter irony that a man could express, and if the world should end and people were asked there, somewhere, 'Well, did you understand your life on earth and what conclusions have you drawn from it?' a person could silently point to Don Quixote: 'Here is my conclusion about life, can you judge me for it?'"[i]

It is characteristic that Dostoevsky structures his evaluation of *Don Quixote* in the form of a typical "threshold dialogue."

To conclude our analysis of carnival (from the vantage point of carnivalized literature), a few words about the carnival square.

The main arena for carnival acts was the square and the streets adjoining it. To be sure, carnival also invaded the home; in essence it was limited in time only and not in space; carnival knows neither stage nor footlights. But the central arena could only be the square, for by its very idea carnival *belongs to the whole people*, it is *universal, everyone* must participate in its familiar contact. The public square was the symbol of communal performance. The carnival square —the square of carnival acts—acquired an additional symbolic overtone that broadened and deepened it. In carnivalized literature the square, as a setting for the action of the plot, becomes two-leveled and ambivalent: it is as if there glimmered through the actual square the carnival square of free familiar contact and communal performances of crowning and decrowning. Other places of action as well (provided they are realistically motivated by the plot, of course) can, if they become meeting- and contact-points for heterogeneous people —streets, taverns, roads, bathhouses, decks of ships, and so on—take on this additional carnival-square significance (for all the naturalistic

---

[i]The comment on Quixote occurs in *The Diary of a Writer*, 1876, March, Ch. II, 1: "Don Carlos and Sir Watkin. Again, Symptoms of 'the Beginning of the End,'" p. 260.

qualities of the representation, the universal symbol-system of carnival is in no danger of naturalism).

Festivities of the carnival type occupied an enormous place in the life of the broadest masses of the people in ancient times—in Greek and even more in Roman life, where the central (but not the sole) festival of the carnival type was the *saturnalia*. These festivals had no less (and perhaps, even more) significance in medieval Europe and during the Renaissance, where they were in part a direct living continuation of Roman saturnalia. In the realm of carnivalistic folk culture there was no break in tradition between antiquity and the Middle Ages. In all epochs of their development, festivities of the carnival type have exercised an enormous influence—as yet insufficiently appreciated and researched—on the development of culture as a whole, including literature, several of whose genres and movements have undergone a particularly intense *carnivalization*. In the ancient period, early Attic comedy and the entire realm of the serio-comical was subjected to a particularly powerful carnivalization. In Rome, the many diverse varieties of satire and epigram were linked, and were designed to be linked, with the saturnalia; they were either written for saturnalia, or at least were created under cover of that legitimized carnival license enjoyed by the festival (all of Martial's* work, for example, was directly connected with the saturnalia).

In the Middle Ages the vast comic and parodic literature in vernacular languages and in Latin was, one way or another, connected with festivals of the carnival type—with carnival proper, with the "Festival of Fools," with free "paschal laughter" (*risus paschalis*), and so forth. Essentially every church holiday in the Middle Ages had its carnivalistic side, the side facing the public square (especially those holidays like Corpus Christi). Many national festivities, such as the bullfight, for example, were of a clearly expressed carnivalistic character. A carnival atmosphere reigned during the days of a fair, on the festival of the harvesting of grapes, on the performance days of miracle plays, mystery plays, *soties*ʲ and so forth; the entire theatrical life of the Middle Ages was carnivalistic. The large cities of the late Middle Ages (such cities as Rome, Naples, Venice, Paris, Lyon, Nuremberg, Cologne) lived a full carnival life on the average of three months out of the year (and sometimes more). It could be said (with certain reservations, of course) that a person of the Middle Ages lived, as it were, *two lives*: one was the *official* life, monolithically serious and gloomy, subjugated to a strict hierarchical order, full of terror, dogmatism, reverence, and piety; the other was the *life of the carnival square*, free and unrestricted, full of ambivalent laughter,

---

ʲ*Soties*: French satirical farces of the medieval period, in which actors (in fool's costume) ridiculed social manners and political events.

blasphemy, the profanation of everything sacred, full of debasing and obscenities, familiar contact with everyone and everything. Both these lives were legitimate, but separated by strict temporal boundaries.

Without taking into account the alternation and mutual estrangement of these two systems of life and thought (the official and the carnivalistic), one cannot understand correctly the peculiar nature of medieval man's cultural consciousness, and cannot make sense of many phenomena in medieval literature—such as, for example, the "parodia sacra."[6]

This epoch also witnessed the carnivalization of the *speech life* of European peoples: whole layers of language, the so-called *familiar speech of the public square*, were permeated with a carnival sense of the world; there came into being an enormous fund of unrestrained carnivalistic gesticulations. The familiar speech of all European peoples is to this day filled with relics of carnival, especially speech of abuse and ridicule; the symbol-system of carnival also fills the abusive, ridiculing gesticulations of today.

During the Renaissance, one could say that the primordial elements of carnival swept away many barriers and invaded many realms of official life and worldview. Most importantly, they took possession of all the genres of high literature and transformed them fundamentally. There occurred a deep and almost total carnivalization of all artistic literature. The carnival sense of the world, with its categories, its carnival laughter, its symbol-system of carnival acts of crowning/decrowning, of shifts and disguises, carnival ambivalence and all the overtones of the unrestrained carnival word—familiar, cynically frank, eccentric, eulogistic-abusive and so on—penetrated deeply into almost all genres of artistic literature. On the basis of this carnival sense of the world, the complex forms of the Renaissance worldview came into being. Even antiquity, as assimilated by the humanists of the epoch, was to a certain extent refracted through the prism of the carnival sense of the world. The Renaissance is the high point of carnival life.[7] Thereafter begins its decline.

Beginning with the seventeenth century, folk-carnival life is on the wane: it almost loses touch with communal performance, its specific weight in the life of people is sharply reduced, its forms are impoverished, made petty and less complex. As early as the Renaissance a *festive court masquerade* culture begins to develop, having absorbed into itself a whole series of carnivalistic forms and symbols (mostly of an externally decorative sort). Later there begins to develop a broader line of festivities and entertainments (no longer limited to the court) which we might call the *masquerade line* of development; it preserved in itself a bit of the license and some faint reflections of the carnival sense of the world. Many carnival forms were completely cut off from their folk base and left the public square to enter this chamber masquerade line, which exists even today. Many ancient forms of carnival were preserved and continue to live and renew themselves in the *farcical* comic antics of the public square, and also in the *circus*. Certain elements of carnival are also preserved in the life of the theater and spectacle in modern times. It is characteristic that the subculture of the theater has even retained something of carnivalistic license, the carnivalistic sense of the world, the fascination of carnival; this was very well illustrated by Goethe in *Wilhelm Meisters Lehrjahre*, and for our time by Nemirovich-Danchenko* in his memoirs.[k] Something of the carnival atmosphere is retained, under certain conditions, among the so-called bohemians, but here in most cases we are dealing with the degradation and trivialization of the carnival sense of the world (there is, for example, not a grain of that carnival spirit of communal performance).

Alongside these later branchings from the basic carnival trunk—branchings that had emaciated the trunk—there continued and still continues to exist a public-square carnival in the proper sense, as well as other festivities of the carnivalistic type, but they have lost their former significance and their former wealth of forms and symbols.

As a consequence, there occurred a deterioration and dissipation of carnival and the carnival sense of the world; it lost that authentic sense of a communal performance on the public square. And thus a change also occurred in the nature of the carnivalization of literature. Until the second half of the seventeenth century, people were *direct participants* in carnivalistic acts and in a carnival sense of the world; they still *lived* in carnival, that is, carnival was one of the forms of life itself. Therefore carnivalization was experienced as something unmediated (several genres in fact directly serviced carnival). *The source of carnivalization was carnival itself.* In addition, carnivalization had genre-shaping significance; that is, it determined not only the content but also the very generic foundations of a work. From the second half of the seventeenth century on, carnival almost completely ceases to be a direct source of carnivalization, ceding its place to the influence of already carnivalized literature; in this way carnivalization becomes a purely literary tradition. Thus in Sorel* and Scarron* we already observe, alongside the direct influence of carnival, the powerful effect of the carnivalized literature of the Renaissance (primarily Rabelais and Cervantes), and this latter influence predominates. Carnivalization, consequently, is already becoming a literary and generic tradition. Carnival elements in this literature—already cut off

[k]See, in English, Vladimir Ivanovich Nemirovich-Danchenko, *My Life in the Russian Theatre*, trans. John Cournos (Boston: Little, Brown & Co., 1936).

from their direct source, carnival—change their appearance somewhat and are reconceptualized.

It is of course true that carnival in the proper sense as well as other festivities of the carnival type (bullfights, for example), the masquerade line, farcical street antics, and other forms of carnivalistic folklore continue to exercise a certain direct influence on literature even to this day. But in the majority of cases this influence is limited to the content of works and does not touch their generic foundation; that is, it is deprived of any genre-shaping power.

We can now return to the carnivalization of genres within the realm of the serio-comical—a realm whose very name already sounds ambivalent, after the manner of carnival.

The carnivalistic base of the Socratic dialogue, despite its very complicated form and philosophical depth, is beyond any doubt. Folk-carnival "debates" between life and death, darkness and light, winter and summer, etc., permeated with the pathos of change and the joyful relativity of all things, debates which did not permit thought to stop and congeal in one-sided seriousness or in a stupid fetish for definition or singleness of meaning—all this lay at the base of the original core of the genre. This distinguishes the Socratic dialogue from the purely rhetorical dialogue as well as from the tragic dialogue; but this carnivalistic base also brings Socratic dialogue close in several respects to the agons of ancient Attic comedy and to the mimes of Sophron (there have even been attempts to reconstruct the mimes of Sophron after certain Platonic dialogues). The Socratic discovery of the dialogic nature of thought, of truth itself, presumes a carnivalistic familiarization of relations among people who have entered the dialogue, it presumes the abolition of all distance between them; moreover, it presumes a familiarizing of attitudes toward the object of thought itself, however lofty and important, and toward truth itself. Several of Plato's dialogues are constructed along the lines of a carnival crowning/decrowning. Characteristic for a Socratic dialogue are unrestrained mésalliances of thoughts and images. "Socratic irony" is reduced carnival laughter.

The image of Socrates himself is of an ambivalent sort—a combination of beauty and ugliness (see the characterization of him by Alcibiades in Plato's *Symposium*); Socrates' own characterizations of himself as a "pander" and "midwife" are also constructed in the spirit of carnival debasings. And the personal life of Socrates was itself surrounded by carnivalistic legends (for example, his relationship with his wife Xanthippe). Carnivalistic legends in general are profoundly different from traditional heroicizing epic legends: carnivalistic legends debase the hero and bring him down to earth, they make him familiar, bring him close, humanize him; ambivalent carnival laughter burns away all that is stilted and stiff, but in no way destroys the heroic core of the image. It should be pointed out that novelistic images of heroes (Gargantua, Eulenspiegel, Don Quixote, Faust, Simplicissimus and others) also coalesced in the atmosphere of carnivalistic legends.

The carnivalistic nature of the menippea is even more pronounced. Carnivalization permeates both its external layers and its deepest core. Certain menippea directly portray festivals of the carnival type (Roman festivals are depicted in two of Varro's satires, for example; in one menippea by Julian the Apostate, there is a depiction of the celebration of saturnalia on Olympus). This is a purely external (so to speak, thematic) connection, but it too is characteristic. More essential is the carnivalistic treatment of the three planes of the menippea: Olympus, the nether world, and earth. The representation of Olympus is clearly carnivalistic: free familiarization, scandals and eccentricities, crownings and decrownings are characteristic for the Olympus of the menippea. Olympus is, as it were, transformed into a carnival square (as, for example, in Lucian's *Juppiter tragoedus*). Olympian scenes are sometimes presented as carnivalistic debasings and bringings-down-to-earth (also in Lucian). Still more interesting is the consistent carnivalization of the nether world. The nether world equalizes representatives of all earthly positions in life; there the emperor and the slave, the rich man and the beggar come together on equal terms and enter into familiar contact; death decrowns all who have been crowned in life. Representation of the nether world often applied the carnivalistic logic of "a world upside down": an emperor in the nether world becomes a slave, a slave an emperor, and so forth. The carnivalized nether world of the menippea determined the medieval tradition of representations of *joyful hell*, a tradition which found its culmination in Rabelais. Characteristic for this medieval tradition is a deliberate confusion of the ancient nether world and Christian hell. In the mystery plays, hell and devils (in the "diableries") are also consistently carnivalized.

The earthly plane in the menippea is also carnivalized: behind almost all scenes and events of real life, most of which are portrayed in a naturalistic manner, there glimmers more or less distinctly the carnival square with its specific carnivalistic logic of familiar contacts, mésalliances, disguises and mystifications, contrasting paired images, scandals, crownings/decrownings, and so forth. Behind all the slum-naturalism scenes of the *Satyricon*, more or less distinctly, the carnival square is glimmering. And in fact the very plot of the *Satyricon* is thoroughly carnivalized. We notice the same thing in Apuleius' *Meta-morphoses* (*The Golden Ass*). Sometimes carnivalization lies buried at deeper levels and permits us to speak only of *carnivalistic overtones* to individual images and events. But sometimes it surfaces, for example in the purely carnivalistic episode of the supposed murder *on the threshold*, when instead of humans Lucius stabs wineskins filled with wine, mistaking the wine for blood, and in the subsequent scene of carnival mystification surrounding his trial. Carnivalistic overtones are heard even in a menippea of so serious a tone as Boethius' *De Consolatione Philosophiae*.

Carnivalization even penetrates the deepest philosophical and dialogic core of the menippea. Characteristic for the genre, as we have seen, is a naked posing of ultimate questions on life and death, a universalism of the most extreme sort (personal problems and elaborate philosophical argumentation are unknown to it). Carnivalistic thought also lives in the realm of ultimate questions, but it gives them no abstractly philosophical or religiously dogmatic resolution; it plays them out in the concretely sensuous form of carnivalistic acts and images. Thus carnivalization made possible the transfer of ultimate questions from the abstractly philosophical sphere, through a carnival sense of the world, to the concretely sensuous plane of images and events— which are, in keeping with the spirit of carnival, dynamic, diverse and vivid. A carnival sense of the world also made it possible to "deck out philosophy in the motley dress of a hetaera." A carnival sense of the world is the drive-shaft between the *idea* and the *artistic image of adventure*. A vivid example of this in European literature of modern times are the philosophical novellas of Voltaire, with their universalism of ideas, their carnivalistic dynamism and motley colors (*Candide*, for example); in very graphic form these novellas reveal the traditions of the menippea and carnivalization.

Carnivalization thus penetrates to the very philosophical core of the menippea.

The following conclusion can now be drawn. We have uncovered in the menippea a striking combination of what would seem to be absolutely heterogeneous and incompatible elements: philosophical dialogue, adventure and fantasticality, slum naturalism, utopia, and so forth. We can now say that the clamping principle that bound all these heterogeneous elements into the organic whole of a genre, a principle of extraordinary strength and tenacity, was carnival and a carnival sense of the world. In the subsequent development of European literature as well, carnivalization constantly assisted in the destruction of all barriers between genres, between self-enclosed systems of thought, between various styles, etc.; it destroyed any attempt on the part of genres and styles to isolate themselves or ignore one another; it brought closer what was distant and united what had been sundered. This has been the great function of carnivalization in the history of literature.

Now a few words about the menippea and carnivalization on Christian soil.

The menippea and kindred genres developing within its orbit exercised a defining influence on emerging ancient Christian literature — Greek, Roman, and Byzantine.

The basic narrative genres of ancient Christian literature — "Gospels," "Acts of the Apostles," "Apocalypse," and "Lives of Saints and Martyrs" — are linked with an ancient aretalogy which in the first centuries A.D. developed within the orbit of the menippea. In the Christian genres this influence was sharply increased, especially at the expense of the *dialogic element* of the menippea. In these genres, and especially in the numerous "Gospels" and "Acts," the classical Christian dialogic syncrises are worked out: that of the tempted (Christ or a righteous man) with the tempter, the believer with the nonbeliever, the righteous man with the sinner, the beggar with the rich man, the follower of Christ with the Pharisee, the apostle (the Christian) with the heathen, and so forth. These syncrises are familiar to everyone through the canonical Gospels and Acts. The corresponding anacrises are also developed (that is, provocation through discourse or plot situation).

In the Christian genres as in the menippea, enormous organizing significance is alloted to the *testing of an idea and its carrier*, testing by means of temptations and martyrdom (especially, of course, in the hagiographic genre). As in the menippea, rulers, rich men, thieves, beggars, hetaerae come together here on equal terms on a single, fundamentally dialogized plane. Here, as in the menippea, considerable importance is given to dream visions, insanity, obsessions of all sorts. And finally, Christian narrative literature also absorbed into itself kindred genres: the symposium (the gospel meals) and the soliloquy.

Christian narrative literature (independently of the influence of carnivalized menippea) was also subjected to direct carnivalization. It is enough to recall the scene of crowning and decrowning the "King of the Jews" in the canonical Gospels. But carnivalization is even more powerfully present in apocryphal Christian literature.

Thus ancient Christian narrative literature (including that which was canonized) is also permeated by elements of the menippea and carnivalization.[8]

These are the ancient sources, the "origins" (the "archaic portion") of that generic tradition, one of whose high peaks was to be the work of Dostoevsky. These "origins" are preserved, in a renewed form, in his work.

But Dostoevsky is separated from these sources by two thousand years, during which time the generic tradition continued to develop, to become more complex, to change its shape and be reconceptualized (while preserving throughout its unity and continuity). A few words now on the further development of the menippea.

We have seen that on ancient soil, including the earliest Christian period, the menippea already manifested an extraordinary "protean" capacity for changing its external form (while preserving its inner generic essence), a capacity to grow into whole novels, to combine with kindred genres, to infiltrate other large genres (for example, the Greek and ancient Christian novel). This capacity manifests itself in the subsequent development of the menippea, in the Middle Ages as well as in modern times.

During the Middle Ages, certain generic features of the menippea continue to live and be renewed in several genres of Latin ecclesiastical literature, directly continuing the tradition of ancient Christian literature, especially in certain varieties of hagiographic literature. In more free and original form the menippea lives on in such dialogized and carnivalized medieval genres as "arguments," "debates," ambivalent "panegyrics" (*desputaisons, dits, débats*),[1] morality and miracle plays, and in the later Middle Ages mystery plays and *soties*. Menippean elements are felt in the intensely carnivalized parodic and semiparodic literature of the Middle Ages: in parodic visions from beyond the grave, in parodic "Gospel readings," and so forth. And finally, as a very important moment in the development of this generic tradition, there is the novelistic literature of the Middle Ages and the early Renaissance—a literature thoroughly permeated with elements of the carnivalized menippea.[9]

The entire medieval development of the menippea is permeated with elements of *local* carnival folklore and reflects the specific features characteristic of various periods in the Middle Ages.

During the Renaissance—an epoch of deep and almost complete carnivalization of literature and worldview—the menippea infiltrates all the large genres of the epoch (the works of Rabelais, Cervantes, Grimmelshausen* and others); there develop at the same time diverse Renaissance forms of the menippea, in most cases combining ancient and medieval traditions of the genre: Des Périers' *Cymbalum mundi*, Erasmus' *The Praise of Folly*, *Novelas ejemplares* of Cervantes*, *Satyre Ménippée de la vertu du Catholicon d'Espagne* (1594, one of the greatest political satires of world literature), the satires of Grimmelshausen, Quevedo,* and others.

---

[1]In medieval literature, the *dit* is a flexible verse composition, either descriptive or didactic. The *débat* is a didactic *dit* in the form of a dialogue, often between personifications (of the seasons, etc.) and frequently on religious themes.

In modern times, while infiltrating deep into other carnivalized genres, the menippea continues its own independent development, in diverse variants and under diverse names: the "Lucianic dialogue," "dialogues of the dead" (varieties in which ancient traditions predominate), the "philosophical tale" (a variety of menippea characteristic for the Enlightenment), the "fantastic story" and "philosophical fairy tale" (forms characteristic for Romanticism — Hoffmann, for example), and others. Here it should be noted that in modern times the generic characteristics of the menippea have been used by various literary movements and creative methods, renewing them, of course, in a variety of ways. Thus, for example, the rationalistic "philosophical tale" of Voltaire and the romantic "philosophical fairy tale" of Hoffmann share common generic features of the menippea and are equally intensely carnivalized, for all the profound differences in artistic intention, the content of their ideas, and, of course, their individuality as creative works of art (it suffices to contrast, for example, *Micromégas* with *Klein Zaches*). It must be said that the menippea has been, in the literature of modern times, the primary conduit for the most concentrated and vivid forms of carnivalization.

In conclusion we consider it necessary to emphasize that the generic label "menippea," like all other generic labels — "epic," "tragedy," "idyll," etc. — is, when applied to the literature of modern times, a means of designating the *essence of a genre*, and not any specific genre canon (as in antiquity).[10]

With this we conclude our digression into the realm of the history of genres and return to Dostoevsky (although throughout this entire digression we have not for a single moment lost sight of him).

We already noted in the course of our digression that the characterization we offered of the menippea and its kindred genres also applies, and almost in its entirety, to the generic features of Dostoevsky's work. We must now illustrate this concretely with an analysis of several of his works that are *key* from the generic standpoint.

Two "fantastic stories" of the late Dostoevsky — "Bobok" (1873) and "The Dream of a Ridiculous Man" (1877) — may be called menippea almost in the strict ancient sense of the term, so precisely and fully manifest in them are the classical characteristic features of the genre. A number of other works ("Notes from Underground," "A Meek One," and others) constitute variants, freer and more distant from the ancient models, of the same generic essence. Finally, the menippea infiltrates all of Dostoevsky's larger works, especially his five mature novels, and infiltrates, moreover, precisely the most fundamental and decisive aspects of the novels. Therefore we can say outright that the menippea essentially sets the tone for Dostoevsky's entire work.

We would hardly be mistaken in saying that "Bobok," in all its depth and boldness, is one of the greatest menippea in all word literature. But the depth of its content will not detain us here; here we are interested only in the particular generic characteristics of the work.

Characteristic first of all is the image of the narrator and the *tone* of his story. The narrator—a "certain person"[11] —is on the *threshold* of insanity (delirium tremens). But that aside, he is already a person *not like everyone else*; that is, he is one who has deviated from the general norm, who has fallen out of life's usual rut, who is despised by everyone and who himself despises everyone—that is, we have before us a new variety of the "underground man." His tone is unstable, equivocal, full of muffled ambivalence, with elements of infernal buffoonery (similar to the devils of mystery plays). Despite the external form of short, "choppy" categorical sentences, he conceals his final word, evades it. He himself quotes a characterization of his style, given by a friend:

"Your style is changing," he said; "it is choppy: you chop and chop—and then a parenthesis, then a parenthesis in the parenthesis, then you stick in something else in brackets, then you begin chopping and chopping again." [SS X, 343]

His speech is internally dialogized and shot through with polemic. The story in fact begins directly on a polemic with one Semyon Ardalionovich, who has accused him of being a drunkard. He also polemicizes with the editors who refuse to print his words (he is an unrecognized author), and with the contemporary public not capable of understanding humor; in fact he polemicizes with all of his contemporaries. And later, when the main action of the story unfolds, he indignantly polemicizes with "contemporary corpses." Such is the dialogized and equivocal verbal style and tone of the story, so typical of the menippea.

At the beginning of the story there is discussion on a theme typical for the carnivalized menippea: the relativity and ambivalence of reason and madness, intelligence and stupidity. Then follows the description of a cemetery and a funeral.

The entire description is permeated with a markedly *familiar* and *profaning* attitude toward the cemetery, the funeral, the cemetery clergy, the deceased, the very "sacrament of death" itself. The entire description is built on oxymoronic combinations and carnivalistic mésalliances; it is full of *debasing* and *bringings-down-to-earth*, full of the *symbol-system* of carnival and at the same time a crude naturalism.

Here are some typical excerpts:

I went out in search of *diversion*, I hit upon a *funeral*. . . . It's been twenty-five years, I think, since I was at the cemetery; *what a wretched place!*

To begin with, the *odor*. About fifteen corpses *arrived. Shrouds at various prices*; there were even two catafalques.

One was a general's and one some lady's. There were many *mourners*, a great deal of feigned mourning and a great deal of *open gaiety*. The clergy have nothing to complain of; it brings them a good *income*. But the *odor*, the *odor*. I should not like to be *in the holy orders* here. [A profanatory pun typical for the genre.] [m]

I kept glancing at the faces of the dead cautiously, distrusting my impressionability. Some had a mild expression, some looked unpleasant. As a rule the *smiles* were disagreeable, and in some cases very much so . . . I went out while the *service* was going on and strolled *outside the gates*. Close by was an alms-house, and a little further off there was a *restaurant*. It was not a bad little restaurant: one could have a snack and everything. There were lots of the *mourners* there. I noticed a great deal of *gaiety* and *genuine heartiness. I had something to eat and drink*. [*SS* X, 343-44]

We have italicized the most striking overtones of familiarization and profanation, the oxymoronic combinations, the mésalliances, bringings-down-to-earth, naturalism and symbolic elements. We see that the text is very strongly saturated with them. Before us is a somewhat condensed model for the style of a carnivalized menippea. We recall the symbolic significance of the ambivalent combination: death—laughter (here, gaiety)—feasting (here, "I had something to eat and drink").

This is followed by a short and vacillating meditation by the narrator, who has sat down on a gravestone, on the theme of *wonder* and *respect*, which his contemporaries have rejected. This meditation is important for an understanding of the author's conception. And then follows this simultaneously naturalistic and symbolic detail:

A half-eaten sandwich was lying on the tombstone near me; stupid and inappropriate. I threw it on the ground, as it was not bread but only a sandwich. Though I believe it is not a sin to throw bread on the earth, but only on the floor. I must look it up in Suvorin's calendar. [*SS* X, 345]

This particularly naturalistic and profaning detail—a half-eaten sandwich on the grave—gives us occasion to touch on a symbolic attribute of the carnival type: throwing bread on the ground is permitted, for that is sowing, fructification; throwing it on the floor is forbidden, for that is barren soil.

Further on begins development of the fantastic plot, which creates

---

[m]The Russian root *dukh* ["animus"] is found in the Russian words for breath, air, spirit, and odor. The pun to which Bakhtin refers here is Dostoevsky's juxtaposition of *dukh* (odor) with *dukhovnoe litso* (spiritual personage or member of the clergy.) There is an additional pun on *dokhody* (income) and perhaps a hidden one on *dokhnut'* (to die, as an animal dies; to croak.)

an *anacrisis* of extraordinary power (Dostoevsky is a great master of the anacrisis). The narrator listens in on a conversation of the dead beneath the earth. It so happens that their lives in the grave continue for a certain time. The deceased philosopher *Platon* Nikolaevich (an allusion to the Socratic dialogue) explained it in this way:

> "He [Platon Nikolaevich—M. B.] explains this by a very simple fact, namely that when we were living on the surface we mistakenly thought that death there was death. The body revives, as it were, here; the remains of life are concentrated, but only in consciousness. I don't know how to express it, but life goes on, as it were, by inertia. In his opinion everything is concentrated somewhere in consciousness and goes on for two or three months . . . sometimes even for half a year. . . . There is one here, for instance, who is almost completely decomposed, but once every six weeks he suddenly utters one word, quite senseless of course, about some *bobok*, 'Bobok bobok,' but even in him, that means, life is still glimmering with an imperceptible spark . . ." [*SS* X, 354]

This creates an extraordinary situation: the *final life of the consciousness* (the two or three months before it falls asleep forever), freed from all the conditions, positions, obligations, and laws of ordinary life, as it were a *life outside of life*. And how will it be used by the "contemporary corpses"? As anacrisis, provoking the consciousnesses of the corpses to reveal themselves with *full*, absolutely unlimited *freedom*. And reveal themselves they do.

What unfolds is the typical carnivalized nether world of the menippea: a rather motley crew of corpses which cannot immediately liberate themselves from their earthly hierarchical positions and relationships, giving rise to comic conflicts, abuse, and scandals; on the other hand, liberties of the carnival type, the awareness of a complete absence of responsibility, open graveyard eroticism, laughter in the coffins (". . . the general's *corpse* shook with agreeable *laughter*"), and so on. The marked carnivalistic tone of this paradoxical "life outside of life" is set from the very beginning, with a game of cards being played in the grave on which the narrator sits (it is of course a make-believe game, played "by heart"). All these are typical traits of the genre.

The "king" of this carnival of the dead is a "scoundrel of pseudo-high society" (as he characterizes himself), one baron Klinevich. We will quote his words, which cast much light on the anacrisis and its use. Having dispensed with the moral interpretations of the philosopher Platon Nikolaevich (paraphrased by Lebezyatnikov), Klinevich declares:

> "Enough; all the rest of it, I am sure, is nonsense. The great thing is that we have two or three months more of life and then—bobok! I propose to spend these two months as agreeably as possible, and so to arrange everything on a new basis. Gentlemen! *I propose to cast aside all shame.*"

Once he obtains the general approval of the dead, he develops his thought somewhat further along these lines:

Though meanwhile *I don't want us to be telling lies*. That's all I care about, for that is one thing that matters. *One cannot exist on the surface without lying, for life and lying are synonymous*, but here we will *amuse ourselves* by not lying. Hang it all, the *grave* has some value after all! *We'll all tell our stories aloud, and we won't be ashamed of anything*. First of all I'll tell you about myself. I am one of the predatory kind, you know. *All that was bound and held in check by rotten cords up there on the surface*. Away with cords and let us spend these two months in *shameless truthfulness! Let us strip and go naked!"*

"Let us go naked, naked!" cried all the voices. [*SS* X, 355-56]

This dialogue of dead people was unexpectedly interrupted in a carnival manner:

And here I suddenly *sneezed*. It happened suddenly and unintentionally, but the effect was striking: all became as silent as a *grave*, it all vanished like a dream. A real silence of the tomb set in.

I shall also quote the narrator's concluding comments, which are interesting for their tone:

No, that I cannot admit, no, I really cannot! It's not bobok that bothers me (so it did turn out to be bobok!).

Depravity in such a place, depravity of the last aspirations, depravity of sodden and rotten corpses—and not even sparing the *last moments of consciousness*! Those moments have been granted, vouchsafed to them, and . . . and, worst of all, in such a place! No, that I cannot admit. [*SS* X, 357-58]

Here the almost pure words and intonations of a completely different voice, that is, the author's voice, break in on the narrator's speech; they break in, but then are immediately broken off on the word "and . . .":

The ending of the story is journalistic, feuilletonistic:

I shall take it to the *Citizen*; the editor there has had his portrait exhibited too. Maybe he will print it.

Such is Dostoevsky's almost classical menippea. The genre is sustained with remarkable integrity. One could even say that the genre of the menippea reveals here its greatest potential, realizes its maximum. Least of all is this a *stylization* of a defunct genre. On the contrary, in Dostoevsky's piece the genre of the menippea *continues to live* its full generic life. For the life of a genre consists in its constant rebirths and renewals in *original* works. Dostoevsky's "Bobok" is, of course, profoundly original. Dostoevsky was not writing a parody on the genre; he was using it in its straightforward sense. However, it should be noted that the menippea—and this includes also its oldest antique forms—to some extent always parodies itself. That is one of the generic characteristics of the menippea. This element of self-parody is one of the reasons for the extraordinary vitality of the genre.

Here we must touch upon the question of Dostoevsky's possible generic sources. The essence of every genre is realized and revealed in all its fullness only in the diverse variations that arise throughout a given genre's historical development. The more accessible all these variants are to the artist, the more richly and flexibly will he command the language of the given genre (for the language of a genre is concrete and historical).

Dostoevsky understood subtly and well all the generic possibilities of the menippea. He possessed an extraordinarily deep and well-differentiated feeling for this genre. To trace all of Dostoevsky's possible contacts with different varieties of the menippea would be a very important task, both for a deeper understanding of the generic characteristics of his works and for a more complete idea of the development of the generic tradition itself, before Dostoevsky.

Dostoevsky was linked with varieties of the ancient menippea most directly and intimately through ancient Christian literature (that is, through the Gospels, the Apocalypse, the Lives of Saints, and so on). But he was doubtless also familiar with the classic models of the ancient menippea. It is very likely that he knew Lucian's menippea *Menippus, or a Journey to the Kingdom of the Dead*, as well as his *Dialogues of the Dead* (a group of small-scale dialogic satires). These works illustrate various types of *behavior of dead people* under the conditions of the Kingdom beyond the Grave, that is, in the carnivalized nether world. It should be pointed out that Lucian—"the Voltaire of antiquity"—was widely known in Russia beginning with the eighteenth century[12] and inspired numerous imitations, and the generic situation of "meetings beyond the grave" became a common one in literature, right down to the level of school exercises.

Dostoevsky was quite possibly also acquainted with Seneca's menippea *Apocolocyntosis*. We find in Dostoevsky three aspects that recall that satire. (1) The "open gaiety" of the mourners at the cemetery in Dostoevsky is, perhaps, evoked by an episode in Seneca: Claudius, flying from Olympus to the nether world via Earth, comes upon his own funeral on Earth and satisfies himself that all the mourners are very cheerful (except the contentious ones); (2) the make-believe game of cards, played "by heart," is perhaps evoked by Claudius' game of dice in the nether world, which is also make-believe (the dice tumble out before they are thrown); (3) the naturalistic decrowning of death in Dostoevsky recalls an even cruder depiction of the death of Claudius, who dies (gives up the ghost) at the moment of defecation.[13]

There is no doubt about Dostoevsky's familiarity—more or less intimate—with other ancient works of the genre: *The Satyricon, The Golden Ass,* and others.[14]

Dostoevsky's European generic sources, those that might have revealed for him the richness and diversity of the menippea, are very numerous and heterogeneous. He probably knew Boileau's literary-polemical menippea *Dialogue des héros de romans,** and perhaps also Goethe's literary-polemical satire *Götter, Helden und Wieland.** He was probably familiar with the "dialogues of the dead" of Fénelon* and Fontenelle* (Dostoevsky had an excellent knowledge of French literature). All these satires are linked through their depiction of the kingdom beyond the grave, and all of them externally sustain the ancient (predominantly Lucianic) form of the genre.

Of fundamental significance for understanding Dostoevsky's generic traditions are the menippea of Diderot, free in their external form but typical in their generic essence. Of course the tone and style of telling in Diderot (sometimes in the spirit of eighteenth-century erotic literature) differs from Dostoevsky. In *Le neveu de Rameau* (also in essence a menippea, but without the fantastic element) the motif of extremely frank confessions without a single grain of remorse recalls "Bobok." And the very image of Rameau's nephew, an openly "rapacious type," who like Klinevich considers social morality "rotten cords" and who recognizes only the "shameless truth," recalls the image of Klinevich.

Dostoevsky was acquainted with another variety of the free menippea through Voltaire's *Contes philosophiques.*[n] This type of menippea was very close to certain sides of his own creative talent (Dostoevsky even had a plan to write the "Russian Candide").

We should keep in mind the enormous significance for Dostoevsky of the *dialogic culture* of Voltaire and Diderot, which had its roots in the Socratic dialogue, the ancient menippea, and somewhat in the diatribe and the soliloquy.

Another type of free menippea, with a fantastic and fairy-tale element, was represented in the work of Hoffmann, who already exercised a significant influence on the early Dostoevsky. Dostoevsky's attention was also attracted by the tales of Edgar Allan Poe, close in essence to the menippea. In his prefatory note "Three Tales of Edgar Poe," Dostoevsky quite correctly noted the characteristics of that writer, so similar to his own:

"He almost always takes the most extraordinary reality, *places his hero in the most extraordinary external or psychological position,*

---

[n] A "conte" is a short fictitious narrative, often didactic, relying on wit, allegory, or titillation to attract the reader and drive home the moral. It was a popular eighteenth-century form. Voltaire's *Candide* is perhaps the most famous example.

and with what power of penetration, with what stunning accuracy does he tell the story of the state of that person's soul!"[15]

To be sure, this definition singles out only one aspect of the menippea—the creation of an extraordinary plot situation, that is, a provocative anacrisis—but precisely this aspect was consistently singled out by Dostoevsky himself as the major distinguishing feature of his own creative method.

Our survey (far from complete) of Dostoevsky's generic sources indicates that he knew, or could have known, diverse variants of the menippea, a genre of very rich and plastic possibilities, extraordinarily well-suited for penetrating into the "depths of the human soul" and for a keen and naked posing of "ultimate questions."

The story "Bobok" demonstrates to what an extent the generic essence of the menippea answered to all the fundamental creative aspirations of Dostoevsky. From the generic standpoint, this story is one of his key works.

Let us attend first to the following observation. Little "Bobok"— one of Dostoevsky's shortest plotted stories—is almost a microcosm of his entire creative output. Very many, and including the most important, ideas, themes and images of his work—both preceding and following "Bobok"—appear here in extremely keen and naked form: the idea that "everything is permitted" if there is no God and no immortality for the soul (one of the leading idea-images of his work); the related theme of confession without repentance and of "shameless truth," which runs through all of Dostoevsky's work beginning with *Notes from Underground*; the theme of the final moments of consciousness (connected in other works with the themes of capital punishment and suicide); the theme of a consciousness on the brink of insanity; the theme of sensuality, penetrating the highest spheres of consciousness and thought; the theme of the total "inappropriateness" and "unseemliness" of life cut off from its folk roots and from the people's faith, and so on—all these themes and ideas, in condensed and naked form, are fitted into the seemingly narrow confines of this story.

The leading images of the story (there are not, to be sure, many of them) also recall other images in Dostoevsky's work: Klinevich in a simplified and intensified form repeats Prince Valkovsky, Svidrigailov, and Fyodor Pavlovich; the narrator ("a certain person") is a variant of the Underground Man; General Pervoedov[16] is also somewhat familiar to us, as are the sensual old official who had squandered a huge sum of public funds earmarked "for widows and orphans," the sycophant Lebezyatnikov, and the engineer and believer in progress who wishes to "arrange life down here on a rational basis."

A special place among the dead is occupied by *"prostoliudin"* (a "simpleman," a well-to-do shopkeeper); he alone has preserved a bond with the common people and their faith, and thus behaves properly even in the grave, accepts death as a sacrament, interprets what is going on around him (among the debauched dead) as "a visitation of tribulations upon their souls," impatiently awaits the *sorokoviny*° ("May our forty days pass quickly, then I shall hear tearful voices over my head, my wife's lament and my children's soft weeping . . ."). The seemliness and highly reverent style of speech of this "simpleman," juxtaposed to the impropriety and familiar cynicism of all the others (both living and dead), anticipate in part the future image of the pilgrim Makar Dolgoruky, although here, under conditions of the menippea, the "seemly" simpleman is presented with a slight overtone of comicality, as if he were somewhat inappropriate.

In addition, the carnivalized nether world of "Bobok" is *internally* profoundly resonant with those scenes of scandal and catastrophe that have such crucial significance in almost all of Dostoevsky's works. These scenes, usually taking place in drawing rooms, are of course considerably more complex, more motley, more full of carnivalized contrasts, abrupt mésalliances and eccentricities, fundamental crownings and decrownings, but their inner essence is analogous: the "rotten cords" of the official and personal lie are snapped (or at least weakened for the moment), and human souls are laid bare, either terrible souls as in the nether world, or else bright and pure ones. People appear for a moment outside the usual conditions of their lives, on the carnival square or in the nether world, and there opens up another — more genuine — sense of themselves and of their relationships to one another.

Of such a sort, for example, is the famous scene at Nastasya Filippovna's name-day party (*The Idiot*). Here there are also external resonances with "Bobok": Ferdyshchenko (a petty mystery-play devil) proposes a *petit-jeu* — everyone is to tell the worst action of his life (cf. Klinevich's proposal: "We'll all tell our stories aloud, and we won't be ashamed of anything"). To be sure, the stories that are told do not justify Ferdyshchenko's expectations, but this *petit-jeu* helps prepare the way for that carnival-square atmosphere in which abrupt carnivalistic changes in the fates and appearances of people can occur, where cynical calculations are exposed, where Natasya Filippovna's familiar and decrowning speech can take on the sound of the carnival square. We are not concerned here, of course, with the profound moral-psychological and social meaning of this scene — what interests us is precisely its generic aspect, those *carnivalistic overtones* that sound in almost every image and word (however realistic and motivated), and that second plane of the carnival square (and the carnivalized

---

°*Sorokoviny*: a commemorative service in the Orthodox Church forty days after a death.

nether world) which, as it were, glimmers through the actual fabric of the scene.

One could also mention the sharply carnivalized scene of scandals and decrownings at the funeral feast for Marmeladov (in *Crime and Punishment*). Or the even more complicated scene in Varvara Petrovna Stavrogina's grand drawing room in *The Possessed*, with the part played by the mad lame girl, the entry of her brother Captain Lebyadkin, the first appearance of the "devil" Pyotr Verkhovensky, the triumphant eccentricity of Varvara Petrovna, the exposure and banishment of Stepan Trofimovich, Liza's hysterics and fainting fit, Shatov's slap in Stavrogin's face, and so on. Here everything is unexpected, out of place, incompatible and impermissible if judged by life's ordinary, "normal" course. It is absolutely impossible to imagine such a scene in, say, a novel by Leo Tolstoy or Turgenev. This is no grand drawing room, it is the public square with all the specific logic of carnivalized public-square life. And finally one must mention the extraordinarily vivid carnivalistic-menippean coloration of the scandal scene in Father Zosima's cell (*The Brothers Karamazov*).

These scandal scenes—and they occupy a very important place in Dostoevsky's works—almost always met with negative criticism from his contemporaries,[17] and continue to do so today. They seemed then, and still seem today, improbable in terms of life and unjustified in terms of art. They were often explained by the author's fondness for purely external and false effects. But in fact these scenes are in the spirit and the style of Dostoevsky's whole work. And they are deeply organic, there is nothing contrived in them: in their entirety as well as *in each detail* they are a result of that consistent artistic logic of carnivalistic acts and categories characterized above—and absorbed over the centuries into the carnivalized line of artistic prose. At their base lies a profound carnivalistic sense of the world, which gives meaning to and unites all the seemingly absurd and unexpected things in these scenes and creates their artistic truth.

"Bobok," thanks to its *fantastic* plot, can present this carnival logic in a somewhat simplified form (as required by the genre), and yet keenly and nakedly, and can therefore serve as a sort of commentary to more complicated but analogous phenomena in Dostoevsky's work.

In the story "Bobok," rays issuing from preceding and subsequent works of Dostoevsky come to a focus. "Bobok" could become such a focus precisely because it is a menippea. All aspects of Dostoevsky's creativity feel in their element here. The narrow framework of that story, as we see, has turned out to be quite spacious indeed.

We remember that the menippea is the *universal genre* of *ultimate questions*. Its action takes place not only in the "here" and the "now," but throughout the world and for all eternity: on earth, in the nether world, and in heaven. In Dostoevsky the menippea is brought close to the mystery play. The mystery play is, after all, nothing other than a modified medieval dramatic variant of the menippea. In Dostoevsky, the participants in the act stand *on the threshold* (on the threshold of life and death, falsehood and truth, sanity and insanity). And they are presented here as *voices*, ringing out, speaking out "before earth and heaven." The central figurative idea here is also that of the mystery play (to be sure, in the spirit of the Eleusinian mysteries): "contemporary dead men" are as sterile seed, cast on the ground, but capable neither of dying (that is, of being cleansed of themselves, of rising above themselves), nor of being renewed (that is, of bearing fruit).

The second key work from the generic standpoint is Dostoevsky's "Dream of a Ridiculous Man" (1877).

In its generic essence this work can also be traced to the menippea, but to different varieties of it: to the "dream satire" and to "fantastic journeys" containing a utopian element. In the subsequent development of the menippea, these two varieties are often combined.

The dream, as something with its own (nonepic) artistic interpretation, first entered European literature, as we have said, in the genre of Menippean satire (and in the realm of the serio-comical in general). Dreams in the epic did not destroy the unity of a represented life and did not create a second plane; they also did not destroy the *simple* integrity of the hero's image. The dream was not counterposed to ordinary life as *another* possible life. Such an opposition (from one or another viewpoint) appears for the first time in the menippea. The dream is introduced there precisely as the *possibility* of a completely different life, a life organized according to laws different from those governing ordinary life (sometimes directly as an "inside-out world"). The life seen in the dream makes ordinary life seem strange, forces one to understand and evaluate ordinary life in a new way (in the light of another glimpsed possibility). The person in a dream becomes another person, reveals in himself new possibilities (both worse and better), tests himself and verifies himself by means of the dream. Sometimes the dream is constructed directly as a crowning/decrowning of the person in life.

Thus an extraordinary situation is created in the dream quite impossible in ordinary life, a situation that serves here the same purpose it serves in the menippea—the testing of an idea and the man of an idea.

The traditional way of using menippean dreams in art continues to live on in the subsequent development of European literature, in diverse variations and with diverse nuances: in the "dream visions" of medieval literature, in the grotesque satires of the sixteenth and seventeenth centuries (especially vividly in Quevedo and Grimmelshausen), in its fairytale-symbolic use by the Romantics (including the highly original dream lyrics of Heinrich Heine), in its psychological and socio-historical application in realistic novels (in George Sand and Chernyshevsky). Special note should be made of the important variation known as *crisis dreams*, which lead a person to rebirth and renewal (the crisis variant was used in dramaturgy as well: in Shakespeare, Calderón, and in the nineteenth century in Grillparzer).

Dostoevsky made very wide use of the artistic possibilities of the dream in almost all its variations and nuances. Indeed, in all of European literature there is no writer for whom dreams play such a large and crucial role as Dostoevsky. We recall the dreams of Raskolnikov, of Svidrigailov, Myshkin, Ippolit, the Adolescent, Versilov, Alyosha and Dmitry Karamazov, and the role which they play in realizing the ideational design of their respective novels. Predominant in Dostoevsky is the crisis variation of the dream. To such a type belongs the dream of the "ridiculous man."

Concerning the generic variety of "fantastic journeys" used in "The Dream of a Ridiculous Man," Dostoevsky may have been acquainted with Cyrano de Bergerac's work *Histoire comique des états et empires de la Lune* [Comical History of the States and Empires of the Moon] (1647-50).* This is a description of an earthly paradise on the moon, from which the narrator has been banished for disrespectfulness. He is accompanied on his journey about the moon by the "demon of Socrates," thus permitting the author to introduce a philosophical element (in the spirit of Gassendi's* materialism). In its external form de Bergerac's work is an entire philosophical-fantastic novel.

Also interesting is Grimmelshausen's menippea *Der fliegende Wandersmann nach dem Monde* (c. 1659), which shares a common source with Cyrano de Bergerac's work. Here the utopian element is of foremost importance. There is a description of the extraordinary purity and truthfulness of the Moon's inhabitants; they know no vices, no crimes, no falsehood; in their country it is eternal spring, they live a long time and greet death with cheerful feasting amid a circle of friends. Children born with evil tendencies are sent off to Earth to prevent them from corrupting society. The precise date of the hero's arrival on the moon is indicated (just as the date of the dream is given in Dostoevsky).

Dostoevsky was undoubtedly familiar with Voltaire's menippea *Micromégas*, belonging to the same fantastic line in the development of the menippea, the line that estranges earthly reality.

In "The Dream of a Ridiculous Man" we are struck, first of all, by the maximal universalism of this work and at the same time by its maximal terseness, its remarkable artistic and philosophical laconicism. There is no developed discursive argumentation in it whatsoever. There is clear evidence here of Dostoevsky's extraordinary capacity to *see* and *feel an idea*, a trait we mentioned in the previous chapter. We have before us an authentic *artist of the idea*.

"The Dream of a Ridiculous Man" presents us with a full and complete synthesis of the universalism of the menippea—a genre of ultimate questions of worldview—with the universalism of the medieval mystery play portraying the fate of mankind: earthly paradise, the Fall, redemption. In "The Dream of a Ridiculous Man" this internal kinship between the two genres emerges very clearly; the genres are, of course, also akin to each other historically and genetically. But from the generic standpoint, the ancient type of menippea is dominant here. And in general what dominates in "The Dream of a Ridiculous Man" is not the Christian but the ancient spirit.

In its style and composition, "The Dream of a Ridiculous Man" differs rather significantly from "Bobok": it contains crucial elements of the diatribe, the confession, and the sermon. Such a complex of genres is in general characteristic of Dostoevsky's work.

The central part of the work is the story of a dream vision. Here we are given a splendid character-sketch, so to speak, of the peculiar compositional nature of the dream:

. . . everything was happening the way it usually happens in dreams when you leap over space and time, over all laws of life and reason, and only pause where your heart's desire bids you pause. [*SS* X, 429]

This is in fact a completely true characterization of the compositional method used for constructing a fantastic menippea. And, with certain limitations and reservations, these characteristics can be applied to Dostoevsky's entire creative method as well. In his works Dostoevsky makes almost no use of relatively uninterrupted historical or biographical time, that is, of strictly epic time; he "leaps over" it, he concentrates action at *points of crisis, at turning points and catastrophes*, when the inner significance of a moment is equal to a "billion years," that is, when the moment loses its temporal restrictiveness. In essence he leaps over space as well, and concentrates action in two "points" only: on the *threshold* (in doorways, entrance ways, on staircases, in corridors, and so forth), where the crisis and the turning point occur, or on the *public square*, whose substitute is usually the drawing room (the hall, the dining room), where the catastrophe, the scandal take place. Precisely this is his artistic conception of time and space. He often leaps over elementary empirical norms of verisimilitude and superficial rational logic as well. This is why he finds the genre of the menippea so congenial.

These words of the Ridiculous Man are also characteristic for the artistic method of Dostoevsky, as an artist of the idea:

. . . I have seen the truth, it was not a figment of my imagination or my mind, I have seen it, seen it, and its **living image** has taken hold of my soul for ever. [*SS* X, 440]

In its subject matter "The Dream of a Ridiculous Man" is practically a complete encyclopedia of Dostoevsky's most important themes, and at the same time all these themes, as well as the means for elaborating them in art, are very characteristic of the carnivalized genre of the menippea. We shall pause on several of them.

1. In the central figure of the Ridiculous Man there are clear traces of the *ambivalent*—serio-comical—image of the "wise fool" and "tragic clown" of carnivalized literature. But such ambivalence—to be sure, usually in more muffled form—is characteristic for all of Dostoevsky's heroes. It might be said that Dostoevsky's mode of artistic thinking could not imagine anything in the slightest way humanly significant that did not have certain elements of *eccentricity* (in all its diverse variations). This is revealed most clearly in the image of Myshkin. But in all other major Dostoevskian heroes—in Raskolnikov, Stavrogin, Versilov, Ivan Karamazov—there is always "something ridiculous," although in a more or less reduced form.

We repeat: Dostoevsky, as an artist, could not imagine human significance as a *single-toned* thing. In the preface to *The Brothers Karamazov* ("From the Author") he even makes a case for the special and vital *historical* importance of eccentricity:

For not only is an eccentric "not always" an isolated case and an exception, but, on the contrary, it happens sometimes that such a person, I dare say, carries within himself the very heart of the whole, and the rest of the men of his epoch have for some reason been temporarily torn from it, as if by a gust of wind . . . [*SS* IX, 9]

In the image of the Ridiculous Man this ambivalence is, in keeping with the spirit of the menippea, laid bare and emphasized.

Also very characteristic for Dostoevsky is the *fullness of self-consciousness* in the Ridiculous Man: he himself knows better than anyone that he is ridiculous (". . . of all the people in the world, I knew best how ridiculous I was . . ."). When he begins to preach *paradise* on earth, he himself understands perfectly that it can never be realized: "I shall go further: let it never, never come true, let paradise never be (after all, I do realize that!), I shall anyway go and spread the word" [*SS* X, 441]. This is an eccentric who is keenly conscious of both himself and everything else; there is not a grain of naiveté in him; it is impossible to finalize him (since there is nothing located external to his consciousness).

2. The story opens with a theme most typical for the menippea, the theme of a person who is *alone* in his knowledge of the truth and who is therefore ridiculed by everyone else as a madman. Here is that splendid opening:

I am a ridiculous man. They call me a madman now. That would be a promotion, if it were not that I remain as ridiculous to them as ever. But I no longer mind—they are all dear to me now, even when they are laughing at me—indeed, something endears them to me particularly then. I would laugh with them—not at myself, that is, but because I love them—I would laugh if I did not feel so sad watching them. What saddens me is that they do not know the Truth, and I do. Oh, how hard it is to be the only one to know the Truth! But they will not understand this. No, they will not. [*SS* X, 420]

This is the typical position of the wise man in the menippea (Diogenes, Menippus, or Democritus from the "Hippocratic novel"). the carrier of truth vis-à-vis all other people who consider the truth either insanity or stupidity; but here this position is, when compared with the ancient menippea, both more complicated and more profound. At the same time this position is, in different variations and with various nuances, characteristic for all of Dostoevsky's major heroes from Raskolnikov to Ivan Karamazov: being possessed by their "truth" defines their relationship to other people and creates the special sort of loneliness these heroes know.

3. Further along in the story there appears a theme very characteristic for the menippea of the Cynics and the Stoics, the theme of absolute indifference to everything in the world:

. . . that hopeless sadness that was mounting in my soul about something that was infinitely greater than myself: this something was a mounting conviction that **nothing mattered**. I had begun to suspect this long ago, but positive conviction came to me all at once, one day last year. I suddenly knew that **I would not have cared** if the world existed at all or if there was nothing anywhere. I began to know and feel with all my being that **nothing in my lifetime had existed**. [*SS* x, 421]

This universal indifference and the premonition of nonexistence leads the Ridiculous Man to thoughts of suicide. Before us is one of Dostoevsky's numerous variations on the theme of Kirillov.

4. There follows the theme of the final hours of life before suicide (one of Dostoevsky's major themes). Here this theme—in keeping with the spirit of the menippea—is laid bare and intensified.

After the Ridiculous Man makes the final decision to kill himself, he meets a little girl on the street who begs him to help her. The

Ridiculous Man shoves her away rudely, since he already feels himself to be outside all norms and obligations of human life (like the dead in "Bobok"). Here are his reflections:

But if I was going to kill myself in a couple of hours from then, why should I be concerned with the girl and what did I care for shame or anything else in the world? . . . Why, the reason I had stamped my feet and shouted so brutally at the poor child was to assert that "far from feeling pity, I could even afford to do something inhumanly vile now, because two hours hence everything would be snuffed out."

This is moral experimentation, characteristic for the genre of the menippea and no less characteristic of Dostoevsky's work. Further along the reflections continue:

For instance, a strange notion like this occurred to me: supposing I had once lived on the moon or Mars and had committed there the foulest and most shameful deed imaginable, and had been put to such shame and disgrace as can be experienced and imagined only sometimes in dreams, in nightmares, and supposing I later found myself on the earth, with the crime committed on that other planet alive in my consciousness and, moreover, knowing there was no return for me, ever, under any circumstances—would I **have cared** or not as I gazed at the moon from this earth? Would I have felt shame for that deed or not? [SS X, 425-26]

In a conversation with Kirillov, Stavrogin puts to himself an absolutely analogous "experimental" question about an act on the moon [SS VII, 250; The Possessed, Part Two, ch. 1, 5]. All this is the familiar problematic posed by Ippolit (The Idiot), Kirillov (The Possessed), by the graveside shamelessness in "Bobok." In fact they are all merely various facets of a leading theme of all Dostoevsky's work, the theme that "all is permitted" (in a world where there is no God and no immortality of the soul) and, linked with it, the theme of ethical solipsism.

5. Further on there unfolds the central (and one might say genre-shaping) *theme of the crisis dream*; more precisely, it is the theme of a man's rebirth and renewal through a dream vision, permitting him *to see* "with his own eyes" the possibility of an entirely different human life on earth.

Yes, I dreamed that dream then, my 3rd of November dream! They all tease me now, telling me it was nothing but a dream. But surely it makes no difference whether it was a dream or not since it did reveal the Truth to me. Because if you have come to know it once and to see it, you will know it is the Truth and that there neither is nor can be any other, whether you are dreaming or awake. Very well, it was a dream—let it be a dream, but the fact remains that this real life which you so extol I was going to snuff out by suicide, whereas my dream, my dream—oh, it revealed to me another life, a great, renewed and powerful life! [SS X, 427]

6. In the "dream" itself there is detailed development of the utopian theme of heaven on earth, experienced by the Riticulous Man and seen with his own eyes on a distant unknown star. The very description of this earthly paradise is sustained in the spirit of the ancient Golden Age, and is thus thoroughly permeated with a carnival sense of the world. The portrayal of this earthly paradise recalls in many ways Versilov's dream (*The Adolescent*). Very characteristic here is the purely carnivalistic faith professed by the Ridiculous Man in the unity of mankind's aspirations and in the goodness of human nature:

> And yet everyone is going towards the same thing, at least all strive for the same thing, all—*from the wise man to the meanest wretch*—only all follow different paths. It's an old truth, but here's something new: I cannot flounder too badly, you know. Because *I have seen the Truth, I have seen it* and I know that people can be beautiful and happy without losing their ability to dwell on this earth. I cannot and will not believe that evil is man's natural state. [*SS* X, 440]

We emphasize again that truth, according to Dostoevsky, can only be the subject of a living vision, not of abstract understanding.

7. At the end of the story there sounds a theme very characteristic for Dostoevsky, the theme of the *instantaneous* transformation of life into paradise (it finds its most profound expression in *The Brothers Karamazov*):

> And yet it could be done so simply: in a single day, in a **single hour** everything would be settled! One should love others as one loves oneself, that is the main thing, that is all, nothing else, absolutely nothing else is needed, and then one would instantly know how to go about it. [*SS* X, 441]

8. We note also the theme of the mistreated little girl, which runs through a series of Dostoevsky's works: we meet her in *The Insulted and the Injured* (Nelly), in Svidrigailov's dream before his suicide, in "Stavrogin's Confession," in "The Eternal Husband" (Liza); the theme of the suffering child is one of the leading themes in *The Brothers Karamazov* (the images of suffering children in the chapter "Rebellion," the image of Ilyushechka, "the babe weeping" in Dmitri's dream).

9. Also present here are elements of slum naturalism: the debauched captain begging for alms on Nevsky Prospect (the image is familiar to us from *The Idiot* and *The Adolescent*), drunkenness, a card game and fighting in the room next door to the little closet where the Ridiculous Man has spent his sleepless nights in the Voltairian armchair, absorbed in solving ultimate questions, and where he dreams his dream about the fate of mankind.

Of course we have not exhausted all the themes in "The Dream of a Ridiculous Man," but even these are sufficient to demonstrate the enormous ideational spaciousness of this particular variety of the menippea and its suitability to Dostoevsky's subject matter.

In "The Dream of a Ridiculous Man" there are no compositionally expressed dialogues (except one half-expressed dialogue with the "unknown being"), but the narrator's entire speech is permeated with interior dialogue: all words are addressed to himself, to the universe, to his creator,[18] to all people. And here, as in a mystery play, the word rings out before heaven and before earth, that is, before the entire world.

Such are the two key works of Dostoevsky that reveal most clearly the generic essence of his creative work, one with great affinity for the menippea and genres kindred to it.

We have offered our analyses of "Bobok" and "The Dream of a Ridiculous Man" from the vantage point of an historical poetics of genre. Of primary interest to us has been the way in which these works manifest the generic essence of the menippea. But at the same time we have tried to show how the traditional features of the genre are organically combined, in Dostoevsky's use of them, with an individual uniqueness and profundity.

We shall touch on several other works of his which are also in their essence close to the menippea, but of a somewhat different type and without the direct fantastic element.

One of the best examples is the story "A Meek One." Here the sharp plot-line anacrisis characteristic for the genre, with its abrupt contrasts, its mésalliances and moral experimentation, is formulated as a soliloquy. The hero of the tale says of himself: "I am a past master at speaking silently, I have spent a lifetime speaking in silence and I have lived through whole dramas by myself and in silence." The image of the hero is revealed precisely through this dialogic relationship to his own self. And he remains almost until the very end by himself, in utter loneliness and hopeless despair. He does not acknowledge any higher judgment on himself. He generalizes from his own loneliness, universalizes it as the ultimate loneliness of the entire human race:

Stagnation! Nature! Men are alone on earth—that's the horror! . . . Everything is dead, and the dead are everywhere. Men are alone, and around them is silence—that is the earth!

Another work close in its essence to the menippea is *Notes from Underground* (1864). It is constructed as a diatribe (a conversation with an absent interlocutor), saturated with overt and hidden polemic, and contains important elements of the confession. A story with an acute anacrisis is introduced into the second part. In *Notes from*

Underground we also find other familiar signs of the menippea: abrupt dialogic syncrises, familiarization and profanation, slum naturalism, and so on. This work too is characterized by an extraordinary ideational spaciousness: almost all the themes and ideas of Dostoevsky's subsequent work are outlined here in simplified and stripped-down form. The verbal style of this work will be dealt with in the following chapter.

We shall touch upon one more work of Dostoevsky with a very characteristic title: "A Nasty Story" (1862).P This *deeply carnivalized* story is also close to the menippea (but of the Varronian type). Serving as plot-center for the ideas is an argument among three generals at a name-day party. Afterwards the hero of the story (one of the three), in order to test his liberal-humanistic idea, drops in on the wedding feast of one of his lowliest subordinates—where, due to inexperience (he is a nondrinker), he gets thoroughly drunk. Everything is built on the extreme *inappropriateness* and *scandalous nature* of all that occurs. Everything is full of sharp carnivalistic contrasts, mésalliances, ambivalence, debasing, and decrownings. There is also an element here of rather cruel moral experimentation. We are not, of course, concerned here with the profound social and philosophical idea present in this work, which even today is not adequately appreciated. The tone of the story is deliberately unsteady, ambiguous and mocking, permeated with elements of hidden socio-political and literary polemic.

Elements of the menippea can be found in all early (that is, pre-exile) works of Dostoevsky (influenced for the most part by the generic traditions of Gogol and Hoffmann).

The menippea, as we have said, also infiltrates Dostoevsky's novels. We shall cite only the most essential instances (without any particular supporting argumentation).

In *Crime and Punishment*, the famous scene of Raskolnikov's first visit to Sonya (with the reading of the Gospel) is an almost perfect Christianized menippea: sharp dialogic syncrises (faith vs. lack of faith, meekness vs. pride), sharp anacrisis, oxymoronic combinations (the thinker-criminal, the prostitute-righteous woman), a naked statement of ultimate questions and a reading of the Gospels in a slum setting. Raskolnikov's dreams are also menippea, as is Svidrigailov's dream before his suicide.

In *The Idiot*, Ippolit's confession ("An Essential Explanation") is a menippea, framed by a carnivalized scene of dialogue on Prince Myshkin's terrace and ending with Ippolit's attempted suicide. In *The Possessed* it is Stavrogin's confession, together with the dialogue

---

P*"Skvernyi anekdot."* The story is variously translated into English as "An Unpleasant Predicament," "A Most Unfortunate Incident," "A Nasty Predicament."

between Stavrogin and Tikhon which frames it. In *The Adolescent* it is Versilov's dream.

In *The Brothers Karamazov* there is a remarkable menippea in the conversation between Ivan and Alyosha in "Metropolis" tavern on the market square of a godforsaken provincial town. Here, to the sounds of the tavern organ, the clacking of billiard balls and uncorking of beer bottles, monk and atheist solve ultimate universal questions. Into this Menippean satire a second satire is inserted—"The Legend of the Grand Inquisitor," which has its own independent significance and is constructed on the syncrisis in the Gospels between Christ and the Devil.[19] Both these interconnected Menippean satires are among the most profound artistic and philosophical works of all world literature. And finally, there is an equally profound menippea in the conversation between Ivan Karamazov and the devil (the chapter: "The Devil. Ivan Fyodorovich's Nightmare").

Of course, all these menippea are subordinated to the polyphonic design of the novelistic whole encompassing them, are determined by it and are inseparable from it.

But in addition to these relatively independent and relatively finalized menippea, all of Dostoevsky's novels are permeated with menippean elements, and with elements of other kindred genres as well— the Socratic dialogue, the diatribe, the soliloquy, the confession. Of course these genres all reached Dostoevsky after thousands of years of intense development, but throughout all changes they retained their generic essence. Sharp dialogic syncrises, extraordinary and provocative plot situations, crises and turning points and moral experimentation, catastrophes and scandals, contrasts and oxymoronic combinations are what determine the entire plot and compositional structure of Dostoevsky's novels.

Without further thorough research into the essence of the menippea and other kindred genres, without research into the history of these genres and their diverse varieties in the literatures of modern times, it is impossible to arrive at a correct historico-genetic explanation of the generic characteristics of Dostoevsky's works (and not only Dostoevsky's works; the problem is of much broader significance).

Analyzing the generic characteristics of the menippea in Dostoevsky, we simultaneously uncovered in it elements of carnivalization. And this is fully understandable, since the menippea is a profoundly carnivalized genre. But the phenomenon of carnivalization in Dostoevsky's work is of course much broader than the menippea; it has additional generic sources and therefore requires special attention.

To say that carnival and its later derivatives (the masquerade line of development, the farcical street comedy, and so on) exercised a direct and vital influence on Dostoevsky is difficult (although real experiences of a carnival type did certainly exist in his life).[20] Carnivalization acted on him, as on the majority of other eighteenth- and nineteenth-century writers, primarily as a literary and generic tradition whose extraliterary source, that is, carnival proper, was perhaps not even perceived by him in any clearly precise way.

But over the long course of centuries carnival, its forms and symbols, and above all a carnival sense of the world, seeped into many literary genres, merged with their features, shaped them, became somehow inseparable from them. Carnival was, as it were, *reincarnated in literature*, and precisely into one specific and vigorous line of its development. Carnival forms, transposed into the language of literature, became a *powerful means* for comprehending life in art, they became a special language whose words and forms possess an extraordinary capacity for *symbolic* generalization, that is, for *generalization in depth*. Many essential sides of life, or more precisely its *layers* (and often the most profound), can be located, comprehended, and expressed only with the help of this language.

In order to master this language, that is, in order to attach himself to the carnivalistic generic tradition in literature, a writer need not know all the links and all the branchings of that tradition. A genre possesses its own organic logic which can to a certain extent be understood and creatively assimilated on the basis of a few generic models, even fragments. *But the logic of genre is not an abstract logic.* Each new variety, each new work of a given genre always enriches it in some way, aids in perfecting the language of the genre. For this reason it is important to know the possible generic sources of a given author, the literary and generic atmosphere in which his creative work was realized. The more complete and concrete our knowledge of an artist's *generic contacts*, the deeper can we penetrate the peculiar features of his generic form and the more correctly can we understand the interrelationship, within it, of tradition and innovation.

All this obliges us—insofar as we are touching here upon questions of *historical* poetics—to characterize at least those basic links in the carnivalistic generic tradition with which Dostoevsky was directly or indirectly connected and which defined the generic atmosphere of his work, in many ways so fundamentally different from the generic atmosphere of Turgenev, Goncharov, or Leo Tolstoy.

One basic source of carnivalization for literature of the seventeenth, eighteenth and nineteenth centuries was the writers of the Renaissance—above all Boccaccio, Rabelais, Shakespeare, Cervantes, and Grimmelshausen.[21] Another such source was the early picaresque novel (directly carnivalized). An additional source of carnivalization for the writers of these centuries was, of course, the carnivalized literature of antiquity (including Menippean satire) and of the Middle Ages.

All the above-named basic sources for the carnivalization of European literature were very well known to Dostoevsky, except, perhaps, Grimmelshausen and the early picaresque novel. But the characteristic features of this type of novel were familiar to him from Lesage's *Gil Blas*,* and he took an intense interest in them. The picaresque novel portrayed life drawn out of its ordinary and (as it were) legitimized rut, it decrowned all hierarchical positions people might hold, and played with these positions; it was filled with sudden shifts, changes and mystifications, it perceived the entire represented world in a zone of familiar contact. As concerns Renaissance literature, its direct influence on Dostoevsky was considerable (especially Shakespeare and Cervantes). We are speaking here not of the influence of individual themes, ideas, or images, but rather of the deeper influence of *a carnival sense of the world itself*, that is, the influence of the very *forms* for visualizing the world and man, and that truly *godlike freedom* in approaching them which is manifest not in the individual thoughts, images, and external devices of construction, but in these writers' work as a *whole*.

The literature of the eighteenth century was of essential importance for Dostoevsky's assimilation of the carnival tradition, and above all Voltaire and Diderot. Characteristic for both was a combination of carnivalization with high dialogic culture, culture raised on antiquity and on the dialogues of the Renaissance. Here Dostoevsky found an organic combination of carnivalization with the rationalistic philosophical idea, and, in part, with the social theme.

The combination of carnivalization with the adventure plot and with pressing social themes of the day was found by Dostoevsky in the social-adventure novels of the nineteenth century, primarily in Frédéric Soulié* and Eugène Sue* (also somewhat in Dumas *fils* and in Paul de Kock*). Carnivalization in these authors is of a more external sort: it is manifested in the plot, in external carnivalistic antitheses and contrasts, in abrupt changes of fate, in mystifications, and so on. A deep and free carnival sense of the world is almost entirely absent. The most essential feature in these novels is an application of carnivalization to the portrayal of contemporary reality and contemporary everyday life; *everyday life* is drawn into the carnivalized action of the plot; the ordinary and constant is combined with the extraordinary and changeable.

A more profound assimilation of the carnival tradition Dostoevsky found in Balzac, George Sand, and Victor Hugo. Here there are considerably fewer external manifestations of carnivalization, but there is a deeper carnival sense of the world, and, most importantly, carnivalization permeates the very construction of the major strong characters and the development of the passions. The carnivalization of passion is evidenced first and foremost in its ambivalence: love is combined with hatred, avarice with selflessness, ambition with self-abasement, and so forth.

A combination of carnivalization with a sentimental perception of life was found by Dostoevsky in Sterne and Dickens.

Finally, the combination of carnivalization with an idea of the romantic type (rather than a rationalistic idea, as in Voltaire and Diderot) Dostoevsky found in Edgar Allan Poe and even more in Hoffmann.

A special place is held by Russian tradition. In addition to Gogol, mention must be made here of the huge influence exercised on Dostoevsky by the most carnivalized works of Pushkin: *Boris Godunov*, *The Tales of Belkin*, the *Little Tragedies* and *The Queen of Spades*.

Our brief survey of the sources of carnivalization does not pretend in any way to be complete. For our purposes it was important to trace only the basic lines of the tradition. We emphasize again that we are not interested in the influence of separate individual authors, individual works, individual themes, ideas, images—what interests us is precisely the influence of the *generic tradition itself* which was transmitted through the particular authors. Throughout this process the tradition is reborn and renewed in each of them in its own way, that is, in a unique and unrepeatable way. This constitutes the life of the tradition. What interests us—we use a comparison here—is the discourse of a *language*, and not its *individual use* in a particular *unrepeatable context*, although, of course, the one cannot exist without the other. It is certainly possible to study individual influences as well, that is, the influence of one individual writer on another (for example, Balzac on Dostoevsky), but this is already a special task and one which we do not set for ourselves here. We are interested only in the tradition itself.

In Dostoevsky's work too, of course, the carnivalistic tradition is reborn in a new way: it takes on its own meaning, combines with other artistic elements, furthers its own particular artistic goals, precisely those goals that we have tried to point out in the preceding chapters. Carnivalization is combined organically with all the other characteristics of the polyphonic novel.

Before moving on to an analysis of the elements of carnivalization in Dostoevsky (we shall concentrate on a few works only), we must first touch upon two additional questions.

To understand correctly the problem of carnivalization, one must dispense with the oversimplified understanding of carnival found in the *masquerade* line of modern times, and even more with a vulgar bohemian understanding of carnival. Carnival is past millennia's way of sensing the world as one great communal performance. This sense of the world, liberating one from fear, bringing the world maximally close to a person and bringing one person maximally close to another (everything is drawn into the zone of free familiar contact), with its joy at change and its joyful relativity, is opposed to that one-sided and gloomy official seriousness which is dogmatic and hostile to evolution and change, which seeks to absolutize a given condition of existence or a given social order. From precisely that sort of seriousness did the carnival sense of the world liberate man. But there is not a grain of nihilism in it, nor a grain of empty frivolity or vulgar bohemian individualism.

One must also dispense with that narrow theatrical-pageantry concept of carnival, so very characteristic of modern times.

For a proper understanding of carnival, one must take it at its *origins* and at its *peaks*, that is, in antiquity, in the Middle Ages and finally in the Renaissance.[22]

The second question concerns literary movements. Carnivalization, once it has penetrated and to a certain extent determined the structure of a genre, can be used by various movements and creative methods. It is quite wrong to see it as no more than a specific characteristic of Romanticism. In fact, every movement and creative method interprets and renews it in its own way. To be persuaded of this, it is enough to contrast carnivalization in Voltaire (Enlightenment realism), the early Tieck* (Romanticism), Balzac (critical realism), and Ponson du Terrail* (pure adventure). The degree of carnivalization in each of the above authors is almost identical, but each is subordinated to its own special artistic tasks (connected with its literary movement) and therefore each "sounds" differently (we are not speaking here of the individual characteristics of these writers). At the same time the presence of carnivalization defines them as belonging to one and the same *generic* tradition and creates, from the point of view of a poetics, a very *fundamental common ground* between them (we repeat, even given all the differences in literary movement, individual personality and artistic merit).

In "Petersburg Visions in Verse and Prose" (1861) Dostoevsky recalls the unique and vivid carnival sense of life experienced by him at the very beginning of his career as a writer. This was above all a special sense of Petersburg, with all its sharp social contrasts, as "a fantastic magical daydream," as "dream," as something standing on the boundary between reality and fantastic invention. An analogous carnival sense of a great city (Paris) can be found in Balzac, Sue,

Soulié, and others, but not as strong or as deep as it is in Dostoevsky; the sources of this tradition go back to the ancient menippea (Varro, Lucian). Building on this sense of the city and the city crowd, Dostoevsky proceeds to give a sharply carnivalized picture of the emergence of his own first literary projects, including a plan for *Poor Folk*:

And I began to look around and suddenly I saw some strange faces. They were all strange, queer, totally prosaic figures, in no way a Don Carlos or a Posa, nothing more than titular counselors, but at the same time they somehow seemed to be fantastic titular counselors. Someone *grimaced* in front of me, hiding behind that *fantastic crowd*, and *jerked at some strings and springs*, and these *puppets* moved, and he guffawed, how he guffawed! And then another story occurred to me, in some dark corners, some titular heart, honest and pure, moral and loyal to the authorities, and alongside it some little girl, mistreated and melancholy, and this whole story rent my heart deeply. And if one could gather together that whole crowd which I dreamed of then, it would make a wonderful *masquerade* . . .[23]

In this way, according to Dostoevsky's own reminiscences, his creative art was born—born, as it were, out of a vivid carnival vision of life ("I call the feeling I had on the Neva a vision," Dostoevsky tells us). Here we have the characteristic accessories of a carnival complex: guffaw and tragedy, a clown, comical street farces, a crowd of masqueraders. But the most important thing here, of course, is that very carnival sense of the world, which thoroughly permeates "Petersburg Dreams." In its generic essence this work is a variety of carnivalized menippea. One should emphasize the central *guffaw* accompanying the vision. We shall see further that Dostoevsky's entire work is in fact permeated with it, though in a reduced form.

The carnivalization of Dostoevsky's early work will not be dealt with in detail. We shall examine only certain elements of carnivalization in some of the individual works published after his exile. Here we set ourselves a limited task—to prove the presence of carnivalization and to uncover its basic functions in Dostoevsky. A deeper and fuller study of the problem, based on all of Dostoevsky's work, is beyond the limits of the present book.

The first work of the second period—"Uncle's Dream"—is remarkable for its vividly expressed, but somewhat simplified and *external*, carnivalization. At its center lies a scandal-catastrophe with a double decrowning—of Moskaleva and the prince. Even the very tone of the story told by Mordasov's chronicler is ambivalent: there is an ironic glorification of Moskaleva, that is, a carnivalistic fusion of praise and abuse.[24]

The scene of the scandal and decrowning of the prince—the carnival king, or more accurately the carnival bridegroom—is consistently portrayed as a *tearing to pieces*, as a typical carnivalistic "sacrificial" dismemberment into parts:

". . . If I'm a tub, then you are a *one-legged cripple!*"

"Me—one-legged—"

"Yes, yes, one-legged and *toothless* into the bargain, that's what you are!"

"And one-eyed, too!" shouted Marya Alexandrovna.

"You have a corset instead of ribs," added Natalya Dmitriyevna.

"Your *face* is on springs!"

"You have no *hair* of your own!"

"And the old fool's *moustache* is artificial, too," screeched Marya Alexandrovna.

"At least leave me my *nose*, Marya Alexandrovna!" cried the Prince, flabbergasted by such unexpected *revelations*. . . .

"Good God," said the unfortunate Prince, ". . . take me away, my good fellow, take me away, or they'll *tear me to pieces* . . ." [*SS* II, 398-99]

We have here a typical "carnival anatomy"—an enumeration of the parts of the dismembered body. Such "enumerations" were a widespread comic device in the carnivalized literature of the Renaissance (it is met very often in Rabelais, and in a somewhat less developed form in Cervantes).

The role of a decrowned carnival king was also played by the heroine of the tale, Marya Alexandrovna Moskaleva:

The guests dispersed with squeals and abuse, and Marya Alexandrovna was at last alone amidst the ruins and fragments of her former glory. Alas! Power, glory, distinction—all had vanished in a single evening. [*SS* II, 399]

But after the scene of the *comic* decrowning of the *old* bridegroom, the prince, there follows a *paired* scene of the tragic self-decrowning and death of the young bridegroom, the schoolteacher Vasya. Such a *pairing* of scenes (and individual images) that reflect one another or shine through one another—one given in the comic plane and the other in the tragic (as in this instance) or one on a lofty and the other on a low plane, or one affirming, the other repudiating, and so forth—is characteristic of Dostoevsky; taken together, these paired scenes create an ambivalent whole. It is evidence of an even deeper influence of the carnival sense of the world. To be sure, in "Uncle's Dream" this characteristic is still expressed somewhat externally.

Carnivalization is much deeper and more substantial in the tale *The Village of Stepanchikovo and its Inhabitants*,q although here,

_____

qOne of Dostoevsky's early post-exile works (1859); translated by Constance Garnett as "The Friend of the Family."

too, there is still much that is external. All life in Stepanchikovo is concentrated around Foma Fomich Opiskin, former *hanger-on* and *buffoon*, who has become the *unlimited despot* on Colonel Rostanev's estate; that is, all life is concentrated around a *carnival king*. Thus all life in the village of Stepanchikovo assumes a carnivalistic character, vividly expressed. This is life that has left its normal rut, almost a "world turned inside out."

And it cannot be otherwise, insofar as the tone is set by a carnival king—Foma Fomich. All the other characters, participants in this life, take on carnival coloration as well: the *mad* rich lady Tatyana Ivanovna, suffering from an erotic mania for falling in love (in the banal-romantic style) and who is at the same time the purest and kindest of souls; the *mad wife of the general* with her adoration and cult of Foma; the little *fool* Falalei with his persistent dream about the white bull and his Kamarinskaya[r]; the *mad lackey* Vidoplyasov, who is constantly changing his name to one more noble—such as "Tantsev," "Esbuketov" (this he must do because the house servants find an indecent rhyme for each new name); the *old man* Gavrila, who is forced in his old age to study French; the malicious *buffoon* Ezhevikin; the *"progressive" fool* Obnoskin who dreams of a wealthy bride; the *bankrupt hussar* Mizinchikov; the *eccentric* Bakhcheev, and others too. These are all people who for one reason or another have left the normal rut of life, who are denied the position in life normal and appropriate for them. The entire action of the tale is an uninterrupted series of scandals, eccentric escapades, mystifications, decrownings and crownings. The work is saturated with parodies and semiparodies, including a parody on Gogol's *Selected Passages from a Correspondence with Friends*; these parodies are organically linked with the carnival atmosphere of the tale as a whole.

Carnivalization allows Dostoevsky to glimpse and bring to life aspects in the character and behavior of people which in the normal course of life could not have revealed themselves. Especially deeply carnivalized is the character of Foma Fomich: he does not coincide with himself, he is not equal to himself, he cannot be given a mono-semantic finalizing definition, and he anticipates in many ways the future heroes of Dostoevsky. He is, incidentally, presented in a carnivalistic contrasting pair with Colonel Rostanev.

We have concentrated on carnivalization in two works of Dostoevsky's second period because there it is more or less external and consequently very visible, obvious to all. In subsequent works carnivalization

---

[r]"Kamarinskaya," native Russian dance, made famous by Glinka's orchestral fantasy of the same name (1848).

recedes into the deeper levels and its nature changes. In particular, the *comic* aspect, here rather loud, is later muffled and reduced almost to the minimum. We must treat this point in somewhat more detail.

We have already made reference to the phenomenon of reduced laughter, so important in world literature. Laughter is a specific aesthetic relationship to reality, but not one that can be translated into logical language; that is, it is a specific means for artistically visualizing and comprehending reality and, consequently, a specific means for structuring an artistic image, plot, or genre. Enormous creative, and therefore genre-shaping, power was possessed by ambivalent carnivalistic laughter. This laughter could grasp and comprehend a phenomenon in the process of change and transition, it could fix in a phenomenon both poles of its evolution in their uninterrupted and creative renewing changeability: in death birth is foreseen and in birth death, in victory defeat and in defeat victory, in crowning a decrowning. Carnival laughter does not permit a single one of these aspects of change to be absolutized or to congeal in one-sided seriousness.

When we say that birth is "foreseen" in death, we inevitably make logical, and thus somewhat distort, carnival ambivalence: for in so doing we sever death from birth and distance them somewhat from each other. In living carnival images, death itself is pregnant and gives birth, and the mother's womb giving birth becomes a grave. Precisely such images are produced by creative ambivalent carnival laughter, in which mockery and triumph, praise and abuse are inseparably fused.

When the images of carnival and carnivalistic laughter are transposed into literature, they are transformed to a greater or lesser degree in keeping with specific artistic and literary tasks. But regardless of the degree or nature of the transformation, ambivalence and laughter remain in the carnivalized image. Under certain conditions and in certain genres, however, laughter can be reduced. It continues to determine the structure of the image, but it itself is muffled down to the minimum: we see, as it were, the track left by laughter in the structure of represented reality, but the laughter itself we do not hear. Thus in Plato's Socratic dialogues (of the first period) laughter is reduced (although not entirely), but it remains in the structure of the image of the major hero (Socrates), in the methods for carrying on the dialogue, and—most importantly—in authentic (not rhetorical) dialogicality itself, immersing thought itself in the joyful relativity of evolving existence and not permitting it to congeal in abstractly dogmatic (monologic) ossification. But here and there in the dialogues of the early period laughter goes beyond the structure of the image and, so to speak, bursts out in a loud register. In the dialogues of the later period, laughter is reduced to a minimum.

In the literature of the Renaissance, laughter is generally not reduced, but certain gradations of "volume" do, of course, exist even here. In Rabelais, for example, it rings out loudly, as is fitting on a public square. In Cervantes there is no longer that public-square intensity of sound, although in the first book of *Don Quixote* laughter is still quite loud, and in the second it is significantly (when compared with the first) reduced. This reduction is also linked with certain changes in the structure of the major hero's image, and with changes in the plot.

In carnivalized literature of the eighteenth and nineteenth centuries, laughter is as a rule considerably muffled—to the level of irony, humor, and other forms of reduced laughter.

Let us return to reduced laughter in Dostoevsky. In the first two works of the second period, as we have said, laughter can still be distinctly heard, for elements of carnival ambivalence are of course still preserved in it.[25] But in Dostoevsky's subsequent great novels, laughter is reduced almost to the minimum (especially in *Crime and Punishment*). In all his novels, however, we find a trace of that ambivalent laughter, absorbed by Dostoevsky together with the generic tradition of carnivalization, performing its work of artistically organizing and illuminating the world. We find such traces in the structure of images, in numerous plot situations, and in certain characteristics of verbal style. But the most important—one could say, the decisive—expression of reduced laughter is to be found in the ultimate position of the author. This position excludes all one-sided or dogmatic seriousness and does not permit any single point of view, any single polar extreme of life or of thought, to be absolutized. All one-sided seriousness (of life and thought), all one-sided pathos is handed over to the heroes, but the author, who causes them all to collide in the "great dialogue" of the novel, leaves that dialogue open and puts no finalizing period at the end.

It should be pointed out that the carnival sense of the world also knows no period, and is, in fact, hostile to any sort of *conclusive conclusion*: all endings are merely new beginnings; carnival images are reborn again and again.

Certain scholars (Vyacheslav Ivanov,[s] Komarovich) apply to Dostoevsky's works the ancient (Aristotelian) term "catharsis" (purification). If this term is understood in a very broad sense, then one can agree with it (without catharsis in the broad sense there is no art at all). But tragic catharsis (in the Aristotelian sense) is not

---

[s]In English, see Vyacheslav Ivanov, *Freedom and the Tragic Life: A Study in Dostoevsky*, pp. 12-14.

applicable to Dostoevsky. The catharsis that finalizes Dostoevsky's novels might be—of course inadequately and somewhat rationalistically—expressed in this way: *nothing conclusive has yet taken place in the world, the ultimate word of the world and about the world has not yet been spoken, the world is open and free, everything is still in the future and will always be in the future.*

But this is, after all, also the *purifying sense* of ambivalent laughter.

It would not, perhaps, be superfluous to emphasize again that we speak here of Dostoevsky the artist. Dostoevsky the journalist was by no means a stranger to cramped and one-sided seriousness, to dogmatism, even to eschatology. But these ideas of the journalist, once introduced into the novel, become there merely one of the embodied voices of an unfinalized and open dialogue.

In Dostoevsky's novels, everything is directed toward that unspoken and as yet unpredetermined *"new word,"* everything waits tensely on that word, and the *author* does not block its path with his own one-sided and monosemantic seriousness.

Reduced laughter in carnivalized literature by no means excludes the possibility of somber colors within a work. For this reason the somber coloration of Dostoevsky's works should not confuse us: it is not their final word.

Sometimes in Dostoevsky's novels reduced laughter rises to the surface, especially in those places where a narrator or a chronicler is introduced whose story is almost always constructed in parodic-ironic ambivalent tones (for example, the ambivalent glorification of Stepan Trofimovich in *The Possessed*, very close in tone to the glorification of Moskaleva in "Uncle's Dream"). This laughter comes to the fore in open or half-concealed parodies that are scattered throughout all of Dostoevsky's novels.[26]

We shall pause on several other characteristics of carnivalization in Dostoevsky's novels.

Carnivalization is not an external and immobile schema which is imposed upon ready-made content; it is, rather, an extraordinarily flexible form of artistic visualization, a peculiar sort of heuristic principle making possible the discovery of new and as yet unseen things. By *relativizing* all that was externally stable, set and ready-made, carnivalization with its pathos of change and renewal permitted Dostoevsky to penetrate into the deepest layers of man and human relationships. It proved remarkably productive as a means for capturing in art the developing relationships under capitalism, at a time when previous forms of life, moral principles and beliefs were being turned into "rotten cords" and the previously concealed, ambivalent, and unfinalized nature of man and human *thought* was being nakedly exposed. Not only people and their actions but even *ideas* had broken out of their self-enclosed hierarchical nesting places and had begun to collide in the familiar contact of "absolute" (that is, completely unlimited) dialogue. Capitalism, similar to that "pander" Socrates on the market square of Athens, brings together people and ideas. In all of Dostoevky's novels, beginning with *Crime and Punishment*, there is a consistent *carnivalization* of dialogue.

We find other instances of carnivalization in *Crime and Punishment*. Everything in this novel—the fates of people, their experiences and ideas—is pushed to its boundaries, everything is prepared, as it were, to pass over into its opposite (but not, of course, in the abstractly dialectical sense), everything is taken to the extreme, to its outermost limit. There is nothing in the novel that could become stabilized, nothing that could justifiably relax within itself, enter the ordinary flow of biographical time and develop in it (the possibility of such a development for Razumikhin and Dounia is only indicated by Dostoevsky at the end of the novel, but of course he does not show it: such life lies outside his artistic world). Everything requires change and rebirth. Everything is shown in a moment of unfinalized transition.

It is characteristic that the very setting for the action of the novel —*Petersburg* (its role in the novel is enormous)—is on the borderline between existence and nonexistence, reality and phantasmagoria, always on the verge of dissipating like the fog and vanishing. Petersburg too is devoid, as it were, of any internal grounds for justifiable stabilization; it too is on the threshold.[27]

The sources of carnivalization for *Crime and Punishment* are no longer provided by Gogol. We feel here in part a Balzacian type of carnivalization, and in part elements of the social-adventure novel (Soulié and Sue). But perhaps the most vital and profound source of carnivalization for this novel was Pushkin's "Queen of Spades."

We shall pause for analysis on only one small episode of the novel, which will permit us to investigate several important characteristics of carnivalization in Dostoevsky, and at the same time clarify our claim concerning Pushkin's influence.

After the first meeting with Porfiry and the appearance of the mysterious artisan with his one word, "Murderer!", Raskolnikov has a *dream* in which he *again* commits the murder of the old woman. We quote the end of this dream:

He stood over her. "She is afraid," he thought. He stealthily took the axe from the noose and struck her one blow, then another on the skull. But strange to say she did not stir, as though she were made of wood. He was frightened, bent down nearer and tried to look at her; but she, too, bent her head lower. He bent right down to the ground and peeped up into her face from below, he peeped and turned cold with horror; the old woman was sitting and *laughing, shaking with noiseless laughter*, doing her utmost that he should not hear it. Suddenly he fancied that the door from the bedroom was opened a little and that there was *laughter* and whispering within. He was overcome with frenzy and he began hitting the old woman on the head with all his force, but at every blow of the axe and the *laughter* and whispering from the bedroom *grew louder* and the old woman was simply shaking with mirth. He was rushing away, but the *passage was full of people, the doors* of the flats stood open and *on the landing, on the stairs* and everywhere below there were people, rows of heads, *all looking*, but huddled together in silence and expectation. Something gripped his heart, his legs were rooted to the spot, they would not move. . . . He tried to scream and woke up. [*SS* V, 288; *Crime and Punishment*, Part III, ch. 6]

Several points are of interest here.

1. The first point is already familiar to us: the fantastic logic of dreams employed here by Dostoevsky. We recall his words: ". . . you *leap over* space and time, *over all laws of life and reason*, and only pause where your *heart's desire* bids you pause" ("Dream of a Ridiculous Man"). This same dream logic made it possible to create here the image of a *laughing murdered old woman, to combine laughter with death and murder*. But this is also made possible by the ambivalent logic of carnival. Before us is a typical carnival combination.

The image of the laughing old woman in Dostoevsky echoes Pushkin's image of the old Countess winking from the coffin, and the winking Queen of Spades on the card (the Queen of Spades is, incidentally, a *carnival double* of the old Countess). We have here a *fundamental* resonance between two images and not a chance external similarity, for it occurs against the background of a general resonance between these two works ("The Queen of Spades" and *Crime and Punishment*). This is a resonance both in the atmosphere of images and in the basic content of ideas: "Napoleonism" on the specific terrain of early Russian capitalism. In both works this concretely historical phenomenon receives a second *carnivalistic plane*, one which recedes into infinite semantic space. The motivation for these two echoing images (the laughing dead woman) is also similar: in Pushkin it is *insanity*, in Dostoevsky, the *delirious dream*.

2. In Raskolnikov's dream it is not only the murdered woman who laughs (in the dream, to be sure, it proves impossible to murder her). Other people are also laughing, elsewhere in the apartment, in the bedroom, and they laugh louder and louder. Then a crowd appears, a multitude of people on the *stairway* and *down below* as well, and in relation to this crowd passing *below*, Raskolnikov is located at the *top of the stairs*. Before us is the image of communal ridicule on the public square decrowning a carnival king-pretender. The public square is a symbol of the communal performance, and at the end of

the novel, Raskolnikov, before going to give himself up at the police station, comes out on the square and bows low to the earth before the whole people. This communal decrowning, which "came to Raskolnikov's heart" in a dream, has no *direct* echo in the "The Queen of Spades," but a distant echo is nevertheless there: Hermann's fainting spell in the presence of the people at the Countess' grave. A fuller echo of Raskolnikov's dream can be found in another of Pushkin's works, *Boris Godunov*. We have in mind the thrice-recurring prophetic *dream* of the Pretender (the scene in the cell of Chudovo Monastery):

> I dreamed I climbed a *crooked stair* that led
> Up to a tower, and there upon that *height*
> I stood, where Moscow like an ant hill lay
> *Under* my feet, and in the *marketplace*
> The *people* stared and pointed at me *laughing;*
> *I felt ashamed, a trembling overcame me,*
> I fell headfirst, and in that fall I woke.[t]

Here is the same carnival logic of self-appointed *elevation*, the communal act of comic *decrowning on the public square*, and a falling *downward*.

3. In Raskolnikov's dream, *space* assumes additional significance in the overall symbol-system of carnival. *Up, down*, the *stairway*, the *threshold*, the *foyer*, the *landing* take on the meaning of a "point" where *crisis*, radical change, an unexpected turn of fate takes place, where decisions are made, where the forbidden line is overstepped, where one is renewed or perishes.

Action in Dostoevsky's works occurs primarily at these "points." The interior spaces of a house or of rooms, spaces distant from the boundaries, that is from the threshold, are almost never used by Dostoevsky, except of course for scenes of scandals and decrownings, when interior space (the drawing room or the hall) becomes a substitute for the public square. Dostoevsky "leaps over" all that is comfortably habitable, well-arranged and stable, all that is far from the threshold, because the life that he portrays does not take place in that sort of space. Dostoevsky was least of all an estate-home-room-apartment-family writer. In comfortably habitable interior space, far from the threshold, people live a biographical life in biographical time: they are born, they pass through childhood and youth, they marry, give birth to children, die. This biographical time Dostoevsky also "leaps over." On the threshold and on the square the only time possible is *crisis time*, in which a *moment* is equal to years, decades,

---

[t]Translation by Paul Schmidt in his *Meyerhold at Work* (Austin: U. of Texas Press, 1980), p. 85.

even to a "billion years" (as in "The Dream of a Ridiculous Man").

If we now turn from Raskolnikov's *dream* to what happens in the waking life of the novel, we will be persuaded that the threshold and its substitutes are the fundamental "points" of action in the novel.

First of all, Raskolnikov lives, in essence, on a threshold: his narrow room, a "coffin" (a carnival symbol here) opens directly onto the *landing of the staircase*, and he never locks his door, even when he goes out (that is, his room is unenclosed interior space). In this "coffin" it is impossible to live a biographical life—here one can experience only crisis, make ultimate decisions, die or be reborn (as in the coffins of "Bobok" or the coffin of the Ridiculous Man). Marmeladov's family lives on the threshold as well, in a walk-through room leading directly onto a staircase (here, on the threshold, while bringing home the drunken Marmeladov, Raskolnikov meets the members of the family for the first time). Raskolnikov experiences terrible moments at the threshold of the murdered pawnbroker's when, on the other side of the door, on the stairway landing, her visitors stand and tug at the bell. It is to this place that he returns and himself rings the bell, in order to relive those moments. The scene of his half-confession to Razumikhin takes place on the threshold in the corridor by a lamp, without words, only in glances. On the threshold, near the doors leading to a neighboring apartment, his conversations with Sonya occur (with Svidrigailov eavesdropping on the other side of the door). There is certainly no need to enumerate further all the "acts" that take place on the threshold, near the threshold, or that are permeated with the living sensation of threshold in this novel.

The threshold, the foyer, the corridor, the landing, the stairway, its steps, doors opening onto the stairway, gates to front and back yards, and beyond these, the city: squares, streets, façades, taverns, dens, bridges, gutters. This is the space of the novel. And in fact absolutely nothing here ever loses touch with the threshold, there is no interior of drawing rooms, dining rooms, halls, studios, bedrooms where biographical life unfolds and where events take place in the novels of writers such as Turgenev, Tolstoy, and Goncharov. Of course, we can uncover just such an organization of space in Dostoevsky's other works as well.

We find a somewhat different nuance of carnivalization in "The Gambler."

It portrays, first of all, the life of "Russians abroad," a special category of people that attracted Dostoevsky's interest. These are people cut off from their native land and folk, whose life ceases to be determined by the norms of people living in their own country;

their behavior is no longer regulated by that position which they had occupied in their homeland, they are not fastened down to their environment. The General, the tutor in the General's house (the hero of the tale), the scoundrel de Grieux, Polina, the courtesan Blanche, the Englishman Astley, and all the others who have come together in the little German town of Roulettenburg make up a sort of *carnival collective*, which seems to a certain extent itself outside the norms and order of ordinary life. Their behavior and their relationships with one another become unusual, eccentric, and scandalous (they live constantly in an atmosphere of scandal).

Secondly, the center of the life portrayed in the tale is the *game of roulette*. This second aspect is a decisive one and determines the special nuance of carnivalization in the work.

Gambling (with dice, cards, roulette, etc.) is by nature carnivalistic. This was clearly recognized in antiquity, the Middle Ages and the Renaissance. Symbols of gambling were always part of the image system of carnival symbols.

People from various (hierarchical) positions in life, once crowded around the roulette table, are made equal by the rules of the game and in the face of fortune, chance. Their behavior at the roulette table in no way corresponds to the role they play in ordinary life. The atmosphere of gambling is an atmosphere of sudden and quick changes of fate, of instantaneous rises and falls, that is, of crownings/decrownings. The *stake* is similar to a *crisis*: a person feels himself *on the threshold*. And the time of gambling is a special time: here, too, a minute is equal to years.

The game of roulette spreads its carnivalizing influence over all life that comes in contact with it, over almost the whole town, which Dostoevsky for good reason called Roulettenburg.

The personalities of the main heroes of the tale also unfold in an intense carnivalized atmosphere—Alexei Ivanovich and Polina, ambivalent and crisis-ridden characters, unfinalized, eccentric, full of unexpected possibilities. In one of his letters from 1863, Dostoevsky characterized in this way the *concept* underlying Alexei Ivanovich's image (considerably changed in the final version of 1866):

"I am taking a direct spontaneous nature, a man however of considerable development, but *in everything incomplete*, a man *who has lost faith* and yet who **does not dare not to believe**, *who rebels against the authorities while fearing them* . . . the main point is that all his vital juices, strength, rebelliousness and daring have gone into **roulette**. He is a gambler, but not an *ordinary gambler*, just as *Pushkin's miserly knight is not an ordinary miser* . . ."

As we have said, the final image of Alexei Ivanovich differs rather considerably from this concept, but the ambivalence mentioned in it not only remains but is even sharply intensified, and incompleteness becomes a consistent and crucial *open-endedness*; in addition, the character of the hero is revealed not only in gambling and in carnival-type scandals and eccentricities, but also in his deeply ambivalent and crisis-ridden passion for Polina.

Dostoevsky's reference to Pushkin's "Miserly Knight," pointed out by us above, is of course no accidental juxtaposition. "The Miserly Knight" exercises a very fundamental influence on all of Dostoevsky's subsequent works, especially on *The Adolescent* and *The Brothers Karamazov* (a maximally profound and universalized treatment of the theme of parricide).

We cite another excerpt from the same letter of Dostoevsky's:

"If *House of the Dead* attracted the public's attention because it portrayed convicts, whom no one had graphically portrayed prior to *House of the Dead*, then this story will be sure to attract attention as a **graphic** and highly detailed *portrayal of the game of roulette . . .* *House of the Dead* was indeed curious. But this is a *description of a sort of hell*, a unique sort of 'prison bathhouse.' "[28]

At superficial glance it may seem strange and far-fetched to juxtapose the game of roulette with penal servitude, and "The Gambler" with "House of the Dead." But in fact the juxtaposition is profoundly appropriate. Both the life of convicts and the life of gamblers — for all their differences in content — are equally *"life taken out of life"* (that is, taken out of common, ordinary life). In this sense both convicts and gamblers are carnivalized collectives.[29] And the *time* of penal servitude and the *time* of gambling are — for all their profound differences — an identical *type of time*, similar to the "final moments of consciousness" before execution or suicide, similar in general to the time of crisis. All this is time on the *threshold*, and not biological time, experienced in the interior spaces of life far from the threshold. It is remarkable that Dostoevsky equates both gambling at roulette and penal servitude equally to *hell*, or as we would say, to the carnivalized nether world of Menippean satire (the "prison bathhouse" is an extraordinary externally visible symbol of this). Dostoevsky's juxtapositions here are to the highest degree characteristic of him, and at the same time have the sound of a typical carnival mésalliance.

In the novel *The Idiot*, carnivalization is present simultaneously with great external visibility, and with the enormous inner depth of a carnival sense of the world (this is in part due to the direct influence of Cervantes' *Don Quixote*).

At the center of the novel stands the carnivalistically ambivalent figure of the "Idiot," Prince Myshkin. This person, in a special and *higher sense*, does not occupy any *position* in life that might define his behavior and limit his *pure humanness*. From the point of view of life's ordinary logic, the entire behavior and all the experiences of Prince Myshkin appear incongruous and eccentric in the extreme. Such, for example, is his brotherly love for his rival, a person who made an attempt on his life and who has become the murderer of the woman he loves; this brotherly love toward Rogozhin in fact reaches its peak immediately after the murder of Nastasya Filippovna and fills Myshkin's "final moments of consciousness" (before he falls into complete idiocy). The final scene of *The Idiot*—the last meeting of Myshkin and Rogozhin beside Nastasya Filippovna's corpse—is one of the most striking in all of Dostoevsky's art.

Just as paradoxical from the point of view of life's normal logic is Myshkin's attempt to *combine in life* his simultaneous love for Nastasya Filippovna and Aglaya. Also outside the logic of ordinary life are Myshkin's relationships to the other characters: to Ganya Ivolgin, Ippolit, Burdovsky, Lebedev, and others as well. One might say that Myshkin is not able to enter into life completely, cannot become completely embodied, cannot accept any definitiveness in life that would limit a personality. He remains, as it were, on a tangent to life's circle. It is as if he lacks the necessary *flesh of life* that would permit him to occupy a specific place in life (thereby crowding others out of that place), and therefore he remains on a tangent to life. But precisely for that reason is he able to "penetrate" through the life-flesh of other people and reach their deepest "I."

In Myshkin this detachment from the ordinary relationships of life, the constant *inappropriateness* of his personality and his behavior impart to him a certain integrity, almost a naiveté; he is precisely an "idiot."

The heroine of the novel, Nastasya Filippovna, also falls out of the ordinary logic and relationships of life. She, too, always and in everything acts *in spite ·of* her position in life. But characteristic for her is the *violent emotional response*. She is "mad."

And around these two central figures of the novel—the "idiot" and the "madwoman"—all of life is carnivalized, turned into a "world inside out": traditional plot situations radically change their meaning, there develops a dynamic carnivalistic play of sharp contrasts, unexpected shifts and changes; secondary characters in the novel take on carnivalistic overtones, form carnival pairs.

A carnivalistic-fantastic atmosphere permeates the entire novel. But around Myshkin this atmosphere is *bright*, almost *joyful*. Around Nastasya Filippovna it is *gloomy, infernal*. Myshkin is in carnival *paradise*, Nastasya Filippovna in carnival *hell*; but this hell and paradise in the novel intersect, intertwine in various ways, and are reflected in each other according to the laws of a profound carnival ambivalence. All this permits Dostoevsky to expose a different side of life to himself and to the reader, to spy upon and depict in that life certain new, unknown depths and possibilities.

But what interests us here is not those depths of life that Dostoevsky *glimpsed*, but only the *form of their visualization*, and the role played in that form by elements of carnivalization.

We shall pause a while longer on the carnivalizing function of the image of Prince Myshkin.

Wherever Prince Myshkin appears, hierarchical barriers between people suddenly become penetrable, an inner contact is formed between them, a carnival frankness is born. His personality possesses the peculiar capacity to relativize everything that disunifies people and imparts a *false seriousness* to life.

The action of the novel begins in a third-class railway car, where "two passengers found themselves opposite each other by the window"—Myshkin and Rogozhin. We have already had occasion to point out that the third-class railway car, like the deck of a ship in the ancient menippea, is a substitute for the *public square*, where people from various positions find themselves in familiar contact with one another. Thus there is a coming together of the *beggar prince* and the *merchant millionaire*. The carnivalistic contrast is emphasized even in their clothing: Myshkin is in a sleeveless cloak of foreign make with an enormous hood, and in gaiters; Rogozhin is in a sheepskin coat and boots.

> The fell into talk. The readiness of the *fair* young man in the Swiss cloak to answer all his *swarthy* companion's inquiries was remarkable. He betrayed no suspicion of the extreme impertinence of some of his misplaced and idle questions. [SS VI, 7; *The Idiot*, Part, I, ch. 1]

This remarkable readiness of Myshkin to open himself up calls forth a reciprocal frankness on the part of the suspicious and withdrawn Rogozhin, and prompts him to relate the story of his passion for Nastasya Filippovna with absolute carnivalistic frankness.

Such is the first carnivalized episode of the novel.

In the second episode, already in the Epanchin's house, Myshkin, waiting to be received, carries on a conversation *in the foyer* with the *butler*, on the inappropriate theme of capital punishment and the final moral torments of the condemned. And he succeeds in entering into inner contact with this stuffy and limited servant.

In the same carnivalistic manner does he penetrate social barriers in his first meeting with General Epanchin.

Of some interest is the carnivalization of the following episode: in Madame Epanchin's living room, Myshkin tells of the *final moments of consciousness* of a man condemned to death (an autobiographical account of something that Dostoevsky had himself experienced). The theme of the threshold intrudes here into the interior space of the drawing room, a space far from the threshold. No less inappropriate here is Myshkin's amazing story about Marie. This whole episode is full of carnivalistic frankness; an odd and in fact suspicious *stranger* — the Prince — is, as swiftly and unexpectedly as in carnival, transformed into an intimate and a friend of the family. The Epanchin household is drawn into Myshkin's carnival atmosphere. Of course, this is facilitated by the childlike and eccentric character of Madame Epanchin herself.

The subsequent episode, which takes place in the Ivolgins' apartment, is remarkable for its even more pronounced external and internal carnivalization. It unfolds from the very beginning in an atmosphere of scandal, which exposes the soul of almost all the participants. Such externally carnivalistic figures as Ferdyshchenko and General Ivolgin make their appearance. The typical carnival mystifications and mésalliances occur. Characteristic is the short, acutely carnivalized scene in the foyer, on the *threshold*, when Nastasya Filippovna, who has appeared unexpectedly, mistakes the prince for a servant and rudely curses him out ("Oaf," "you should be fired," "what an idiot!"). This abuse, which contributes to a thickening of the carnival atmosphere of the scene, is completely out of keeping with Nastasya Filippovna's actual treatment of servants. The scene in the foyer prepares for the subsequent scene of mystification in the living room, where Nastasya Filippovna plays out the role of a heartless and cynical courtesan. Then occurs the exaggeratedly carnivalistic scene of the scandal: the appearance of the tipsy general with his carnivalistic story, his exposure, the appearance of Rogozhin's motley and drunken crew, Ganya's clash with his sister, the slap in the prince's face, the provocative behavior of the petty carnival demon Ferdyshchenko, and so forth. The Ivolgins' living room is transformed into a carnival square, where for the first time Myshkin's carnival paradise intersects and intertwines with Nastasya Filippovna's carnival hell.

After the scandal, there is the Prince's penetrating conversation with Ganya and the latter's frank confession, then a carnivalistic journey through Petersburg with the drunken general, and, finally, the evening at Nastasya Filippovna's with the culminating scandal-catastrophe, which we have already analyzed in its place. Thus ends the first part, and with it the first *day* of the novel's action.

The action of the first part began at dawn and ended late in the evening. But this is not, of course, the day of tragedy ("from the rising to the setting of the sun"). The time here is neither tragic time (although it is close to it in type), nor is it epic time, nor biographical time. This is a day in special carnival time, excluded, as it were, from historical time, flowing according to its own special carnival laws and finding room in itself for an unlimited numer of radical shifts and metamorphoses.[30] Precisely this sort of time—to be sure, not carnival time in the strict sense but rather carnivalized time—was necessary to Dostoevsky for the fulfillment of his special artistic tasks. Those events that Dostoevsky portrayed on the *threshold* or on the *public square*, with their profound inner meaning, and likewise such heroes of his as Raskolnikov, Myshkin, Stavrogin, Ivan Karamazov, could not have been explored in ordinary biographical and historical time. And in fact polyphony itself, as the event of interaction between autonomous and internally unfinalized consciousnesses, demands a different artistic conception of time and space; to use Dostoevsky's own expression, a "non-Euclidian" conception.

On this we may conclude our analysis of carnivalization in Dostoevsky's works.

In the subsequent three novels we will find the same features of carnivalization,[31] although in a more complex and intensified form (especially in *The Brothers Karamazov*). In concluding the present chapter we will touch upon one aspect only, which is most vividly expressed in the later novels.

We have already spoken of the structural characteristics of the carnival image: it strives to encompass and unite within itself both poles of becoming or both members of an antithesis: birth-death, youth-old age, top-bottom, face-backside, praise-abuse, affirmation-repudiation, tragic-comic, and so forth, while the upper pole of a two-in-one image is reflected in the lower, after the manner of the figures on playing cards. It could be expressed this way: opposites come together, look at one another, are reflected in one another, know and understand one another.

And in just this way could one define the basic principle of Dostoevsky's art. Everything in his world lives on the very border of its opposite. Love lives on the very border of hate, knows and understands it, and hate lives on the border of love and also understands it (the love-hate of Versilov, the love of Katerina Ivanovna toward Dmitri Karamazov; to a certain extent also both Ivan's love for Katerina Ivanovna and Dmitri's love for Grushenka). Faith lives on the very border of atheism, sees itself there and understands it, and atheism lives on the border of faith and understands it.[32] Loftiness and nobility live on the border of degradation and vulgarity (Dmitri Karamazov). Love for life neighbors upon a thirst for self-destruction (Kirillov). Purity and chastity understand vice and sensuality (Alyosha Karamazov).

We are, of course, simplifying and coarsening somewhat the very complex and subtle ambivalence of Dostoevsky's later novels. In Dostoevsky's world all people and all things must know one another and know about one another, must enter into contact, come together face to face and *begin to talk* with one another. Everything must be reflected in everything else, all things must illuminate one another dialogically. Therefore all things that are disunified and distant must be brought together at a single spatial and temporal "point." And what is necessary for this is carnival *freedom* and carnival's artistic conception of space and time.

Carnivalization made possible the creation of the *open* structure of the great dialogue, and permitted social interaction between people to be carried over into the higher sphere of the spirit and the intellect, which earlier had always been primarily the sphere of a single and unified monologic consciousness, a unified and indivisible spirit unfolding within itself (as, for example, in Romanticism). A carnival sense of the world helps Dostoevsky overcome gnoseological as well as ethical solipsism. A single person, remaining alone with himself, cannot make ends meet even in the deepest and most intimate spheres of his own spiritual life, he cannot manage without *another* consciousness. One person can never find complete fullness in himself alone.

Carnivalization, in addition, makes it possible to extend the narrow scene of a personal life in one specific limited epoch to a maximally universal *mystery play scene*, applicable to all humanity. Dostoevsky strove for this in his later novels, especially in *The Brothers Karamazov*.

In *The Possessed*, Shatov tells Stavrogin before the beginning of their heart-to-heart conversation:

> . . . we are two *beings*, and have come together *in infinity* . . . for the *last time in the world*. Drop your tone, and speak like a *human being*! Speak, if only for once in your life, with the voice of a man. [SS VII, 260-61; *The Possessed*, Part Two, ch. 1]

All *decisive* encounters of man with man, consciousness with consciousness, always take place in Dostoevsky's novels "in infinity" and "for the last time" (in the ultimate moments of crisis), that is, they take place in *carnival-mystery play* space and time.

The aim of our entire work has been to explore the inimitable uniqueness of Dostoevsky's poetics, "to show the Dostoevsky in Dostoevsky." But if such a *synchronic* task is properly resolved, then it should help us feel out and trace Dostoevsky's generic tradition back to its sources in antiquity. We have tried to do just that in the present chapter, although, to be sure, in a somewhat general and almost schematic form. We believe our diachronic analysis confirms the results of the synchronic one. Or more precisely, the results of both analyses mutually verify and confirm one another.

Having linked Dostoevsky with a specific tradition, it goes without saying that we have not in the slightest degree limited the profound originality and individual uniqueness of his work. Dostoevsky is the creator of *authentic polyphony*, which, of course, did not and could not have existed in the Socratic dialogue, the ancient Menippean satire, the medieval mystery play, in Shakespeare and Cervantes, Voltaire and Diderot, Balzac and Hugo. But polyphony was prepared for in a *fundamental* way by this line of development in European literature. This entire tradition, beginning with the Socratic dialogue and the menippea, was reborn and renewed in Dostoevsky in the uniquely original and innovative form of the polyphonic novel.

NOTES

1. Leonid Grossman, *Poetika Dostoevskogo* [The Poetics of Dostoevsky] (Moscow: GAKhN, 1925), pp. 53, 56-57.

2. Ibid., pp. 61, 62.

3. His satires have not survived, but their titles are mentioned by Diogenes Laertius.

4. The phenomenon of reduced laughter is of considerable importance in world literature. Reduced laughter is denied direct expression, which is to say "it does not ring out," but traces of it remain in the structure of an image or a discourse and can be detected in it. Paraphrasing Gogol, one can speak of "laughter invisible to the world." We shall meet it in the works of Dostoevsky.

5. In *Eumenides* (fragments) Varro portrays as insanity such passions as ambition, acquisitiveness, and so on.

6. Two lives—the official and the carnivalistic—also existed in the ancient world, but there was never such a sharp break between them (especially in Greece).

7. My work *Rabelais and the Folk Culture of the Middle Ages and the Renaissance* (1940), at the present time [1963] being prepared for publication, is devoted to the carnivalistic folk culture of the Middle Ages and the Renaissance. It provides a special bibliography on the question. [Bakhtin's book on Rabelais, submitted as a doctoral dissertation in 1940, was not published until 1965. It exists in English as Mikhail Bakhtin, *Rabelais and His World*, trans. Hélène Iswolsky (Cambridge, MA: MIT Press, 1968).]

8. Dostoevsky was very familiar not only with canonical Christian literature, but with the apocrypha as well.

9. Mention must be made here of the enormous influence exerted by the novella "The Widow of Ephesus" (from the *Satyricon*) on the Middle Ages and the Renaissance. This inserted novella is one of the greatest menippea of antiquity. [See Bakhtin's extensive analysis in "Forms of Time and Chronotope in the Novel," *The Dialogic Imagination*, pp. 221-24.]

10. The application of such terms as "epic," "tragedy," "idyll" to modern literature has become generally accepted and customary, and we are not in the least confused when *War and Peace* is called an epic, *Boris Godunov* a tragedy, "Old-World Landowners" an idyll. But the generic term "menippea" is not customary (especially in our literary scholarship), and therefore its application to works of modern literature (Dostoevsky, for example), may seem somewhat strange and strained.

11. In *Diary of a Writer* he appears again in "A Certain Person's Half-letter." [See *The Diary of a Writer*, 1873, pp. 65-74.]

12. In the eighteenth century, *Dialogues of the Dead* were written by Sumarokov and even by A. V. Suvorov, the future Field Commander (see his *Razgovor v tsarstve mertvykh mezhdu Aleksandrom Makedonskim i Gerostratom* [A Conversation in the Kingdom of the Dead Between Alexander the Great and Herostratus], 1755).

13. It is true that juxtapositions of this sort cannot decisively prove anything. All these similar elements could have been engendered by the logic of the genre itself, particularly by the logic of carnivalistic decrownings, debasings, and mésalliances.

14. The possibility cannot be discounted, although it is doubtful, that Dostoevsky was familiar with the satires of Varro. A complete scholarly edition of Varro's fragments was published in 1965 (Riese, *Varronis Saturarum Menippearum relinquiae*, Leipzig, 1865). The book aroused interest beyond the narrow philological circles, and Dostoevsky might have gained a secondhand acquaintance of it during his stay abroad, or perhaps through his Russian philologist friends.

15. *PS* XIII, 523. [The note was published in Dostoevsky's journal *Vremia* (Time) in January, 1861, as an editor's foreword to a Russian translation of three Poe stories ("The Black Cat," "The Tell-tale Heart," "The Devil in the Belfry"). Contrasting Poe and Hoffmann, Dostoevsky distinguishes between two types of fantasticality: the direct reproduction of the otherworldly realm, and—more his own practice—an indirect, external and "materialized" form of fantasticality that functions as a literary device, and as a principle for structuring the plot or image. The Russian text can be found in *F. M. Dostoevskii ob iskusstve* (Moscow: Iskusstvo, 1973), pp. 114-17.]

16. General Pervoedov ["he who eats first"] even in the grave could not renounce the consciousness of his general's dignity, and in the name of that dignity he categorically protests against Klinevich's proposal ("to cease to be ashamed"), announcing, "I have served my monarch." In *The Possessed* there is an analogous situation, but on the real-life earthly plane: General Drozdov, finding himself among nihilists, for whom the very word "general" is a word of abuse, defends his dignity as a general with the very same words. Both episodes are handled in a comic way.

17. Even from such well-meaning and competent contemporaries as A. N. Maikov.*

18. "And suddenly I called out, not with my voice for I could not move, but with the whole of my being, to the master of all that was befalling me" [*SS* X, 428].

19. On the generic and thematic sources of the "Legend of the Grand Inquisitor" (*Histoire de Jenni, ou L'Athée et le Sage* of Voltaire, Victor Hugo's *Le Christe au Vatican*), see the works of L. P. Grossman.

20. Gogol was still subject to the direct and vital influence of Ukrainian carnivalistic folklore.

21. Grimmelshausen is already beyond the limits of the Renaissance, but his work reflects the deep and direct influence of carnival no less than does the work of Shakespeare and Cervantes.

22. It cannot be denied, of course, that a certain degree of special fascination is inherent in all contemporary forms of carnivalistic life. It is enough to name *Hemingway*, whose work, on the whole deeply carnivalized, was strongly influenced by contemporary forms and festivals of a carnival type (especially the bullfight). He had a very keen ear for everything carnivalistic in contemporary life.

23. *PS* XIII, pp. 158-59. ["Petersburg Dreams in Verse and Prose" was published as a feuilleton in Dostoevsky's journal *Vremia (Time)* in 1861.]

24. Here the model for Dostoevsky was Gogol, namely the ambivalent tone of "The Story about how Ivan Ivanovich Quarreled with Ivan Nikiforovich."

25. During this period Dostoevsky was working on a large comic epic, of which "Uncle's Dream" is an episode (according to his own statement in a letter). As far as we know, Dostoevsky never subsequently returned to a plan for a large, purely comic work.

26. Thomas Mann's novel *Doktor Faustus*, which reflects the powerful influence of Dostoevsky, is also thoroughly permeated with reduced ambivalent laughter, sometimes

breaking through to the surface, especially in the narrator Zeitblom's story. Thomas Mann himself, in his history of the creation of the novel, writes of it this way: "Therefore I must introduce as much jesting, as much ridicule of the biographer, as much *anti-self-important mockery as possible* — as much of that as was humanly possible!" (T. Mann, "Istoriia *Doktora Faustusa.* Roman odnogo romana," *Sobranie sochinenii* [The History of Doktor Faustus. The Novel of a Novel, Collected Works] [Moscow: Golitizdat, 1960], vol. 9, p. 224). Reduced laughter, primarily of the parodic type, is in general characteristic of all of Mann's work. In comparing his style with that of Bruno Frank, Mann makes a very characteristic admission: "He [that is, B. Frank—M. B.] uses the humanistic narrative style of Zeitblom with *complete seriousness* as his own: In *matters of style I really no longer admit anything but parody"* (ibid., p. 235). It should be pointed out that Thomas Mann's work is profoundly carnivalized. Carnivalization occurs in most vivid external form in Mann's novel *Die Bekentnisse des Hochstaplers Felix Krull* (where Professor Kuckuck becomes the mouthpiece for a sort of philosophy of carnival and carnival ambivalence). [See, in English, Mann's discussion of Zeitblom as narrator in Thomas Mann, *The Story of a Novel: The Genesis of Doctor Faustus,* trans. Richard and Clara Winston (New York: Knopf, 1961). The passages Bakhtin cites occur on p. 38 and 54.]

27. A carnivalized sense of Petersburg first appears in Dostoevsky in his novella *A Faint Heart* (1847), and was later powerfully developed, in ways applicable to all of Dostoevsky's early works, in "Petersburg Visions in Verse and Prose."

28. Pis'ma, I, 333-34 [Dostoevsky to N. N. Strakhov, from Rome, 18/30 September 1863].

29. In penal servitude too, people of various positions find themselves in familiar contact who under conditions of normal life would not have been able to meet on equal terms on a single plane.

30. For example, the beggar prince, who in the morning had nowhere to lay his head, becomes by the end of the day a millionaire.

31. In the novel *The Possessed*, for example, all life that is penetrated by devils is portrayed as a carnival nether world. The entire novel is thoroughly permeated by the theme of crowning-decrowning and pretendership (for example, Stavrogin's decrowning by the lame woman and Pyotr Verkhovensky's idea to crown him "Ivan the Tsarevich"). For an analysis of external carnivalization, *The Possessed* offers very rewarding material. *The Brothers Karamazov* is also very rich in external carnival accessories.

32. In his conversation with the devil, Ivan Karamazov asks him:

"Fool! did you ever tempt those holy men who ate locusts and prayed seventeen years in the wilderness till they were overgrown with moss?"

"My dear fellow, I've done nothing else. One forgets the whole world and all the worlds, and sticks to one such saint, because he is a very precious diamond. *One such soul, you know, is sometimes worth a whole constellation. We have our arithmetic, you know.* The conquest is precious! And some of them, on my word, are not inferior to you in culture, though you won't believe it. *They can contemplate such depths of belief and disbelief at the same moment* that sometimes it really seems that they are within a hairsbreadth of being 'turned upside down,' as the actor Gorbunov says." [*SS* X, 174; *The Brothers Karamazov,* Book Eleven, ch. IX]

It should be noted that Ivan's conversation with the devil is full of images of cosmic space and time: "quadrillions of kilometers" and "billions of years," "whole constellations," etc. All these cosmic magnitudes are mixed together here with elements of the most immediate present-day reality ("the actor Gorbunov") and with details of local setting and everyday life — all that is organically combined under the conditions of carnival time.

Chapter Five
Discourse in Dostoevsky

i. Types of Prose Discourse. Discourse in Dostoevsky

A few preliminary remarks on methodology.

We have entitled our chapter "*Discourse* in Dostoevsky," for we have in mind *discourse*, that is, language in its concrete living totality, and not language as the specific object of linguistics, something arrived at through a completely legitimate and necessary abstraction from various aspects of the concrete life of the word. But precisely those aspects in the life of the word that linguistics makes abstract are, for our purposes, of primary importance. Therefore the analyses that follow are not linguistic in the strict sense of the term. They belong rather to metalinguistics, if we understand by that term the study of those aspects in the life of the word, not yet shaped into separate and specific disciplines, that exceed—and completely legitimately— the boundaries of linguistics. Of course, metalinguistic research cannot ignore linguistics and must make use of its results. Linguistics and metalinguistics study one and the same concrete, highly complex, and multi-faceted phenomenon, namely, the word—but they study it from various sides and various points of view. They must complement one another, but they must not be confused. In practice, the boundaries between them are very often violated.

From the vantage points provided by *pure* linguistics, it is impossible to detect in belletristic literature any really essential differences between a monologic and a polyphonic use of discourse. In Dostoevsky's multi-voiced novels, for example, there is significantly less language differentiation, that is, fewer language styles, territorial and social dialects, professional jargons and so forth, than in the work of many writer-monologists—Leo Tolstoy, Pisemsky,* Leskov and others. It might even seem that the heroes of Dostoevsky's novels all speak one and the same language, namely the language of their author. For this monotony of language many reproached Dostoevsky, including Leo Tolstoy.

But the fact is that language differentiation and the clear-cut "speech characterizations" of characters have the greatest artistic significance precisely in the creation of objectified and finalized images of people. The more objectified a character, the more sharply his speech physiognomy stands out. To be sure, language diversity and speech characterizations remain important in a polyphonic novel, but this importance is diminished, and most important, the artistic functions of these phenomena change. For what matters here is not the mere presence of specific language styles, social dialects, and so forth, a presence established by purely linguistic criteria; what matters is the *dialogic angle* at which these styles and dialects are juxtaposed or counterposed in the work. Yet this dialogic angle is precisely what cannot be measured by purely linguistic criteria, because dialogic relationships, although belonging to the realm of the *word*, do not belong to the realm of its purely linguistic study.

Dialogic relationships (including the dialogic relationships of a speaker to his own discourse) are the subject of metalinguistics. And it is precisely these relationships, determining the characteristic features of verbal structure in Dostoevsky's work, that interest us here.

In language as the object of linguistics, there are not and cannot be any dialogic relationships: they are impossible both among elements in a system of language (for example, among words in a dictionary, among morphemes, and so forth), and among elements of a "text" when approached in a strictly linguistic way. These sorts of relationships cannot exist among units on a single level, nor among units on various levels. Nor can they exist, of course, among syntactic units, among prepositions for example, when they are approached in a strictly linguistic way.

Nor can there be any dialogic relationships among texts when approached in a strictly linguistic way. Any purely linguistic juxtaposition and grouping of given texts must necessarily abstract itself from any dialogic relationships that might be possible among them as whole utterances.

Linguistics recognizes, of course, the compositional form of "dialogic speech" and studies its syntactic and lexical-semantic characteristics. But it studies these as purely linguistic phenomena, that is, on the level of language, and is utterly incapable of treating the specific nature of dialogic relationships between rejoinders in a dialogue. Thus, when studying "dialogic speech," linguistics must utilize the results of metalinguistics.

Dialogic relationships, therefore, are extralinguistic. But at the same time they must not be separated from the realm of *discourse*, that is, from language as a concrete integral phenomenon. Language lives only in the dialogic interaction of those who make use of it. Dialogic interaction is indeed the authentic sphere where language *lives*. The entire life of language, in any area of its use (in everyday life, in business, scholarship, art, and so forth), is permeated with dialogic relationships. But linguistics studies "language" itself and the logic specific to it in its capacity as a *common ground*, as that which *makes possible* dialogic interaction; consequently, linguistics distances itself from the actual dialogic relationships themselves. These relationships lie in the realm of discourse, for discourse is by its very nature dialogic; they must therefore be studied by metalinguistics, which exceeds the limits of linguistics and has its own independent subject matter and tasks.

Dialogic relationships are reducible neither to logical relationships nor to relationships oriented semantically toward their referential object, relationships *in and of themselves* devoid of any dialogic element. They must clothe themselves in discourse, become utterances, become the positions of various subjects expressed in discourse, in order that dialogic relationships might arise among them.

"Life is good." "Life is not good." We have before us two judgments, possessing specific logical form and specific content oriented semantically toward a referential object (philosophical judgments on the value of life). Between these two judgments there exists a specific logical relationship: one is the negation of the other. But between them there are not and cannot be any dialogic relationships; they do not argue with one another in any way (although they can provide the referential material and logical basis for argument). Both these judgments must be embodied, if a dialogic relationship is to arise between them and toward them. Thus, both these judgments can, as thesis and antithesis, be united in a single utterance of a single subject, expressing his unified dialectical position on a given question. In such a case no dialogic relationships arise. But if these two judgments are separated into two different utterances by two different subjects, then dialogic relationships do arise.

"Life is good." "Life is good." Here are two absolutely identical judgments, or in fact one singular judgment written (or pronounced) by us *twice*; but this "twice" refers only to its verbal embodiment and not to the judgment itself. We can, to be sure, speak here of the logical relationship of identity between two judgments. But if this judgment is expressed in two utterances by two different subjects, then dialogic relationships arise between them (agreement, affirmation).

Dialogic relationships are absolutely impossible without logical relationships or relationships oriented toward a referential object, but they are not reducible to them, and they have their own specific character.

As we have already said, logical and semantically referential relationships, in order to become dialogic, must be embodied, that is, they must enter another sphere of existence: they must become *discourse*, that is, an utterance, and receive an *author*, that is, a creator of the given utterance whose position it expresses.

Every utterance in this sense has its author, whom we hear in the very utterance as its creator. Of the real author, as he exists outside the utterance, we can know absolutely nothing at all. And the forms of this real authorship can be very diverse. A given work can be the product of a collective effort, it can be created by the successive efforts of generations, and so forth—but in all cases we hear in it a unified creative will, a definite position, to which it is possible to react dialogically. A dialogic reaction personifies every utterance to which it responds.

Dialogic relationships are possible not only among whole (relatively whole) utterances; a dialogic approach is possible toward any signifying part of an utterance, even toward an individual word, if that word is perceived not as the impersonal word of language but as a sign of someone else's semantic position, as the representative of another person's utterance; that is, if we hear in it someone else's voice. Thus dialogic relationships can permeate inside the utterance, even inside the individual word, as long as two voices collide within it dialogically (microdialogue, of which we spoke earlier).

On the other hand, dialogic relationships are also possible between language styles, social dialects, and so forth, insofar as they are perceived as semantic positions, as language worldviews of a sort, that is, as something no longer strictly within the realm of linguistic investigation.

Finally, dialogic relationships are also possible toward one's own utterance as a whole, toward its separate parts and toward an individual word within it, if we somehow detach ourselves from them, speak with an inner reservation, if we observe a certain distance from them, as if limiting our own authorship or dividing it in two.

In conclusion, we remind the reader that dialogic relationships in the broad sense are also possible among different intelligent phenomena, provided that these phenomena are expressed in some *semiotic* material. Dialogic relationships are possible, for example, among images belonging to different art forms. But such relationships already exceed the limits of metalinguistics.

The chief subject of our investigation, one could even say its chief hero, will be *double-voiced discourse,* which inevitably arises under conditions of dialogic interaction, that is, under conditions making possible an authentic life for the word. Linguistics does not recognize double-voiced discourse. But precisely it, in our opinion, must become one of the chief objects of study for metalinguistics.

This concludes our preliminary remarks on methodology. What we have in mind will become clear from our further concrete analyses.

There exists a group of artistic-speech phenomena that has long attracted the attention of both literary scholars and linguists. By their very nature these phenomena exceed the limits of linguistics; that is, they are metalinguistic. These phenomena are: stylization, parody, *skaz,* and dialogue (compositionally expressed dialogue, broken down into rejoinders).

All these phenomena, despite very real differences among them, share one common trait: discourse in them has a twofold direction—it is directed both toward the referential object of speech, as in ordinary discourse, and toward *another's discourse,* toward *someone else's speech.* If we do not recognize the existence of this second context of someone else's speech and begin to perceive stylization or parody in the same way ordinary speech is perceived, that is, as speech directed only at its referential object, then we will not grasp these phenomena in their essence: stylization will be taken for style, parody simply for a poor work of art.

This twofold directedness of discourse is less obvious in *skaz* and in dialogue (within the limits of a single rejoinder). *Skaz* may in fact sometimes have only a single direction—toward its referential object. A single rejoinder in a dialogue may also strive for direct and unmediated referential significance. But in the majority of cases both *skaz* and the rejoinder of a dialogue are oriented toward someone else's speech: *skaz* by stylizing that speech, the rejoinder by taking it into account, responding to it, anticipating it.

These phenomena are of far-reaching and fundamental significance. They require a completely new approach to speech, one that does not fit within the limits of ordinary stylistic and linguistic purview. For the usual approach treats discourse within the limits of a *single monologic context.* Discourse therefore is defined in relation to its referential object (the study of tropes, for example) or in relation to other discourses within the same context or the same speech (stylistics in the narrow sense). Lexicology, to be sure, does profess a somewhat different attitude toward discourse. The lexical nuance of a word, an archaism or regionalism for example, does point to some other context in which the given word *normally* functions (ancient literary texts, regional speech), but this other context is one of language and not of speech (in the strict sense); it is not someone else's utterance but impersonal language material and not organized into a concrete utterance. If, however, this lexical nuance is individualized to the slightest degree, that is, if it points to another's specific utterance from which a given word is borrowed or in whose spirit it is constructed, then we already have stylization, parody, or some analogous phenomenon. Thus lexicology too remains essentially within the limits of a single monologic context, and recognizes only the direct unmediated orientation of discourse toward its referential object, without taking into account anyone else's discourse or any second context.

The very fact of the existence of double-directed discourses, incorporating a relationship to someone else's utterance as an indispensable element, creates for us the necessity of providing a full and exhaustive classification of discourses from the vantage point of this new principle, a principle not taken into account by stylistics, lexicology, or semantics. It can be easily demonstrated that in addition to object-directed discourses, and discourses directed toward someone else's discourse, there is yet a third type. But even double-directed discourses (those taking into account someone else's word), which include such heterogeneous phenomena as stylization, parody, and dialogue, are in need of some differentiation. The fundamental varieties must be delineated (from the vantage point of this same principle). And then the question inevitably arises of the possibility and means for combining discourses belonging to various types within the limits of a single context. On this ground new stylistic problems arise, problems which up to now have scarcely been taken into account by stylistics. To understand the style of prose speech, precisely these problems are of paramount importance.[1]

Alongside direct and unmediated object-oriented discourse—naming, informing, expressing, representing—intended for equally unmediated, object-oriented understanding (the first type of discourse), we can also observe represented or objectified discourse (the second type). By far the most typical and widespread form of represented objectified discourse is the *direct speech of characters*. Such speech has direct referential meaning, but it does not lie in the same plane with the author's speech; it observes, as it were, a certain distance and perspective. Such speech is meant to be understood not only from the point of view of its own referential object, but is itself, as characteristic, typical, colorful discourse, a referential object toward which something is directed.

Whenever we have within the author's context the direct speech of, say, a certain character, we have within the limits of a single context two speech centers and two speech unities: the unity of the author's utterance and the unity of the character's utterance. But the second unity is not self-sufficient; it is subordinated to the first and incorporated into it as one of its components. The stylistic treatment of the two utterances differs. The hero's discourse is treated precisely as someone else's discourse, as discourse belonging to some specific characterological profile or type; that is, it is treated as an object of authorial understanding, and not from the point of view of its own referential intention. The author's discourse, on the contrary, is treated stylistically as discourse directed toward its own straightforward referential meaning. It must be adequate to its object (cognitive, poetic, or whatever). It must be expressive, forceful, significant, elegant, etc., from the vantage point of the direct referential task it fulfills—to signify, express, inform, represent something. And its stylistic treatment is oriented purely toward an understanding of the referent. Should authorial discourse be treated in such a way that it is felt to be characteristic or typical for a specific person, a specific social position, or a specific artistic manner, then we already have stylization: either ordinary literary stylization, or stylized *skaz*. Of these, already a *third* type, we shall speak later.

Direct referentially oriented discourse recognizes only itself and its object, to which it strives to be maximally adequate. If in the process it imitates someone or learns from someone, this does not change things in the slightest: that is merely the scaffolding, which is not incorporated into the architectural whole even though it is indispensable and taken into account by the builder. The act of imitating someone else's discourse and the presence of various influences from other people's words, while recognizably clear to the historian of literature and to any competent reader, do not enter into the project that discourse has set itself. If they do enter in, that is, if the discourse itself does contain a deliberate reference to someone else's words, then again we would have before us discourse of the third type, and not the first.

The stylistic treatment of objectified discourse, that is, of a character's discourse, is subject—as if to a higher and ultimate authority—to the stylistic tasks of the author's context. This fact gives rise to a number of stylistic problems connected with the introduction and organic incorporation of a character's direct speech into the author's context. Ultimate semantic authority, and consequently ultimate stylistic authority as well, resides in the direct speech of the author.

An ultimate semantic authority requiring purely referential understanding is, of course, present in every literary work, but it is not always represented by direct authorial discourse. The latter may be absent altogether, compositionally replaced by the discourse of a narrator, or, as in drama, there may be no compositional equivalent at all. In such instances the entire verbal material of the work belongs to the second or third type of discourse. Drama is almost always constructed out of represented, objectified discourses. In Pushkin's *Tales of Belkin*, for another example, the story (Belkin's words) is constructed out of discourses of the third type; the characters' words belong, of course, to the second type. The absence of direct object-oriented discourse is a common phenomenon. Ultimate semantic authority—the author's intention—is realized not in his direct discourse but with the help of other people's words, created and distributed specifically as the words of others.

The degree to which a character's represented discourse is objectified may vary. It is enough, for example, to compare the words of Tolstoy's Prince Andrei with those of Gogol's characters, for instance Akaky Akakievich. As the direct, referential impulse of a character's words is intensified and their objectification correspondingly decreased, the internal interrelationship between authorial speech and a character's speech begins to approach the interrelationship between two rejoinders in a dialogue. The perspectival relationship weakens, and they may come to occupy a single plane. To be sure, this is present only as a tendency, as a striving toward a limit which is never quite achieved.

The scholarly article—where various authors' utterances on a given question are cited, some for refutation and others for confirmation and supplementation—is one instance of a dialogic interrelationship among directly signifying discourses within the limits of a single context. The relationships of agreement/disagreement, affirmation/supplementation, question/answer, etc., are purely dialogic relationships, although not of course between words, sentences, or other elements of a single utterance, but between whole utterances. In dramatic dialogue or a dramaticized dialogue introduced into the author's context, these relationships link together represented, objectified utterances and therefore are themselves objectified. This is not a clash of two ultimate semantic authorities, but rather an objectified (plotted) clash of two represented positions, subordinated wholly to the higher, ultimate authority of the author. The monologic context, under these circumstances, is neither broken nor weakened.

The weakening or destruction of a monologic context occurs only when there is a coming together of two utterances equally and directly oriented toward a referential object. Two discourses equally and directly oriented toward a referential object within the limits of a single context cannot exist side by side without intersecting dialogically, regardless of whether they confirm, mutually supplement, or (conversely) contradict one another, or find themselves in some other dialogic relationship (that of question and answer, for example). Two equally weighted discourses on one and the same theme, once having come together, must inevitably orient themselves to one another. Two embodied meanings cannot lie side by side like two objects—they must come into inner contact; that is, they must enter into a semantic bond.

Unmediated, direct, fully signifying discourse is directed toward its referential object and constitutes the ultimate semantic authority within the limits of a given context. Objectified discourse is likewise directed exclusively toward its object, but is at the same time the object of someone else's intention, the author's. But this other intention does not penetrate inside the objectified discourse, it takes it as a whole and, without changing its meaning or tone, subordinates it to its own tasks. It does not invest it with another referential meaning. Discourse that has become an object is, as it were, itself unaware of the fact, like the person who goes about his business unaware that he is being watched; objectified discourse sounds as if it were direct single-voiced discourse. Discourses of both the first and second type have in fact only one voice each. These are *single-voiced discourses*.

But the author may also make use of someone else's discourse for his own purposes, by inserting a new semantic intention into a discourse which already has, and which retains, an intention of its own. Such a discourse, in keeping with its task, must be perceived as belonging to someone else. In one discourse, two semantic intentions appear, two voices. Parodying discourse is of this type, as are stylization and stylized *skaz*. Here we move on to the characteristics of the third type of discourse.

Stylization presupposes style; that is, it presupposes that the sum total of stylistic devices that it reproduces did at one time possess a direct and unmediated intentionality and expressed an ultimate semantic authority. Only discourses of the first type can be the object of stylization. Stylization forces another person's referential (artistically referential) intention to serve its own purposes, that is, its new intentions. The stylizer uses another's discourse precisely as other, and in so doing casts a slight shadow of objectification over it. To be sure, the discourse does not become an object. After all, what is important to the stylizer is the sum total of devices associated with the other's speech precisely as an expression of a particular point of view. He works with someone else's point of view. Therefore a certain shadow of objectification falls precisely on that very point of view, and consequently it becomes conditional. The objectified speech of a character is never conditional. A character always speaks in earnest. The author's attitude does not penetrate inside his speech—the author observes it from without.

Conditional discourse is always double-voiced discourse. Only that which was at one time unconditional, in earnest, can become conditional. The original direct and unconditional meaning now serves new purposes, which take possession of it from within and render it conditional. This is what distinguishes stylization from imitation. Imitation does not render a form conditional, for it takes the imitated material seriously, makes it its own, directly appropriates to itself someone else's discourse. What happens in that case is a complete merging of voices, and if we do hear another's voice, then it is certainly not one that had figured in to the imitator's plan.

Thus, while a clear-cut semantic boundary exists between stylization and imitation, historically there exists between them extremely subtle and sometimes imperceptible transitions. As the seriousness of a style is weakened in the hands of its epigone-imitators, its devices become more conventional, and imitation becomes semistylization. On the other hand, stylization may also become imitation, should the stylizer's enthusiasm for his model destroy the distance and weaken the deliberate sense of a reproduced style as *someone else's* style. For precisely distance had created the conventionality.

An analogous case to stylization is the narration of a narrator, when it functions as a compositional substitute for the author's word. A narrator's narration may be developed in forms of literary discourse (Belkin, or the narrator-chroniclers in Dostoevsky) or in forms of oral speech—*skaz* in the strict sense of the word. Here, too, someone else's verbal manner is utilized by the author as a point of view, as a position indispensable to him for carrying on the story. But the shadow of objectification falling on the narrator's discourse is much denser than in stylization, and the conventionality much weaker. Of course, the degree of both may vary greatly. But the narrator's discourse can never become purely objectified, even when he himself is one of the characters and takes upon himself only part of the narration. His importance to the author, after all, lies not only in his individual and typical manner of thinking, experiencing, and speaking, but above all in his manner of seeing and portraying: in this lies his direct function as a narrator replacing the author. Therefore the author's attitude, as in stylization, penetrates inside the narrator's discourse, rendering it to a greater or lesser degree conventional. The author does not display the narrator's discourse to us (as he does the objectified discourse of a hero), but utilizes it from within for his own purposes, forcing us to be acutely aware of the distance between him and this alien discourse.

An element of *skaz*, that is, an orientation toward oral speech, is necessarily inherent in any narrated story. The narrator, although he might write his story down and give it a certain literary polish, is nonetheless not a literary professional, he commands no specific style but only a socially and individually specific manner of storytelling, one that gravitates toward oral *skaz*. If he does command a specific literary style, a style reproduced by the author in the narrator's name, then we have before us a stylization and not a narrated story (stylization may in fact be introduced and motivated in various ways).

Both the narrated story and even pure *skaz* may lose all trace of conventionality and become direct authorial discourse, expressing without mediation the author's intention. This is almost always the case with *skaz* in Turgenev. When introducing a narrator, Turgenev in most instances makes no attempt to stylize *another person's* distinctly individual and social manner of storytelling. The story in "Andrei Kolosov," for example, is narrated by an intelligent and literary man of Turgenev's own circle. Thus would Turgenev himself have spoken, and spoken of the most serious matters in his own life. There is no orientation here toward a socially foreign *skaz* tone, nor toward a socially foreign manner of seeing and conveying what is seen. There is also no orientation toward any individually characteristic manner. Turgenev's *skaz* signifies autonomously; there is one voice in it and this voice directly expresses the intention of the author. We have here a simple compositional device. Narration in *First Love* is of a similar sort (presented by the narrator in written form.)[2]

The same cannot be said of Belkin as a narrator: he is important to Pushkin as another person's voice, first and foremost as a socially defined person with a corresponding spiritual level and approach to the world, but also as an individually characteristic image. What happens in the *Tales of Belkin*, consequently, is a refraction of the author's intention through the words of a narrator; discourse here is double-voiced.

The problem of *skaz* was first brought to the fore in our scholarship by Boris Eikhenbaum.[3] He perceives *skaz* as an *orientation toward the oral form of narration*, an orientation toward oral speech and its corresponding language characteristics (oral intonation, the syntactic construction of oral speech, the corresponding lexicon, etc.). He completely fails to take into account the fact that in the majority of cases *skaz* is above all an orientation toward *someone else's speech*, and only then, as a consequence, toward oral speech.

For a proper treatment of the historico-literary problem of *skaz*, we believe that the understanding of *skaz* offered by us here is much more to the point. It seems to us that in most cases *skaz* is introduced precisely for the sake of *someone else's voice*, a voice socially distinct, carrying with it precisely those points of view and evaluations necessary to the author. What is introduced here, in fact, is a storyteller, and a storyteller, after all, is not a literary person; he belongs in most cases to the lower social strata, to the common people (precisely this is important to the author)—and he brings with him oral speech.

Direct authorial discourse is not possible in every epoch, nor can every epoch command a style—for style presupposes the presence of authoritative points of view and authoritative, stabilized ideological value judgments. Such epochs can either go the route of stylization, or can resort to extraliterary forms of narration that possess a specific manner of seeing and portraying the world. Where there is no adequate form for the unmediated expression of an author's thoughts, he must resort to refracting them in someone else's discourse. Sometimes the artistic tasks themselves are such that they can be realized only by means of double-voiced discourse (as we shall see, such exactly was the case with Dostoevsky).

Leskov, we believe, resorted to a narrator largely for the sake of a socially foreign discourse and socially foreign worldview, and only secondarily for the sake of oral *skaz* (since he was interested in the discourse of the common people). Turgenev, on the contrary, sought in a narrator precisely the oral form of narration, but for a *direct* expression of his own intentions. Characteristic for him, in fact, is an orientation toward oral speech but not toward another person's discourse. To refract his own thoughts in another's discourse was something Turgenev did not like to do, and did not know how to do. Double-voiced discourse did not turn out well in his work (consider the satiric and parodying passages in *Smoke*). For that reason he chose narrators from his own social circle. Such narrators inevitably had to speak a literary language, since they could not reliably sustain oral *skaz*. For Turgenev it was important only to enliven his literary speech with oral intonations.

This is not the place to document all the historico-literary claims we have made above. Let them remain assumptions. But on one point we do insist: a strict distinction in *skaz* between an orientation toward another person's discourse and an orientation toward oral speech is absolutely indispensable. To see in *skaz* only oral speech is to miss the main point. What is more, a whole series of intonational, syntactic, and other *language* phenomena in *skaz* (when the author is oriented toward another person's speech) can be explained precisely by its double-voicedness, by the intersection within it of two voices and two accents. We will be persuaded of this in our analysis of narration in Dostoevsky. There are no similar phenomena, for example, in Turgenev, although his narrators tend more strongly toward precisely oral speech than do Dostoevsky's narrators.

Analogous to narrator's narration is the *Ich-Erzählung* form (narration from the first person): sometimes it is defined by its orientation toward another's discourse, and sometimes, as with narration in Turgenev, it can approach and ultimately fuse with direct authorial discourse, that is, operate alongside single-voiced discourse of the first type.

One must keep in mind that compositional forms in and of themselves do not yet resolve the question of discourse type. Such definitions as *Ich-Erzählung*, narrator's narration, author's narration, and so forth are purely compositional definitions. These compositional forms do gravitate, to be sure, toward specific types of discourse, but they are not obligatorily connected with them.

All instances of the third type of discourse so far discussed — stylization, narrated story, *Ich-Erzählung* — share one common feature, by virtue of which they constitute a special (the first) variety of the third type. That common feature is an intention on the part of the author to make use of someone else's discourse in the direction of its own particular aspirations. Stylization stylizes another's style in the direction of that style's own particular tasks. It merely renders those tasks conventional. Likewise a narrator's narration, refracting in itself the author's intention, does not swerve from its own straight path and is sustained in tones and intonations truly characteristic of it. The author's thought, once having penetrated someone else's discourse and made its home in it, does not collide with the other's thought, but rather follows after it in the same direction, merely making that direction conventional.

The situation is different with parody. Here, as in stylization, the author again speaks in someone else's discourse, but in contrast to stylization parody introduces into that discourse a semantic intention that is directly opposed to the original one. The second voice, once having made its home in the other's discourse, clashes hostilely with its primordial host and forces him to serve directly opposing aims. Discourse becomes an arena of battle between two voices. In parody, therefore, there cannot be that fusion of voices possible in stylization or in the narration of a narrator (as in Turgenev, for example); the voices are not only isolated from one another, separated by a distance, but are also hostilely opposed. Thus in parody the deliberate palpability of the other's discourse must be particularly sharp and clearly marked. Likewise, the author's intentions must be more individualized and filled with specific content. The other's style can be parodied in various directions and may have new accents introduced into it, but it can be stylized essentially only in one direction—in the direction of its own particular task.

Parodistic discourse can be extremely diverse. One can parody another person's style as a style; one can parody another's socially typical or individually characterological manner of seeing, thinking, and speaking. The depth of the parody may also vary: one can parody merely superficial verbal forms, but one can also parody the very deepest principles governing another's discourse. Moreover, parodistic discourse itself may be used in various ways by the author: the parody may be an end in itself (for example, literary parody as a genre), but it may also serve to further other positive goals (Ariosto's* parodic style, for example, or Pushkin's). But in all possible varieties of parodistic discourse the relationship between the author's and the other person's aspirations remains the same: these aspirations pull in different directions, in contrast to the unidirectional aspirations of stylization, narrated story, and analogous forms.

Thus a very fundamental distinction must be drawn between parodistic *skaz* and simple *skaz*. The battle between two voices in parodistic *skaz* gives rise to those very specific language phenomena mentioned by us above. To ignore in *skaz* its orientation toward someone else's discourse and, consequently, its double-voicedness, is to be denied any understanding of those complex interrelationships into which voices, once they have become vari-directional, may enter within the limits of *skaz* discourse. Inherent in most cases of contemporary *skaz* is a slight parodic overtone. In Dostoevsky's stories, as we shall see, parodistic elements of a special type are always present.

Analogous to parodistic discourse is ironic, or any other double-voiced, use of someone else's words; in those instances too another's discourse is used for conveying aspirations that are hostile to it. In the ordinary speech of our everyday life such a use of another's words is extremely widespread, especially in dialogue, where one speaker very often literally repeats the statement of the other speaker, investing it with new value and accenting it in his own way—with expressions of doubt, indignation, irony, mockery, ridicule, and the like.

In his book on the characteristic features of conversational Italian, Leo Spitzer says the following:

When we reproduce in our own speech a portion of our partner's utterance, then by virtue of the very change in speakers a change in tone inevitably occurs: *the words of "the other person" always sound on our lips like something alien to us, and often have an intonation of ridicule, exaggeration, or mockery.*

I should like to point out here the facetious or sharply ironic repetition of the partner's question-verb in the subsequent reply. Here we will observe that one can employ not only grammatically correct constructions but also constructions that are very bold, even impossible, for the sake of repeating somehow a portion of our partner's speech and giving it an ironic flavor.[4]

Someone else's words introduced into our own speech inevitably assume a new (our own) interpretation and become subject to our evaluation of them; that is, they become double-voiced. All that can vary is the interrelationship between these two voices. The transmission of someone else's statement in the form of a question already leads to a clash of two intentions within a single discourse: for in so doing we not only ask a question, but make someone else's statement problematical. Our practical everyday speech is full of other people's words: with some of them we completely merge our own voice, forgetting whose they are; others, which we take as authoritative, we use to reinforce our own words; still others, finally, we populate with our own aspirations, alien or hostile to them.

Let us proceed to the first variety of the third type. In both stylization and parody, that is, in both of the preceding varieties of the third type, the author makes use precisely of other people's words for the expression of his own particular intentions. In the third variety, the other person's discourse remains outside the limits of the author's speech, but the author's speech takes it into account and refers to it. Another's discourse in this case is not reproduced with a new intention, but it acts upon, influences, and in one way or another determines the author's discourse, while itself remaining outside it. Such is the nature of discourse in the hidden polemic, and in most cases in the rejoinder of a dialogue as well.

In a hidden polemic the author's discourse is directed toward its own referential object, as is any other discourse, but at the same time every statement about the object is constructed in such a way that, apart from its referential meaning, a polemical blow is struck at the other's discourse on the same theme, at the other's statement about the same object. A word, directed toward its referential object, clashes with another's word within the very object itself. The other's discourse is not itself reproduced, it is merely implied, but the entire structure of speech would be completely different if there were not this reaction to another person's implied words. In stylization the actual reproduced model—someone else's style—also remains outside the author's context and is only implied. Likewise in parody the specific actual parodied discourse is only implied. But in these instances authorial discourse itself either poses as someone else's, or claims someone else's discourse as its own. In any case it works directly with the other's words, while the implied model (the other person's actual discourse) merely provides the material; it functions as a document confirming the fact that the author is indeed reproducing another person's specific discourse. In a hidden polemic, on the other hand, the other's words are treated antagonistically, and this antagonism, no less than the very topic being discussed, is what determines the author's discourse. This radically changes the semantics of the discourse involved: alongside its referential meaning there appears a second meaning—an intentional orientation toward someone else's words. Such discourse cannot be fundamentally or fully understood if one takes into consideration only its direct referential meaning. The polemical coloration of the discourse appears in other purely language features as well: in intonation and syntactic construction.

To draw a clear-cut boundary between hidden and obvious open polemic in any concrete instance sometimes proves quite difficult. But the semantic distinctions here are very fundamental. Overt polemic is quite simply directed at another's discourse, which it refutes, as if at its own referential object. In the hidden polemic, however, discourse is directed toward an ordinary referential object, naming it, portraying, expressing, and only indirectly striking a blow at the other's discourse, clashing with it, as it were, within the object itself. As a result, the other person's discourse begins to influence authorial discourse from within. For this reason, hidden polemical discourse is double-voiced, although the interrelationship of the two voices here is a special one. The other's thought does not personally make its way inside the discourse, but is only reflected in it, determining its tone and its meaning. One word acutely senses alongside it someone else's word speaking about the same object, and this awareness determines its structure.

Internally polemical discourse—the word with a sideward glance at someone else's hostile word—is extremely widespread in practical everyday speech as well as in literary speech, and has enormous style-shaping significance. Here belong, in everyday speech, all words that "make digs at others" and all "barbed" words. But here also belongs all self-deprecating overblown speech that repudiates itself in advance, speech with a thousand reservations, concessions, loopholes and the like. Such speech literally cringes in the presence or the anticipation of someone else's word, reply, objection. The individual manner in which a person structures his own speech is determined to a significant degree by his peculiar awareness of another's words, and by his means for reacting to them.

In literary speech the significance of the hidden polemic is enormous. In every style, strictly speaking, there is an element of internal polemic, the difference being merely one of degree and character. Every literary discourse more or less sharply senses its own listener, reader, critic, and reflects in itself their anticipated objections, evaluations, points of view. In addition, literary discourse senses alongside itself another literary discourse, another style. An element of so-called reaction to the preceding literary style, present in every new style, is an example of that same internal polemic; it is, so to speak, a hidden anti-stylization of someone else's style, often combining with a clear parodying of that style. The style-shaping significance of internal polemic is extremely great in autobiographies and in *Ich-Erzählung* forms of the confessional type. It is enough to mention Rousseau's *Confessions.*

Analogous to the hidden polemic is a rejoinder from any real and profound dialogue. Every word of that rejoinder, directed toward its referential object, is at the same time reacting intensely to someone else's word, answering it and anticipating it. An element of response and anticipation penetrates deeply inside intensely dialogic discourse. Such a discourse draws in, as it were, sucks in to itself the other's replies, intensely reworking them. The semantics of dialogic discourse are of an utterly special sort. (The extremely subtle changes in meaning that occur in the presence of intense dialogicality have unfortunately not yet been studied.) Taking the counterstatement (*Gegenrede*) into account produces specific changes in the structure of dialogic discourse, making it the inner scene for an event and illuminating the very object of discourse in a new way, uncovering in it new sides inaccessible to monologic discourse.

Especially significant and important for our further purposes is the phenomenon of hidden dialogicality, a phenomenon quite different from hidden polemic. Imagine a dialogue of two persons in which the statements of the second speaker are omitted, but in such a way that the general sense is not at all violated. The second speaker is present invisibly, his words are not there, but deep traces left by these words have a determining influence on all the present and visible words of the first speaker. We sense that this is a conversation, although only one person is speaking, and it is a conversation of the most intense kind, for each present, uttered word responds and reacts with its every fiber to the invisible speaker, points to something outside itself, beyond its own limits, to the unspoken words of another person. We shall see below that in Dostoevsky this hidden dialogue occupies a very important place and is very profoundly and subtly developed.

This third variety, as we see, differs sharply from the preceding two varieties of the third type. This final variety might be called *active*, in contrast to the preceding *passive* varieties. And so it is: in stylization, in the narrated story and in parody the other person's discourse is a completely passive tool in the hands of the author wielding it. He takes, so to speak, someone else's meek and defenseless discourse and installs his own interpretation in it, forcing it to serve his own new purposes. In hidden polemic and in dialogue, on the contrary, the other's words actively influence the author's speech, forcing it to alter itself accordingly under their influence and initiative.

In all manifestations of the second variety of the third type, however, a heightening of activity on the part of the other person's discourse is also possible. When parody senses a fundamental resistance, a certain strength and depth to the parodied words of the other, the parody becomes complicated by tones of hidden polemic. Such parody already has a different sound to it. The parodied discourse rings out more actively, exerts a counterforce against the author's intentions. There takes place an internal dialogization of the parodistic discourse. Similar processes occur whenever the hidden polemic is coupled with a narrated story, and in general in all examples of the third type when there is a divergence in direction between the author's and the other person's aspirations.

To the extent that the objectification of another's discourse is decreased—objectification being, as we know, inherent to a certain extent in all discourses of the third type, and in unidirectional discourses (stylizations and unidirectional narration)—there tends to occur a merging of the author's and the other person's voice. The distance between the two is lost; stylization becomes style; the narrator is transformed into a mere compositional convention. In vari-directional discourse, on the other hand, a decrease in objectification and a corresponding heightening of activity on the part of the aspirations of the other discourse lead inevitably to an internal dialogization of discourse. In such discourse, the author's thought no longer oppressively dominates the other's thought, discourse loses its composure and confidence, becomes agitated, internally undecided and two-faced. Such discourse is not only double-voiced but also double-accented; it is difficult to speak it aloud, for loud and living intonation excessively monologizes discourse and cannot do justice to the other person's voice present in it.

This internal dialogization—connected with a decrease in objectification in vari-directional discourses of the third type—does not, of course, constitute a new variety of that type. It is only a tendency, inherent in every example of the type (given the condition of vari-directionality). At its outer limit this tendency leads to a disintegration of double-voiced discourse into two discourses, into two fully isolated independent voices. The other tendency, which is inherent in unidirectional discourses provided there is a decrease in the objectification of the other's discourse, leads at its outer limit to a complete fusion of voices, and consequently to single-voiced discourse of the first type. Between these two limits fluctuate all manifestations of the third type.

Of course we have far from exhausted all the possible examples of double-voiced discourse, or all the possible means of orienting toward another's discourse, processes that complicate the ordinary referential orientation of speech. It would be possible to create a more far-reaching and subtle classification with a greater number of varieties, perhaps even of types. But for our purposes the classification we have offered is sufficient.

We represent it schematically below.

The classification offered below is of course somewhat abstract in character. A concrete discourse may belong simultaneously to different varieties and even types. Moreover, interrelationships with another person's discourse in a concrete living context are of a dynamic and not a static character: the interrelationship of voices in discourse may change drastically, unidirectional words may turn into varidirectional ones, internal dialogization may become stronger or weaker, a passive type may be activized, and so forth.

I. Direct, unmediated discourse directed exclusively toward its referential object, as an expression of the speaker's ultimate semantic authority

II. Objectified discourse (discourse of a represented person)
 1. With a predominance of socio-typical determining factors
 2. With a predominance of individually characteristic determining factors

 } Various degrees of objectification.

III. Discourse with an orientation toward someone else's discourse (double-voiced discourse)

 1. Unidirectional double-voiced discourse:
    a. Stylization;
    b. Narrator's narration;
    c. Unobjectified discourse of a character who carries out (in part) the author's intentions;
    d. *Ich-Erzählung*

    } When objectification is reduced, these tend toward a fusion of voices, i.e., toward discourse of the first type.

 2. Vari-directional double-voiced discourse:
    a. Parody with all its nuances;
    b. Parodistic narration;
    c. Parodistic *Ich-Erzählung*;
    d. Discourse of a character who is parodically represented;
    e. Any transmission of someone else's words with a shift in accent

    } When objectification is reduced and the other's idea activated, these become internally dialogized and tend to disintegrate into two discourses (two voices) of the first type.

 3. The active type (reflected discourse of another)
    a. Hidden internal polemic;
    b. Polemically colored autobiography and confession;
    c. Any discourse with a sideward glance at someone else's word;
    d. A rejoinder of a dialogue;
    e. Hidden dialogue

    } The other discourse exerts influence from without; diverse forms of interrelationship with another's discourse are possible here, as well as various degrees of deforming influence exerted by one discourse on the other.

The plane of investigation proposed by us here, an investigation of discourse from the point of view of its relationship to someone else's discourse, has, we believe, exceptionally great significance for an understanding of artistic prose. Poetic speech in the narrow sense requires a uniformity of all discourses, their reduction to a common denominator, although that denominator can either be discourse of the first type, or can belong to certain weakened varieties of the other types. Of course, even in poetic speech works are possible that do not reduce their entire verbal material to a single common denominator, but in the nineteenth century such instances were rare and rather specific. To this group belong, for example, the "prosaic" lyric of Heine, Barbier,* some works of Nekrasov, and others (not until the twentieth century is there a drastic "prosification" of the lyric). The possibility of employing on the plane of a single work discourses of various types, with all their expressive capacities intact, without reducing them to a common denominator—this is one of the most fundamental characteristic features of prose. Herein lies the profound distinction between prose style and poetic style. But even in poetry a whole series of fundamental problems cannot be solved without some attention to the above-mentioned plane for investigating discourse, because different types of discourse in poetry require different stylistic treatments.

Contemporary stylistics, which ignores this plane of investigation, is in essence a stylistics based on the first type of discourse alone, that is, on the direct referentially oriented discourse of the author. Contemporary stylistics, whose roots go back to the poetics of classicism, has been unable to this day to free itself from the specific orientations and limitations of that poetics. The poetics of classicism are oriented toward direct referentially oriented discourse, slanted somewhat in favor of conventionalized stylized discourse. Semi-conventionalized, semi-stylized discourse sets the tone in classical poetics. And to this day stylistics is oriented toward this semi-conventionalized direct discourse, which has in fact been identified with poetic discourse as such. For classicism, only the word of language exists, "no one's word," a material word which is part of the poetic lexicon, and this word passes directly from the treasurehouse of poetic language into the monologic context of a given poetic utterance. Thus a stylistics nurtured on the soil of classicism recognizes only the life of a word in a single self-enclosed context. It ignores those changes that take place in a word during its passage from one concrete utterance to another, and while these utterances are in the process of orienting to one another. It recognizes only those changes that come about when a word is transferred from the system of language into a monologic poetic utterance. The life and functions of a word in the *style* of a concrete utterance are perceived against the background of its life and functions in *language*. The internally dialogic relationships between one word and the same word in someone else's context, on someone else's lips, are ignored. Within this framework stylistics has continued to operate up to the present time.

Romanticism brought with it direct, fully signifying discourse without any inclination toward conventionality. Characteristic for Romanticism is direct authorial discourse, expressive to the point of self-oblivion, which did not cool itself down by any refraction through someone else's verbal medium. Of considerable significance in romantic poetics were discourses of the second and even more of the final varieties of the third type,[5] but nevertheless direct expressive discourse, discourse of the first type taken to its extreme limits, dominated to such an extent that on romantic soil too no significant progress on this question was made. On this point the poetics of classicism was hardly disturbed at all. But it should be noted that contemporary stylistics is far from adequate even for Romanticism.

Prose, and especially the novel, is completely beyond the reach of such a stylistics. The latter can treat with some degree of success only certain small portions of prose literature, portions which are for prose insignificant and the least characteristic. For the prose artist the world is full of other people's words, among which he must orient himself and whose speech characteristics he must be able to perceive with a very keen ear. He must introduce them into the plane of his own discourse, but in such a way that this plane is not destroyed.[6] He works with a very rich verbal palette, and he works exceptionally well with it.

And we, when perceiving prose, orient ourselves very subtly among all the types and varieties of discourse analyzed above. Moreover, in real life as well we very keenly and subtly hear all these nuances in the speech of people surrounding us, and we ourselves work very skillfully with all these colors on the verbal palette. We very sensitively catch the smallest shift in intonation, the slightest interruption of voices in anything of importance to us in another person's practical everyday discourse. All those verbal sideward glances, reservations, loopholes, hints, thrusts do not slip past our ear, are not foreign to our own lips. All the more astonishing, then, that up to now all this has found no precise theoretical cognizance, nor the assessment it deserves!

Theoretically we analyze only the stylistic interrelationships of elements within the limits of a self-enclosed utterance, against the background of abstractly linguistic categories. Only such single-voiced phenomena as these are within the reach of that superficial linguistic stylistics which, until now, for all its linguistic merit, has been unable to do more in the realm of artistic creativity than to register the traces and residue of artistic tasks unknown to it on the verbal periphery of literary works. The authentic life of prose discourse cannot be fit within this framework. The framework is even too confining for poetry.[7]

Stylistics must be based not only, and even *not as much*, on linguistics as on *metalinguistics*, which studies the word not in a system of language and not in a "text" excised from dialogic interaction, but precisely within the sphere of dialogic interaction itself, that is, in that sphere where discourse lives an authentic life. For the word is not a material thing but rather the eternally mobile, eternally fickle medium of dialogic interaction. It never gravitates toward a single consciousness or a single voice. The life of the word is contained in its transfer from one mouth to another, from one context to another context, from one social collective to another, from one generation to another generation. In this process the word does not forget its own path and cannot completely free itself from the power of these concrete contexts into which it has entered.

When a member of a speaking collective comes upon a word, it is not as a neutral word of language, not as a word free from the aspirations and evaluations of others, uninhabited by others' voices. No, he receives the word from another's voice and filled with that other voice. The word enters his context from another context, permeated with the interpretations of others. His own thought finds the word already inhabited. Therefore the orientation of a word among words, the varying perception of another's word and the various means for reacting to it, are perhaps the most fundamental problems for the metalinguistic study of any kind of discourse, including the artistic. Every social trend in every epoch has its own special sense of discourse and its own range of discursive possibilities. By no means all historical situations permit the ultimate semantic authority of the creator to be expressed without mediation in direct, unrefracted, unconditional authorial discourse. When there is no access to one's own personal "ultimate" word, then every thought, feeling, experience must be refracted through the medium of someone else's discourse, someone else's style, someone else's manner, with which it cannot immediately be merged without reservation, without distance, without refraction.[8]

If there is at the disposal of a given epoch some authoritative and stabilized medium of refraction, then conventionalized discourse in one or another of its varieties will dominate, with a greater or lesser degree of conventionality. If there is no such medium, then varidirectional double-voiced discourse will dominate, that is, parodistic discourse in all its varieties, or a special type of semi-conventionalized, semi-ironic discourse (that of late classicism, for example). In such epochs, and especially in epochs dominated by conventionalized

refracted P

discourse, the direct, unconditional, unrefracted word appears barbaric, raw, wild. Cultured discourse is discourse refracted through an authoritative and stabilized medium.

What kind of discourse dominates during a given epoch in a given social trend, what forms exist for the refraction of discourse, what serves as the medium of refraction — all these questions are of paramount importance for the study of artistic discourse. Here, of course, we can only briefly and in passing make note of these problems, note them without documenting them, without elaborating them on the basis of concrete material — this is not the place for an examination of these problems in depth.

Let us return to Dostoevsky.

Dostoevsky's works astound us first of all by their extraordinary diversity of types and varieties of discourse, types and varieties, moreover, that are present in their most extreme expression. Clearly predominant is vari-directional double-voiced discourse, in particular internally dialogized discourse and the reflected discourse of another: hidden polemic, polemically colored confession, hidden dialogue. In Dostoevsky almost no word is without its intense sideward glance at someone else's word. At the same time there are almost no objectified words in Dostoevsky, since the speech of his characters is constructed in a way that deprives it of all objectification. What also astounds us is the continual and abrupt alternation of the most varied types of discourse. Sharp and unexpected transitions from parody to internal polemic, from polemic to hidden dialogue, from hidden dialogue to stylization in serene hagiographic tones, then back again to parodistic narration and finally to an extremely intense open dialogue — such is the agitated verbal surface of his works. All this is interwoven with the deliberately dull thread of informative documentary discourse, the ends and beginnings of which are difficult to catch; but even this dry documentary discourse registers the bright reflections or dense shadows of nearby utterances, and this gives it as well a peculiar and ambiguous tone.

What is important here, of course, is not only the diversity and abrupt shift of discursive types, nor the predominance among them of double-voiced, internally dialogized discourses. The uniqueness of Dostoevsky lies in his special distribution of these discursive types and varieties among the basic compositional elements of a given work.

How and in what aspects of the verbal whole is the author's ultimate semantic authority implemented? For the monologic novel, this question is very easily answered. Whatever discourse types are introduced by the author-monologist, whatever their compositional distribution, the author's intentions and evaluations must dominate over all the others and must form a compact and unambiguous whole. Any intensification of others' intonations in a certain discourse or a certain section of the work is only a game, which the author permits so that his own direct or refracted word might ring out all the more energetically. Every struggle between two voices within a single discourse for possession or dominance in that discourse is decided in advance, it only appears to be a struggle; all fully signifying authorial interpretations are sooner or later gathered together in a single speech center and a single consciousness; all accents are gathered together in a single voice.

The artistic task Dostoevsky takes on is completely different. He does not fear the most extreme activization of vari-directional accents in double-voiced discourse; on the contrary, such activization is precisely what he needs to achieve his purpose. A plurality of voices, after all, is not meant to be eliminated in his works but in fact is meant to triumph.

The stylistic significance of the *other person's discourse* in Dostoevsky's works is enormous. Here it lives an extremely intense life. The stylistic bonds most basic to Dostoevsky are not bonds between words on the level of a single monologic utterance—basic for him rather are dynamic, vibrantly intense bonds between utterances, between independent and autonomous speech and semantic centers, not subordinated to the verbal and semantic dictatorship of a monologic, unified style and a unified tone.

Discourse in Dostoevsky, its life in the work and its functions in the realization of the polyphonic project, shall be investigated by us here in connection with those compositional unities within which discourse functions: the unity of a character's monologic self-utterance, the unity of the story—narrator's narration or narration by the author—and, finally, the unity of the dialogue among characters. This also will be the sequence of our investigations.

ii. The Hero's Monologic Discourse and Narrational Discourse in Dostoevsky's Short Novels

Dostoevsky began with the *refracting word*—with the epistolary form. Apropos of *Poor Folk* he wrote his brother: "They [the public and the critics—M. B.] have grown used to seeing in everything the author's mug; I didn't show mine. And it doesn't even occur to them that Devushkin is speaking and not I, and that Devushkin cannot speak in any other way. They find the novel long-winded, but there is not a superfluous word in it."[9]

It is Makar Devushkin and Varenka Dobroselova who speak in the work, and the author merely distributes their words: his concepts and aspirations are refracted through the words of the hero and heroine. The epistolary form is a variety of *Ich-Erzählung*. Discourse here is double-voiced, and in most cases unidirectional. As such it functions as a compositional surrogate of the author's discourse, which is absent. We shall see that authorial understanding is very subtly and carefully refracted through the words of the hero-narrators, even though the entire work is filed with overt and hidden parodies, with overt and hidden (authorial) polemic.

But for now we are interested in Makar Devushkin's speech only as the monologic utterance of a character, and not as the speech of a narrator in an *Ich-Erzählung* — a function which it in fact fulfills (since, outside the characters, there are no other carriers of discourse here). For after all, the discourse of any narrator employed by the author to realize his artistic plan belongs in its own right to some specific discursive type, quite apart from the type determined by its function as narration. Of what type, then, is Devushkin's monologic utterance?

The epistolary form in and of itself does not predetermine the type of discourse. In general this form permits broad discursive possibilities, but it is best suited to discourse of the final variety of the third type, that is, the reflected discourse of another. A characteristic feature of the letter is an acute awareness of the interlocutor, the addressee to whom it is directed. The letter, like a rejoinder in a dialogue, is addressed to a specific person, and it takes into account the other's possible reactions, the other's possible reply. This reckoning with an absent interlocutor can be more or less intensive. In Dostoevsky it is extremely intense.

In his first work, Dostoevsky develops that speech style so characteristic of his entire creative art, a style defined by the intense anticipation of another's words. The significance of this style in his subsequent work is enormous: his heroes' most important confessional self-utterances are permeated with an intense sensitivity toward the anticipated words of others about them, and with others' reactions to their own words about themselves. Not only the tone and style but also the internal semantic structure of these self-utterances are defined by an anticipation of another person's words, from Golyadkin's tension-filled reservations and loopholes to the ethical and metaphysical loopholes of Ivan Karamazov. In *Poor Folk* Dostoevsky begins to work out the "degraded" variety of this style — discourse that cringes with a timid and ashamed sideward glance at the other's possible response, yet contains a muffled challenge.

This "sideward glance" manifests itself above all in two traits characteristic of the style: a certain halting quality to the speech, and its interruption by reservations.

I live in the kitchen, or rather, to be more accurate, there is a room near the kitchen (and our kitchen, I ought to tell you, is clean, light and very nice), a little room, a modest corner . . . or rather the kitchen is a big room of three windows so I have a partition running along the inside wall, so that it makes as it were another room, an extra lodging; it is roomy and comfortable, and there is a window and all—in fact, every convenience. Well, so that is my little corner. So don't you imagine, my darling, there is anything else about it, any mysterious significance in it; "here he is living in the kitchen!" Well, if you like, I really am living in the kitchen, behind the partition, but that is nothing. I am quite private, apart from everyone, quiet and snug. I have put in a bed, a table, a chest of drawers and a couple of chairs, and I have hung up the ikon. It is true there are better lodgings—perhaps there may be much better, but convenience is the great thing; I have arranged it all for my own convenience, you know, and you must not imagine it is for anything else. [*SS* I, 82; *Poor Folk*, Letter of April 8]

After almost every word Devushkin casts a sideward glance at his absent interlocutor: he is afraid she will think he is complaining, he tries in advance to destroy the impression that will be created by the news that he lives in the kitchen, he does not want to distress her, and so forth. The repetition of words results from his trying to intensify their accent or to give them a new nuance in light of his interlocutor's possible reaction.

In the above excerpt, the reflected discourse turns out to be the potential words of the addressee, Varenka Dobroselova. In most cases Makar Devushkin's speech about himself is determined by the reflected discourse of another, "other person," a stranger. Here is how he defines this stranger: "And what will you do out there among strangers?" he asks Varenka Dobroselova.

I expect you don't know yet what strangers are like . . . You had better ask me and I will tell you what strangers are like. I know them, my darling, I know them very well, I've had to eat their bread. They are spiteful, Varenka, spiteful; so spiteful that you would have no heart left, they would torment it so with reproach, upbraiding and ill looks. [*SS* I, 240; *Poor Folk*, Letter of July 1]

A poor man, but a man "with ambition"—such is Makar Devushkin according to Dostoevsky's concept; he constantly senses the "ill look" of this other upon him, a glance which is either reproachful or—perhaps even worse in his eyes—mocking (for heroes of the prouder type, the worst glance another could cast is a compassionate one). Under this other's glance even Devushkin's speech cringes. He, like the hero from the underground, is constantly eavesdropping on others' words about him. "The poor man is exacting; he takes a different view of God's world, and looks askance at every passer-by and turns a troubled gaze about him and looks to every word, wondering whether people are not talking about him . . ." [*SS* I, 153; *Poor Folk*, Letter of August 1].

This sideward glance at a socially alien discourse determines not only the style and tone of Makar Devushkin's speech, but also his very manner of thinking and experiencing, of seeing and understanding himself and the little world that surrounds him. Between the most superficial elements of a character's manner of speech, the form in which he expresses himself, and the ultimate foundations of his worldview Dostoevsky always creates a profound organic bond. A person is wholly present in his every gesture. And the orientation of one person to another person's discourse and consciousness is, in essence, the basic theme of all of Dostoevsky's works. The hero's attitude toward himself is inseparably bound up with his attitude toward another, and with the attitude of another toward him. His consciousness of self is constantly perceived against the background of the other's consciousness of him — "I for myself" against the background of "I for another." Thus the hero's words about himself are structured under the continuous influence of someone else's words about him.

This theme is developed in various works through various forms, filled with varying content and on various spiritual levels. In *Poor Folk*, the self-consciousness of a poor man unfolds against the background of a consciousness about him that is socially alien to him. His affirmation of self sounds like a continuous hidden polemic or hidden dialogue with some other person on the theme of himself. In Dostoevsky's early works this is still given rather simple and direct expression — dialogue has not yet gone within, not yet, so to speak, entered the very atoms of thought and experience. The heroes' world is still small, and the heroes are not yet ideologists. Even the very social degradation of the characters makes their internal sideward glance and internal polemic quite direct and clear-cut, without the highly complex internal loopholes that grow into whole ideological constructions in Dostoevsky's final works. But the profound dialogic and polemical nature of self-awareness and self-affirmation is already revealed here with the utmost clarity.

A day or two ago, in private conversation, Yevstafy Ivanovich said that the most important virtue in a citizen was to earn money. He said in jest (I know it was in jest) that morality consists in not being a burden to anyone. Well, I'm not a burden to anyone. My crust of bread is my own; it is true it is a plain crust of bread, at times a dry one; but there it is, earned by my toil and put to lawful and irreproachable use. Why, what can one do? I know very well, of course, that I don't do much by copying; but all the same I am proud of working and earning my bread in the sweat of my brow. Why, what if I am a copying clerk, after all? What harm is there in copying, after all? "He's a copying clerk," they say, but what is there discreditable in that? . . . So I see now that I am necessary, that I am indispensable, and that it's no use to worry a man with nonsense. Well, let me be a rat if you like, since they see a resemblance! But the rat is necessary, but

208 □ DISCOURSE IN DOSTOEVSKY

the rat is of service, but the rat is depended upon, but the rat is given a reward, so that's the sort of rat he is!

Enough about that subject though, my own! I did not intend to talk about that at all, but I got a little heated. Besides, it's pleasant from time to time to do oneself justice. [*SS* I, 125-26; *Poor Folk*, Letter of June 12]

In an even sharper polemic, Makar Devushkin's self-awareness is revealed when he recognizes himself in Gogol's "Overcoat"; he perceives the story as someone else's words about him personally, and he seeks to destroy those words polemically as something not adequate to him.

But let us now take a closer look at the very structure of this "word with a sideward glance."

In the first excerpt cited, where Devushkin is casting an anxious sideward glance at Varenka Dobroselova while he informs her of his new room, we already notice the peculiar interruptions in speech that determine its syntactic and accentual structure. The other's rejoinder wedges its way, as it were, into his speech, and although this rejoinder is in fact absent, its influence brings about a radical accentual and syntactic restructuring of that speech. The rejoinder is not actually present, but its shadow, its trace, falls on his speech, and that shadow, that trace is real. But sometimes the other's rejoinder, quite apart from its influence on the accentual and syntactic structure, leaves behind in Makar Devushkin's speech one or two of its own words, and sometimes a whole sentence: "So don't you imagine, my darling, there is anything else about it, any mysterious significance in it; 'here he is living in the *kitchen*!' Well, if you like, I really am living in the kitchen, behind the partition, but that is nothing . . ." The word "kitchen" bursts into Devushkin's speech from out of the other's potential speech, which Devushkin anticipates. This word is presented with the other's accent, which Devushkin somewhat exaggerates polemically. He does not accept this accent, although he cannot help recognizing its power, and he tries to evade it by all sorts of reservations, partial concessions and extenuations, all of which distort the structure of his speech. From this other discourse embedded in him, circles fan out, as it were, across the smooth surface of his speech, furrowing it. Apart from this obviously alien discourse with its obviously alien accent, the majority of words in the quoted passage are chosen by the speaker from two points of view simultaneously: as he himself understands them and wants others to understand them, and as another might actually understand them. Here the other's accent is only hinted at, but it already gives rise to a reservation or a hesitation in speech.

The embedding of words and especially of accents from the other's rejoinder in Makar Devushkin's speech is even more marked and obvious in the second of the quoted passages. The words containing the other's polemically exaggerated accent are even enclosed here in quotation marks: "He's a copying clerk . . ." In the preceding lines the word "copy" is repeated three times. In each of these three instances the other's potential accent is present in the word "copy," but it is suppressed by Devushkin's own accent; however, it becomes constantly stronger, until it finally breaks through and assumes the form of the other's direct speech. We are presented here, therefore, with gradations of gradual intensification in the other's accent: "I know very well, of course, that I don't do much by *copying* . . . [then follows a reservation—M. B.] Why, what if I am a *copying* clerk, after all? What harm is there in *copying*, after all? 'He's a *COPYING* clerk!' . . ." We have indicated by italics and underscoring the other's accent and its gradual intensification, which finally dominates utterly the line of discourse enclosed in quotation marks. But even in these final words, obviously belonging to the other, Devushkin's own voice is present too, for he polemically exaggerates the other's accent. As the other person's accent intensifies, so does Devushkin's counter-accent.

We can descriptively define all the above-mentioned phenomena in the following way: the hero's self-awareness was penetrated by someone else's consciousness of him, the hero's own self-utterance was injected with someone else's words about him; the other's consciousness and the other's words then give rise to specific phenomena that determine the thematic development of Devushkin's self-awareness, its breaking points, loopholes and protests on the one hand, and on the other the hero's speech with its accentual interruptions, syntactic breaking points, repetitions, reservations, and long-windedness.

We might offer this graphic definition and explanation of the same phenomena: let us imagine two rejoinders of the most intense dialogue—a discourse and a counter-discourse—which, instead of following one after the other and being uttered by two different mouths, are superimposed one on the other and merge into a *single* utterance issuing from a *single* mouth. These two rejoinders move in opposite directions and clash with one another; therefore their overlapping and merging into a single utterance results in a most intense mutual interruption. This collision of two rejoinders—each integral in itself and single-accented—is now transformed, in the new utterance resulting from their fusion, into the most acute interruption of voices, contradictory in every detail, in every atom of the utterance. The dialogic collision has gone within, into the subtlest structural elements of speech (and correspondingly, of consciousness).

The above-quoted passage could be approximately paraphrased in the following crude dialogue between Makar Devushkin and the "other person":

THE OTHER: One must know how to earn a lot of money. One shouldn't be a burden to anyone. But you are a burden to others.

MAKAR DEVUSHKIN: I'm not a burden to anyone. I've got my own piece of bread.

THE OTHER: But what a piece of bread it is! Today it's there, and tomorrow it's gone. And it's probably a dry one, at that!

MAKAR DEVUSHKIN: It is true it is a plain crust of bread, at times a dry one, but there it is, earned by my toil and put to lawful and irreproachable use.

THE OTHER: But what kind of toil! All you do is copy. You're not capable of anything else.

MAKAR DEVUSHKIN: Well, what can one do! I know very well, of course, that I don't do much by copying, but all the same I am proud of it.

THE OTHER: Oh, there's something to be proud of, all right! Copying! It's disgraceful!

MAKAR DEVUSHKIN: Well, in fact really, so what if I am just a copying clerk! . . . [etc.]

It is as if the overlapping and merging of these sides of dialogue into a single voice had resulted in Devushkin's self-utterance quoted above.

Of course this imagined dialogue is extremely primitive, just as the content of Devushkin's consciousness is still primitive. For this is ultimately still an Akaky Akakievich, enlightened by self-consciousness, who has acquired speech and is "elaborating a style." But then the formal structure of his self-consciousness and self-utterances is, because of its primitiveness and crudeness, extremely well-marked and clear. For this reason we are examining it in such detail. All the truly essential self-utterances of Dostoevsky's later heroes could also be turned into dialogues, since all of them arose, as it were, out of two merged rejoinders, but the interruption of voices in them goes so deep, into such subtle elements of thought and discourse, that to turn them into a visible and crude dialogue such as we have done with Devushkin's self-utterance is of course utterly impossible.

The phenomena which we have examined here, the result of a second and alien discourse functioning inside the consciousness and speech of the hero, are presented in *Poor Folk* in the stylistic garb of the speech of a petty Petersburg clerk. The structural characteristics we have noted—"the word with a sideward glance," discourse concealing a hidden polemic, internally dialogic discourse—are refracted

character's monologue

here in a strictly and skillfully sustained manner that is sociotypical of Devushkin's speech.[10] For this reason all these phenomena of language—reservations, repetitions, diminutives, the diversity of particles and interjections—would not be possible, in the form in which they occur here, in the mouths of other Dostoevskian heroes belonging to another social world. The same phenomena would appear in a different sociotypical and individually characteristic speech profile. But their essence remains the same: the crossing and intersection, in every element of consciousness and discourse, of two consciousnesses, two points of view, two evaluations—two voices interrupting one another intra-atomically.

In the same sociotypical speech environment, but in a different individually characteristic manner, Dostoevsky constructs the discourse of Golyadkin. In *The Double*, the characteristic trait of consciousness and speech that we examined above is expressed with a sharpness and clarity not found in any other work of Dostoevsky's. The tendencies already embedded in Makar Devushkin are developed here with extraordinary boldness and consistency, carried to their conceptual limits, on the basis of the same deliberately primitive, simple, and crude material.

We cite below the semantic structure and speech profile of Golyadkin's discourse in a parodic stylization done by Dostoevsky himself, in a letter written to his brother while working on *The Double*. As in any parodic stylization, there is an obvious and crude emphasis upon the basic characteristics and tendencies of Golyadkin's discourse.

> "**Yakov Petrovich Golyadkin** holds his own completely. He's a terrible scoundrel and there's no approaching him; he refuses to move forward, pretending that he's not ready yet, that for the present he's on his own, he's all right, nothing is the matter, but that if it comes to that, then he can do that too, why not, what's to prevent it? He's just like everyone else, he's nothing special, just like everyone else. What's it to him! A scoundrel, a terrible scoundrel! He'll never agree to end his career before the middle of November. He's just now spoken with his Excellency, and he just may (and why shouldn't he) be ready to announce his retirement."[11]

As we shall see, *The Double* itself is narrated in this same style, parodying the hero. But to that narration we shall return later.

The influence of another person's words on Golyadkin's speech is absolutely obvious. We immediately sense that his speech, like Devushkin's, gravitates neither toward itself nor toward its referential object. Golyadkin's interrelationships with another's speech and another's consciousness are, however, quite different from Devushkin's. And for this reason the traits in Golyadkin's style produced by the other's discourse are of a different sort.

Golyadkin's speech seeks, above all, to simulate total independence

from the other's words: "He's on his own, he's all right." This simulation of independence and indifference also leads to endless repetitions, reservations, and long-windedness, but here they are directed
not outward, not toward another, but toward Golyadkin's own self:
he persuades himself, reassures and comforts himself, plays the role
of another person vis-à-vis himself. Golyadkin's comforting dialogues
with himself are the most prominent trait of the whole story. Along
with a simulation of indifference, however, goes another attitude
toward the other's discourse: the desire to hide from it, to avoid at-
tracting attention to himself, to bury himself in the crowd, to go unnoticed: "After all he's just like everyone else, he's nothing special,
just like everyone else." But in this he is trying to convince not himself, but another. Finally, there is a third attitude toward the other's
discourse: concession, subordination to it, a submissive assimilation
of it, as if Golyadkin thought the same way himself and sincerely
agreed with it: "If it comes to that, then he can do that too, why not,
what's to prevent it?"

Such are Golyadkin's three general lines of orientation, and they
are complicated by other secondary but rather important ones. Each
of these three lines in itself gives rise to very complex phenomena in
Golyadkin's consciousness and discourse.

We shall concentrate primarily on his simulation of independence
and composure.

monologue

The pages of *The Double* are filled, as we have said, with the hero's
dialogues with himself. It could be said that Golyadkin's entire inner
life develops dialogically. We quote two examples of such dialogue:

"Will it be all right, though?" went on our hero, stepping out of his carriage at
the porch of a five-story house on Litciny Street, beside which he had ordered
the vehicle to stop; "will it be all right? Is it a proper thing to do? Will this be the
right time? However, does it really matter?" he continued as he mounted the
stairs, breathing hard and trying to control the beating of his heart, which always
seemed to beat hard on other people's stairs; "does it matter? I've come about
my own business, after all, and there's nothing reprehensible in that. . . . It
would be stupid to try to keep anything from him. So I'll just make it appear
that it's nothing special, I just happened to be driving past. . . . He will see
that's how it must have been." [*SS* I, p. 215; *The Double*, ch. i]

The second example of interior dialogue is considerably more
complex and pointed. Golyadkin conducts it after the appearance of
the double; that is, after the second voice has already become objectified for him within his own field of vision.

Thus Mr. Golyadkin's delighted mood expressed itself, but all the time something went on nagging away at the back of his mind, a kind of ache, which sometimes so drained his spirits that Mr. Golyadkin did not know where to turn for
consolation. "However, we'll wait a day, and then we can be happy. Still, what

does it amount to, after all? Well, we'll think about it, and we'll see. Well, let's think it over, my young friend, let's discuss it. Well, he's a man like you to begin with, exactly the same. Well, what of that? If that's what he is, ought I to weep over it? What's it got to do with me? I'm outside it; I just whistle, that's all! Let him work! Well, it's something strange and queer; just like the Siamese twins, as they call them. . . . Well, why them, the Siamese twins? — all right, they're twins, but even the very greatest people have seemed a bit queer sometimes. Why, even in history, it's well known the famous Suvorov crowed like a cock. . . . Well, but that was all for political reasons; and great generals . . . but why talk about generals? I go my own way, that's all, and I don't want to know anybody, and in my innocence I scorn my enemies. I am no intriguer, and I'm proud to say it. Honest, straightforward, orderly, agreeable, mild . . ." [SS I, pp. 268-69; The Double, ch. vi]

The first question that arises concerns the function of this dialogue with the self in Golyadkin's spiritual life. The question can be briefly answered thus: *the dialogue allows him to substitute his own voice for the voice of another person.*

This substituting function of Golyadkin's second voice is felt in everything. Without understanding it we cannot understand his interior dialogues. Golyadkin addresses himself as if addressing another person ("my young friend"), he praises himself as only another person could, and verbally caresses himself with tender familiarity: "Yakov Petrovich, my dear fellow, you little Golyadka you, what a nice little name you have!";[a] he reassures and encourages himself with the authoritative tone of an older, more self-confident person. But this second voice of Golyadkin's, confident and calmly self-satisfied, cannot possibly merge with his first voice, the uncertain timid one; the dialogue cannot be transformed into the integral and confident monologue of a single Golyadkin. Moreover, that second voice is to such a degree unable to merge with the first, it feels so threateningly independent, that in place of comforting and encouraging tones there begin to appear teasing, mocking, and treacherous ones. With astonishing tact and artistry Dostoevsky transfers — almost imperceptibly to the reader — Golyadkin's second voice from his interior dialogue to the narration itself: it begins to sound like an outside voice, the voice of the narrator. But of the narration we shall speak somewhat later.

Golyadkin's second voice must compensate for the inadequate recognition he receives from the other person. Golyadkin wants to get by without such recognition, wants to get by, so to speak, on his

---

[a]The name in Russian suggests *golyada*, "tramp" or "beggar," derived from the adjective *golyi*, "naked, bare." The Coulson translation incorrectly reflects the intonation here (ch. 4, p. 158) by rendering the line as "You . . . you — Golyadkin! (What a name!)." The tone is in fact the opposite: it is tender and protective, as Bakhtin points out, and as the narrator confirms in the subsequent sentence: "However, these flattering remarks addressed to himself at this moment did not mean anything . . ."

own. But this "on his own" inevitably takes the form of "you and I, my friend Golyadkin"; that is, it takes dialogic form. In actual fact Golyadkin lives only in another, lives by his reflection in another: "Will it be all right? Is it a proper thing to do?" And this question is always answered from the possible and presumed point of view of another person: Golyadkin *will pretend* that nothing is the matter, that he just happened to be driving by, and the other person will see that "that's how it must have been." It is in the reaction of the other person, in his discourse and his response, that the whole matter lies. There is no way that the confidence of Golyadkin's second voice can rule all of him, nor can it actually take the place of another real person. For him, another's words are the most important thing.

> Although Mr. Golyadkin had said all this [about his independence–M. B.] with the utmost possible distinctness and clarity, confidently, weighing his words and calculating their probable effect, nevertheless it was now with anxiety, with the utmost anxiety, that he gazed at Christian Ivanovich. Now he had become all eyes, and awaited Christian Ivanovich's answer with sad and melancholy impatience. [*SS* I, pp. 220-21; *The Double*, ch. ii]

In this second excerpt of interior dialogue, the substituting functions of the second voice are absolutely clear. But here there appears in addition a third voice, the direct voice of the other, interrupting the second merely substitute voice. Thus elements appear here that are completely analogous to those we analyzed in Devushkin's speech —words of the other, words partially belonging to the other, and the corresponding accentual interruptions:

> Well, it's something strange and queer; just like the Siamese twins, as they call them. . . . Well, why them, the Siamese twins?—all right, they're twins, but even the very greatest people have seemed a bit queer sometimes. Why, even in history, it's well known the famous Suvorov crowed like a cock. . . . Well, but that was all for political reasons; and great generals . . . but why talk about generals?

Everywhere here, but especially where ellipses appear, the anticipated responses of others wedge themselves in. This passage too could be unfolded in the form of a dialogue. But here it is more complex. While in Devushkin's speech a single integrated voice polemicized with the "other person," here there are two voices: one confident, even too confident, and the other too timid, giving in to everything, capitulating totally.[12]

Golyadkin's second voice (the voice substituting for another person), his first voice hiding away from the other's word ("I'm like everyone else," "I'm all right") and then finally giving in to that other word ("In that case, I'm ready") and, finally, that genuinely other voice forever resounding in him—these three voices are so complexly interrelated that the material provided by them is adequate for the entire intrigue and permits the whole novel to be constructed on them alone. The actual event, namely the unsuccessful courting of Klara Olsufievna, and all the circumstances accompanying it are in fact not represented in the novel at all: they serve only as the stimulus setting inner voices in motion, they make immediate and intensify that inner conflict that is the real object of representation in the novel.

Except for Golyadkin and his double, no other characters take any real part whatsoever in the intrigue, which unfolds entirely within the bounds of Golyadkin's self-consciousness; the other characters merely provide raw material, add, as it were, the fuel necessary for the intense work of that self-consciousness. The external, intentionally obscure intrigue (everything of importance has already taken place before the novel begins) serves also as a firm, barely discernible frame for Golyadkin's inner intrigue. The novel tells the story of Golyadkin's desire to do without the other's consciousness, to do without recognition by another, his desire to avoid the other and assert his own self, and what resulted from this. Dostoevsky intended *The Double* as a "confession"[13] (not in the personal sense, of course), that is, as the representation of an event that takes place within the bounds of self-consciousness. *The Double* is the *first dramatized confession* in Dostoevsky's work.

At the base of the intrigue, therefore, lies Golyadkin's attempt—in view of the total nonrecognition of his personality on the part of others—to find for himself a substitute for the other. Golyadkin plays at being an independent person; his consciousness plays at confidence and self-sufficiency. At the dinner party where Golyadkin is publicly humiliated, this new and acute experience of collision with another person intensifies the split in his personality. Golyadkin's second voice overexerts itself in a desperate simulation of self-sufficiency, in order to save Golyadkin's face. It is impossible for this second voice to merge with Golyadkin; on the contrary, treacherous tones of ridicule grow louder and louder in it. It provokes and teases Golyadkin, it casts off its mask. The double appears. The inner conflict is dramatized; Golyadkin's intrigue with the double begins.

The double speaks in Golyadkin's own words, bringing with him no new words or tones. At first he pretends to be a cringing Golyadkin, Golyadkin surrendering. When Golyadkin brings the double home with him, the latter looks and behaves like the first and uncertain voice in Golyadkin's internal dialogue ("Will it be all right, is it a proper thing to do," etc.)

The visitor [the double—M. B.] evidently felt highly embarrassed and extremely shy; he humbly followed his host's every movement and caught his every look, apparently trying to guess his thoughts from them. All his gestures expressed something meek, downtrodden, and cowed, so that at that moment he was, if the comparison is permissible, like a man who for want of his own clothes is wearing somebody else's; the sleeves have crept half-way up his arms, the waist is almost round his neck, and he is either constantly tugging at the too-short waistcoat, or sliding away somewhere out of the way, or striving to find somewhere to hide, or looking into everybody's eyes and straining to hear whether people are talking about his plight and laughing at him or ashamed of him; and the poor man blushes, he loses his presence of mind, his pride suffers. . . . [SS I, 270-71; The Double, ch. vii]

This is a characterization of the cringing and self-effacing Golyadkin. The double speaks, too, in the tones and style of Golyadkin's first voice. The part of the second voice—confident and tenderly reassuring in its relation to the double—is played by Golyadkin himself, who this time seems to have merged totally with that voice:

"Well, you know, Yakov Petrovich, you and I are going to get on well together," said our hero; "you and I, Yakov Petrovich, will get on like a house on fire, we'll live together like brothers; the two of us will be very clever, old chap, very clever we're going to be; we'll be the ones to intrigue against them . . . intrigue against them, that's what we'll do. After all, I know you, Yakov Petrovich, I understand what you're like; you blurt out everything straight away, like the honest soul that you are. You just keep away from all of them, old man" [SS I, 276; The Double, ch. vii] [14]

But later on the roles change: the treacherous double takes over the tone of Golyadkin's second voice, parodically exaggerating its affectionate familiarity. At their very next meeting in the office the double has already assumed this tone, and he sustains it until the end of the story, now and then himself emphasizing the identity between expressions from his own speech and Golyadkin's words (the words spoken by him during their first conversation). During one of their meetings at the office, the double, familiarly poking Golyadkin, said to him:

with a smile full of the most venomous and far-reaching implications: "Oh no, you don't, Yakov Petrovich, my little friend, oh no, you don't. We'll dodge you, Yakov Petrovich, we'll dodge you." [SS I, 289; The Double, ch. viii]

Or a little later, before their eye-to-eye confrontation in the coffee-house:

". . . You've talked me over, my dear boy," said Mr. Golyadkin junior, climbing down from the cab and shamelessly clapping him on the shoulder, "you're such a good sort; for you, Yakov Petrovich, I'm willing to take a side-street (as you so rightly remarked that time, Yakov Petrovich). You're a sly one, you know, you do whatever you like with a man." [SS I, 337; The Double, ch. xi]

This transferral of words from one mouth to another, where the content remains the same although the tone and ultimate meaning are changed, is a fundamental device of Dostoevsky's. He forces his heroes to recognize themselves, their idea, their own words, their orientation, their gesture in another person, in whom all these phenomena change their integrated and ultimate meaning and take on a different sound, the sound of parody or ridicule.[15]

Almost all of Dostoevsky's major heroes, as we have said elsewhere, have their partial double in another person or even in several other people (Stavrogin and Ivan Karamazov). In his last work Dostoevsky again returned to the device of fully embodying the second voice, this time, to be sure, on deep and more subtle grounds. In its externally formal plan Ivan Karamazov's dialogue with the devil is analogous to those interior dialogues that Golyadkin conducts with himself and with his double; for all the dissimilarity in situation and in ideological content, essentially one and the same artistic task is being solved here.

Thus does Golyadkin's intrigue with his double unfold, and it unfolds as the dramatized crisis of his self-consciousness, as a dramatized confession. The action cannot go beyond the bounds of self-consciousness, since the *dramatis personae* are no more than isolated elements of that self-consciousness. The actors here are the three voices into which Golyadkin's voice and consciousness have been dismantled: his "I for myself," which cannot manage without another person and without that person's recognition; his fictitious "I for the other" (reflections in the other), that is, Golyadkin's second substituting voice; and finally the genuinely other voice which does not recognize Golyadkin and yet is not depicted as actually existing outside Golyadkin, since there are no other autonomous characters in the work.[16] What results is a peculiar sort of mystery play, or rather morality play, in which the actors are not whole people but rather the spiritual forces battling within them, a morality play, however, stripped of any formalism or abstract allegorizing.

But who tells the story in *The Double*? What is the positioning of the narrator and what sort of voice does he have?

In the narration too we do not find a single element that exceeds the bounds of Golyadkin's self-consciousness, not a single word or a single tone that could not have been part of his interior dialogue with himself or his dialogue with his double. The narrator picks up on Golyadkin's words and thoughts, intensifies the teasing, mocking tones embedded in them, and in these tones portrays Golyadkin's every act, every gesture, every movement. We have already said that Golyadkin's second voice, through imperceptible transitions, merges with the voice of the narrator; one gets the impression that *the narration is dialogically addressed to Golyadkin himself*, it rings in Golyadkin's own ears as another's voice taunting him, as the voice of his double, although formally the narration is addressed to the reader.

This is how the narrator describes Golyadkin's behavior at the most fateful moment in his escapades, when he tries, uninvited, to gain entrance to the ball at Olsufy Ivanovich's:

Let us rather turn to Mr. Golyadkin, the real and sole hero of our true to life story.

The fact is that he is now in a position that is, to say the least, extremely strange. He is here too, ladies and gentlemen, that is to say not at the ball, but almost at the ball; he is all right, ladies and gentlemen; he may be on his own, yet at this moment he stands upon a path that is not altogether straight; he stands now—it is strange even to say it—he stands now in the passage from the back entrance of Olsufy Ivanovich's flat. But that he is standing there means nothing; he is all right. He is standing, though, ladies and gentlemen, in a corner, lurking in a much darker, if no warmer, place, half concealed by an enormous cupboard and an old screen, among every kind of dusty rubbish, trash, and lumber, hiding until the proper time and meanwhile only watching the progress of the general business in the capacity of casual looker-on. He is only watching now, ladies and gentlemen; but, you know, he may also go in, ladies and gentlemen . . . why not? He has only to take a step, and he is in, and in very neatly. [*SS* I, 239-40; *The Double*, ch. iv]

In the structure of this narration we observe two voices interrupting each other, and the same merging of two rejoinders that we had earlier observed in the utterances of Makar Devushkin. But here the roles have changed: here it is as if the other person's rejoinder has swallowed up the rejoinder of the hero. The narration glitters with Golyadkin's own words: "he is all right," "he's on his own," etc. But these words are uttered by the narrator with ridicule, with ridicule and somewhat with reproach, directed at Golyadkin himself and constructed in a form meant to touch his sore spots and provoke him. The mocking narration imperceptibly passes over into the speech of Golyadkin himself. The question "Why not?" belongs to Golyadkin himself, but is given in the teasing, aggressive intonation of the narrator. Even this intonation, however, is not in essence alien to the consciousness of Golyadkin himself. All this could ring in his own head, as his second voice. In fact the author could at any point insert quotation marks without changing the tone, voice, or construction of the sentence.

Somewhat further he does exactly that:

So there he is now, ladies and gentlemen, waiting for the chance to do things quietly, and he has been waiting for exactly two and a half hours. Why not wait? Villèle himself used to wait. "But what's Villèle got to do with this?" thought Mr. Golyadkin. "Who's Villèle, anyhow? And what if I were to . . . just go through . . .? Oh you, bit player, you!" [*SS* I, 241; *The Double*, ch. iv]

But why not insert quotation marks two sentences earlier, before the words "Why not wait?", or even earlier, changing the words "So there he is now, ladies and gentlemen. . . ." to "Golyadka, old boy," or some other form of address by Golyadkin to his own self? Of course the quotation marks are not inserted at random. They are inserted in such a way as to make the transition especially subtle and imperceptible. Villèle's name appears in the narrator's last sentence and in the hero's first. Golyadkin's words seem to continue the narration uninterruptedly and answer it in an interior dialogue. "Villèle himself used to wait." "'But what's Villèle got to do with this!'" These are in fact detached rejoinders in Golyadkin's interior dialogue with himself: one side entered the narration, the other remained with Golyadkin. A phenomenon has occurred that is quite the reverse of what we had observed earlier, when we witnessed the interruption-prone merging of two rejoinders. But the result is the same: a double-voiced, interruption-prone construction with all the accompanying phenomena. The field of action is the same, too: a single self-consciousness. Authority in that consciousness, however, has been seized by the other's discourse, which has made its home in it.

We shall quote another example with the same vacillating borders between the narration and the hero's discourse. Golyadkin has made up his mind and has at last entered the hall where the ball is going on, and finds himself before Klara Olsufievna:

> There is not the slightest doubt he could most gladly have sunk through the floor at that moment without so much as blinking; but what's done can't be undone . . . no, indeed it can't. What was he to do? "If things go wrong, stand your ground; if all goes well, stand firm." Mr. Golyadkin, of course, was "not an intriguer, nor was he good at polishing the parquet with his shoes. . . ." Well, now the worst had happened. And besides, the Jesuits were mixed up in it somehow. . . . However, Mr. Golyadkin had no time for them now! [SS I, 242-43; *The Double*, ch. iv]

The passage is interesting because it contains no grammatically direct discourse belonging to Golyadkin himself, and thus there is no justification for setting off words in quotation marks. The portion of the narration in quotation marks here was set that way, apparently, through a mistake of the editor. Dostoevsky probably set off only the proverb: "If things go wrong, stand your ground; if all goes well, stand firm." The next sentence is given in the third person, although, of course, it belongs to Golyadkin himself. Further on, the pauses marked by ellipses also belong to Golyadkin's inner speech. The sentences preceding and following these ellipses, judging by their accents, relate to one another as do rejoinders in an interior dialogue. The two adjacent sentences with the Jesuits are completely analogous to the above-quoted sentences on Villèle, set off from one another by quotation marks.

Finally, one more excerpt, where perhaps the opposite mistake was committed: quotation marks were not inserted where grammatically they should have been. Golyadkin, driven from the ball, rushes home through a snowstorm and meets a passer-by who later turns out to be his double:

> It was not that he feared this might be some bad character, it was simply perhaps . . . "And besides, who knows?" — the thought came unbidden into Mr. Golyadkin's mind — "perhaps this passer-by is — he, himself, perhaps he is here and, what matters most, he is not here for nothing, he has a purpose, he is crossing my path, he will brush against me." [SS I, 252; The Double, ch. v]

Here the ellipsis serves as a dividing line between the narration and Golyadkin's direct inner speech, which is structured in the first person ("*my* path" "brush against *me*"). But they are merged so closely here that one really does not want to insert quotation marks. For this sentence, after all, must be read with a single voice, albeit an internally dialogized one. Stunningly successful here is the transition from the narration to the hero's speech: we feel, as it were, the wave of a single speech current, one that carries us without dams or barriers from the narration into the hero's soul and out again into the narration; we feel that we are moving essentially within the circle of a single consciousness.

One could cite many more examples proving that the narration is a direct continuation and development of Golyadkin's second voice and that it is addressed dialogically to the hero, but even the above examples are sufficient. The whole work is constructed, therefore, entirely as an interior dialogue of three voices within the limits of a single dismantled consciousness. Every essential aspect of it lies at a point of intersection of these three voices, at a point where they abruptly, agonizingly interrupt one another. Invoking our image, we could say that this is not yet polyphony, but no longer homophony. One and the same word, idea, phenomenon is passed through three voices and in each voice sounds differently. The same set of words, tones, inner orientations is passed through the outer speech of Golyadkin, through the speech of the narrator and through the speech of the double, and these three voices are turned to face one another, they speak not about each other but with each other. Three voices sing the same line, but not in unison; rather, each carries its own part.

But these voices have not yet become fully independent real voices, they are not yet three autonomous consciousnesses. This occurs only in Dostoevsky's longer novels. In *The Double* there is no monologic discourse gravitating solely toward itself and its referential object. Each word is dismantled dialogically, each word contains an interruption of voices, but there is not yet an authentic dialogue of unmerged consciousnesses such as will later appear in the novels. Already the rudiments of counterpoint are here: it is implied in the very structure of the discourse. The analyses of the sort we have offered here are already, as it were, contrapuntal analyses (speaking figuratively, of course). But these new connections have not yet gone beyond the bounds of monologic material.

Relentlessly ringing in Golyadkin's ears are the provocative and mocking voice of the narrator and the voice of the double. The narrator shouts into Golyadkin's ear Golyadkin's own words and thoughts, but in another, hopelessly alien, hopelessly censuring and mocking tone. This second voice is present in every one of Dostoevsky's heroes, and in his final novel, as we have said, it again takes on an independent existence. The devil shouts into Ivan Karamazov's ear Ivan's very own words, commenting mockingly on his decision to confess in court and repeating in an alien tone his most intimate thoughts. We shall not take up here the actual dialogue between Ivan and the devil, since the principles of authentic dialogue will concern us further on. But we shall quote the passage immediately following this dialogue, Ivan's agitated story to Alyosha. Its structure is analogous to the previously analyzed structure of *The Double*. The same principle obtains for combining voices, although to be sure everything here is deeper and more complex. In this story Ivan passes his own personal thoughts and decisions simultaneously through two voices; he transmits them in two different tonalities. In the quoted excerpt we omit Alyosha's side of the dialogue, for his real voice does not yet fit into our scheme. What interests us now is only the intra-atomic counterpoint of voices, their combination solely within the bounds of a single dismantled consciousness (that is, a microdialogue). *micro dialogue*

"He's been teasing me. And you know he does it so cleverly, so cleverly. 'Conscience! What is conscience? I make it up for myself. Why am I tormented by it? From habit. From the universal habit of mankind for seven thousand years. So let us give it up, and we shall be gods.' It was he who said that, it was he who said that!" . . .

"Yes, but he is spiteful. He laughed at me. He was impudent, Alyosha," Ivan said, with a shudder of offense. "But he was unfair to me, unfair to me about lots of things. He told lies about me to my face. 'Oh, you are going to perform an act of heroic virtue: to confess you murdered your father, that the lackey murdered him at your instigation.'" . . .

"That's what he says, he, and he knows it. 'You are going to perform an act of heroic virtue, and you don't believe in virtue; that's what tortures you and makes you angry, that's why you are so vindictive.' He said that to me about me and he knows what he says." . . .

"Yes, he knows how to torment one. He's cruel," Ivan went on, unheeding.

"I had an inkling from the first what he came for. 'Granting that you go through pride, still you had a hope that Smerdyakov might be convicted and sent to Siberia, and Mitya would be acquitted, while you would only be punished with **moral** condemnation' ('Do you hear?' he laughed then—'and some people will praise you. But now Smerdyakov's dead, he has hanged himself, and who'll believe you alone? But yet you are going, you are going, you'll go all the same, you've decided to go. What are you going for now?' That's awful, Alyosha. I can't endure such questions. Who dare ask me such questions?" [SS X, 184-85; *The Brothers Karamazov*, Part IV, Book 11, ch. 10]

All the loopholes in Ivan's thoughts, all his sideward glances at another's words and another's consciousness, all his attempts to get around the other's words and to replace them in his soul with an affirmation of his own self, all the reservations of his conscience that serve to interrupt his every thought, his every word and experience, condense and thicken here into the completed replies of the devil. Ivan's words and the devil's replies do not differ in content but only in tone, only in accent. But this change of accent changes their entire ultimate meaning. The devil, as it were, transfers to the main clause what had been for Ivan merely a subordinate clause, uttered under his breath and without independent accent, and the content of the main clause he makes into an unaccented subordinate clause. Ivan's reservation concerning the main motive for his decision is transformed by the devil into the main motive, and the main motive becomes merely a reservation. What results is a combination of voices that is highly intense and maximally eventful, but which at the same time is not dependent on any opposition in content or plot.

But of course this full dialogization of Ivan's consciousness is—as is always the case with Dostoevsky—prepared for in a leisurely fashion. The other's discourse gradually, stealthily penetrates the consciousness and speech of the hero: now in the form of a pause where one would not be appropriate in monologically confident speech, now in the form of someone else's accent breaking up the sentence, now in the form of an abnormally heightened, exaggerated, or anguished personal tone, and so on. From Ivan's first words and from his entire inner orientation in Zosima's cell, through his conversations with Alyosha, with his father, and especially with Smerdyakov before his departure to Chermashnya, and finally through his three meetings with Smerdyakov after the murder, this process of the gradual dialogic dismantling of Ivan's consciousness stretches out, a process more profound and ideologically complicated than was the case with Golyadkin, but structurally fully analogous to it.

Someone else's voice whispering into the ear of the hero his own words with a displaced accent, and the resulting unrepeatably unique combination of vari-directional words and voices within a single word, a single speech, the intersection of two consciousnesses in a single consciousness—in one form or another, to one degree or another, in one ideological direction or another—all this is present in every one of Dostoevsky's works. This contrapuntal combination of vari-directional voices within the bounds of a single consciousness also serves him as the basis, the ground, on which he introduces other real voices as well. But we will return to that later. At this point we would like to quote one passage from Dostoevsky where, with stunning artistic power, he offers a musical image for the interrelationship of voices analyzed by us above. This page from *The Adolescent* is all the more interesting because in his works Dostoevsky, with the exception of this passage, almost never speaks of music.

Trishatov is telling the adolescent of his love for music, and explains to him his plan for an opera:

"Tell me, do you like music? I'm crazy about music. I'll play you something when I come to see you. I've studied piano for years seriously, and I can play really well. If I were to compose an opera, I'd choose a theme from *Faust*. I love *Faust*. I keep composing music for that scene in the cathedral—oh, just in my head, of course. . . . The interior of that Gothic cathedral, the choir, the hymns. . . . In comes Gretchen . . . the choir is medieval—you can hear the fifteenth century at once. Gretchen is in despair. First, a recitative, played very softly, but full of suffering and terror, while the choir thunders grimly, sternly, and impersonally, *'Dies irae, dies illa!' And then, all of a sudden, the devil's voice sings the devil's song. You can't see him, there's only his song mingling with the hymns, almost blending into them, although it's completely different from them—I must manage to convey that somehow.* The devil's song is long, persistent. A tenor—it absolutely must be a tenor. It begins softly and tenderly: 'Do you remember, Gretchen, when, still an innocent child, you came here with your mother and lisped your prayers from the old prayer book?' But the devil's voice grows louder, more passionate, more intense, it floats on higher notes that contain despair, tears, and infinite, irretrievable hopelessness: 'There's no forgiveness, Gretchen, no forgiveness here for you!' Gretchen wants to pray but only cries of pain come from her breast—you know, the breast shaken by sobs and convulsions. . . . And all this time the devil's song continues and pierces her soul deeper and deeper like a spear—the notes get higher and higher and then, suddenly, it all breaks off in a shriek: 'Accursed one, this is the end!' . . . Gretchen falls on her knees, her hands clasped in front of her. And then comes her prayer. Something very short, a semi-recitative, but completely simple, without ornamentation, again very medieval, only four lines—Stradella has a passage with a score a bit like that. . . . And then, on the last note, she faints! There's general confusion, they pick her up, and suddenly the choir thunders forth. It must sound like an explosion of voices, an inspirational, triumphant, irresistible outburst, somewhat like 'Borne on high by angels . . .' So that everything is shaken to its foundations and it all merges into one single overwhelming, exalted

'Hosanna!'—like an outcry from the whole universe. . . . And they carry Gretchen off, and just at that moment the curtain must fall . . ." [*SS* VII, 482-83; *The Adolescent*, Part III, ch. 5, iii]

A part of that musical plan—although in the form of literary works —was indisputably realized by Dostoevsky, and realized quite frequently and with the most varied material.[17]

But let us return to Golyadkin, we have not yet finished with him; or rather, we have not yet finished with the narrator's discourse. From an utterly different point of view—namely the point of view of linguistic stylistics—a definition of narration in *The Double* analogous to ours has been provided by V. Vinogradov in his article "The Style of the Petersburg Poem *The Double*."[18]

Here is Vinogradov's basic claim:

The introduction of "interjections" and expressions from Golyadkin's speech into the narrational *skaz* achieves an effect whereby it seems, from time to time, that hidden behind the narrator's mask Golyadkin himself begins to appear, narrating his own adventures. In *The Double* this convergence of Mr. Golyadkin's controversial speech with the narrational *skaz* of the storyteller is further intensified, because in indirect speech Golyadkin's style remains unchanged, falling, therefore, to the author's responsibility. And since Golyadkin says the same thing over and over not only with his language but also with his glance, his appearance, his gestures and movements, it is fully understandable why almost all the descriptions (significantly making reference to the 'perpetual habits' of Mr. Golyadkin) glitter with unmarked citations from his speech.

After citing a series of examples where the narrator's speech coincides with Golyadkin's speech, Vinogradov continues:

This number of excerpts could be considerably increased, but even the ones we have cited, illustrating this combination of Golyadkin's self-definitions and the minor verbal brush-strokes of a detached observer, stress clearly enough the idea that the 'Petersburg poem,' at least in many parts, expresses itself as a story about Golyadkin told by his 'double,' that is, by 'a person with his language and concepts.' The use of this innovative device explains the failure of *The Double*.[9]

Vinogradov's analysis is subtle and well-substantiated and his conclusions are correct, but he remains, of course, within the bounds of his chosen method, and what is most important and fundamental simply cannot be fit within those bounds.

Vinogradov, it seems to us, could not perceive the real uniqueness of syntax in *The Double*, because syntactic structure here is not determined by the *skaz* in and of itself, nor by a clerk's conversational dialect, nor by official bureaucratese, but first and foremost by the collision and interruption of various accents within the bounds of a single syntactic whole, that is, precisely by the fact that this whole, while being one, accommodates in itself the accents of two voices. Furthermore, there is no understanding or indication of the fact that the narration is *dialogically addressed* to Golyadkin, a fact manifest in very clear external features: for example, in the fact that the first line Golyadkin speaks is quite often an obvious response to the sentence preceding it in the narration. There is no understanding, finally, of the fundamental connection between the narration and Golyadkin's interior dialogue: the narration, after all, makes no attempt to reproduce Golyadkin's speech in general, but directly continues only the speech of his second voice.

On the whole it is impossible, while remaining within the limits of linguistic stylistics, to tackle the proper artistic problem of style. No single formal linguistic definition of a word can cover all its artistic functions in the work. The authentic style-generating factors remain outside the field of vision available to linguistic stylistics.

The style of the narration in *The Double* contains yet another very fundamental feature, also correctly noted by Vinogradov but not explained by him. "In the narrational *skaz*," he says, "there is a predominance of motor images, and its basic stylistic device is the registering of movements independent of their repetitiveness."[20]

In fact the narration does, with the most tedious precision, register all the minutest movements of the hero, not sparing endless repetitions. The narrator is literally fettered to his hero; he cannot back off from him sufficiently to give a summarizing and integrated image of his deeds and actions. Such a generalizing image would already lie outside the hero's own field of vision, and on the whole such images presume some stable position on the outside. The narrator does not have access to such a position, he has none of the perspective necessary for an artistically finalizing summation of the hero's image or of his acts as a whole.[21]

This peculiar feature of narration in *The Double* is, with certain modifications, preserved throughout all of Dostoevsky's subsequent work. Narration in Dostoevsky is always narration without perspective. Employing a term from art criticism, we could say that Dostoevsky had no "distance perspective" on the hero and the event. The narrator finds himself in immediate proximity to the hero and to the ongoing event, and it is from this maximally close, aperspectival point of view that he structures their representation. It is true that Dostoevsky's chroniclers write their notes after events have already come to a close and as if from a certain temporal perspective. The narrator of *The Possessed*, for example, quite often says: "now, after everything is over," "now, when we remember all this," etc., but in fact he structures his narration without any significant perspective at all.

However, in contrast to narration in *The Double*, Dostoevsky's later narrations make no effort to register all the minutest movements of the hero, they are not at all long-winded, and are completely devoid of any repetitions. Narration in Dostoevsky's later period is brief, dry, and even somewhat abstract (especially in those places where information is provided about earlier events). But this brevity and dryness of narration, "sometimes bordering on Gil Blas," results not from perspective, but on the contrary, from a lack of perspective. Such deliberate lack of perspective is preordained by Dostoevsky's entire artistic plan, for, as we know, a firm and finalized image of the hero and the event is excluded in advance from that plan.

But let us return again to narration in *The Double*. In addition to its above-mentioned relationship to the hero's speech, we notice in it yet another parodic intention. In the narration of *The Double*, as in Devushkin's letters, there are clear elements of literary parody.

As early as *Poor Folk* the author was already using the voice of his hero to refract parodic intentions. This he achieved by various means: the parodies were either simply introduced into Devushkin's letters and motivated by the plot (the excerpts from Ratazyaev's compositions: parodies on the high society novel, on the historical novel of the time, and finally on the Naturalist School), or parodic brush strokes were made part of the very structure of the story (for example, "Teresa and Faldoni"). And he introduced into the story, finally, a polemic with Gogol directly refracted through the hero's voice, a polemic parodically colored (Devushkin's reading of "The Overcoat" and his indignant reaction to it. In the subsequent episode, where the general helps the hero, there is a hidden juxtaposition to the episode with the "important personage" in Gogol's "Overcoat").[22]

In *The Double*, a parodic stylization of the "high style" from *Dead Souls* is refracted through the narrator's voice; in general, *The Double* is sprinkled with parodic and semiparodic allusions to various works of Gogol. It should be noted that these parodic tones in the narration are directly interwoven with a mimicry of Golyadkin.

To introduce a parodic and polemical element into the narration is to make it more multi-voiced, more interruption-prone, no longer gravitating toward itself or its referential object. But literary parody, on the other hand, strengthens the element of literary conventionality in the narrator's discourse, depriving it even more of its independence and finalizing power in relation to the hero. In subsequent works as well, this element of literary conventionality, and the various forms used to expose it, always served to intensify greatly the direct and autonomous signifying power of the hero and the independence of the hero's position. In this sense literary conventionality, in Dostoevsky's overall plan, not only did not reduce the signifying- and idea-content of his novels, but on the contrary could only increase it (as was also the case, incidentally, with Jean Paul and even with Sterne). Dostoevsky's destruction in his works of the usual mono- logic orientation led him to exclude altogether from his construction certain elements of this monologic orientation, and conscientiously to neutralize others. One means of neutralization was literary con- ventionality, that is, introducing into the narration or into the prin- ciples of construction a conventionalized discourse, stylized or parodic.[23]

As concerns a dialogic addressing of the narration to the hero, this feature did of course remain in Dostoevsky's subsequent works, but it changed shape and became deeper and more complex. No longer is every word of the narrator addressed to the hero, but rather the nar- ration as a whole, the very orientation of the narration. Within the narration, speech in most cases is dry and colorless: the best defini- tion for it is "documentary style." But this documentation taken as a whole functions basically to expose and to provoke; it is addressed to the hero, speaking as it were to him and not about him, speaking however with its entire mass and not with its individual elements. To be sure, even in the latest works individual heroes are illuminated by a style that directly parodies and taunts them, a style that sounds like an exaggerated rejoinder from their own interior dialogue. Thus, for example, is the narrative of *The Possessed* constructed in relation to Stepan Trofimovich, but only in relation to him. Isolated notes of this taunting style are scattered throughout the other novels as well. They are present even in *The Brothers Karamazov*. But on the whole they are considerably weakened. A basic tendency of Dostoevsky in his later period is to make his style and tone dry and precise, to neutralize it. But wherever this predominating, documentarily dry and neutralized narration is replaced by sharply accented tones col- ored with value judgments, those tones are invariably addressed to the hero and are born out of a rejoinder in his potential interior dia- logue with himself.

From *The Double* we move immediately to "Notes from Under- ground," passing over a whole series of intervening works.

"Notes from Underground" is a confessional *Ich-Erzählung*. Orig- inally the work was entitled "A Confession."[24] And it is in fact an authentic confession. Of course, "confession" is understood here not in the personal sense. The author's intention is refracted here, as in any *Ich-Erzählung*; this is not a personal document but a work of art.

In the confession of the Underground Man what strikes us first of all is its extreme and acute dialogization: there is literally not a single monologically firm, undissociated word. From the very first sentence the hero's speech has already begun to cringe and break under the influence of the anticipated words of another, with whom the hero, from the very first step, enters into the most intense internal polemic.

"I am a sick man . . . I am a spiteful man. I am an unpleasant man." Thus begins the confession. The ellipsis and the abrupt change of tone after it are significant. The hero began in a somewhat plaintive tone "I am a sick man," but was immediately enraged by that tone: it looked as if he were complaining and needed sympathy, as if he were seeking that sympathy in another person, as if he needed another person! And then there occurs an abrupt dialogic turnaround, one of those typical breaks in accent so characteristic of the whole style of the "Notes," as if the hero wants to say: You, perhaps, were led to believe from my first word that I am seeking your sympathy, so take this: I am a spiteful man. I am an unpleasant man!

Characteristic here is a gradual increase in negative tone (to spite the other) under the influence of the other's anticipated reaction. Such breaks in accent always lead to an accumulation of ever-intensifying abusive words or words that are, in any case, unflattering to the other person, as in this example:

To live longer than forty years is bad manners; it is vulgar, immoral. Who does live beyond forty? Answer that, sincerely and honestly. I will tell you who: fools and worthless people do. I tell all old men that to their face, all those respectable old men, all those silver-haired and reverend old men! I tell the whole world that to its face. I have a right to say so, for I'll go on living to sixty myself. I'll live till seventy! Till eighty! Wait, let me catch my breath. [SS IV, 135; "Notes," Part One, 1]

In the opening words of the confession, this internal polemic with the other is concealed. But the other's words are present invisibly, determining the style of speech from within. Midway into the first paragraph, however, the polemic has already broken out into the open: the anticipated response of the other takes root in the narration, although, to be sure, still in a weakened form. "No, I refuse to treat it out of spite. You probably will not understand that. Well, but I understand it."

At the end of the third paragraph there is already a very characteristic anticipation of the other's reaction:

Well, are you not imagining, gentlemen, that I am repenting for something now, that I am asking your forgiveness for something? I am sure you are imagining that. However, I assure you it does not matter to me if you are.

At the end of the next paragraph comes the above-quoted polemical attack against the "reverend old men." The following paragraph begins directly with the anticipation of a response to the preceding paragraph:

No doubt you think, gentlemen, that I want to amuse you. You are mistaken in that, too. I am not at all such a merry person as you imagine, or as you may imagine; however, if irritated by all this babble (and I can feel that you are irritated) you decide to ask me just who I am—then my answer is, I am a certain low-ranked civil servant.

The next paragraph again ends with an anticipated response:

. . . I'll bet you think I am writing all this to show off, to be witty at the expense of men of action; and what is more, that out of ill-bred showing-off, I am clanking a sword, like my officer.

Later on such endings to paragraphs become more rare, but it remains true that all basic semantic sections of the work become sharper and more shrill near the end, in open anticipation of someone else's response.

Thus the entire style of the "Notes" is subject to the most powerful and all-determining influence of other people's words, which either act on speech covertly from within as in the beginning of the work, or which, as the anticipated response of another person, take root in the very fabric of speech, as in those above-quoted ending passages. The work does not contain a single word gravitating exclusively toward itself and its referential object; that is, there is not a single monologic word. We shall see that this intense relationship to another's consciousness in the Underground Man is complicated by an equally intense relationship to his own self. But first we shall make a brief structural analysis of this act of anticipating another's response.

Such anticipation is marked by one peculiar structural trait: it tends toward a vicious circle. The tendency of these anticipations can be reduced to a necessity to retain for oneself the final word. This final word must express the hero's full independence from the views and words of the other person, his complete indifference to the other's opinion and the other's evaluation. What he fears most of all is that people might think he is repenting before someone, that he is asking someone's forgiveness, that he is reconciling himself to someone else's judgment or evaluation, that his self-affirmation is somehow in need of affirmation and recognition by another. And it is in this direction that he anticipates the other's response. But precisely in this act of anticipating the other's response and in responding to it he again demonstrates to the other (and to himself) his own dependence on this other. He *fears* that the other might think he *fears* that other's opinion. But through this fear he immediately demonstrates his own dependence on the other's consciousness, his own inability to be at peace with his own definition of self. With his refutation, he confirms precisely what he wishes to refute, and he knows it. Hence the inescapable circle in which the hero's self-consciousness and discourse are trapped: "Well, are you not imagining, gentlemen, that I am repenting for something now? . . . I am sure you are imagining that. However, I assure you it does not matter to me if you are. . . ."

During that night out on the town, the Underground Man, insulted by his companions, wants to show them that he pays them no attention:

> I smiled contemptuously and walked up and down the other side of the room, opposite the sofa, along the wall, from the table to the stove and back again. I tried my very utmost to show them that I could do without them, and yet I purposely stomped with my boots, thumping with my heels. But it was all in vain. They paid no attention at all. [SS IV, 199; "Notes," Part Two, ch. IV]

Meanwhile our underground hero recognizes all this perfectly well himself, and understands perfectly well the impossibility of escaping from that circle in which his attitude toward the other moves. Thanks to this attitude toward the other's consciousness, a peculiar *perpetuum mobile* is achieved, made up of his internal polemic with another and with himself, an endless dialogue where one reply begets another, which begets a third, and so on to infinity, and all of this without any forward motion.

Here is an example of that inescapable *perpetuum mobile* of the dialogized self-consciousness:

> You will say that it is vulgar and base to drag all this [the hero's dreaming— M. B.] into public after all the tears and raptures I have myself admitted. But why is it base? Can you imagine that I am ashamed of it all, and that it was stupider than anything in your life, gentlemen? And I can assure you that some of these fancies were by no means badly composed. Not everything took place on the shores of Lake Como. And yet you are right—it really is vulgar and base. And what is most base of all is that I have now started to justify myself to you. And even more base than that is my making this remark now. But that's enough, or, after all, there will be no end to it; each step will be more base than the last. [SS IV, 181; "Notes," Part Two, ch. II]

Before us is an example of a vicious circle of dialogue which can neither be finished nor finalized. The formal significance of such inescapable dialogic oppositions in Dostoevsky's work is very great. But nowhere in his subsequent works does this opposition appear in such naked, abstractly precise, one could even say directly mathematical, form.[25]

As a result of the Underground Man's attitude toward the other's consciousness and its discourse—extraordinary dependence upon it and at the same time extreme hostility toward it and nonacceptance of its judgments—his narration takes on one highly essential artistic characteristic. This is a deliberate clumsiness of style, albeit subject to a certain artistic logic. His discourse does not flaunt itself and cannot flaunt itself, for there is no one before whom it can flaunt. It does not, after all, gravitate naively toward itself and its referential object. It is addressed to another person and to the speaker himself (in his internal dialogue with himself). And in both of these directions it wants least of all to flaunt itself and be "artistic" in the usual sense of the word. In its attitude toward the other person it strives to be deliberately inelegant, to "spite" him and his tastes in all respects. But this discourse takes the same position even in regard to the speaker himself, for one's attitude toward oneself is inseparably interwoven with one's attitude toward another. Thus discourse is pointedly cynical, calculatedly cynical, yet also anguished. It strives to play the holy fool, for holy-foolishness is indeed a sort of form, a sort of aestheticism—but, as it were, in reverse.

As a result, the prosaic triteness of the portrayal of his inner life is carried to extreme limits. In its material, in its theme, the first part of "Notes from Underground" is lyrical. From a formal point of view, this is the same prose lyric of spiritual and emotional quest, of spiritual unfulfillment that we find, for example, in Turgenev's "Phantoms" or "Enough,"[b] or in any lyrical page from a confessional *Ich-Erzählung* or a page from *Werther*. But this is a peculiar sort of lyric, analogous to the lyrical expression of a toothache.

This expression of a toothache, oriented in an internally polemical way toward the listener and toward the sufferer, is spoken by the Underground Hero himself, and he speaks of it, of course, not by chance. He suggests eavesdropping on the groans of an "educated man of the nineteenth century" who suffers from a toothache, on the second or third day of his illness. He tries to expose the peculiar sensuality behind this whole cynical expression of pain, an expression intended for the "public":

His moans become nasty, disgustingly spiteful, and go on for whole days and nights. And, after all, he himself knows that he does not benefit at all from his moans; he knows better than anyone that he is only lacerating and irritating himself and others in vain; he knows that even the audience for whom he is exerting himself and his whole family now listen to him with loathing, do not believe him for a second, and that deep down they understand that he could moan differently, more simply, without trills and flourishes, and that he is only indulging himself like that out of spite, out of malice. Well, sensuality exists precisely in all these consciousnesses and infamies. "It seems I am troubling you, I am lacerating your hearts, I am keeping everyone in the house awake. Well, stay awake then, you, too, feel every minute that I have a toothache. I am no longer the hero to you now that I tried to appear before, but simply a nasty person, a

b"Phantoms," the least successful of Turgenev's several stories on the supernatural; "Enough" (1865) is one of Turgenev's periodic gestures of withdrawal, a sort of prose poem announcing to his public his disillusionment with life and art. Both pieces, and their author, are vigorously parodied by Dostoevsky in the character of Karmazinov in *The Possessed*.

scoundrel. Well, let it be that way, then! I am very glad that you see through me. Is it nasty for you to hear my foul moans? Well, let it be nasty. Here I will let you have an even nastier flourish in a minute. . . ." [*SS* IV, 144; "Notes," Part One, ch. IV]

Of course any implied comparison here between the structure of the Underground Man's confession and the expression of a toothache is on the level of parodic exaggeration, and in this sense is cynical. But the orientation of this expression of a toothache, with all its "trills and flourishes," nevertheless does, in its relation to the listener and to the speaker himself, reflect very accurately the orientation of discourse in a confession—although, we repeat, it reflects not objectively but in a taunting, parodically exaggerating style, just as *The Double* reflected the internal speech of Golyadkin.

The destruction of one's own image in another's eyes, the sullying of that image in another's eyes as an ultimate desperate effort to free oneself from the power of the other's consciousness and to break through to one's self for the self alone—this, in fact, is the orientation of the Underground Man's entire confession. For this reason he makes his discourse about himself deliberately ugly. He wants to kill in himself any desire to appear the hero in others' eyes (and in his own): "I am no longer the hero to you now that I tried to appear before, but simply a nasty person, a scoundrel. . . ."

To accomplish this he must banish from his discourse all epic and lyrical tones, all "heroizing" tones; he must make his discourse *cynically* objective. A soberly objective definition of himself, without exaggeration or mockery, is impossible for a hero from the underground, because such a soberly prosaic definition would presuppose a word without a sideward glance, a word without a loophole; neither the one nor the other exist on his verbal palette. True, he is continually trying to break through to such a word, to break through to spiritual sobriety, but for him the path lies through cynicism and holy-foolishness. He has neither freed himself from the power of the other's consciousness nor admitted its power over him,[26] he is for now merely struggling with it, polemicizing with it maliciously, not able to accept it but also not able to reject it. In this striving to trample down his own image and his own discourse as they exist in and for the other person, one can hear not only the desire for sober self-definition, but also a desire to annoy the other person; and this forces him to overdo his sobriety, mockingly exaggerating it to the point of cynicism and holy-foolishness: "Is it nasty for you to hear my foul moans? Well, let it be nasty. Here I will let you have an even nastier flourish in a minute. . . ."

But the underground hero's word about himself is not only a word with a sideward glance; it is also, as we have said, a word with a loophole. The influence of the loophole on the style of his confession is so great that his style cannot be understood without a consideration of its formal activity. The word with a loophole has enormous significance in Dostoevsky's works in general, especially in the later works. And here we pass on to another aspect of the structure of "Notes from Underground": the hero's attitude toward his own self, which throughout the course of the entire work is interwoven and combined with his dialogue with another.

What, then, is this loophole of consciousness and of the word?

A loophole is the retention for oneself of the possibility for altering the ultimate, final meaning of one's own words. If a word retains such a loophole this must inevitably be reflected in its structure. This potential other meaning, that is, the loophole left open, accompanies the word like a shadow. Judged by its meaning alone, the word with a loophole should be an ultimate word and does present itself as such, but in fact it is only the penultimate word and places after itself only a conditional, not a final, period.

For example, the confessional self-definition with a loophole (the most widespread form in Dostoevsky) is, judging by its meaning, an ultimate word about oneself, a final definition of oneself, but in fact it is forever taking into account internally the responsive, contrary evaluation of oneself made by another. The hero who repents and condemns himself actually wants only to provoke praise and acceptance by another. Condemning himself, he wants and demands that the other person dispute this self-definition, and he leaves himself a loophole in case the other person should suddenly in fact agree with him, with his self-condemnation, and not make use of his privilege as the other.

Here is how the hero from the underground tells of his "literary" dreams:

> I, for instance, was triumphant over everyone; everyone, of course, lay in the dust and was *forced* to recognize my superiority *spontaneously*, and I forgave them all. I, a famous poet, and a courtier, fell in love; I inherited countless millions and immediately devoted them to humanity, and *at the same time I confessed before all the people my shameful deeds, which, of course, were not merely shameful, but contained an enormous amount of "the sublime and the beautiful," something in the Manfred style. Everyone would weep and kiss me (what idiots they would be if they did not)*, while I would go barefoot and hungry preaching new ideas and fighting a victorious Austerlitz against the reactionaries. [*SS* IV, 181; "Notes," Part Two, ch. II]

Here he ironically relates dreams of heroic deeds with a loophole, dreams of confession with a loophole. He casts a parodic light on these dreams. But his very next words betray the fact that his repentant confession of his dreams has its own loophole, too, and that he himself is prepared to find in these dreams and in his very confessing of them something, if not in the Manfred style, then at least in the realm of "the sublime and the beautiful," if anyone should happen to agree with him that the dreams are indeed base and vulgar: "You will say that it is vulgar and base to drag all this into public after all the tears and raptures I have myself admitted. But why is it base? Can you imagine that I am ashamed of it all, and that it was stupider than anything in your life, gentlemen? And I can assure you that some of these fancies were by no means badly composed. . . ."

And this passage, already cited by us above, is caught up in the vicious circle of self-consciousness with a sideward glance.

The loophole creates a special type of fictive ultimate word about oneself with an unclosed tone to it, obtrusively peering into the other's eyes and demanding from the other a sincere refutation. We shall see that the word with a loophole achieves especially sharp expression in Ippolit's confession, but it is to one degree or another inherent in all the confessional self-utterances of Dostoevsky's heroes.[27] The loophole makes all the heroes' self-definitions unstable, the word in them has no hard and fast meaning, and at any moment, like a chameleon, it is ready to change its tone and its ultimate meaning.

The loophole makes the hero ambiguous and elusive even for himself. In order to break through to his self the hero must travel a very long road. The loophole profoundly distorts his attitude toward himself. The hero does not know whose opinion, whose statement is ultimately the final judgment on him: is it his own repentant and censuring judgment, or on the contrary is it another person's opinion that he desires and has compelled into being, an opinion that accepts and vindicates him? The image of Nastasya Filippovna, for example, is built almost entirely on this motif alone. Considering herself guilty, a fallen woman, she simultaneously assumes that the other person, precisely as the other, is obliged to vindicate her and cannot consider her guilty. She genuinely quarrels with Myshkin, who vindicates her in everything, but she equally genuinely despises and rejects all those who agree with her self-condemnation and consider her a fallen woman. Ultimately Nastasya Filippovna does not know even her own final word on herself: does she really consider herself a fallen woman, or does she vindicate herself? Self-condemnation and self-vindication, divided between two voices—I condemn myself, another vindicates me—but anticipated by a single voice, create in that voice interruptions and an internal duality. An anticipated and obligatory vindication by the other merges with self-condemnation, and both tones begin to sound simultaneously in that voice, resulting in abrupt interruptions and sudden transitions. Such is the voice of Nastasya Filippovna, such is the style of her discourse. Her entire inner life (and, as we shall see, her outward life as well) is reduced to a search for herself and for her own undivided voice beneath the two voices that have made their home in her.

The Underground Man conducts the same sort of inescapable dialogue with himself that he conducts with the other person. He cannot merge completely with himself in a unified monologic voice simply by leaving the other's voice entirely outside himself (whatever that voice might be, without a loophole), for, as is the case with Golyadkin, his voice must also perform the function of surrogate for the other person. He cannot reach an agreement with himself, but neither can he stop talking with himself. The style of his discourse about himself is organically alien to the period, alien to finalization, both in its separate aspects and as a whole. This is the style of internally endless speech which can be mechanically cut off but cannot be organically completed.

But precisely for that reason is Dostoevsky able to conclude his work in a way so organic and appropriate for the hero; he concludes it on precisely that which would foreground the tendency toward eternal endlessness embedded in his hero's notes.

> But enough; I don't want to write more from "underground" . . .
> The "notes" of this paradoxalist do not end here, however. He could not resist and continued them. But it also seems to me that we may stop here. [*SS* IV, 224; "Notes," Part Two, ch. X]

In conclusion we will comment upon two additional characteristics of the Underground Man. Not only his discourse but his face too has its sideward glance, its loophole, and all the phenomena resulting from these. It is as if interference, voices interrupting one another, penetrate his entire body, depriving him of self-sufficiency and unambiguousness. The Underground Man hates his own face, because in it he senses the power of another person over him, the power of that other's evaluations and opinions. He himself looks on his own face with another's eyes, with the eyes of the other. And this alien glance interruptedly merges with his own glance and creates in him a peculiar hatred toward his own face:

> For instance, I hated my face; I thought it disgusting, and even suspected that there was something base in its expression and therefore every time I turned up at the office I painfully tried to behave as independently as possible so that I might not be suspected of being base, and to give my face as noble an expression as possible. "Let my face even be ugly," I thought, "but let it be noble, expressive, and above all, **extremely** intelligent." But I was absolutely and painfully certain that my face could never express those perfections; but what was worst of all, I thought it positively stupid-looking. And I would have been quite satisfied if I could have looked intelligent. In fact, I would even have put up with looking base if, at the same time, my face could have been thought terribly intelligent. [*SS* IV, 168, "Notes," Part Two, ch. I]

Just as he deliberately makes his discourse about himself unattractive, so is he made happy by the unattractiveness of his face:

> I happened to look at myself in the mirror. My harassed face struck me as extremely revolting, pale, spiteful, nasty, with disheveled hair. "No matter, I am glad of it," I thought; "I am glad that I shall seem revolting to her; I like that." [*SS* IV, 206; "Notes," Part Two, Ch. V]

This polemic with the other on the subject of himself is complicated in "Notes from Underground" by his polemic with the other on the subject of the world and society. The underground hero, in contrast to Devushkin and Golyadkin, is an ideologist.

In his ideological discourse we can easily uncover the same phenomena that are present in his discourse about himself. His discourse about the world is both overtly and covertly polemical; it polemicizes not only with other people, with other ideologies, but also with the very subject of its thinking—with the world and its order. And in this discourse on the world there are two voices, as it were, sounding for him, among which he cannot find himself and his own world, because even the world he defines with a loophole. Just as his body has become an "interrupted" thing in his own eyes, so is the world, nature, society perceived by him as "interrupted." In each of his thoughts about them there is a battle of voices, evaluations, points of view. In everything he senses above all *someone else's will* predetermining him. It is within the framework of this alien will that he perceives the world order, nature with its mechanical necessity, the social order. His own thought is developed and structured as *the thought of someone personally insulted by the world order*, personally humiliated by its blind necessity. This imparts a profoundly intimate and passionate character to his ideological discourse, and permits it to become tightly interwoven with his discourse about himself. It seems (and such indeed was Dostoevsky's intent) that we are dealing here with a single discourse, and only by arriving at himself will the hero arrive at his world. Discourse about the world, just like discourse about oneself, is profoundly dialogic: the hero casts an energetic reproach at the world order, even at the mechanical necessity of nature, as if he were talking not about the world but with the world. Of these peculiarities of ideological discourse we will speak below, when we take up the general issue of hero-ideologists and Ivan Karamazov in particular; in him these features are especially acute and clear-cut.

The discourse of the Underground Man is entirely a discourse-address. To speak, for him, means to address someone; to speak about himself means to address his own self with his own discourse; to speak about another person means to address that other person; to speak about the world means to address the world. But while speaking with himself, with another, with the world, he simultaneously addresses a third party as well: he squints his eyes to the side, toward the listener, the witness, the judge.[28] This simultaneous triple-directedness of his discourse and the fact that he does not acknowledge any object without addressing it is also responsible for the extraordinarily vivid, restless, agitated, and one might say, obtrusive nature of this discourse. It cannot be seen as a lyrical or epic discourse, calmly gravitating toward itself and its referential object; no, first and foremost one reacts to it, responds to it, is drawn into its game; it is capable of agitating and irritating, almost like the personal address of a living person. It destroys footlights, but not because of its concern for topical issues or for reasons that have any direct philosophical significance, but precisely because of that formal structure analyzed by us above.

The element of *address* is essential to every discourse in Dostoevsky, narrative discourse as well as the discourse of the hero. In Dostoevsky's world generally there is nothing merely thing-like, no mere matter, no object—there are only subjects. Therefore there is no word-judgment, no word about an object, no secondhand referential word—there is only the word as address, the word dialogically contacting another word, a word about a word addressed to a word.

iii. The Hero's Discourse and Narrative Discourse in Dostoevsky

We now move on to the novels. We shall spend less time on them, since what is new in them is manifested in dialogue and not in the monologic utterance of the characters, which becomes here more complex and subtle but which is not in general enriched by any fundamentally new structural elements.

What strikes us especially about Raskolnikov's monologic discourse is its extreme internal dialogization and the vivid personal address it makes to everything he thinks and speaks about. For Raskolnikov as well, to conceive of an object means to address it. He does not think about phenomena, he speaks with them.

In this way also does he address himself (often in the second person singular, as if to another person), he tries to persuade himself, he taunts, exposes, ridicules himself and so forth. Here is an example of one such dialogue with himself:

"It shall not be? But what are you going to do to prevent it? You'll forbid it? And what right have you? What can you promise them on your side to give you such a right? Your whole life, your whole future, you will devote to them **when you have finished your studies and obtained a post?** Yes, we have heard all that before, and that's all **words**, but now? Now something must be done, now, do you understand that? And what are you doing now? You are living upon them. They borrow on their hundred roubles pension. They borrow from the Svidrigaïlovs. How are you going to save them from the Svidrigaïlovs, from Afanasy Ivanovich Vahrushin, oh future millionaire Zeus who would arrange their lives for them? In another ten years? In another ten years, mother will be blind with knitting shawls, maybe with weeping too. She will be worn to a shadow with fasting; and my sister? Imagine for a moment what may have become of your sister in ten years? What may happen to her during those ten years? Can you fancy?"

So he tortured himself, fretting himself with such questions, and finding a kind of enjoyment in it. [*SS* V, 50; *Crime and Punishment*, Part I, ch. 4]

Such is the dialogue he conducts with himself throughout the entire novel. To be sure, the questions change, the tone changes, but the structure remains the same. Characteristically, his inner speech is filled with other people's words that he has just recently heard or read: from his mother's letter, from things Luzhin, Dunechka, Svidrigailov had said that were quoted in the letter, from Marmeladov's speech which he had just heard, from Sonechka's words which he heard from Marmeladov, etc. He inundates his own inner speech with these words of others, complicating them with his own accents or directly reaccenting them, entering into a passionate polemic with them. Consequently his inner speech is constructed like a succession of living and impassioned replies to all the words of others he has heard or has been touched by, words gathered by him from his experience of the immediately preceding days. He addresses everyone with whom he polemicizes in the second singular "you," and to almost all of them he returns their own words, with altered tone and accent. Thus every individual, every new person immediately becomes for him a symbol, and their names become common nouns: the Svidrigailovs, the Luzhins, the Sonechkas, and so forth. "Hey! You Svidrigailov! What do you want here?" he shouts to the dandy who is trying to proposition the drunken girl. Sonechka, whom he knows from Marmeladov's stories, constantly figures in his inner speech as a symbol of unnecessary and senseless sacrifice. Likewise, but with a different nuance, Dounia also figures, and the symbol of Luzhin has its own special meaning too.

Each individual, however, enters Raskolnikov's inner speech not as a character or a type, not as a personage in the plot of his life (sister, sister's fiancé, etc.), but as a symbol of a certain orientation to life and an ideological position, the symbol of a specific real-life solution to those same ideological questions that torment him. It is enough for a person to appear in his field of vision to become for him instantly an embodied solution to his own personal question, a solution different from the one at which he himself had arrived; therefore every person touches a sore spot in him and assumes a firm role in his inner speech. He relates all these persons to one another, juxtaposes or counterposes them, forces them to answer one another, to echo each other's words or to expose one another. As a result his inner speech unfolds like a philosophical drama, where the *dramatis personae* are embodied points of view on life and on the world, realized in living situations.

All the voices that Raskolnikov introduces into his inner speech come into a peculiar sort of contact, one that would be impossible among voices in an actual dialogue. Because they all sound within a single consciousness, they become, as it were, reciprocally permeable. They are brought close to one another, made to overlap; they partially intersect one another, creating the corresponding interruptions in areas of intersection.

We have already noted above that Dostoevsky's work contains no evolution of thought, not even within the boundaries of the consciousness of individual heroes (with very rare exceptions). Semantic material is always given to the hero's consciousness all at once and in its entirety, and given not as individual thoughts and propositions but as the semantic orientations of whole human beings, as voices; it remains only to make a choice among them. That internal ideological struggle which the hero wages is a struggle for a choice among already available semantic possibilities, whose quantity remains almost unchanged throughout the entire novel. The motifs "I didn't know that," "I didn't see that," "that was revealed to me only later," are absent from Dostoevsky's world. His hero knows and sees everything from the very beginning. This is why it is so common for heroes (or for a narrator speaking about a hero) to announce, after a catastrophe, that they had known and foreseen everything in advance. "Our hero shrieked and clutched at his head. Alas! That was what he had known for a long time would happen!" Thus ends *The Double*. The Underground Man is constantly emphasizing that he knew everything and foresaw everything. "I saw everything myself, all my despair was as clear as day!" exclaims the hero of "A Meek One." It is true, as we shall soon see, that the hero very often hides from himself what he knows, and pretends to himself that he does not see what in fact is constantly before his very eyes. But in such cases this characteristic trait stands out all the more sharply.

Almost no evolution of thought takes place under the influence of new material, new points of view. All that matters is the choice, the resolution of the question "Who am I" and "With whom am I?" To find one's own voice and to orient it among other voices, to combine it with some and to oppose it to others, to separate one's voice from another voice with which it has inseparably merged—these are the tasks that the heroes solve in the course of the novel. And this determines the hero's discourse. It must find itself, reveal itself among other words, within an intense field of interorientations. And all these discourses are usually given in their entirety at the very start. Throughout the entire internal and external action of the novel they are merely distributed in various ways in relation to one another, they enter into various combinations, but their quantity, given from the very start, remains unchanged. We could put it this way: from the very beginning a certain stable semantic multiplicity exists, with unchanging content, and all that occurs within it is a rearrangement of accents. Even before the murder Raskolnikov recognizes Sonya's voice from Marmeladov's stories, and immediately decides to go to her. From the very beginning her voice and her world enter Raskolnikov's field of vision, and are attached to his interior dialogue.

"Then, Sonya," [Raskolnikov says after his final confession to her] "when I used to lie there in the dark and all this became clear to me, was it a temptation of the devil, eh?"

"Hush, don't laugh, blasphemer! You don't understand, you don't understand! Oh God! He won't understand!"

"Hush, Sonya! I am not laughing. I know myself that it was the devil leading me. Hush, Sonya, hush!" he repeated with gloomy insistence. "I know it all, *I have thought it all over and over and whispered it all over to myself, lying there in the dark. . . . I've argued it all over with myself, every point of it and I know it all, all!* And how sick, how sick I was then of going over it all! I kept wanting to forget it and make a new beginning, Sonya, and leave off thinking. . . . I wanted to find out something else: it was something else led me on. *I wanted to find out then and quickly whether I was a louse like everybody else or a man.* Whether I can step over barriers or not, whether I dare stoop to pick up or not, whether I am a trembling creature or whether I have the **right** . . . I want to prove one thing only, that *the devil led me on then and he has shown me since that I had not the right to take that path, because I am just such a louse as all the rest. He was mocking me and here I've come to you now!* Welcome your guest! If I were not a louse, should I have come to you? Listen: when I went then to the old woman's I only went to **try**. . . . you may be sure of that!" [*SS* V, 436-38; *Crime and Punishment*, Part V, ch. 4]

In these whisperings of Raskolnikov, as he lay alone in the darkness, all the voices were already reverberating—and Sonya's voice as well. Among them he was searching for himself (and the crime was a breaking-through to himself), he was orienting his own accents. Now their reorientation is taking place; that dialogue, from which we quoted an excerpt above, occurs at a moment of transition in this process of rearranging accents. The voices in Raskolnikov's soul have already shifted, and now they intersect one another in a different way. But the interruption-free voice of the hero will not be heard by us within the bounds of the novel; its possibility is only hinted at in the Epilogue.

Of course this far from exhausts the characteristics of Raskolnikov's discourse, with the multiplicity of stylistic phenomena peculiar to it.

We will later return to the extraordinarily intense life this discourse leads in the dialogues with Porfiry.

We shall spend even less time on *The Idiot*, since it contains almost no fundamentally new stylistic phenomena.

The inserted narrative of Ippolit's Confession ("An Essential Explanation") is a classic example of the confession with a loophole, just as the unsuccessful suicide itself was by its very intent a suicide with a loophole. Ippolit's intent is on the whole correctly defined by Myshkin. In answer to Aglaya, who assumes that Ippolit wanted to shoot himself so that afterwards she would read his confession, Myshkin says:

"That is . . . how shall I tell you . . . it is very difficult to explain. Only he certainly wanted every one to come round him and tell him that they loved him very much and respected him; he longed for them all to beg him to remain alive. It may very well be that he had you in his mind more than anyone, because he mentioned you at such a moment . . . though, perhaps, he didn't know himself that he had you in mind." [*SS* VI, 484; *The Idiot*, Part Three, ch. 8]

This is, of course, no crude calculation but precisely a loophole that Ippolit's will has left for itself, and it confuses Ippolit's attitude toward his own self as much as it confuses his attitude toward others.[29] Therefore Ippolit's voice is just as internally open-ended, just as unacquainted with the period, as is the voice of the Underground Man. It is no accident that his final word (which is what he intended his confession to be) turned out to be in fact not final at all, since the suicide did not succeed.

Contradicting this hidden orientation toward recognition by another—an orientation that defines the entire style and tone of the whole—there are the open pronouncements by Ippolit that determine the content of his confession: independence from another's judgment, indifference toward it, display of his self-will. "I don't want to go away without leaving some word in response," he says, " a free word, not forced out of me, and not to justify myself—oh, no! . . . Simply because I want to" [Part III, ch. 7]. On that contradiction his entire image is built, and it determines his every thought and every word.

Ippolit's personal discourse on himself is interwoven with an ideological discourse which is, as with the Underground Man, addressed to the universe, addressed with a protest; the expression of this protest was to be suicide. His thought about the world develops in the form of a dialogue with some higher power that has insulted him.

The interorientations among Myshkin's speech and others' words are also intense, although of a somewhat different character. Myshkin's inner speech also develops dialogically, in relation to his own self as well as to the other. He also speaks not about himself or about another but with himself and with another, and these interior dialogues are marked by a great anxiety. But he is guided more by fear of his own word (in relation to another person) than by fear of the other's word. His reservations, hesitations, and the like can be explained in most cases by precisely this fear; beginning with his simple tact in dealing with others and ending with his deep and fundamental horror at speaking a decisive and ultimate word about another person. He is afraid of his own thoughts about the other, afraid of his own suspicions and presumptions. Very typical in this respect is his interior dialogue before Rogozhin's attempt on his life.

It is true that according to Dostoevsky's plan Myshkin was already the carrier of the *penetrated word*, that is, a word capable of actively and confidently interfering in the interior dialogue of the other person, helping that person to find his own voice. At one of those moments when the interruption of voices within Nastasya Filippovna is at its most acute, when she is desperately playing out the role of "fallen woman" in Ganichka's apartment, Myshkin introduces an almost decisive tone into her interior monologue:

> "Aren't you ashamed? Surely you are not what you are pretending to be now? It isn't possible!" cried Myshkin suddenly with deep and heartfelt reproach.
> Nastasya Filippovna was surprised, and smiled, seeming to hide something under her smile. She looked at Ganya, rather confused, and walked out of the drawing-room. But before reaching the entry, she turned sharply, went quickly up to Nina Alexandrovna, took her hand and raised it to her lips.
> "I really am not like this, he is right," she said in a rapid eager whisper, flushing hotly; and turning around, she walked out so quickly that no one had time to realise what she had come back for. [SS VI, 136; *The Idiot*, Part One, ch. 10]

He manages to say similar words, and with the same effect, to Ganya, Rogozhin, Elizaveta Prokofievna and others. But this penetrative word, once having made its appeal to one of the voices (to the genuine voice) within the other person, is—in keeping with Dostoevsky's plan—never, in the case of Myshkin, a decisive voice. It is denied any real ultimate confidence and sovereignty, and is often simply allowed to drop. A firm and integral monologic discourse is unknown to him too. The internal dialogism of his discourse is just as great and anxiety-ridden as that of the other characters.

Let us move on to *The Possessed*. We will deal only with Stavrogin's confession.

The stylistic aspect of Stavrogin's confession attracted the attention of Leonid Grossman, who devoted to this question an article entitled "Stavrogin and his Stylistics (Toward a Study of the New Chapter in *The Possessed*)."[30]

Here is a summary of his analysis:

Such is the unusual and subtle compositional system of Stavrogin's "Confession." Acute self-analysis of the criminal consciousness and a merciless recording of all its most minute ramifications made necessary in the very tone of the narration some new principle for stratifying discourse and splitting up smooth, integral speech. Throughout most of the narration one senses a disintegration of harmonious narrative style. The murderously analytical theme of a terrible sinner's confession required just such a dismembered and, as it were, constantly disintegrating embodiment. The synthetically finished, fluid and well-balanced speech of literary description would have been the least appropriate mode for this chaotically sinister and frantically unstable world of the criminal spirit. All the monstrous ugliness and inexhaustible horror of Stavrogin's reminiscences necessitated this disordering of traditional discourse. The nightmarishness of the theme stubbornly sought new devices to achieve the distorted and irritating phrase.

"Stavrogin's Confession" is a remarkable stylistic experiment in which the classical prose of the Russian novel was for the first time shaken, distorted and shifted in the direction of some unknown future achievement. Only against the background of contemporary European art can one find the criteria for evaluating all the prophetic devices of this disorganized style.[31]

Leonid Grossman took the style of Stavrogin's Confession to be a monological expression of Stavrogin's consciousness; this style, in his opinion, is adequate to the theme, that is, to the crime itself and to Stavrogin's soul. Grossman thus applied to the confession the principles of ordinary stylistics, which takes into account only the direct word, the word that recognizes only itself and its referential object. In actual fact the style of Stavrogin's Confession is determined above all by its internally dialogic orientation vis-à-vis the other person. Precisely this sideward glance at the other person determines the breaks in its style and its whole specific profile. Tikhon had precisely this in mind when he began directly with an "aesthetic critique" of the style of the confession. It is characteristic that Grossman ignores altogether and does not quote in his article what is most important in Tikhon's critique, and deals only with secondary features. Tikhon's critique is very important, for it doubtless expresses the artistic intention of Dostoevsky himself.

What does Tikhon see as the chief shortcoming of the confession? Tikhon's first words upon reading Stavrogin's notes were:

"And would it be possible for you to make a few corrections in this document?"

"Why? I wrote it honestly," Stavrogin answered.

"Something in the diction . . ."[32]

Thus the diction (style) and its unattractiveness is what struck Tikhon above all in the confession. We quote an excerpt from their dialogue which reveals the true essence of Stavrogin's style:

"It's as if you deliberately want to represent yourself more coarsely than

your heart would wish it . . ." said Tikhon, growing more and more bold. Apparently the "document" had made a strong impression on him.

"Represent? I repeat: I did not 'represent myself' and in particular I did not 'put on airs.'"

Tikhon quickly lowered his eyes.

"This document comes straight from the needs of a heart mortally wounded —do I understand you correctly?" he said insistently and with unusual fervor. "Yes, this is penitence and the natural need for it which has overwhelmed you, and you have entered upon a noble path, an unprecedented path. *But you seem to despise and disdain in advance all who will read what is written here, and you are calling them to battle.* You are not ashamed of confessing your crime, *so why are you ashamed of repentance?*"

"Ashamed?"

"You are *ashamed* and *afraid!*"

"Afraid?"

"Mortally. *Let them stare at me, you say; well, but you yourself, how are you going to look at them?* Certain places in your account are even intensified in diction, as if you admire your own psychology and grasp at every trifle in order to astound *the reader* with an insensitivity which you may well not have. *What is this, if not a prideful challenge from a guilty man to a judge?*" ["Dokumenty . . .", p. 33]

Stavrogin's confession, like the confessions of Ippolit and the Underground Man, is a confession intensely oriented toward another person, without whom the hero could not manage but whom at the same time he despises and whose judgment he does not accept. Stavrogin's confession, therefore, like the other confessions discussed earlier, is deprived of any finalizing force and tends toward that same vicious circle that marked the speech of the Underground Man. Without recognition, and affirmation by another person Stavrogin is incapable of accepting himself, but at the same time he does not want to accept the other's judgment of him.

"But as far as I am concerned there will remain those who will know everything and who will stare at me, and I at them. I want everyone to stare at me. Whether or not this will make it easier for me I do not know. I resort to it as the last means."

At the same time, however, the style of his confession is dictated by his hatred and nonacceptance of this "everyone."

Stavrogin's attitude toward himself and toward the other person is locked into that same vicious circle which the Underground Man had tread, "paying no attention to his companions" and at the same time stomping his boots so they could not fail to notice that he was paying them no attention. Here it is presented through different material, very far removed from the realm of the comic. But Stavrogin's position is nevertheless comical. "Even in the *form* of this great confession there is something *ridiculous*," Tikhon says.

But if we turn to the "Confession" itself, we must admit that judged by external indicators of style it differs sharply from "Notes from Underground." No one else's word, no one else's accent forces its way into the fabric. There is not a single reservation, not a single repetition, not a single ellipsis. No external signs of the overwhelming influence of another's word appear to register here at all. Here, indeed, the other's word has penetrated so deeply within, to the very atoms of the construction, the conflicting rejoinders overlap one another so densely that discourse appears on the surface monologic. But nevertheless even the careless ear can catch in it sharp and irreconcilable voices interrupting one another, as was pointed out immediately by Tikhon.

The style is determined above all by a cynical ignoring of the other person, an ignoring that is pointedly deliberate. Sentences are crudely abrupt and cynically precise. This is not sober-minded strictness or precision, this is not documentation in the usual sense, because that sort of realistic documentation is oriented toward its referential object and, for all the dryness of its style, does strive to be adequate to all aspects of the object. Stavrogin attempts to present his word without any evaluative accent, to make it intentionally wooden, to eliminate all human tones in it. He wants everyone to stare at him, but at the same time he repents in an immobile and deathly mask. This is why he rearranges every sentence so that his personal tone does not surface, so that his repentant, or perhaps simply agitated, accent does not slip through. That is why he breaks up his sentences, because a normal sentence is too flexible and subtle in its transmission of the human voice.

We cite a single example:

"I, Nikolai Stavrogin, a retired officer, was living in Petersburg in 186-, indulging in lewdness in which I found no pleasure. For some time I had had three apartments. I myself was living in one of them, in a hotel, with board and maid-service, where at that time Marya Lebyadkin, now my lawful wife, was, too. I rented both my other apartments by the month for love-affairs: in one I received a certain lady who loved me and, in the other, her maid, and for a while I was very much occupied with the effort to bring them both together so that the lady and the girl would meet at my place. Knowing both their characters, I expected some pleasure for myself from this stupid joke." ["Dokumenty . . .", p. 15]

The sentence breaks off, as it were, at just that point where a living human voice begins. Stavrogin seems to turn away from us as soon as he casts a word our way. It is noteworthy that he even tries to omit the word "I" when speaking of himself, where "I" is not the simple formal subject of the verb but where it might carry some especially strong and personal accent (for example, in the first and last sentences of the quoted excerpt).[c] All those syntactical peculiarities mentioned by Grossman—the broken sentence, the deliberately lackluster or deliberately cynical word, etc.—are in fact proof of Stavrogin's fundamental effort to eliminate, emphatically and aggressively, any living personal accent from his own voice, to speak with his back turned to the listener. Alongside this element, of course, we also find in Stavrogin's "Confession" several phenomena familiar to us from previous monologic utterances of characters, but they are present in weakened form and are in any case subordinated to this other basic dominating tendency.

The narration of *The Adolescent*, especially in the beginning, seems to take us back to "Notes from Underground": the same hidden and open polemic with the reader, the same reservations, ellipses, the same infiltration of anticipated responses, the same dialogization of all attitudes toward oneself and toward the other. The same traits, of course, characterize the discourse of the Adolescent as a hero.

Somewhat different phenomena surface in Versilov's discourse. His discourse is restrained and, as it were, thoroughly aesthetic. But in fact it too lacks a genuine attractiveness. It is entirely constructed in such a way as to muffle, deliberately, emphatically, with a restrained and disdainful challenge to the other person, all personal tones and accents. This distresses and offends the adolescent, who yearns to hear Versilov's own true voice. With great mastery Dostoevsky permits that voice too in rare moments to break through, with new and unexpected intonations. For a long time Versilov stubbornly avoids meeting the adolescent face to face without the verbal mask he has perfected and always wears with such elegance. Here is one of the meetings where Versilov's voice breaks through:

"Ah, these staircases . . ." Versilov moaned, dragging out his vowels endlessly, probably trying to fill the silence so as not to say something he would regret later or to prevent me from saying something he didn't want me to say. "I'm no longer used to stairs . . . that's three floors . . . but don't bother, I'm sure I'll be able to find my way in the dark now. . . . Thank you, go back now, my boy, don't catch cold. . . ." [. . .]

He was silent as I followed him all the way to the outer door. He opened it. A rush of wind blew out my candle. I suddenly seized his hand. It was completely dark. He started but said nothing. I pulled his hand to my mouth and kissed it. I kissed it again and again, many times, fervently.

"My dear little boy, what have I done that you should love me so much?" he

---

[c]Russian has a highly inflected verb system, and personal pronouns can be easily omitted without any disorienting effects. In the above example, the first-singular pronoun is absent at the end of the first sentence (". . . in which [I] found no pleasure"); and at the end of the last (". . . characters, [I] expected some pleasure for myself from this stupid joke").

said now in a quite different voice. There was a quiver in it and a certain ring that was new to me; it was as if someone else had spoken. [*SS* VIII, 229-30; *The Adolescent*, Part Two, ch. 1, II]

The interruption of two voices within Versilov's voice is particularly abrupt and strong in his relationship to Akhmakova (love-hate) and also in part to the adolescent's mother. This interrupting activity results in the complete temporal disintegration of these voices—a doubling.

In *The Brothers Karamazov* a new element appears in the structure of a character's monologic speech, and we must briefly consider it, although strictly speaking it is already fully revealed in dialogue.

We have said that Dostoevsky's heroes know everything from the very outset, and need only make their choice from among fully available semantic material. But sometimes they conceal from themselves what they in fact already know and see. The simplest expressions of this are the dual thoughts so characteristic of Dostoevsky's heroes (even Myshkin and Alyosha). One of the thoughts is obvious, determining the *content* of speech; the other is hidden, but nevertheless determines the *structuring* of speech, casting its shadow upon it.

The story "A Meek One" is directly structured on the motif of conscious ignorance. The hero conceals from himself and carefully eliminates from his own discourse the very thing that is constantly before his eyes. His entire monologue can be reduced to his forcing himself to see and admit what he has in fact known and seen from the very beginning. Two-thirds of the monologue is defined by the hero's desperate attempt to get around what already internally determines his thought and speech as an invisibly present "truth." At first he tries to "bring his thoughts to a focus" that lies on the far side of that truth. But all the same he is ultimately forced to gather his thoughts together at what is for him a terrible point of "truth."

This stylistic motif is developed most profoundly in the speech of Ivan Karamazov. First his desire for his father's death and then his participation in the murder are the facts that invisibly determine his discourse, although of course in tight and inseparable connection with his doubled ideological orientation in the world. To a considerable extent the process of Ivan's inner life as depicted in the novel is the process of his recognition and affirmation, for himself and for others, of what he has in fact already long known.

We repeat, this process unfolds primarily in dialogues, and above all in dialogues with Smerdyakov. Smerdyakov gradually gains control over that voice of Ivan's which Ivan is hiding from his own self. Smerdyakov is able to govern that voice precisely because Ivan's consciousness does not look in that direction and does not wish to look there. He finally extracts from Ivan the deed and the word he needs. Ivan leaves for Chermashnya, where Smerdyakov had been insistently directing him.

> When he had seated himself in the carriage, Smerdyakov jumped up to arrange the rug.
>
> "You see . . . I am going to Chermashnya," broke suddenly from Ivan Fyodorovich. Again, as the day before, the words seemed to drop of themselves, and he laughed, too, a peculiar, nervous laugh. He remembered it long after.
>
> "It's a true saying then, that 'it's always worthwhile speaking to a clever man,'" answered Smerdyakov firmly, looking significantly at Ivan Fyodorovich. [SS IX, 351; *The Brothers Karamazov*, Part Two, Book Five, ch. 7]

This process of self-elucidation and gradual realization of what he in fact already knew, what his second voice was saying, makes up the content of the subsequent parts of the novel. The process remained unfinished. It was interrupted by Ivan's mental illness.

Ivan's ideological discourse, the personal orientation of this discourse and its dialogic addressivity toward its referential object, stand out with extraordinary clarity and vividness. It is not a judgment about the world but rather a personal nonacceptance of the world, a rejection of it, addressed to God as the guilty party responsible for the world order. But this ideological discourse of Ivan's develops, as it were, in a double dialogue: inserted into the dialogue between Ivan and Alyosha is the dialogue (more accurately a dialogized monologue) that Ivan creates between the Grand Inquisitor and Christ.

We shall touch briefly upon one other variety of discourse in Dostoevsky—hagiographic discourse. It appears in the speech of the cripple Maria Lebyadkina, in Makar Dolgoruky, and finally in the Life of Zosima. Its first appearance was perhaps in Myshkin's stories (especially in the episode with Marie). The hagiographic word is a word without a sideward glance, calmly adequate to itself and its referential object. But in Dostoevsky this discourse is of course stylized. A monologically firm and self-confident voice for the hero never really appears in his works, but a certain tendency toward it is clearly felt in several rare instances. When a hero, in keeping with Dostoevsky's plan, comes close to the truth about himself, makes peace with the other and takes possession of his own authentic voice, his style and tone begin to change. When, for example, the hero of "A Meek One" arrives, according to plan, at the truth: "the truth irresistibly ennobles his heart and mind. Toward the end the very tone of his narrative becomes different from its incoherent beginning" (from Dostoevsky's Foreword).

Here is the hero's changed voice on the last page of the story:

> She's blind, blind! She's dead, she cannot hear. You do not know that I would have built a paradise for you to dwell in. For I had a paradise in my heart,

and I would have lavished it on you. Granted you would not have given me your love—never mind, what of it? Everything would have remained **like that**, it would have gone on being **like that**. You would have spoken to me as to a friend; we would have delighted in our talks and laughed together, looking happily into each other's eyes, that's all. And that's how it would have been. And even if you came to love another, why—never mind, never mind! You would have walked along with him and smiled, while I would have looked at you from across the street. . . . Oh, never mind anything, if only she would open her eyes just once! For one single moment, just one! If she would only look at me the way she had done earlier today when she stood before me and swore to be a faithful wife to me! Oh, in that single glance she would have understood everything. [*SS* X, 419]

Analogous words, in the same style but in tones of fulfillment, can be heard in the speech of "the young brother of the Elder Zosima," in the speech of Zosima himself after his victory over himself (the episode with the orderly and the duel), and finally in the speech of the "mysterious visitor" after he has made his confession. But all this speech is to a greater or lesser degree subordinated to the stylized tones of a clerical-hagiographic or clerical-confessional style. In the narration itself these tones appear only once: in *The Brothers Karamazov*, in the chapter "Cana of Galilee."

A special place must also be allotted to *penetrated discourse*, which has its own functions in Dostoevsky's works. It is, according to Dostoevsky's plan, a firmly monologic, undivided discourse, a word without a sideward glance, without a loophole, without internal polemic. But such a discourse is only possible in actual dialogue with another person.

In general, the reconciliation and merging of voices even within the bounds of a single consciousness—according to Dostoevsky's plan and in accordance with his basic ideological premises—cannot be a monologic act, but rather presumes the attachment of the hero's voice to the chorus; for this to happen, however, it is necessary to subdue and muffle the fictive voices that interrupt and mock a person's genuine voice. On the level of Dostoevsky's social ideology, this expressed itself as a demand for the intelligentsia to merge with the common people: "Humble thyself, proud man; above all, subdue thy pride! Humble thyself, idle man, and first of all labor on thy native land!"[d] On the level of his religious ideology this meant to join the chorus and proclaim with them "Hosanna!" In this chorus the word passes from mouth to mouth in identical tones of praise, joy and gladness. But what unfolds on the level of his novels is not a polyphony

[d]From Dostoevsky's Pushkin Speech (1880). Dostoevsky is discussing Aleko, hero of Pushkin's narrative poem *The Gypsies* (1824). See *The Diary of a Writer*, 1880, August, ch. II, p. 970.

of reconciled voices but a polyphony of battling and internally divided voices. These latter voices were no longer present on the level of Dostoevsky's narrowly ideological aspirations but were present in the actual reality of his time. The social and religious utopia inherent in his ideological views did not swallow up or dissolve in itself his objectively artistic vision.

A few words about the narrator's style.

In the later works as well the narrator's discourse does not, if compared with the characters' discourse, introduce any new tones or fundamentally new orientations. It is, as before, one discourse among many discourses. In general the narration moves between two poles: between a drily informative, documentary discourse that hardly represents at all, and the discourse of the character. But where narration tends in the direction of a character's discourse, it gives that discourse a displaced or altered accent (mocking, polemical, ironic) and only in the rarest instances attempts any single-accented merging with it.

Between these two poles the narrator's discourse moves in every novel.

The influence of these two poles is clearly visible even in the titles of the chapters. Some of the titles are taken directly from the characters' words (but as chapter titles these words, of course, take on a different accent); others are given in the style of a character; others are of a strictly informative character; still others are of the conventionally literary sort. Here is an example of each out of *The Brothers Karamazov*: in Book Two, ch. IV: "Why Is Such a Man Alive" (Dmitry's words); in Book One, ch. II: "He Gets Rid of his Eldest Son" (in the style of Fyodor Pavlovich); in Book One, ch. I: "Fyodor Pavlovich Karamazov" (informative title); in Book Five, ch. VI: "For a While a Very Obscure One" (a conventionally literary title). The chapter titles of *The Brothers Karamazov* comprise, as if in microcosm, the whole multiplicity of tones and styles incorporated into the novel.

In no novel is this multiplicity of tones and styles reduced to a single common denominator. Nowhere is there a discourse-*dominant*, be it authorial discourse or the discourse of a major hero. Unity of style in this monologic sense does not exist in Dostoevsky's novels. As concerns the positioning of the narration as a whole, it is, as we know, dialogically addressed to the hero. A thoroughgoing dialogization of all elements of the work without exception is an essential aspect of the author's design.

Wherever the narration does not interfere as an alien voice in the heroes' interior dialogue, does not enter into an interruption-ridden union with the speech of one or another of the characters, then it presents facts without voice, without intonation or with conventional intonation. Dry, informative, documentary discourse is, as it were, voiceless discourse, raw material for the voice. But a voiceless and accentless fact is presented in such a way that it can enter the hero's field of vision and can become material for his own personal voice, material for the judgment he passes on himself. The author does not insert into this material any judgment or evaluation of his own. This is why the narrator has no surplus field of vision, no perspective.

Thus certain words directly and openly participate in the interior dialogue of the hero, and others do so only potentially: the author structures them in such a way that they can be controlled by the consciousness and voice of the hero himself, their accent is not predetermined, a place is left open for it.

Thus Dostoevsky's works contain no final, finalizing discourse that defines anything once and for ever. Thus there can be no firm image of the hero answering to the question "Who is *he*?" The only questions here are "Who am *I*?" and "Who are *you*?". But even these questions reverberate in a continuous and open-ended interior dialogue. Discourse of the hero and discourse about the hero are determined by an open dialogic attitude toward oneself and toward the other. Authorial discourse cannot encompass the hero and his word on all sides, cannot lock in and finalize him from without. It can only address itself to him. All definitions and all points of view are swallowed up by dialogue, drawn into its becoming. Secondhand discourse—discourse which, without interfering in the interior dialogue of the hero, would neutrally and objectively structure his finalized image—is unknown to Dostoevsky. "Secondhand" discourse providing a final summary of personality does not enter into his design. Whatever is firm, dead, finished, unable to respond, whatever has already spoken its final word, does not exist in Dostoevsky's world.

iv. Dialogue in Dostoevsky

A character's self-consciousness in Dostoevsky is thoroughly dialogized: in its every aspect it is turned outward, intensely addressing itself, another, a third person. Outside this living addressivity toward itself and toward the other it does not exist, even for itself. In this sense it could be said that the person in Dostoevsky is the *subject of an address*. One cannot talk about him; one can only address oneself to him. Those "depths of the human soul," whose representation Dostoevsky considered the main task of his realism "in a higher sense," are revealed only in an intense act of address. It is impossible to master the inner man, to see and understand him by making him into an object of indifferent neutral analysis; it is also impossible to master him by merging with him, by empathizing with him. No, one can approach him and reveal him—or more precisely, force him to reveal himself—only by addressing him dialogically. And to portray the inner man, as Dostoevsky understood it, was possible only by portraying his communion with another. Only in communion, in the interaction of one person with another, can the "man in man" be revealed, for others as well as for oneself.

It is fully understandable that at the center of Dostoevsky's artistic world must lie dialogue, and dialogue not as a means but as an end in itself. Dialogue here is not the threshold to action, it is the action itself. It is not a means for revealing, for bringing to the surface the already ready-made character of a person; no, in dialogue a person not only shows himself outwardly, but he becomes for the first time that which he is—and, we repeat, not only for others but for himself as well. To be means to communicate dialogically. When dialogue ends, everything ends. Thus dialogue, by its very essence, cannot and must not come to an end. At the level of his religious-utopian worldview Dostoevsky carries dialogue into eternity, conceiving of it as eternal co-rejoicing, co-admiration, con-cord. At the level of the novel, it is presented as the unfinalizability of dialogue, although originally as dialogue's vicious circle.

Everything in Dostoevsky's novels tends toward dialogue, toward a dialogic opposition, as if tending toward its center. All else is the means; dialogue is the end. A single voice ends nothing and resolves nothing. Two voices is the minimum for life, the minimum for existence.

The potential endlessness of dialogue in Dostoevsky's design already in itself answers the question why such dialogue cannot be plot-dependent in the strict sense of the word, for a plot-dependent dialogue strives toward conclusion just as inevitably as does the plot of which it is in fact a component. Therefore dialogue in Dostoevsky is, as we have said, always external to the plot, that is, internally independent of the plot-related interrelationships of the speakers—although, of course, dialogue is prepared for by the plot. Myshkin's dialogue with Rogozhin, for example, is a dialogue "man to man," but in no sense is it a dialogue of two rivals, although rivalry is precisely what has brought them together. The nucleus of the dialogue is always external to the plot, no matter how intensely it is motivated by the plot (for example, Aglaya's dialogue with Nastasya Filippovna). The shell of the dialogue, however, is always intimately plot-related. Only in Dostoevsky's early works are dialogues of a somewhat abstract nature and not firmly inserted in the framework of the plot.

The basic scheme for dialogue in Dostoevsky is very simple: the opposition of one person to another person as the opposition of "I" to "the other."

In Dostoevsky's early works this "other person" is still rather abstract: it is another person as such. "I'm alone, and they are everyone else," thought the Underground Man in his youth. But he continues to think in essentially the same way throughout the rest of his life. The world for him falls into two camps: in one, "I," in the other, "they," that is, all "others" without exception, no matter who they are. Every person exists for him, first and foremost, as "the other person." And this definition of the person directly conditions all the Underground Man's attitudes toward him. He reduces all people to a single common denominator—"the other." School friends, fellow civil servants, his servant Apollon, the woman who has fallen in love with him, even the creator of the world order with whom he polemicizes, all are reduced to this category by the Underground Man, and his primary reaction to them is as "others" in relation to himself.

Such abstractness is provided for by the entire plan of the work. The life of the Underground Man is absolutely devoid of any plot. A plotted life in which there are friends, brothers, parents, wives, rivals, mistresses, etc., and in which he himself could be a brother, a son, a husband, is experienced by him only in his dreams. In his actual life there are no real human categories. This is why the internal and external dialogues in this work are so abstract and so classically precise that they can be compared only with dialogues in Racine. The endlessness of the external dialogue emerges here with the same mathematical clarity as does the endlessness of internal dialogue. A real-life other voice inevitably fuses with the other voice already ringing in the hero's ears. And the real-life discourse of the "other person" is also drawn into the movement of a *perpetuum mobile*, as are all anticipated replies. The hero demands from that discourse full recognition and affirmation, but at the same time does not accept that recognition and affirmation, for in that discourse he is the weak and passive party: he is the one who is understood, accepted, forgiven. His pride cannot bear that.

"And I will never forgive you for the tears I could not help shedding before you just now, like some silly old woman put to shame. And for what I am confessing to you now I shall never forgive you either!" he shouts, during his confession to the girl who has fallen in love with him.

"Do you understand how I will hate you now after saying this, for having been here and listening? After all, a man speaks out like this once in a lifetime and then it is in hysterics! What more do you want? Why, after all, do you still stand there in front of me? Why do you torment me? Why don't you go?" [SS IV, 237-38; "Notes," Part Two, ch. IX]

But she did not go. Something still worse happened: she understood him and accepted him as he was. Her sympathy and acceptance were intolerable to him.

To my overwrought brain the thought also occurred that our parts were after all completely reversed now, that she was now the heroine, while I was just a crushed and humiliated creature as she had been before me that night—four days before . . . And all this came into my mind during the minutes I was lying face down on the sofa!

My God! surely I was not envious of her then?

I don't know, to this day I cannot decide, and at the time, of course, I was still less able to understand what I was feeling than now. I cannot get on without domineering and tyrannizing over someone, after all, but—but, after all, there is no explaining anything by reasoning and consequently it is useless to reason. [SS, 239; "Notes," Part Two, ch. IX]

The Underground Man remains in his inescapable opposition to the "other person." A real-life human voice and the other's anticipated reply are equally incapable of finalizing his endless internal dialogue.

We have already said that internal dialogue (that is, microdialogue) and the principles for constructing it served as the basis on which Dostoevsky originally introduced other real voices. This interrelationship between internal dialogue and exterior, compositionally expressed dialogue we should now examine more carefully, for it contains the essence of Dostoevsky's handling of dialogue.

We saw that in *The Double* the second hero (the double) was directly introduced by Dostoevsky as the personified second internal voice of Golyadkin himself. The narrator's voice was also of such a sort. But Golyadkin's internal voice was itself only a substitute, a specific surrogate for the actual voice of another person. This helped to bring about a very close bond between voices and the extreme (to be sure, here one-sided) intensity of their dialogue. The other's (the double's) response could not avoid touching Golyadkin's sore spots, for it was nothing other than his own word in someone else's mouth —but it was, so to speak, his own word turned inside out, with a shifted and maliciously distorted accent.

This principle of voice combination is preserved, although in more complex and profound form, in all of Dostoevsky's subsequent works. To it he is indebted for the extraordinary power of his dialogues. Two characters are always introduced by Dostoevsky in such a way that each of them is intimately linked with the internal voice of the other, although a direct personification of this voice never again appears (with the exception of Ivan Karamazov's devil). In their dialogue, therefore, the rejoinders of the one touch and even partially coincide with the rejoinders of the other's interior dialogue. A deep essential bond or partial coincidence between the borrowed words of one hero and the internal and secret discourse of another hero—this is the indispensable element in all Dostoevsky's crucial dialogues; the major dialogues are structured directly on this principle.

We shall quote a brief but very vivid dialogue from *The Brothers Karamazov*.

Ivan Karamazov still fully believes in Dmitry's guilt. But in the depths of his soul, as yet almost hidden from himself, he begins to pose the question of his own guilt. The internal struggle in his soul is extremely intense. It is at this moment that the following dialogue with Alyosha takes place.

Alyosha categorically denies Dmitry's guilt.

"Who is the murderer then, according to you?" he [Ivan—M. B.] asked, with apparent coldness. There was even a supercilious note in his voice.

"You know who," Alyosha pronounced in a low penetrating voice.

"Who? You mean the myth about that crazy idiot, the epileptic, Smerdyakov?" Alyosha suddenly felt himself trembling all over.

"You know who," broke helplessly from him. He could scarcely breathe.

"Who? Who?" Ivan cried almost fiercely. All his restraint suddenly vanished.

"I only know one thing," Alyosha went on, still almost in a whisper, "it **wasn't you** who killed father."

"Not you! What do you mean by 'not you'?" Ivan was thunderstruck.

"It was not you who killed father, not you!" Alyosha repeated firmly.

The silence lasted for half a minute.

"I know I didn't. Are you raving?" said Ivan, with a pale, distorted smile. His eyes were riveted on Alyosha. They were standing again under a lamp post.

"No, Ivan. You've told yourself several times that you are the murderer."

"When did I say so? I was in Moscow. . . When have I said so?" Ivan faltered helplessly.

"You've said so to yourself many times, when you've been alone during these two dreadful months," Alyosha went on softly and distinctly as before. Yet he was speaking now, as it were, not of himself, not of his own will, but obeying some irresistible command. "You have accused yourself and have confessed to yourself that you are the murderer and no one else. But you didn't do it: you are mistaken: you are not the murderer. Do you hear? It was not you! God has sent me to tell you so." [*SS* X, 117-18; *The Brothers Karamazov*, Part Four, Book Eleven, ch. V]

Here Dostoevsky's device is laid bare and exposed to full view in the very content itself. Alyosha says openly that he is answering a question that Ivan has asked himself in an internal dialogue. This excerpt is a highly typical example of the penetrative word and its artistic role in dialogue. The following is very important. Ivan's own secret words on someone else's lips evoke in him repulsion and hatred toward Alyosha, and precisely because they have touched a sore spot they are indeed an answer to his question. He has now come to the point where he refuses, in general, any discussion of his internal affairs by others. Alyosha understands this perfectly well, but he foresees that Ivan—the "profound conscience"—will inevitably sooner or later give himself the categorically affirmative answer: I am the murderer. In keeping with Dostoevsky's plan, Ivan could not have given himself any other answer. And that is why Alyosha's word must make itself useful precisely as the word of *another*:

> "Brother," Alyosha began again, in a shaking voice, "I have said this to you, because you'll believe my word, I know that. I tell you once and for all, it was **not you.** You hear, once for all! God has put it into my heart to say this to you, even though it may make you hate me from this hour."

Alyosha's words, intersecting with Ivan's inner speech, must be juxtaposed to the words of the devil, which also repeat the words and thoughts of Ivan himself. The devil introduces into Ivan's internal dialogue accents of mockery and hopeless condemnation, similar to the voice of the devil in Trishatov's projected opera, whose song "mingles with the hymns, almost blending with them, although it's completely different from them." The devil speaks as Ivan and at the same time as "the other person," hostilely exaggerating and distorting his accents. "You are me, my own self," Ivan tells the devil, "only with a different face." Alyosha also introduces into Ivan's interior dialogue someone else's accents, but in precisely the opposite direction. Alyosha, as "other," carries tones of love and reconciliation, which are of course impossible on Ivan's lips in relationship to himself. Alyosha's speech and the speech of the devil, identically repeating Ivan's words, impart to those words diametrically opposed accents. One intensifies one side of his internal dialogue, the other another.

For Dostoevsky this distribution of characters and the interrelationship of their discourses is typical to the highest degree. In Dostoevsky's dialogues, collision and quarreling occurs not between two integral monologic voices, but between two divided voices (one of those voices, at least, is divided). The open rejoinders of the one answer the hidden rejoinders of the other. The opposition of one hero to two other heroes, each of which is linked with a contrary rejoinder in the internal dialogue of the first hero, is for Dostoevsky a most typical group.

For a correct understanding of Dostoevsky's plan, it is very important to consider the value he placed on the role of the other person as "another," since Dostoevsky's basic artistic effects are achieved by passing one and the same word through various voices all counterposed to one another. As a parallel to the above-quoted dialogue between Alyosha and Ivan, we quote an excerpt from Dostoevsky's letter to G. A. Kovner (1877):

> I found not quite to my liking the two lines in your letter where you say that you

feel no remorse at all for the act you committed in the bank. There is something higher than the conclusions of reason and the ever-present extenuating circumstances, something to which everyone is subject (that is, again something similar to a **banner**). Perhaps you are sufficiently intelligent not to take offense at the frankness and **unsolicited** nature of my remark. First of all, I myself am no better than you or anyone else (and this is not at all false modesty, what would that bring me?), and secondly, if I justify you in my own way in my heart (as I invite you to justify me), then it is still better if I justify you rather than you justify yourself.[33]

Analogous to this is the distribution of characters in *The Idiot*. Here there are two main groups: Nastasya Filippovna, Myshkin, and Rogozhin are one group; Myshkin, Nastasya Filippovna, and Aglaya are the other. We shall pause briefly only on the first group.

Nastasya Filippovna's voice, as we have seen, is divided between the voice that pronounces her a guilty "fallen woman" and the voice that vindicates and accepts her. Her speech is full of the interruption-prone combination of these two voices; first one predominates, then the other, but neither can ultimately defeat the other. The accents of each voice are intensified or interrupted by the real voices of other people. Condemnatory voices force her to exaggerate the accents of her accusatory voice in order to spite others. Thus her confession begins to sound like Stavrogin's confession, or—in a stylistically closer example—like the confession of the Underground Man. When she comes to Ganya's apartment, where she is, as she knows, condemned, she plays the role of the courtesan out of spite, and only Myshkin's voice, intersecting with her internal dialogue in another direction, forces her to abruptly change that tone and to respectfully kiss the hand of Ganya's mother, whom she had just mocked. The place of Myshkin and of his real voice in Nastasya Filippovna's life is determined by his connection with one of the rejoinders in her internal dialogue.

". . . Haven't I dreamed of you myself? You are right, I dreamed of you long ago, when I lived five years all alone in his country home. I used to think and dream, think and dream, and I was always imagining some one like you, kind, good and honest and so stupid that he would come forward all of a sudden and say, 'You are not to blame, Nastasya Filippovna, and I adore you.' I used to dream like that, till I nearly went out of my mind. . . ." [*SS* VI, 197; *The Idiot*, Part One, ch. 16]

It was this anticipated reply of the other that she had heard in the actual voice of Myshkin, who repeats it almost word for word on that fateful evening at Nastasya Filippovna's.

The positioning of Rogozhin is somewhat different. From the very beginning he becomes for Nastasya Filippovna the symbol for the embodiment of her second voice. "I'm Rogozhin's woman," she keeps repeating. To carouse with Rogozhin, to go to Rogozhin means for her to embody and realize wholly her second voice. Rogozhin's bartering and buying her, Rogozhin's drinking bouts are a maliciously exaggerated symbol of her fall. This is unjust to Rogozhin, for he, especially at the beginning, is not at all inclined to condemn her, although he is capable of hating her. Rogozhin means the knife, and she knows it. Thus is this group constructed. The real-life voices of Myshkin and Rogozhin are interwoven and intersect with the voices in Nastasya Filippovna's internal dialogue. The interruptions in her own voice are transformed into interruptions in her plot relationships with Myshkin and Rogozhin: her frequent flights from the altar with Myshkin to Rogozhin, and from him back again to Myshkin, her hatred and love toward Aglaya.[34]

Of a somewhat different sort are Ivan Karamazov's dialogues with Smerdyakov. Here Dostoevsky reaches the summit of his mastery in handling dialogue.

The interorienting relationships between Ivan and Smerdyakov are very complex. We have already said that the desire for his father's death, invisible and half hidden from Ivan himself, determines some of Ivan's speech in the beginning of the novel. This hidden voice is co-opted, however, by Smerdyakov, and co-opted with absolute precision and self-assurance.[35]

Ivan, according to Dostoevsky's plan, wants his father murdered, but he wants it under the condition that he himself remain not only externally but even *internally* uninvolved in it. He wants the murder to occur as an inevitability of fate, not only *apart from his will*, but *in opposition to it*. "Be sure," he says to Alyosha, "I shall always defend him [father—M. B.]. But in my wishes I reserve myself full latitude in this case."[e] The internally dialogic dissociation of Ivan's will might be presented in the form of two such rejoinders in a dialogue:

"I do not desire my father's murder. If it happens, it will be against my will."

"But I desire that the murder take place against my will, because then I will be internally uninvolved in it and will have nothing with which to reproach myself."

Thus is Ivan's internal dialogue with himself constructed. Smerdyakov guesses or, more precisely, hears clearly the second rejoinder of this dialogue, but he understands the loophole contained in it in his own way: as Ivan's striving not to provide any evidence that might prove his participation in the crime, as the extreme external and internal caution of a "clever man" who avoids all direct words that might expose him, and with whom, therefore, "it's always worthwhile speaking," because it is possible to speak with him by hints alone.

---

[e]Book Three, ch. IX.

Ivan's voice seems to Smerdyakov before the murder to be absolutely integral and undivided. Ivan's desire for the death of his father seems to him an absolutely simple and natural deduction drawn from his ideological views, from his assertion that "all is permitted." The first rejoinder in Ivan's internal dialogue Smerdyakov does not hear, and to the very end he does not believe that Ivan's first voice really and seriously did not wish the death of his father. In Dostoevsky's plan this voice was indeed serious, and it is this voice that gives Alyosha grounds for vindicating Ivan, in spite of the fact that Alyosha himself is perfectly well aware of that second, "Smerdyakovian" voice in him.

Smerdyakov self-confidently and firmly controls Ivan's will, or more precisely, invests that will with the concrete forms of a specific volitional statement. Through Smerdyakov, Ivan's internal rejoinder is transformed from a desire into a deed. Smerdyakov's dialogues with Ivan before the latter's departure to Chermashnya are in fact embodiments, astonishing in their artistic effect, of a conversation between Smerdyakov's open and conscious will (encoded in hints) and Ivan's hidden will (hidden even from himself), taking place, as it were, without the participation of Ivan's open and conscious will. Smerdyakov speaks directly and confidently, addressing his hints and equivocations to Ivan's second voice; Smerdyakov's words intersect with the second rejoinder in Ivan's internal dialogue. Ivan's first voice answers him. Therefore Ivan's words, which Smerdyakov understands as an allegory with the opposite meaning, are in fact not allegories at all. They are Ivan's direct words. But the voice that answers Smerdyakov is interrupted here and there by the hidden rejoinder of his second voice. Thanks to these interruptions, Smerdyakov remains fully convinced of Ivan's compliance.

These interruptions in Ivan's voice are very subtle, and express themselves not so much in words as in pauses quite inappropriate from the point of view of the meaning of his speech, in changes of tone that are incomprehensible from the point of view of his first voice, in his unexpected and inappropriate laughter, and so on. If the voice in which Ivan answers Smerdyakov were his only and integral voice, that is, if it were a purely monologic voice, all these phenomena would be impossible. They are the result of the interruption, the interference of two voices within a single voice, of two rejoinders within a single rejoinder. Thus are Ivan's dialogues with Smerdyakov structured before the murder.

After the murder, the structure of the dialogues is different. Here Dostoevsky forces Ivan to recognize, by degrees, dimly and ambiguously at first and then clearly and distinctly, his own hidden will in another person. What had seemed to him a knowingly inactive and therefore innocent desire, well-hidden even from himself, turns out to be, for Smerdyakov, a clear and distinctly expressed desire directing Ivan's actions. Ivan's second voice, so it turns out, was sounding forth and issuing orders and Smerdyakov was only an executor of its will, its "faithful servant Licharda." In the first two dialogues, Ivan becomes convinced that he had been in any case internally involved in the murder, for he had actually desired it and had unambiguously expressed this will to another. In the final dialogue he comes to realize the fact of his external involvement in the murder as well.

We should attend to the following point. At first Smerdyakov took Ivan's voice for an integrated monologic voice. He heard his confession about "all is permitted" as the word of a teacher, chosen and self-confident. At first he did not understand that Ivan's voice was bifurcated and that its convincing, self-confident tone was meant to convince Ivan himself, and certainly not to transmit his words in a fully convinced way to another person.

Analogous to this is the attitude of Shatov, Kirillov, and Pyotr Verkhovensky toward Stavrogin. Each of them follows Stavrogin as if he were a teacher, taking his voice as integrated and self-confident. All of them think that he spoke with them as a mentor speaks with a pupil; in actual fact he had made them participants in his own inescapable internal dialogue, in which he was trying to convince himself, not them. Now Stavrogin hears from each of them his own words, but with a firm and monologized accent. He himself can now repeat these words only with an accent of mockery, not conviction. He had not succeeded in convincing himself of anything, and it is painful for him to listen to people whom he has convinced. On this base Stavrogin's dialogues are constructed with each of his three followers.

"Do you know [Shatov says to Stavrogin—M. B.] who are the only 'god-bearing people' on earth, destined to regenerate and save the world in the name of a new God, and to whom are given the keys of life and a new word[f] . . . Do you know which is that people and what is its name?"

"From your manner I am forced to conclude, and I think I may as well do so at once, that it is the Russian people."

"And you can laugh, oh, what a race!" Shatov burst out.

"Calm yourself, I beg of you; on the contrary, I was expecting something of the sort from you."

"You expected something of the sort? And don't you know those words yourself?"

"I know them very well. I see only too well what you're driving at. All your phrases, even the expression 'god-bearing people' is only a sequel to our talk two years ago, abroad, not long before you went to America. . . . At least, as far as I can recall it now."

"It's your phrase altogether, not mine. Your own, not simply the sequel of

---

[f]The Constance Garnett translation gives this incorrectly as "the keys of life and of the new world." Here it is precisely *slovo*, a new *word*.

our conversation. 'Our' conversation it was not at all. It was a teacher uttering weighty words, and a pupil who was raised from the dead. I was that pupil
and you were the teacher." [SS VII, 261-62; The Possessed, Part Two, ch.
1, 7]

The convinced tone in which Stavrogin had spoken abroad about
the "god-bearing" people, the tone of the "teacher who uttered
weighty words," can be explained by the fact that he was actually
still trying to convince only himself. His words with their convincing
accent were addressed to himself, they were a loud rejoinder from his
own internal dialogue: "'I wasn't joking with you then; in persuading
you I was perhaps more concerned with myself than with you,'
Stavrogin pronounced enigmatically."

Accents of the most profound conviction in the speech of Dostoevsky's heroes are, in the huge majority of cases, solely the result
of the fact that these words are actually one side of an internal dialogue and meant to convince the speaker himself. The intensification
of a convincing tone indicates an internal resistance on the part of
the hero's other voice. A word completely alien to any internal struggle is almost never found in Dostoevsky's heroes.

In Kirillov's and Verkhovensky's speech as well Stavrogin hears his
own voice, with an altered accent: in Kirillov the accent is maniacal
conviction, in Pyotr Verkhovensky, cynical exaggeration.

A special type of dialogue is present in Raskolnikov's dialogues with
Porfiry, although externally they are extraordinarily similar to Ivan's
dialogues with Smerdyakov before the murder of Fyodor Pavlovich.
Porfiry speaks in hints, addressing himself to Raskolnikov's hidden
voice. Raskolnikov tries to perform his role with calculation and precision. Porfiry's goal is to force Raskolnikov's inner voice to break
out into the open, to create interruptions in his deliberate and skillfully performed replies. For this reason the words and intonations
of Raskolnikov's role are continually invaded by the real words and
intonations of his true voice. Porfiry too occasionally allows his true
face, the face of a man already certain, to peek out from behind his
assumed role of unsuspecting investigator; suddenly, amid each con-
versant's fictive replies, two real rejoinders, two real discourses, two
real human views meet and intersect each other. As a result the dialogue from one plane—the role-playing plane—passes from time to
time to another plane—the real, but only for a moment. And only in
the final dialogue does the effective destruction of the role-playing
plane occur, and with it the full and final emergence of the word
into the plane of reality.

Here is that unexpected breakthrough into the plane of reality.
Porfiry Petrovich, at the beginning of his conversation with Raskolnikov after Mikolka's confession, has apparently withdrawn all his

suspicions, but then, unexpectedly for Raskolnikov, announces that Mikolka could not have done the killing:

". . . No, this is not the work of a Mikolka, my dear Rodion Romanovich, there is no Mikolka here!"

All that had been said before had sounded so like a recantation that these words were too great a shock. Raskolnikov shuddered as though he had been stabbed.

"Then . . . who then . . . is the murderer?" he asked in a breathless voice, unable to restrain himself.

Porfiry Petrovich sank back in his chair, as though he were amazed at the question.

"Who is the murderer?" he repeated, as though unable to believe his ears. "Why, **you**, Rodion Romanovich! You are the murderer," he added, almost in a whisper, in a voice of genuine conviction.

Raskolnikov leapt from the sofa, stood up for a few seconds and sat down again without uttering a word. His face twitched convulsively. . . .

"I didn't do it," Raskolnikov whispered, as frightened children do when caught in the act. [*SS* V, 476; *Crime and Punishment*, Part Six, ch. 2]

Of enormous importance in Dostoevsky is the confessional dialogue. The role of the other person as "the other," whoever it may be, emerges here with special clarity. Let us pause briefly on Stavrogin's dialogue with Tikhon as a maximally pure model of the confessional dialogue.

The entire orientation of Stavrogin in this dialogue is determined by his dual attitude toward the "other person": by the impossibility of managing without his judgment and forgiveness, and at the same time by a hostility toward him and resistance to his judgment and forgiveness. This is what determines all the interruptions in his speech, in his facial expressions and gestures, the abrupt shifts of mood and tone, his ceaseless reservations, his anticipation of Tikhon's replies and abrupt refutation of these imagined replies. It is as if two persons were speaking with Tikhon, merged interruptedly into one. Tikhon is confronted with two voices, into whose internal struggle he is drawn as a participant.

After the first salutations, unintelligible and uttered for some reason with haste and with obvious, mutual awkwardness, Tikhon took his guest into his study, and, still in apparent haste, sat him down on the sofa in front of the table and settled himself beside him in one of the wicker chairs. At this point Nikolai Vsyevolodovich, to his surprise, lost control of himself completely. It seemed as if he were getting ready, with all his strength, to dare something extraordinary and unquestionable, and at the same time, almost impossible for him. He looked around the study for a moment, obviously not noticing what he had seen; he became lost in thought, but, perhaps, not knowing what he was thinking about. The quiet waked him, and it suddenly seemed to him as if Tikhon were sheepishly lowering his eyes and smiling a completely needless smile. This instantly aroused a feeling of disgust and rebellion in him; he wanted to get up and go out; in his opinion, Tikhon was absolutely drunk. But the latter suddenly raised his eyes and looked at him so strongly and so thoughtfully, and at the same time with such an unexpected and enigmatic expression, that he almost winced, and now it suddenly seemed to him something completely different: that Tikhon already knew what he had come for, that he had been forewarned (although nobody in the whole world could know the reason), and if he was not first to start a conversation, it was because he was sparing him, afraid of humiliating him.[36]

The abrupt changes in Stavrogin's mood and tone determine the entire subsequent dialogue. Sometimes one voice wins out, sometimes the other, but more often Stavrogin's rejoinder is structured as an interruption-prone merging of the two voices.

These revelations [of Stavrogin's visitation by the devil—M. B.] were wild and confused and really did seem to come from a madman. But at the same time Nikolai Vsyevolodovich spoke with such a strange frankness, unprecedented for him, with such ingenuousness, completely unnatural for him, that it seemed as if his former self had suddenly and unexpectedly vanished. He was in no way ashamed to display that fear with which he talked about his ghost. But all this was instantaneous and vanished as suddenly as it had appeared.

"This is all nonsense," he said quickly and with awkward annoyance, catching himself up. "I'm going to a doctor."

And somewhat further on:

". . . but it's all nonsense. I'm going to a doctor. It's really all nonsense, terrible nonsense. It's me myself in different aspects, and nothing else. Since I added this . . . sentence just now, you almost certainly think that I'm still doubtful and not sure that it's me and not in fact a devil?"[37]

In the beginning, one of Stavrogin's voices wins out completely and it seems that "his former self had suddenly and unexpectedly vanished." But then the second voice emerges again, causes an abrupt change of tone and breaks apart his reply. There occurs one of Stavrogin's typical anticipations of Tikhon's reaction, and all the accompanying phenomena already familiar to us.

Before he finally hands Tikhon the pages of his confession, Stavrogin's second voice abruptly interrupts his speech and his intentions, proclaiming its independence from the other, its contempt for the other, thus directly contradicting by its tone the very purpose of the confession.

"Listen, I don't like spies and psychologists, at least those who poke into my soul. I don't ask anyone into my soul, I don't need anyone, I can get along by myself. Maybe you think I'm afraid of you." He raised his voice and lifted his face up defiantly. "Maybe you're now completely convinced that I came to tell you some 'terrible' secret and you're waiting for it with all the monkish curiosity of which you're capable? Well, you may be sure that I'm not going to reveal anything to you, no kind of secret, because I can get along perfectly without you . . ."

The structure of this reply and its positioning within the whole dialogue are completely analogous to the phenomena we analyzed in "Notes from Underground." The tendency toward a vicious circle in one's attitude toward "the other" appears here in perhaps even more acute form.

"Answer me one question, but sincerely, only to me, or as if to yourself, in the dark of the night," Tikhon began in an inspired voice. "If someone forgave you this (he pointd to the sheets), and not someone you respect or are afraid of, but a stranger, a man you'll never know, reading your terrible confession silently to himself, would the idea of this make it easier for you or would it be all the same? If it might be hard for your self-respect to give an answer, don't say anything but only think it to yourself."

"Easier," Stavrogin answered in a low voice. "If you forgave me, it would be much easier for me," he added, with downcast eyes.

"I will, if you forgive me too," Tikhon said emphatically.[38]

What emerges here in all its clarity are the functions of the other person in dialogue, the other person as such, deprived of any social or pragmatic real-life concretization. This other person — "a stranger, a man you'll never know" — fulfills his functions in dialogue outside the plot and outside his specificity in any plot, as a pure "man in man," a representative of "all others" for the "I." As a consequence of such a positioning of "the other," communion assumes a special character and becomes independent of all real-life, concrete social forms (the forms of family, social or economic class, life's stories).[39] We will pause on one passage where this function of "the other" as such, whoever he may be, is revealed with extraordinary clarity.

The "mysterious visitor," after confessing his crime to Zosima and on the eve of his public penance, returns to Zosima at night to murder him. What guided him in this was a pure hatred toward "the other" as such. Here is how he depicts his condition:

"I went out from you then into the darkness, I wandered about the streets, struggling with myself. And suddenly I hated you so that I could hardly bear it. Now, I thought, he is all that binds me, and he is my judge. I can't refuse to face my punishment tomorrow, for he knows all. It was not that I was afraid you would betray me (I never even thought of that) but I thought, 'How can I look him in the face if I don't proclaim my crime?' And if you had been at the other end of the earth, but alive, it would have been all the same, the thought was unendurable that you were alive knowing everything and condemning me. I hated you as though you were the cause, as though you were to blame for everything."
[SS IX, 390-91; *The Brothers Karamazov*, Part Two, Book Six, ch. 2]

The voice of the actual "other" in confessional dialogues is always given in an analogous setting, one pointedly external to the plot. And, albeit not in such naked form, this same setting for "the other" determines all of Dostoevsky's crucial dialogues without exception: they are prepared for by the plot, but their culminating points—the peaks of the dialogues—rise above the plot in the abstract sphere of pure relationship, one person to another.

With this we conclude our survey of types of dialogue, although we have far from exhausted all of them. Moreover, each type has numerous varieties which we have not touched upon at all. But the principle of construction is everywhere the same. Everywhere there is an *intersection, consonance, or interruption of rejoinders in the open dialogue by rejoinders in the heroes' internal dialogue.* Everywhere *a specific sum total of ideas, thoughts, and words is passed through several unmerged voices, sounding differently in each.* The object of authorial aspirations is certainly not this sum total of ideas in itself, as something neutral and identical with itself. No, the object is precisely *the passing of a theme through many and various voices*, its rigorous and, so to speak, irrevocable *multi-voicedness* and *vari-voicedness*. The very distribution of voices and their interaction is what matters to Dostoevsky.

Thus external dialogue, expressed compositionally in the text, is inseparably connected with internal dialogue, that is, with micro-dialogue, and to a considerable extent depends on it. And both are just as inseparably connected with the great dialogue of the novel as a whole that encompasses them. Dostoevsky's novels are thoroughly dialogical.

A dialogic feeling for the world, as we have seen, permeates all Dostoevsky's other works as well, beginning with *Poor Folk*. Thus the *dialogic nature of the word* is revealed in his work with enormous force and with an acute palpability. Metalinguistic research into the nature of this dialogicality, and especially into the diverse varieties of *double-voiced discourse* and its influence on various aspects of the structure of speech, finds in Dostoevsky's creative art extraordinarily rich material.

Like every great artist of the word, Dostoevsky knew how to detect and guide to artistically creative consciousness new aspects of discourse, new depths within it, which had been utilized only in a very weak and muffled way by other artists before him. What is important for Dostoevsky is not only the representational and expressive functions of the word, ordinary concerns for any artist, and not only the ability to recreate in an objectified way the social and individual uniqueness of his characters' speech—most important for him is the dialogic interaction of these various speeches, whatever their linguistic characteristics. For the main object of his representation is the word itself, and specifically the *fully signifying* word. Dostoevsky's works are a word about a word addressed to a word. The represented word comes together with the representing word on one level and on equal terms. They penetrate one another, overlap one another at various dialogic angles. As a result of this encounter, new aspects and new functions of the word are revealed and brought to the fore, and these we have tried to characterize in the present chapter.

NOTES

1. The classification of types and varieties of discourse offered below will not be illustrated by any examples, because we shall in due course provide abundant material from Dostoevsky for each of the instances mentioned here.

2. B. M. Eikhenbaum, absolutely correctly but from a different point of view, remarked on this characteristic of Turgenev's narration: "Extremely widespread is that form, authorially motivated, which introduces a special narrator to whom the narration is entrusted. But very often this form has a completely conventional character (as in Maupassant or Turgenev), testifying to no more than the vitality of the tradition of a narrator as a special personage in the story. In such cases the narrator remains the author, and the motivation for introducing this narrator plays the role of a simple introduction." (B. M. Eikhenbaum, *Literatura* [Literature], Leningrad, "Priboi," 1927, p. 217.)

3. First in the article "Kak sdelana 'Shinel'" [How the Overcoat Is Made], in *Poetika* (1919). Later, see especially the article "Leskov i sovremennaia proza" [Leskov and Contemporary Prose] (see *Literatura*, pp. 210 ff.) [The article on Gogol is available in English: Boris Eichenbaum, "How Gogol's 'Overcoat' Is Made," in Robert A. Maguire, ed. and trans., *Gogol from the Twentieth Century* (Princeton U. Press, 1974).]

4. Leo Spitzer, *Italienische Umgangssprache* (Leipzig: 1922), pp. 175-76. [Bakhtin is rather free in his rendering. The first sentence is, more literally: "The taking over (*Übernahme*) of a portion of our partner's utterance brings with it—due to the change in speaking individuals—a transposition in tone: the words of 'the other' always sound strange in our mouth, even slightly sarcastic, caricatured, grotesque."]

5. In connection with the interest in "folk culture" (not as an ethnographic category), Romanticism attached enormous significance to various forms of *skaz*, seen as refracting alien discourse with a weak degree of objectification. For classicism, "folk discourse" (in the sense of a socially typical and individually characteristic alien discourse) was a purely objectified discourse (in the low genres). Among discourses of the third type, special importance was granted in Romanticism to internally polemical *Ich-Erzählung* (especially the confessional type).

6. The majority of prose genres, in particular the novel, are constructive in character: their structural elements are *whole utterances*, although these utterances are not autonomous and are subordinated to a monologic unity.

7. Out of all contemporary linguistic stylistics—both Soviet and foreign—a special place must be given to the outstanding works of V. V. Vinogradov, who, working with an enormous amount of material, uncovers all the fundamental contradictoriness and multistyled nature of artistic prose, and all the complexity of the author's position ("the image of the author") in it—although, it seems to us, Vinogradov somewhat underestimates the significance of dialogic relationships among speech styles (to the extent that these relationships exceed the boundaries of linguistics). [For a listing of the major contributions of Vinogradov to stylistics, see Victor Erlich, *Russian Formalism: History-Doctrine*, 3rd ed. (New Haven: Yale U. Press, 1965), p. 293.]

8. We recall Thomas Mann's very characteristic admission cited by us on pp. 179-80 [ch. 4, n. 26].

9. *Pis'ma*, I, p. 86. [Letter of 1 February 1846, to Mikhail Dostoevsky]

10. A splendid analysis of Makar Devushkin's speech as that of a specific *social character* is given by V. V. Vinogradov in his book *O jazyke khudozhestvennoi literatury* [On the Language of Artistic Literature], (Moscow, Goslitizdat, 1959), pp. 477-92.

11. *Pis'ma*, I, pp. 81-82. [Letter to Mikhail Dostoevsky, 8 October 1845]

12. There were, to be sure, already rudiments of interior dialogue in Devushkin as well.

13. Working on *Netochka Nezvanova*, Dostoevsky writes his brother: "But soon you shall read *Netochka Nezvanova*. It will be a confession, like *Golyadkin*, although of a different tone and sort." [*Pis'ma*, I, p. 108; letter to Mikhail Dostoevsky, Jan.-Feb. 1847.]

14. Not long before Golyadkin had said that to himself: "That's just like you! . . . You go plunging straight in, you're delighted! you guileless creature."

15. In *Crime and Punishment*, for example, there is one such literal repetition by Svidrigailov (Raskolnikov's partial double) of Raskolnikov's most intimate words, spoken by him to Sonya, a repetition with a meaningful wink. We quote this passage in its entirety:

"Ah! you sceptical person!" laughed Svidrigaïlov, "I told you I had no need of that money. Won't you admit that it's simply done from humanity? She wasn't 'a louse', you know" (he pointed to the corner where the dead woman lay), "was she, like some old pawnbroker woman? Come, you'll agree, is Luzhin to go on living and doing wicked things or is she to die? And if I didn't help them, Polenka would go the same way."

He said this with an air of a sort of gay winking slyness, keeping his eyes fixed on Raskolnikov, who turned white and cold, hearing his own phrases, spoken to Sonya. [*SS* V, 455; *Crime and Punishment*, Part V, ch. 5]

16. Other autonomous consciousnesses appear only in the longer novels.

17. In Thomas Mann's novel *Doktor Faustus*, a very great deal was suggested by Dostoevsky and precisely by Dostoevsky's *polyphony*. I quote here an excerpt from a description of one of the composer Adrian Leverkühn's works, very close to Trishatov's "musical idea":

"Everywhere is Adrian Leverkühn great in *making unlike the like*. . . . So here—but nowhere else as here is the effect so profound, mysterious and great. Every word that turns into sound the idea of Beyond, of transformation in the mystical sense, and thus of change, transformation, transfiguration, is here exactly reproduced. The passages of horror just before heard are given, indeed, to the indescribable children's chorus at quite a different pitch, and in changed orchestration and rhythms; but in *the searing, susurrant tones of spheres and angels there is not one note which does not occur, with rigid correspondence, in the hellish laughter*." [Bakhtin cites from a Russian translation of *Doktor Faustus* (Moscow, 1959, pp. 440-41); the passage above is the H. T. Lowe-Porter translation of Thomas Mann, *Doctor Faustus* (Vintage Books, 1948), ch. XXXIV (conclusion), pp. 378-79.]

18. The first to note this characteristic of the narration in *The Double* was Belinsky, but he offered no explanation for it.

19. See *F. M. Dostoevskii, Stat'i i materialy*, I, ed. A. S. Dolinin (Moscow-Leningrad: "Mysl'," 1922), p. 241-42. [The article is V. V. Vinogradov, "K morfologii natural'nogo stilia" (Toward a Morphology of the Naturalist Style). A portion of this article has been translated by Stephen Rudy in Priscilla Meyer and Stephen Rudy, eds., *Dostoevsky & Gogol: Texts and Criticism* (Ann Arbor: Ardis, 1979), pp. 217-28.

20. Ibid. p. 248.

21. This perspective is absent even for the generalizing "authorial" construction of the hero's indirect speech.

22. On the literary parodies and literary polemic in *Poor Folk*, there are some very

valuable historico-literary remarks in Vinogradov's article in *Tvorcheskii put' Dostoevskogo* [Dostoevsky's Creative Path] (ed. by N. L. Brodskii, Leningrad, "Seyatel'," 1924).

23. These stylistic peculiarities too are all connected with the tradition of carnival and with reduced ambivalent laughter.

24. "Notes from Underground" was originally announced by Dostoevsky under this title in "Time."

25. This can be explained by the generic similarities between "Notes from Underground" and Menippean satire.

26. According to Dostoevsky, such an admittance would also serve to calm down the discourse and purify it.

27. Exceptions will be pointed out below.

28. We recall the characterization that Dostoevsky himself gave to the hero's speech in "A Meek One:"

". . . he either argues with himself or addresses some unseen listener, a judge as it were. However, it is always like that in real life."

29. Myshkin guesses correctly at this as well: ". . . Besides, perhaps he didn't think like that at all, but only wanted it . . . He longed for the last time to come near to men, to win their respect and love" [VI, 484-85; *The Idiot*, Part Three, ch. 8]

30. L. Grossman, "Stilistika Stavrogina (K izucheniiu novoi glavy *Besov*)," in *Poetika Dostoevskogo* (Moscow, 1925). The article was originally published in the second volume of *Dostoevskii. Stat'i i materialy*, A. S. Dolinin, ed. (Moscow-Leningrad, 1924).

31. Leonid Grossman, *Poetika Dostoevskogo*, p. 162.

32. *Dokumenty po istorii literatury i obshchestvennosti*, issue I, "F. M. Dostoevskii," (Moscow: izd. Tsentrarkhiv RSFSR, 1922), p. 32 [The above passage does not appear in the variant of Stavrogin's Confession translated by F. D. Reeve and appended to the Garnett translation of *The Possessed*. For the complete text, see volume 11 of the most recent Collected Works (*F. M. Dostoevskii: Polnoe sobranie sochinenii* in 30 vv. [Leningrad: Nauka, 1974], p. 23)

33. *Pis'ma*, III, p. 256. [Dostoevsky to G. A. Kovner, 14 February 1877.]

34. In his article "The Thematic Composition of the Novel *The Idiot*" [Tematicheskaia kompozitsiia romana *Idiota*], A. P. Skaftymov is quite correct in his understanding of the role of the "other" (in its relation to the "I"). "Dostoevsky," he says, "in both Nastasya Filippovna and Ippolit (and in all his prideful characters) exposes the torments of anguish and loneliness, which are expressed in an inexorable craving for love and sympathy, and thereby suggests that a person, confronting himself in the most intimate inner way, **cannot accept himself**, and, unable to sanctify himself, hurts terribly and seeks sanctification and sanctions for himself in the heart of another. It is as a function of purification through forgiveness that the image of Marie is presented in Prince Myshkin's story."

Here is how he defines the positioning of Nastasya Filippovna vis-à-vis Myshkin: "Thus the author himself reveals the inner meaning of Nastasya Filippovna's unstable attitudes toward Prince Myshkin: while being drawn toward him (thirst after an ideal, after love and forgiveness), she is also repelled, first out of feelings of her own unworthiness (consciousness of her guilt, and purity of her soul), then out of feelings of pride (the inability to forget herself and to accept love and forgiveness)." See *Dostoevsky's Creative Path* [Tvorcheskii put' Dostoevskogo], ed. N. L. Brodskii (Leningrad, "Seyatel'," 1924), pp. 153 and 148.

Skaftymov remains, however, on the level of purely psychological analysis. He does not investigate the underlying artistic significance of this element in the structuring of a group of heroes or the structuring of dialogue.

35. From the very beginning Alyosha, too, clearly detects this voice of Ivan's. We quote one of his brief dialogues with Ivan after the murder. This dialogue is generally analogous in structure to the dialogue analyzed above, although there are some differences.

"Do you remember [Ivan asks—M. B.] when Dmitry burst in after dinner and beat father, and afterwards I told you in the yard that I reserved 'the right to desire' . . . tell me, did you think then that I desired father's death or not?"

"I did think so," answered Alyosha, softly.

"It was so, too; it was not a matter of guessing. But didn't you fancy then that what I wished was just that 'one reptile should devour another'; that is, just that Dmitry should kill father, and as soon as possible . . . and that I myself was even prepared to help to bring that about?"

Alyosha turned rather pale, and looked silently into his brother's eyes.

"Speak!" cried Ivan, "I want above everything to know what you thought then. I want the truth, the truth!" He drew a deep breath, looking angrily at Alyosha before his answer came.

"Forgive me, I did think that, too, at the time," whispered Alyosha, and he did not add a single "mitigating circumstance." [SS X, 130-31; *The Brothers Karamazov*, Part Four, Book Eleven, ch. VI]

36. *Dokumenty po istorii literatury i obshchestvennosti*, op. cit., p. 6.

37. Ibid., pp. 8-9.

38. Ibid., p. 35. It is interesting to compare this passage with the excerpt quoted above from Dostoevsky's letter to Kovner.

39. This is, as we know, a departure into carnival and mystery-play time and space, where the ultimate event of interaction among consciousnesses is accomplished in Dostoevsky's novels.

Conclusion

In this book we have sought to reveal the uniqueness of Dostoevsky *as an artist*, an artist who brought with him new forms of artistic visualization and was therefore able to open up and glimpse new sides of the human being and his life. Our attention has been concentrated on that new artistic position which permitted him to broaden the horizon of artistic visualization, which permitted him to look at the human being from a different artistic angle of vision.

While continuing the "dialogic line" in the development of European artistic prose, Dostoevsky created a new generic variety of the novel—the polyphonic novel—whose innovative features we have tried to illuminate in this book. We consider the creation of the polyphonic novel a huge step forward not only in the development of novelistic prose, that is, of all genres developing within the orbit of the novel, but also in the development of the *artistic thinking* of humankind. It seems to us that one could speak directly of a special *polyphonic artistic thinking* extending beyond the bounds of the novel as a genre. This mode of thinking makes available those sides of a human being, and above all the *thinking human consciousness and the dialogic sphere of its existence*, which are not subject to *artistic* assimilation from *monologic positions*.

At the present time, Dostoevsky's novel is perhaps the most influential model in the West. Dostoevsky the artist is followed by people with the most varied ideologies, often deeply hostile to the ideology of Dostoevsky himself: they are enthralled by his artistic will, by the new principle of artistic visualization that he discovered.

But does this mean that the polyphonic novel, once discovered, supplants monologic forms of the novel, making them obsolete and unnecessary? Of course not. A newly born genre never supplants or replaces any already existing genres. Each new genre merely supplements the old ones, merely widens the circle of already existing genres. For every genre has its own predominant sphere of existence, in which it is irreplaceable. Thus the appearance of the polyphonic novel does not nullify or in any way restrict the further productive development of monologic forms of the novel (biographical, historical, the novel of everyday life, the novel-epic, etc.), for there will always continue to exist and expand those spheres of existence, of man and nature, which require precisely objectified and finalizing, that is monological, forms of artistic cognition. But again we repeat: *the thinking human consciousness and the dialogic sphere in which this consciousness exists*, in all its depth and specificity, cannot be reached through a monologic artistic approach. It becomes the object of authentic artistic visualization for the first time in Dostoevsky's polyphonic novel.

Thus no new artistic genre ever nullifies or replaces old ones. But at the same time each fundamentally and significantly new genre, once it arrives, exerts influence on the entire circle of old genres: the new genre makes the old ones, so to speak, more conscious; it forces them to better perceive their own possibilities and boundaries, that is, to overcome their own *naiveté*. Such, for example, was the influence of the novel as a new genre on all the old literary genres: on the novella, the narrative poem, the drama, the lyric. Moreover, a new genre can have a positive influence on old genres, to the extent, of course, that their generic natures permit it; thus, for example, one can speak of a certain "novelization" of old genres in the epoch of the novel's flowering. The effect of new genres on old ones in most cases[1] promotes their renewal and enrichment. This of course also applies to the polyphonic novel. Against the background of Dostoevsky's work, many old monologic forms of literature began to look naive and simplistic. In this respect the influence of Dostoevsky's polyphonic novel on the monologic forms of literature has been very fruitful.

The polyphonic novel makes new demands on aesthetic thought as well. Raised on monologic forms of artistic visualization, thoroughly steeped in them, aesthetic thought tends to absolutize those forms and not see their boundaries.

This is why the tendency to monologize Dostoevsky's novel

remains to this day so strong. It is expressed in a striving, through analysis, to give finalizing definitions to the heroes, to find without fail a definite monologic authorial idea, to seek everywhere a superficial real-life verisimilitude, and so forth. The rigorous unfinalizability and dialogic openness of Dostoevsky's artistic world, that is, its very essence, is ignored or rejected.

The *scientific* consciousness of contemporary man has learned to orient itself among the complex circumstances of "the probability of the universe"; it is not confused by any "indefinite quantities" but knows how to calculate them and take them into account. This scientific consciousness has long since grown accustomed to the Einsteinian world with its multiplicity of systems of measurement, etc. But in the realm of *artistic* cognition people sometimes continue to demand a very crude and very primitive definitiveness, one that quite obviously could not be true.

We must renounce our monologic habits so that we might come to feel at home in the new artistic sphere which Dostoevsky discovered, so that we might orient ourselves in that incomparably more complex *artistic model of the world* which he created.

NOTE

1. If they don't themselves die a "natural death."

Appendixes

In the final decade of his life, Bakhtin saw much of his work—the product of a half-century of creative activity—finally in print. The 1929 Dostoevsky book was revised and expanded for a second edition in 1963. The book on Rabelais, after twenty years in limbo, was published in 1965. A collection of his essays "from various years" (*Voprosy literatury i estetiki*) came out in 1975. Then, four years after Bakhtin's death, the devoted efforts of his disciples in the Soviet Union made possible the publication of a second volume of essays and fragments (M. M. Bakhtin, *Estetika slovesnogo tvorchestva* [Moscow: Iskusstvo, 1979]). Two selections from this most recent volume are directly relevant to the Dostoevsky book, and have been translated here: "Iz knigi *Problemy tvorchestva Dostoevskogo*" (pp. 181-87) appears as Appendix I; "K pererabotke knigi o Dostoevskom" (pp. 308-27) as Appendix II.

A note on the apparatus. Some of the footnotes were provided by S. S. Averintsev and S. G. Bocharov, editors and annotators of the Soviet edition; others have been added for the convenience of the non-Russian reader. The former are identified by [A/B].

Appendix I
Three Fragments
from the 1929 Edition
Problems of Dostoevsky's Art

The passages below appear in the original edition of the Dostoevsky book (*Problemy tvorchestva Dostoevskogo* [Leningrad: Priboi, 1929], pp. 3-4, 100-02, 238-41), but were not included by Bakhtin in his expanded second edition of 1963. The two texts differ considerably in context and tone. Bakhtin's interests and essays during the thirty intervening years left their mark on the revised edition. The 1929 book was a monograph on Dostoevky's novel; the 1963 book was more a study of Dostoevsky's place in the history of novelness. The fourth chapter, substantially rewritten, now included a discussion of the sources and tradition of Menippean satire, and chapter 5 was greatly enriched with refined categories of dialogic discourse. But these many expansions were accompanied by some cuts. Among them are the passages translated here: on Dostoevsky's links with European Romanticism, the internal dialogization of the "Legend of the Grand Inquisitor," Bakhtin's concept of dialogue as contrasted with Platonic and Biblical dialogue, and the utopian striving of Dostoevsky's heroes for a "community in the world." They help to place the Dostoevsky book more securely in the context of Bakhtin's other philosophical interests of the 1920s—especially his huge, unfinished masterwork on the nature of art and moral responsibility, a project with which Bakhtin's research into Dostoevsky was intimately connected.

Foreword

The present book is limited solely to theoretical problems of Dostoevsky's art. We have had to exclude all historical problems. This does not mean, however, that we consider such an approach to the material methodologically correct or normal. On the contrary, we think that every theoretical problem must without fail be oriented historically. Between the synchronic and diachronic approach to a literary work there must be an indissoluble bond and a strict reciprocity. But such is the methodological ideal. It is not always realized in practice. Purely technical considerations sometimes force us to isolate abstractly a theoretical, synchronic problem and develop it independently. Thus have we proceeded here. But the historical point of view has always been taken into account; moreover, it has served as a backdrop against which we have perceived each of the phenomena examined here. The backdrop itself, however, has not entered the book.

But even theoretical problems have been no more than posited within the limits of the present work. To be sure, we have tried to indicate their solutions, but still we do not feel we have the right to call our book anything other than "Problems of Dostoevsky's Art."

At the basis of our analysis lies the conviction that every literary work is internally and immanently sociological. Within it living social forces intersect; each element of its form is permeated with living social evaluations. For this reason a purely formal analysis must take each element of the artistic structure as a point of refraction of living social forces, as a synthetic crystal whose facets are structured and ground in such a way that they refract specific rays of social evaluations, and refract them at a specific angle.

Dostoevsky's work has been, up to now, the object of a narrowly ideological approach and treatment. Of greatest interest has been the ideology that found its direct expression in the pronouncements of Dostoevsky (or more precisely of his characters). The ideology that determined his artistic form, his extraordinarily complex and completely new novelistic construction, has remained to this day almost completely unexamined. A narrowly formalistic approach is almost incapable of reaching further than the periphery of that form. Such narrow ideologism, seeking above all purely philosophical postulates and insights, cannot deal with precisely that aspect of Dostoevsky's work that has outlived his philosophical and sociopolitical ideology — his revolutionary innovation in the realm of the novel as an artistic form.

In the first part of our book we give a general idea of the new type of novel that Dostoevsky created. In the second half we develop our thesis in detail with concrete analyses of discourse and its artistic-social functions in Dostoevsky's works.

From the Chapter "The Functions of the Adventure Plot in Dostoevsky's Work"

Plot in Dostoevsky is absolutely devoid of any sort of finalizing functions. Its goal is to place a person in various situations that expose and provoke him, to bring people together and make them collide in conflict—in such a way, however, that they do not remain within this area of plot-related contact but exceed its bounds. The real connections begin where the ordinary plot ends, having fulfilled its service function.

Before the beginning of their intimate conversation, Shatov tells Stavrogin: "We are two beings and have come together in infinity . . . for the last time in the world. Drop your tone, and speak like a human being! Speak, if only once in your life, with the voice of a man."[1]

In essence all of Dostoevsky's heroes come together outside of time and space, as two beings in infinity.[2] Their consciousnesses, each with its own world, intersect; their integral fields of vision intersect. At the points where their fields of vision intersect lie the culminating points of the novel. At these points also lie the clamps holding together the novelistic whole. They are external to the plot and cannot be subsumed by any of the schemas for constructing a European novel. Of what sort are they? To this basic question we will not give an answer here. The principles for voice combination can be revealed only after a careful analysis of discourse in Dostoevsky. After all, the issue here concerns the combination of characters' fully weighted words about themselves and about the world, words provoked by the plot but not embedded in the plot. The following part of our work is devoted to an analysis of discourse.

In his notebooks Dostoevsky gives us a remarkable definition of the distinguishing features of his literary art: "With full realism, to find the man in man . . . I am called a psychologist: that is not true, I am only a realist in the higher sense, that is, I portray all the depths of the human soul."[3]

"The depths of the human soul," or what the idealist-Romantics meant by "spirit" in contrast to soul, become in Dostoevsky's work the subject of objectively realistic, sober, prosaic depiction. The depths of the human soul in the sense of a sum total of all higher ideological acts—cognitive, ethical, and religious—had been, in literary art, merely an object of direct emotional expression, or else had determined this creativity as its basic principle. Spirit was presented either as the spirit of the author himself, objectified in the whole of the artistic work he had created, or as the lyrics of the author, as his direct confessional statement in categories of his own consciousness. In both instances it was "naive," and even romantic irony itself could not eliminate this naiveté, for romantic irony remained within the bounds of the same spirit.

Dostoevsky is deeply and intimately connected with European Romanticism, but that which the Romantic approached from within, in categories of his own "I" by which he was obsessed, Dostoevsky approached from without—in such a way, however, that this objective approach did not reduce by one iota the spiritual problematics of Romanticism, nor transform it into psychology. Dostoevsky, while objectifying the thought, the idea, the experience, never has anything up his sleeve, never attacks from behind. From the first to the final pages of his artistic work he was guided by the principle: never use for objectifying or finalizing another's consciousness anything that might be inaccessible to that consciousness, that might lie outside its field of vision. Even in his pamphlets he never resorts to exposing a person through something which that person does not see or does not know (with, perhaps, very rare exceptions); he does not use a person's back to expose his face. In Dostoevsky's works there is literally not a single significant word about a character that the character could not have said about himself (from the standpoint of content, not tone). Dostoevsky is no psychologist. But at the same time Dostoevsky is objective, and has every right to call himself a realist.

On the other hand, Dostoevsky also objectifies the entire realm of the author's creative subjectivity which autocratically colors the represented world in a monologic novel, thereby making what was once a form of perception into the object of perception. In this way he moves his own form (and the authorial subjectivity inherent in it) deeper and further, so far that it can no longer find its expression in style or tone. His hero is an ideologist. The consciousness of the ideologist, with all its passionate seriousness, with all its loopholes, with all its rigor and depth and with all its isolation from real existence, enters so fundamentally into the content of Dostoevsky's novel that direct, unmediated monologic ideologism can no longer determine its artistic form. Monologic ideologism after Dostoevsky becomes "Dostoevskyism." Thus Dostoevsky's own monologic position and his ideological value judgments did not obscure the objectivism of his artistic vision. His artistic methods for depicting the inner man, the "man in man," remain in their objectivism exemplary for any epoch and under any ideology.

From the Chapter "Dialogue in Dostoevsky"

With this we conclude our survey of types of dialogue, although we have far from exhausted all of them. Moreover, each type has numerous varieties which we have not touched upon at all. But the principle of construction is everywhere the same. Everywhere there is an intersection, consonance, or interruption of rejoinders in the open dialogue by rejoinders in the heroes' internal dialogues. Everywhere a *specific sum total of ideas, thoughts, and words is passed through several unmerged voices, sounding differently in each*. The object of authorial intentions is certainly not this sum total of ideas in itself, as something neutral and identical to itself. No, the object of intentions is precisely the *passing of a theme through many and various voices*, its rigorous and, so to speak, irrevocable *multi-voicedness* and *vari-voicedness*. The very distribution of voices and their interaction is what matters to Dostoevsky.[4]

Ideas in the narrow sense, that is, the views of the character as an ideologist, enter dialogue under the same principle. Ideological views, as we have seen, are also internally dialogized, and in external dialogue they are always linked with the internal rejoinders of another person, even where they assume a finished, externally monologic form of expression. Of such a sort is the celebrated dialogue between Ivan and Alyosha in the tavern, and the "Legend of the Grand Inquisitor" inserted into it.[5] A more detailed analysis of this dialogue and of the "Legend" itself would show a profound participation of all elements of Ivan's worldview in his internal dialogue with himself and in his internally polemical interrelations with others. For all its external proportionality, the "Legend" is nevertheless full of interruptions; both the very form of its construction as the Grand Inquisitor's dialogue with Christ and at the same time with himself, and, finally, the very unexpectedness and duality of its finale, indicate an internally dialogic disintegration at its very ideological core. A thematic analysis of the "Legend" would reveal the deep essential relevance of its dialogic form.

The idea in Dostoevsky is never cut off from the voice. For this reason it is radically wrong to claim that Dostoevsky's dialogues are dialectical. If that were the case we would have to assert that Dostoevsky's underlying idea is a dialectical synthesis of, for example, the theses of Raskolnikov and the antithesis of Sonya, the theses of Alyosha and the antithesis of Ivan, and so forth. Such an understanding is absurd in the extreme. For Ivan is disputing not with Alyosha but above all with himself, and Alyosha is not disputing with Ivan as an integral and unified voice but rather intervenes in his internal dialogue, trying to reinforce one of its rejoinders. And there can be no talk here of any sort of synthesis; one can talk only of the victory of one or another voice, or of a combination of voices in those places where they agree. It is not the idea as a monologic deduction, even if dialectical, but the event of an interaction of voices that is the ultimate given for Dostoevsky.

This is what distinguishes Dostoevsky's dialogue from Platonic dialogue. In the latter, while it is not a thoroughly monologized pedagogical dialogue, all the same the multiplicity of voices is extinguished in the idea. The idea is conceived by Plato not as an event, but as existence.[6] To participate in the idea means to participate in its existence. But all hierarchical interrelation between perceiving

Communion "of I fother?

human beings, created by the varying degrees of their participation in the idea, are ultimately extinguished in the fullness of the idea itself. The very juxtaposition of Dostoevsky's dialogue with Plato's dialogue seems to us in general superficial and unproductive,[7] for Dostoevsky's dialogue is not at all a purely cognitive, philosophical dialogue. More to the point would be its juxtaposition to Biblical and evangelical dialogue. The influence on Dostoevsky of Job's dialogue and several evangelical dialogues is indisputable, while Platonic dialogues simply lay outside the sphere of his interest. In its structure Job's dialogue is internally endless, for the opposition of the soul to God—whether the opposition be hostile or humble—is conceived in it as something irrevocable and eternal. However, Biblical dialogue will also not lead us to the most fundamental artistic features of Dostoevsky's dialogue. Before posing any questions of influence or structural similarity, we must examine those features in the material itself before us.

The "man with man" dialogue analyzed by us[8] is a highly interesting sociological document. An exceptionally keen sense of the other person as *another* and of one's *I* as a naked *I* presupposes that all those definitions which clothe the *I* and the *other* in socially concrete flesh—family, social, and economic class definitions—and all variants on these definitions, have lost their authoritativeness and their form-shaping force. A person, as it were, senses himself in the world as a whole, without any intervening stages, apart from any social collective to which he might belong. And the communion of this *I* with *another* and with *others* takes place directly on the territory of ultimate questions, bypassing all intermediate and more familiar forms.[9] Dostoevsky's heroes are heroes of accidental families and accidental collectives. They are deprived of any actual and self-evident communion in which their life and their interrelations might unfold. This communion has been transformed for them from an indispensable prerequisite for life into a postulate; it has become the utopian goal of all their aspirations. And Dostoevsky's heroes are indeed motivated by the utopian dream of creating some sort of human community that lies beyond existing social forms. To create a human community in the world, to join several people together outside the framework of available social forms, is the goal of Myshkin, of Alyosha, and in a less conscious and clear-cut form of all Dostoevsky's other heroes. The community of boys that Alyosha establishes after Ilyusha's funeral, united only by the memory of a martyred boy,[10] Myshkin's utopian dream of joining Aglaya and Nastasya Filippovna in a union of love, Zosima's idea of the church, Versilov's and the "Ridiculous Man's" dream about a Golden Age—all these are phenomena of the same order. Communion has been deprived, as it were, of

how?

postulate — hypothesis

its real-life body and wants to create one arbitrarily, out of purely human material. All this is a most profound expression of the social disorientation of the classless intelligentsia, which feels itself dispersed throughout the world and whose members must orient themselves in the world one by one, alone and at their own risk. A firm monologic voice presupposes a firm social support, presupposes a *we* —it makes no difference whether this "we" is acknowledged or not. The solitary person finds that his own voice has become a vacillating thing, his own unity and his internal agreement with himself has become a postulate.

NOTES

1. Fyodor Dostoevsky, *The Possessed*, Part Two, ch. 1, 6.

2. In the revised edition of the book, this breakdown of empirical space and time in the *"decisive* meetings of man with man" is proclaimed in Shatov's words, and characterized as a "departure into carnival-mystery play space and time." (See *Problems of Dostoevsky's Poetics*, p. 177 [A/B].

3. *Biografiia, pis'ma i zametki iz zapisnoi knizhki F. M. Dostoevskogo*, ed. N. N. Strakhov (St. Petersburg, 1883), p. 373 [A/B].

4. This paragraph does in fact appear verbatim in the second edition; see *Problems of Dostoevsky's Poetics*, ch. 5, p. 265.

5. *The Brothers Karamazov*, Part Two, Book Five: "Pro and Contra," ch. 4 and 5.

6. *"ne kak sobytie, a kak bytie."* The Russian plays on *bytie* (being, existence) and *sobytie* (event), giving the latter overtones of *so-bytie*, "co-existence, co-being, shared existence of being *with* another." Being can be static; an event is always interaction.

7. Bakhtin rethought the relationship between Dostoevsky's dialogue and Platonic dialogue for the second edition of the book, in connection with his analysis there of Dostoevsky's generic sources and the "genre memory" embedded in and echoing throughout Dostoevsky's work. The Socratic dialogue is understood there as one of the sources of the "dialogic" line in the development of European prose leading to Dostoevsky. (See *Problems of Dostoevsky's Poetics*, pp. 109-12) [A/B].

8. Bakhtin apparently has in mind his preceding discussion of the "Legend of the Grand Inquisitor."

9. See Bakhtin's somewhat adjusted view on the correlation between "ultimate questions" and "intervening links" in Dostoevsky in his notes "Toward a Reworking of the Dostoevsky Book" (Appendix II, p. 286) [A/B].

10. Cf. in Bakhtin's lectures on the history of Russian literature: "On Ilyusha's grave a little child's church is erected. And this, as it were, is an answer to Ivan. . . . The only harmony that has a living soul is harmony created on living suffering. Around the suffering and death of a martyred boy a union is formed . . . So the episode with the boys reproduces, on a small scale, the novel." [A/B]

[On Bakhtin's Russian history lectures, the editors of *Estetika slovesnogo tvorchestva* have this to say (pp. 412-13):

In the 1920s Bakhtin delivered many public lectures on literary and philosophical themes in the various auditoriums of Vitebsk and Leningrad, and delivered as well various cycles of lectures on the history of philosophy, on aesthetics, and on literature in a more domestic setting. One of these cycles was delivered in a study circle on Russian literature, set up by youthful auditors in Vitebsk; for some of these auditors, the lectures were then continued in Leningrad. One of the participants, Rakhail Moiseevna Mirkina, preserved her notes from these lectures, which covered the history of Russian literature from the 18th c. to the most recent works of the Soviet 1920s. "It should be emphasized," Mirkina writes in her reminiscences of Bakhtin, "that these notes were taken first by a schoolgirl, and then by a student in the beginning classes. The lectures are of course abbreviated here, and preserve to only a slight extent the style and spirit of Bakhtin."

Portions of Mirkina's notes are published in *Estetika*, pp. 374-83 (on Vyacheslav Ivanov), and in *Prometei. Istoriko-biograficheskii almankh*, 12 [Moscow, 1980], pp. 257-68 (on Tolstoy).]

Appendix II
"Toward a Reworking of the Dostoevsky Book" (1961)

The set of notes below are dated 1961 (first published posthumously in *Kontekst-1976*, and reprinted in *Estetika slovesnogo tvorchestva*, 1979). While clearly intended as guidelines for the second revised edition of the Dostoevsky book (a task that occupied Bakhtin in 1961-62), these notes are both that, and considerably more. Major themes do appear here that are generously developed in the 1963 edition: the idea of the word as the major guarantor of human freedom; the communal basis of self-consciousness; promise of an expanded typology of discourses; a discussion of Dostoevsky's generic traditions (which became the basis for a substantially rewritten chapter 4); the position of the author in relation to the hero. The latter area was for Bakhtin especially in need of clarification. The position of the author in the polyphonic novel, Bakhtin wrote to his disciple and colleague V. V. Kozhinov in July 1961, "has more than anything else given rise to objections and misunderstanding."

However, much suggested in these notes did not find its way into the second edition. Among the intriguing topics Bakhtin touches upon here (but does not ultimately develop) are a discussion of psychological approaches to Dostoevsky, a typology of people based on their attitude toward ultimate value, the role of catastrophe in Dostoevsky, and a long excursus on the theme of death in Dostoevsky and Tolstoy. Especially productive is Bakhtin's distinction between the *concept* and the *image* of a depicted person, with its correlate distinction between character and personality.

The style of these notes is characteristic of Bakhtin in a genre we might call "critical meditation." Thoroughly worked-out arguments, sometimes stretching over several pages, alternate with incomplete phrases that contain the kernel of a large thought or suggest a sequence of associations. Every attempt has been made to preserve this striking unevenness of pace and style. As could be said of the notebooks of Dostoevsky himself, these notes offer a glimpse into the peculiar fertility of a mind that worked much less as a system than as a generative center of ideas.

Rework the chapter on plot in Dostoevsky. Adventurism of a special sort. The problem of Menippean satire. The concept of artistic space.

The public square in Dostoevsky. Sparks of carnival fire. Scandals, eccentric escapades, mésalliances, hysterics and so forth in Dostoevsky. Their source: the carnival square. An analysis of Nastasya Filippovna's name-day party. The game of confessions (cf. "Bobok"). The transformation of a beggar into a millionaire, a prostitute into a princess, and so forth. The worldwide, one might even say universal, character of conflict in Dostoevsky. "The conflict of ultimate problems." The boundlessness of contacts among all things in the world. Ivan's characterization of Russian youth. As major heroes Dostoevsky portrays only those people in his work with whom argument has not yet ended (for indeed it is not yet ended in the world). The problem of the open hero. The problem of the author's position. The problem of the third party in a dialogue. Various resolutions to this problem in contemporary novelists (Mauriac, Graham Greene and others).

Thomas Mann's *Doktor Faustus* as an indirect confirmation of my idea. Dostoevsky's influence. Conversation with the devil. The narrator-chronicler and the main hero. The complex authorial position (cf. Mann's letters). Retellings (verbal transpositions) of musical works: in *Netochka Nezvanova*, but especially in the retelling of Trishatov's opera[1] (here there is a literal coincidence of texts about the devil's voice); finally, retellings of Ivan Karamazov's poems. The hero-author. The main thing: the problem of polyphony.

A completely new structure for the image of a human being—a full-blooded and fully signifying other consciousness which is not inserted into the *finalizing* frame of reality, which is not finalized by anything (not even death), for its meaning cannot be resolved or abolished by reality (to kill does not mean to refute). This other consciousness is not inserted into the frame of authorial consciousness, it is revealed from within as something that stands *outside* and *alongside* and with which the author can enter into dialogic relations. The author, like Prometheus, creates (or rather re-creates) living beings who are independent of himself and with whom he is on equal terms. He cannot finalize them, for he has discovered what distinguishes personality from all that is not personality. Objective reality has no power over it. Such is the artist's first discovery.

The second discovery is the *depiction* (or rather the re-creation) of the *self-developing* idea (inseparable from personality). The idea becomes the object of artistic depiction and is revealed not at the level of a system (philosophical or scientific), but on the level of a human *event*.

The artist's third discovery is dialogicality as a special form of interaction among autonomous and equally signifying consciousnesses.

All three discoveries are essentially one: they are three facets of one and the same phenomenon.

These discoveries affect both form and content. Their contribution to questions of *form* is more profound, more condensed, more general than is the concretely ideological, changeable content that fills them in Dostoevsky. The content of autonomous consciousnesses changes, ideas change, the content of the dialogues changes, but the new forms Dostoevsky discovered for the artistic cognition of the human world remain the same. If, for example, in Turgenev one were to cast out the content of the disputes between Bazarov and Pavel Petrovich Kirsanov,[2] no new structural forms would remain (the dialogues unfold in old, uniplanar forms). The comparison with forms of language and forms of logic, but what matters here are *artistic* forms. The chess image in Saussure.[3] Dostoevsky destroys the flatness of the earlier artistic depiction of the world. Depiction becomes for the first time multidimensional.

After my book (but independently of it) the ideas of polyphony, dialogue, unfinalizability, etc., were very widely developed. This is explained by the growing influence of Dostoevsky, but above all, of course, by those changes in reality itself which Dostoevsky (in this sense prophetically) succeeded in revealing earlier than the others.

Surmounting monologism. What monologism is, in the highest sense. A denial of the equal rights of consciousnesses vis-à-vis truth (understood abstractly and systemically). God can get along without man, but man cannot get along without Him. The teacher and the disciple (Socratic dialogue).

Our point of view in no way assumes a passivity on the part of the author, who would then merely assemble others' points of view, others' truths, completely denying his own point of view, his own truth. This is not the case at all; the case is rather a completely new and special interrelationship between the author's and the other's truth. The author is profoundly *active*, but his activity is of a special *dialogic* sort. It is one thing to be active in relation to a dead thing, to voiceless material that can be molded and formed as one wishes, and another thing to be active *in relation to someone else's living, autonomous consciousness*. This is a questioning, provoking, answering, agreeing, objecting activity; that is, it is dialogic activity no less active than the activity that finalizes, materializes, explains, and kills causally, that drowns out the other's voice with nonsemantic arguments. Dostoevsky frequently interrupts, but he never drowns out the other's voice, never finishes it off "from himself," that is, out of his own and alien consciousness. This is, so to speak, the activity of God in His relation to man, a relation allowing man to reveal himself utterly (in his immanent development), to judge himself, to refute himself. This is activity of a higher quality. It surmounts not the resistance of dead material, but the resistance of another's consciousness, another's truth. In other writers too we encounter dialogic activity in relation to those heroes who exert some internal resistance (for example, in Turgenev with regard to Bazarov[4]). But there this dialogism is a dramatic game, completely eliminated in the work as a whole.

In his article on *The Idiot*[5], Fridlender, while demonstrating the activity and intervention of the author, demonstrates in the majority of cases precisely this sort of dialogic activity and thus only confirms my conclusions.

True dialogic relations are possible only in relation to a hero who is a carrier of his own truth, who occupies a *signifying* (ideological) position. If an experience or a deed does not pretend to some *signifying power* (agreement/disagreement), but only to *reality* (evaluation), then the dialogic relationship can be minimal.

But can a *signifying* meaning become the object of *artistic depiction*? With a more profound understanding of artistic depiction, the *idea* can become such an object for it. This is Dostoevsky's second discovery.

Every novel depicts a "self-developing life," "re-creates" it. This self-development of life is independent of the author, of his conscious will and tendencies. But this is an independence of *existence*, of reality (of event, character, deed). This is the logic of an *existence* totally independent of the author, but it is not the logic of meaning-consciousness. Meaning-consciousness in its ultimate instancing belongs to the author and only to him. And this meaning relates to existence, and not to *another's* meaning (to another's equally privileged consciousness).

A creator re-creates the logic of the subject itself, but does not create that logic or violate it. Even a child playing games re-creates the logic of the game he is playing. But Dostoevsky is revealing a new subject and the new logic of that subject. He discovered personality and the self-developing logic of personality, one that occupies positions and makes decisions concerning the ultimate questions of the universe. Meanwhile the intervening links, including the most intimate and ordinary everyday links, are not omitted, but are interpreted in the light of ultimate questions as stages or symbols of an *ultimate solution*. Previously, all this existed on the plane of monologism, on the plane of a single consciousness. Here, a multiplicity of consciousnesses is opened up.

A higher type of disinterested artist who takes nothing from the world. Such consistent antihedonism is no longer anywhere to be found.

Dostoevsky "only projected the landscape of his own soul" (Lettenbauer).[6]

The expression in an artistic work of the writer's *I*. The monologization of Dostoevsky's art. Not an analysis of consciousness in the form of a sole and single *I*, but precisely an analysis of the interactions of many consciousnesses; not many people in the light of a single consciousness, but precisely an analysis of many equally privileged and fully valid consciousnesses. Nonself-sufficiency, the impossibility of the existence of a single consciousness. I am conscious of myself and become myself only while revealing myself for another, through another, and with the help of another. The most important acts constituting self-consciousness are determined by a relationship toward another consciousness (toward a *thou*). Separation, dissociation, and enclosure within the self as the main reason for the loss of one's self. Not that which takes place within, but that which takes place on the *boundary* between one's own and someone else's consciousness, on the *threshold*. And everything internal gravitates not toward itself but is turned to the outside and dialogized, every internal experience ends up on the boundary, encounters another, and in this tension-filled encounter lies its entire essence. This is the highest degree of sociality (not external, not material, but internal). Thus does Dostoevsky confront all decadent and idealistic (individualistic) culture, the culture of essential and inescapable solitude. He asserts the impossibility of solitude, the illusory nature of solitude. The very being of man (both external and internal) is the *deepest communion. To be* means *to communicate*. Absolute death (nonbeing) is the state of being unheard, unrecognized, unremembered (Ippolit). To be means to be for another, and through the other, for oneself. A person has no internal sovereign territory, he is wholly and always on the boundary;[7] looking inside himself, he looks *into the eyes of another* or *with the eyes of another.*

All this is no philosophical theory of Dostoevsky's—it is the way he artistically visualized the life of human consciousness, a visualization embodied in the form of a content. In no sense is *confession* a *form* or an ultimate whole of his art (it is neither his goal nor a mode of relating to himself, of visualizing himself)—confession is the *object* of his artistic vision and depiction. He depicts confession and the confessional consciousnesses of others in order to reveal their internally social structure, in order to show that they (confessions) are nothing other than an event of interaction among consciousnesses, in order to show the interdependence of consciousnesses that is revealed during confession. I cannot manage without another, I cannot become myself without another; I must find myself in another by finding another in myself (in mutual reflection and mutual acceptance). Justification cannot be · *self*-justification, recognition cannot be *self*-recognition. I receive my name from others, and it exists for others (self-nomination is imposture). Even love toward one's own self is impossible.

Capitalism created the conditions for a special type of inescapably solitary consciousness. Dostoevsky exposes all the falsity of this consciousness, as it moves in its vicious circle.

Hence the depiction of the sufferings, humiliations, and *lack of recognition* of man in class society. Recognition has been taken away from him, his name has been taken away. He has been driven into forced solitude, which the unsubmissive strive to transform into *proud solitude* (to do without recognition, without others).

The complex problem of humiliation and the humiliated.

No human events are developed or resolved within the bounds of a single consciousness. Hence Dostoevsky's hostility to those worldviews which see the final goal in a merging, in a dissolution of consciousnesses in one consciousness, in the removal of individuation. No Nirvana is possible for a *single* consciousness. A single consciousness is *contradictio in adjecto*. Consciousness is in essence multiple. *Pluralia tantum*. Dostoevsky also does not accept those worldviews that recognize the right of a higher consciousness to make decisions for lower ones, to transform them into voiceless things.

I translate into the language of an abstract worldview that which was the object of concrete and living artistic visualization and which then became a principle of form. Such a translation is always inadequate.

Not another *person* remaining the object of my consciousness, but another autonomous consciousness standing alongside mine, and my own consciousness can exist only in relation to it.

Dostoevsky made spirit, that is, the ultimate semantic position of the personality, the object of aesthetic contemplation, he was able to *see* spirit in a way in which previously only the body and soul of man could be seen. He moved aesthetic visualization into the depths, into deep new strata, but not into the depths of the unconscious; rather, into the depths of the heights of consciousness. The depths of consciousness are simultaneously its peaks[8] (up and down in the cosmos and in the microworld are relative). Consciousness is much more terrifying than any unconscious complexes.

The assertion that all Dostoevsky's work is one single unified confession. While in actual fact confessions (and not a single confession) are not the form of the whole here, but the object of depiction. Confession is shown from within and from without (in its unfinalizability).

The Underground Man at the mirror.

After Dostoevsky's confessions "by others," the old genre of confession became in essence impossible. Also no longer possible were the naively direct aspect of confession, its rhetorical element, its generally conventional element (with all the traditional devices and stylistic forms). Also no longer possible was a direct relationship to the self in confession (from self-love to self-denial). The role of the other person was revealed, in whose sole light could any word about oneself be constructed. Revealed here as well was the complexity of the simple phenomenon of looking at oneself in the mirror: with one's own and with others' eyes simultaneously, a meeting and interaction between the others' and one's own eyes, an intersection of worldviews (one's own and the other's), an intersection of two consciousnesses.

Unity not as an innate one-and-only, but as a dialogic *concordance* of unmerged twos or multiples.

"He projected the landscape of his own soul." But what does "projected" mean, and what is the meaning of "his own"? Projection cannot be understood mechanically, as a change of name, external life circumstances, the finale of a life (or of an event), etc. Nor can it be understood as a sort of generalized human content, isolated from any relation to *I* or *other*, that is, as an objective, neutral internal given. Emotional experience arises inside boundaries of an objectively determined sort, and not on the boundary between the *I* and the *other*, that is, at a point of interaction of consciousnesses. And *one's own* cannot be understood as a relative and contingent form of belonging, which could easily be replaced by a belonging to another or a third person (it is not like changing owners or changing addresses).

The depiction of death in Dostoevsky and Tolstoy. In Dostoevsky there are considerably fewer deaths than in Tolstoy—and in most cases Dostoevsky's deaths are murders and suicides. In Tolstoy there are a great many deaths. One could even speak of his passion for depicting death. Moreover—and this is very characteristic—Tolstoy depicts death not only from the outside looking in but also from the inside looking out, that is, from the very consciousness of the dying person, *almost* as a fact of that consciousness. Tolstoy is interested in death *for the person's own sake*, that is, for the dying person himself, and not for others, not for those who remain behind. He is in fact profoundly indifferent to one's own death as it exists for others.[9] "It is myself alone who must live, and myself alone who must die." In order to depict death from within, Tolstoy does not hesitate to violate sharply the real-life verisimilitude of the narrator's position (precisely as if the deceased himself had told him the story of his own death, as Agamemnon did to Odysseus). How consciousness dies out for the conscious person himself. This is possible only thanks to a certain materialization of consciousness. Consciousness here is given as something objective (object-like) and almost neutral with respect to the unbridgable (absolute) boundary between *I* and *another*. Tolstoy passes from one consciousness to another as if going from one room to another; he does not know an ultimate threshold.

Dostoevsky *never* depicts death from within. Final agony and death are observed by others. Death cannot be a fact of consciousness itself. And this is not, of course, because Dostoevsky feared for the verisimilitude of the narrator's position (he never feared to use the fantastic here when he needed it). It is rather because consciousness, by its very nature, cannot have a consciously perceived (that is, a consciousness-finalizing) beginning, nor can it have an end located in a sequence of consciousness as its ultimate link and made out of the same material as other elements of consciousness. A beginning and an end, a birth and a death are possessed by a person, a life, a fate, but not by consciousness, which by its very nature is infinite, revealing itself only from within, that is, only for consciousness itself. Beginnings and ends lie in the objective (and object-like) world for others, but not for the conscious person himself. What matters here is not simply that one cannot spy upon death from within, cannot see it, just as one cannot see the back of one's own head without resorting to a mirror. The back of one's head exists objectively and can be seen by others. But death from within, that is, one's own death consciously perceived, does not exist for anyone: not for the dying person, nor for others; it does not exist at all. Precisely this consciousness for its own sake, which neither knows nor has the ultimate word, is the object of depiction in Dostoevsky's world. This is why death-from-within cannot enter this world; such death is alien to its internal logic. Death in Dostoevsky's world is always an objective fact for other consciousnesses; what Dostoevsky foregrounds are the privileges of the other. In Tolstoy's world, another's consciousness is always depicted possessing a certain minimum of materialization (objectification); thus there is no unbridgable chasm between death from within (for the dying person himself) and death from without (for another): in fact they converge.

In Dostoevsky's world death finalizes nothing, because death does not affect the most important thing in this world—consciousness for its own sake. In Tolstoy's world, however, death possesses considerable finalizing and resolving power.

Dostoevsky gives all this an idealistic cast, draws ontological and metaphysical conclusions (the immortality of the soul, and so forth). But the discovery of the internal uniqueness of consciousness does not contradict materialism. Consciousness comes second, it is born at a specific stage in the development of the material organism, it is born objectively, and it dies (also objectively) together with the material organism (sometimes even before it); it dies objectively. But consciousness has a uniqueness, a subjective side; for its own self, in terms of its own consciousness, it can have neither beginning nor end. This subjective side is objective (but not object-like, not reified). The absence of consciously perceived death (death for its own sake) is just as much an objective fact as is the absence of a consciously perceived birth. Herein lies the uniqueness of consciousness.

The problem of the *addressed word*. Chernyshevsky's idea for a novel without authorial evaluations or authorial intonations.[10]

Dostoevsky's influence has still far from reached its culmination. The most essential and far-reaching aspects of his artistic vision, the revolution he brought about in the genre of the novel and in the area of literary art generally, have yet to be fully assimilated and realized. We are even today still being drawn into his dialogue on transient themes, but the dialogism he revealed to us, the dialogism of artistic thinking and of an artistic picture of the world, his new model of the internally dialogized world, has not yet been thoroughly examined. Socratic dialogue, which replaced tragic dialogue, was the first step in the history of the new genre of the novel. But that was mere dialogue, little more than an external form of dialogism.

The more stable elements of form and content, prepared and provided for by the ages (and for the ages), are born only in specific highly favorable moments and in a highly favorable historical location (Dostoevsky's epoch in Russia). Dostoevsky on Balzac's images and their preparation.[11] Marx on antique art.[12] A transient epoch giving birth to transient values. When Shakespeare became Shakespeare. Dostoevsky has not yet become Dostoevsky, he is still becoming him.

In the first part—the birth of a new form of novel (a new form of visualization and a new human being-personality; overcoming materialization). In the second part—the problem of language and style (a new mode for wearing the clothing of the word, the clothing of language, a new mode for wearing one's own body, one's embodiment).

In the first part—a radical change in the position of the author (in relation to the people he depicts, who are transformed from materialized people into personalities). The dialectic of the external and internal in a human being. Criticism of Gogol's authorial position in "The Overcoat" (the beginning, still fairly naive, of the hero's transformation into a personality). The crisis of the author's position and the author's emotion, the author's discourse.

The materialization of a human being. Social and ethical conditions, and the forms of their materialization. Dostoevsky's hatred of capitalism. The artistic discovery of the human being-personality. The dialogic relationship as the only form of relationship toward the human being-personality preserving its freedom and open-endedness. Criticism of all *external* forms of relationship and interaction, from violence to authority; artistic finalization as a variety of violence. The impermissibility of discussing the inner personality (Lise on Snegiryov in *The Karamazovs*,[13] Aglaya on Ippolit in *The Idiot*,[14] cf. the grosser forms of this in Thomas Mann's *Der Zauberberg* with Frau Chauchat and Peeperkorn; the psychologist as spy). Personality (or development of personality) cannot be pre-shaped, cannot be subordinated to one's own plan. One cannot spy or eavesdrop upon personality, cannot force it to reveal itself. The problems of confession and *another person*. One cannot force or pre-shape *confessions* (Ippolit). Persuasion through love.

The creation of a new novel (polyphonic) and the change in all of literature. The transforming influence of the novel on all other genres, their "novelization."

All these structural aspects of the interdependence of consciousnesses (personalities) are translated into the language of social relationships and individual-life relationships (plot relations in the broad sense of the word).

Socratic dialogue and the carnival square.

Materializing, objectified, finalizing definitions of Dostoevsky's heroes are not adequate to their essence.

Overcoming the monologic model of the world. The rudiments of this in Socratic dialogue.

The carnivalistic drawing-out of man from the usual, normal rut of life, out of "his own environment," his loss of his hierarchical place (already with utter precision in *The Double*). Carnival motifs in "The Landlady."

Dostoevsky and sentimentalism. The discovery of the *human being-personality* and his *consciousness* (not in the psychological sense) could not have been accomplished without the discovery of new aspects in the *word*, in a person's means of speech expression. Opening up the *profound dialogism of the word*.

In Dostoevsky a person is always depicted on the threshold, or, in other words, in a state of crisis.

The expansion of the concept of consciousness in Dostoevsky. Consciousness is in essence identical with the *personality* of an individual: everything in a person determined by the words "I myself" or "you yourself," everything in which a person finds himself and senses himself, everything he answers for, everything between birth and death.

Dialogic relations presuppose a communality of the object of intention (directionality).

Monologism, at its extreme, denies the existence outside itself of another consciousness with equal rights and equal responsibilities, another *I* with equal rights (*thou*). With a monologic approach (in its extreme or pure form) *another person* remains wholly and merely an *object* of consciousness, and not another consciousness. No response is expected from it that could change everything in the world of my consciousness. Monologue is finalized and deaf to the other's response, does not expect it and does not acknowledge in it any *decisive* force. Monologue manages without the other, and therefore to some degree materializes all reality. Monologue pretends to be the *ultimate word*. It closes down the represented world and represented persons.

The biographical (and autobiographical) integrity of a person's image, incorporating into itself that which can never be the subject of one's own personal experience, that which is received through the consciousness and thought of others (one's birth, external appearance, and so forth). The mirror. The disintegration of this integral image. That which one receives from another and in the tones of another and for which there is no personal tone.

The dialogic nature of consciousness, the dialogic nature of human life itself. The single adequate form for *verbally expressing* authentic human life is the *open-ended dialogue*. Life by its very nature is dialogic. To live means to participate in dialogue: to ask questions, to heed, to respond, to agree, and so forth. In this dialogue a person participates wholly and throughout his whole life: with his eyes, lips, hands, soul, spirit, with his whole body and deeds. He invests his entire self in discourse, and this discourse enters into the dialogic fabric of human life, into the world symposium.

Reified (materializing, objectified) images are profoundly inadequate for life and for discourse. A reified model of the world is now being replaced by a dialogic model. Every thought and every life merges in the open-ended dialogue. Also impermissible is any materialization of the word: its nature is also dialogic.

Dialectics is the abstract product of dialogue.

The definition of voice. This includes height, range, timbre, aesthetic category (lyric, dramatic, etc.). It also includes a person's worldview and fate. A person enters into dialogue as an integral voice. He participates in it not only with his thoughts, but with his fate and with his entire individuality.

The image of myself for myself, and my image for another. In actuality a person exists in the forms *I* and *another*[15] ("thou," "he" or *man*[16]). But we can conceive of a person irrespective of these forms of his existence, as we can any phenomenon or thing. What matters, however, is that only I myself am a person, which is to say, only a person, and not some other phenomenon conceived by me, exists in the form *I* and *another*. Literature creates utterly specific images of people, where *I* and *another* are combined in a special and unrepeatable way: *I* in the form of *another* or *another* in the form of *I*. This is not a concept of a person (in the way that things or phenomena are concepts), but an *image* of a person; and the image of a person cannot exist irrespective of the form of its existence (that is, irrespective of *I* or *other*). Thus complete materialization of the image of a person, as long as it remains an image, is impossible. But in giving an "objective" sociological (or any other scientific) analysis of this image we transform it into a concept, we place it outside the realm of the "*I-other*" relationship and materialize it. A form of "anotherness" does, of course, still prevail in the image; *I* remains the only one in the world (cf. the theme of the double). But a person's image is a path to the *I* of *another*, a step toward [illegible]. All these problems inevitably arise while analyzing the creative art of Dostoevsky, who sensed exceptionally keenly the form of a person's existence as *I* or as *another*.

Not theory (transient content), but a "sense of theory."

Confession as a higher form of a person's *free* self-revelation *from within* (and not his finalizing from without) confronted Dostoevsky from the very beginning of his literary career. Confession as an encounter of the *deepest I* with *another* and with *others* (with the folk), as an encounter of *I* and *other* on the highest level or in the ultimate instance. But the *I* in this encounter must be the pure, deep *I* from within oneself, without any admixture of presumed and forced or naively assimilated points of view and evaluations from another, that is, without any visualization of the self through the eyes of another. Without a *mask* (an external profile *for another*, the shaping of the self not from within but from without, and this also refers to any speech or stylistic mask), without loopholes, without a false ultimate word, that is, without all that is externalizing and false.

Not faith (in the sense of a specific faith in orthodoxy, in progress, in man, in revolution, etc.), but a *sense of faith*, that is, an integral attitude (by means of the whole person) toward a higher and ultimate value. Atheism is often understood by Dostoevsky as a lack of faith in this sense, as indifference toward an ultimate value which makes demands on the whole man, as a rejection of an ultimate position in the ultimate whole of the world. Dostoevsky's vacillations as regards the *content* of this ultimate value. Zosima on Ivan. The type of people who cannot live without an ultimate value and yet at the same time cannot make a final choice among values. The type of people who construct their lives without any attitude toward ultimate value: plunderers, amoralists, philistines, conformists, careerists, the dead, etc. Dostoevsky almost does not recognize any middle type.

The exceptionally keen sense of *one's own* and *the other* in the word, in style, in the most subtle nuances and twists of style, in intonation, in the speech gesture, in the body (mimic) gesture, in the expression of the eyes, the face, the hands, the entire external appearance, in the very way the body is carried. Shyness, self-confidence, rude and boorish behavior (Snegiryov), mincing and cringing (the body contorts and twists in the presence of another), and so forth. In everything a person uses to express himself on the outside (and consequently, for *another*)—from the body to the word—an intense interaction takes place between *I* and *other*: their struggle (honest struggle or mutual deception), balance, harmony (as an ideal), naive ignorance of one another, deliberate ignoring of one another, challenge, absence of recognition (the Underground Man, who "does not pay attention," etc.) and so forth. We repeat, this struggle takes place in everything a person uses to express (reveal) himself on the outside (for others)—from the body to the word, including the ultimate confessional word. Social graces as a worked-out, ready-made, congealed and (mechanically) assimilated external form for expressing oneself on the outside (control over one's body, gesture, voice, word, etc.), where a full and dead balance is achieved, where there is no struggle, where there is no living *I* and *other*, no living and lasting interaction between them. Opposed to this dead form are "seemliness" and harmony, achieved on the basis of a common higher idea (value, goal), on the basis of a *free* agreement about the higher idea ("The Golden Age," "The Kingdom of God," and so forth).

Dostoevsky had an exceptionally observant eye and keen ear with which to see and hear this highly intense struggle of *I* and *other* in every external manifestation of a person (in each face, gesture, word), in every contemporary living form of communion. All expression—expressive form—had lost its naive integrity, had fallen apart and disintegrated, just as the "connecting link of time had fallen apart" in the sociohistorical world of his time. Eccentricity, scandals, hysterics, etc., in Dostoevsky's world. This is neither psychology nor psychopathology, for the issue here is *personality* and not the *reified* layers of a person, free self-disclosure and not the second-hand objectified analysis of a materialized person.

The concept of man and the image of man in Tolstoy. "Caius is mortal" and *I* (Ivan Ilych).[17] The concept of man and the living man in the form of *I*.

The task of the present introductory article is to reveal the uniqueness of Dostoevsky's artistic vision, to reveal the artistic unity of the world he created, to show the types (varieties) of novel genres he created and his special attitude toward the word as the material of artistic creativity. Problems of literary history in the strict sense will concern us only insofar as they are indispensable for a proper treatment of this uniqueness.

Confession for oneself as an attempt at an objective attitude toward oneself irrespective of the forms *I* and *another*. But when one abstracts oneself from these forms, the most essential thing is immediately lost (the distinction between *I-for-myself* and *I-for-another*). A neutral position in relation to *I* and *another* is impossible in the living image and in the ethical idea. They cannot be equated (as right and left are in geometrical identity). Every person is an *I* for himself, but in the concrete and unrepeatable event of life *I* for oneself is the only *I*, and everyone else are others for me. And this sole and irreplaceable position in the world cannot be abolished through any conceptual, generalizing (and abstracting) interpretive activity.

Not types of peoples and fates finalized in an objectified way, but *types of worldviews* (Chaadaev, Herzen, Granovsky, Bakunin, Belinsky, the Nechaev circle, the Dolgushin* circle, etc.). And Dostoevsky understands worldview not as an abstract unity and sequence in a system of thoughts and positions, but as an ultimate position in the world in relation to higher values. Worldviews embodied in voices. A dialogue among such embodied worldviews, in which he himself participated. In the rough drafts, in the early stages of shaping his plan, these names (Chaadaev, Herzen, Granovsky and others) are given directly, and then, as the plot and *plot fates* take shape, they are replaced by invented names. From the *beginning* of the plan, whole *worldviews* make their appearance, and only then the plot and the plot fates of the heroes ("moments" facing them in which their positions are most vividly revealed). Dostoevsky begins not with the idea, but with idea-heroes of a dialogue. He seeks the integral voice, and fate and event (the fates and events of the plot) become means for expressing voices.

Interest in suicides as conscious deaths, as links in the conscious chain where a man finalizes himself from within.

Finalizing moments, since they are perceived by the person himself, are included in the chain of his consciousness, become transient self-definitions and lose their finalizing force. "A fool who has admitted that he is a fool is no longer a fool"—this deliberately primitive thought, presented in an ironically parodic manner (Alyosha from *The Insulted and the Injured*)[18] nevertheless expresses the essence of the matter.

The finalizing words of an author (without a trace of addressivity), the secondhand words of a third person which as a matter or principle the hero himself cannot hear, cannot understand; he cannot make of them an aspect of his own self-consciousness, cannot respond to them. Such words would lie beyond the dialogic whole. Such words would materialize and debase the human being-personality.

The ultimate whole in Dostoevsky is dialogic. All his major heroes are participants in dialogue. They hear everything that is said by others about them, and respond to everything (nothing is said about them secondhand or behind closed doors). And the author is only a participant in this dialogue (and its organizer). There are very few secondhand, materializing words sounding outside dialogue, and such words have an essential finalizing significance only for secondary, objectified personages (who are depicted essentially beyond the boundaries of dialogue, depicted as extras who do not have their own word with which to enrich or change the meaning of the dialogue).

Forces that lie outside consciousness, externally (mechanically) defining it: from environment and violence to miracle, mystery, and authority. Consciousness under the influence of these forces loses its authentic freedom, and personality is destroyed. There, among these forces, must one also consign the unconscious (the "id").

The sentimental-humanistic dematerialization of man, which remains objectified: pity, the lower forms of love (for children, for everything weak and small). A person ceases to be a thing, but does not become a personality, that is, remains an object lying in the zone of *another*, experienced in the pure form of *another*, distanced from the zone of *I*. In Dostoevsky's early work many heroes are presented in this way, as are secondary characters in his later work (Katerina Ivanovna, children, and others).

Satirical objectification and the destruction of personality (Karmazinov, Stepan Trofimovich in part, and others).

After enthusiastic co-philosophizing and philosophizing with heroes "apropos of . . . ," there began objective research on the actual historical reality lying outside the art work but determining it, that is, on the real outside world pre-existing the aesthetic or creative act. This was both necessary and very productive.

The closer the image to the zone *I-for-myself*, the less there is of the object-like and finalized in it, the more it becomes an image of personality, free and open-ended. Askoldov's classification, for all its depth, transforms the distinguishing features of personality (various degrees of personality-ness) into the objectified indicators of a person, while the fundamental distinction between character and personality (very profoundly and correctly understood by Askoldov[19]) is determined not by qualitative (objectified) indicators, but by the *position* of the image (whatever it may be, according to its characterological features) in the system of coordinates "*I-for-myself* and *another person* (in all its varieties)." The zone of freedom and open-endedness.

In everything that is secret, dark, mystical, to the extent that it could exert a defining influence on *personality*, Dostoevsky saw *violence* destroying the individual. The contradictory understanding of the institution of the elder. The odor of corruption[20] (a miracle would have enslaved). This is precisely what determined Dostoevsky's artistic vision (but not always his ideology).

The materialization of man under conditions of class society, carried to its extreme under capitalism. This materialization is accomplished (realized) by external forces acting on the personality from without and from within; this is violence in all possible forms of its realization (economic, political, ideological), and these forces can be combated only from the outside and with equally externalized forces (justified revolutionary violence); the goal is personality.

The problem of catastrophe. Catastrophe is not finalization. It is the culmination, in collision and struggle, of points of view (of equally privileged consciousnesses, each with its own world). Catastrophe does not give these points of view resolution, but on the contrary reveals their incapability of resolution under earthly conditions; catastrophe sweeps them all away without having resolved them. Catastrophe is the opposite of triumph and apotheosis. By its very essence it is denied even elements of catharsis.

The tasks that confront the author and his consciousness in a polyphonic novel are considerably more complex and profound than in a homophonic (monologic) novel. The unity of the Einsteinian world is more complex and profound than that of the Newtonian world, it is a unity of a higher order (a qualitatively different unity).

Examine in detail the distinction between *character* and *personality*. Even character is to some extent independent of the author (Tatyana's marriage, which Pushkin did not expect),[21] but this independence (its own logic) has an objectified character. The independence of personality is of a qualitatively different nature: personality is not subordinate to (that is, it resists) objectified cognition and reveals itself only freely and dialogically (as *thou* for *I*). The author is a participant in the dialogue (on essentially equal terms with the characters), but he also fulfills additional, very complex functions (he holds the reins between the ideal dialogue of the work and the actual dialogue of reality).

Dostoevsky uncovered the dialogic nature of societal life, of the life of a human being. Not ready-made existence, whose meaning the writer must uncover, but open-ended dialogue with an evolving multivoiced meaning.

The unity of the whole in Dostoevsky is not a matter of plot nor of monologic idea, that is, not mono-ideational. It is a unity above plot and above idea.

The struggle between objectified *characterological* definitions (embodied for the most part in speech styles) and *personality* elements (open-endedness) in Dostoevsky's early works (*Poor Folk, The Double*, and others). The birth of Dostoevsky out of Gogol, the birth of personality out of character.

An analysis of Nastasya Filippovna's nameday party. An analysis of Marmeladov's funeral feast.

The disintegration of the epic wholeness of a person's image. Subjectivity, noncoincidence with one's own self. Bifurcation.

Not merging with another, but preserving one's own position of *extralocality* and the *surplus* of vision and understanding connected with it. But the real question is Dostoevsky's use of this surplus. Not for materialization and finalization. The most important aspect of this surplus is love (one cannot love oneself, love is a coordinate relationship), and then, confession, forgiveness (Stavrogin's conversation with Tikhon), finally, simply an active (not a duplicating) understanding, a willingness to listen. This surplus is never used as an ambush, as a chance to sneak up and attack from behind. This is an open and honest surplus, dialogically revealed to the other person, a surplus expressed by the addressed and not by the secondhand word. Everything essential is dissolved in dialogue, positioned face to face.

The threshold, the door, and the stairway. Their chronotopic significance. The possibility of transforming hell into paradise in a single instant (that is, passing from one to the other, cf. "the mysterious visitor"[22]).

The logic governing the development of the idea itself, taken independently of individual consciousness (the idea in itself, or in consciousness generally, or in the spirit generally), that is, its referentially logical and systemic development, and then the special logic governing the development of an idea embodied in personality. Here the idea, insofar as it is embodied in personality, is regulated by the coordinates *I* and *another*, refracted variously in different zones. This is the special logic revealed in Dostoevsky's works. Thus these ideas cannot be adequately understood and analyzed in the usual referentially logical, systematic plane (as ordinary philosophical theories).

The "final significance" of a monument in a specific epoch, the interests and demands of that epoch, its historical strength and weakness. Final significance is limited significance. The phenomenon here is equal to itself, coincides with itself.

But in addition to the monument's final significance there is also its living, growing, evolving, changing significance. It is not (fully) born in the limited epoch of the monument's birth—it is prepared for in the course of centuries prior to its birth and continues to live and develop centuries after its birth. This growing significance cannot be portrayed and explained solely within the limited conditions of a single given epoch, the epoch of the monument's birth. Cf. Karl Marx on antique art. This growing significance is in fact the discovery made by every great work of art. Like all discoveries (scientific ones, for example), it is prepared for by centuries, but is accomplished under the optimal conditions of the single specific epoch during which it ripened. These optimal conditions must be explored, but they do not of course exhaust the growing and nontransient significance of the work of art.

Introduction: the goal, tasks and limitations of the introductory research. The discovery made by Dostoevsky. The three main facets of this discovery. But first let us give a brief survey of the literature on Dostoevsky from the perspective of this discovery.

The word, the living word, inseparably linked with dialogic communion, by its very nature wants to be heard and answered. By its very dialogic nature it presupposes an ultimate dialogic instancing. To receive the word, to be heard. The impermissibility of *second-hand* resolution. My word remains in the continuing dialogue, where it will be heard, answered and reinterpreted.

In Dostoevsky's world, strictly speaking, there are no deaths as objectified and organic facts in which a person's responsively active consciousness takes no part; in Dostoevsky's world there are only murders, suicides, and insanity, that is, there are only death-acts, responsively conscious. A special place is occupied by the death-departures of righteous men (Makar, Zosima, his younger brother, the mysterious visitor). For the death of consciousness (organic death, that is, the death of the body, did not interest Dostoevsky), the person himself (or another person, a murderer, even an executioner) is always responsible. The only ones who organically die are the objectified personages, the ones who do not take part in the great dialogue (the ones who merely serve as the material or the paradigm for dialogue). Dostoevsky does not acknowledge death as an organic process, as something happening to a person without the participation of his responsive consciousness. Personality does not die. Death is a departure. The person *himself* departs. Only such death-departure can become an object (a fact) of fundamental artistic visualization in Dostoevsky's world. The person has departed, having spoken his word, but the word itself remains in the open-ended dialogue.

On Askoldov: personality is not an object but another subject. The depiction of personality requires above all a radical change in the position of the depicting author—it requires *addressivity* to a *thou*. It is not a matter of noticing new objectified features, but a matter of changing the very artistic approach to the depicted person, changing the system of coordinates.

Expand on the problem of the *author's position* in the homophonic and polyphonic novel. Give a definition of monologism and dialogicality, at the end of the second chapter. The *image of personality* (that is, not an objectified image, but a word). Dostoevsky's (artistic) discovery. In the same chapter, the depiction of deaths in Tolstoy and Dostoevsky. Here also the internal open-endedness of the hero. In the beginning of the chapter, in the transition from Gogol to Dostoevsky, show the necessity of the appearance of a hero-ideologist who takes an ultimate position in the world, the type of person who takes an ultimate decision (Ivan in Zosima's characterization of him[23]). The hero of the accidental family[24] is not defined by a socially stable existence, but makes the ultimate decision for himself. Detailed treatment of this in the third chapter.

In the second chapter, on the plan for an "objective novel" (that is, the novel without an authorial point of view) in Chernyshevsky (according to V. V. Vinogradov). The difference between that plan and the authentically polyphonic plan of Dostoevsky. Chernyshevsky's plan lacks the dialogism (the appropriate counterpoint) of a polyphonic novel.

NOTES

1. See F. M. Dostoevsky, *The Adolescent*, Part Three, ch. 5, III. Bakhtin quotes Trishatov's plan for an opera in chapter 5 of this volume, pp. 223-24.

2. In Turgenev's *Fathers and Sons*, especially ch. 10.

3. Bakhtin is referring to Saussure's analogy between language and chess, which illustrated for him the idea of relational identity: the physical properties of individual chess pieces are of no importance as long as all pieces performing one function in the game are distinguishable from other pieces. See Ferdinand de Saussure, *Course in General Linguistics*, (New York: McGraw-Hill, 1966), p. 110. See also the good discussion in Jonathan Culler, *Ferdinand de Saussure* (Penguin Books, 1976), p. 20, on the moral of the chess analogy: "Identity is wholly a function of differences within a system." [A/B cite Saussure in its Russian edition, *Trudy po jazykoznaniiu*, pp. 120-22.]

4. Cf. the comment on Bazarov in Bakhtin's lectures on the history of Russian literature: "But he cannot cope with a hero in whom the author saw strength and wanted to heroicize. Everyone gives in to Bazarov, even Turgenev himself prevaricates and wants to flatter him, but at the same time hates him." [A/B]

5. Fridlender, G. M. "Roman *Idiot*" in *Tvorchestvo F. M. Dostoevskogo* (Moscow: 1959), pp. 173-214. [A/B]

6. Cf. Lettenbauer, W. *Russische Literaturgeschichte* (Frankfurt/Main-Wien, 1955), p. 250. [A/B]

7. See Bakhtin's 1924 article, "The Problem of Content, Material and Form in Verbal Artistic Creativity": "One must not, however, imagine the realm of culture as some sort of spatial whole, having boundaries but also having internal territory. The realm of culture has no internal territory: it is entirely distributed along the boundaries, boundaries pass everywhere, through its every aspect, the systematic unity of culture extends into the very atoms of cultural life, it reflects like the sun in each drop of that life. Every cultural act lives essentially on the boundaries: in this is its seriousness and its significance; abstracted from boundaries, it loses its soil, it becomes empty, arrogant, it degenerates and dies" (M. Bakhtin, *Voprosy literatury i estetiki* [Moscow: 1975], p. 25). Characteristic of Bakhtin's thought is a unity between the structural understanding of human personality and of culture, a unity

in approach to the problems of philosophical anthropology and to the problems of the history of culture. [A/B]

8. Cf. a similar drawing together of concepts in Dostoevsky's statement about his "realism in a *higher sense*" as a depiction "of all the *depths* of the human soul" (*Biografiia, pis'ma i zametki iz zapisnoi knizhki F. M. Dostoevskogo*, St. Petersburg, 1883, p. 373), which was Bakhtin's starting point for his ideas about Dostoevsky's art. [A/B]

9. On death for oneself and death for others, see Bakhtin's essay "Author and Hero in Aesthetic Activity," the chapter "The Temporal Whole of the Hero" [in M. M. Bakhtin, *Estetika slovesnogo tvorchestva*, pp. 88-120]. [A/B]

10. On Chernyshevsky's *Pearl of Creation*, see this volume, pp. 65-67. [A/B]

11. Dostoevsky wrote to his brother Mikhail on 9 August 1838: "Balzac is great! His characters are the work of a cosmic mind! Not the spirit of the time, but thousands of years have prepared with their struggle for such a dénouement in the human soul" F. M. Dostoevskii, *Pis'ma*, ed. A. S. Dolinin, vol. I [Leningrad, 1928], p. 47) [A/B]

12. See *K. Marks i F. Engels ob iskusstve* (in two volumes, vol. 1, Moscow, 1957), pp. 134-36. [A/B]

13. Reference is to a scene in *The Brothers Karamazov*, Book Five: Pro and Contra, I: "The Engagement."

14. Reference is to *The Idiot*, Part Three, ch. 7. Aglaya says to Myshkin:

"It's very brutal to look on and judge a man's soul, as you judge Ippolit. You have no tenderness, nothing but truth, and so you judge unjustly."

15. *ja i drugoi*. Russian distinguishes between *drugoi* (another, other person) and *chuzhoi* (alien, strange; also, the other). The English pair "I/other," with its intonations of alienation and opposition, has specifically been avoided here. The *another* Bakhtin has in mind is not hostile to the *I* but a necessary component of it, a friendly other, a living factor in the attempts of the *I* toward self-definition.

16. *Man* (the substantivized indefinite personal pronoun in German) is a category in the philosophy of Martin Heidegger. *Man* is an impersonal force defining the everyday existence of a person. [A/B]

17. Reference is to Leo Tolstoy, "The Death of Ivan Ilych," beginning of ch. 6.

18. See *The Insulted and Humiliated*, Part III, ch. 2.

19. Cf. Askol'dov, S. "Religiozno-eticheskoe znachenie Dostoevskogo," in *F. M. Dostoevskii, Stat'i i materialy*, ed. A. S. Dolinin, vol. I (St. Petersburg, 1922). Bakhtin offers a critical appraisal of this article in *Problems of Dostoevsky's Poetics*, ch. 1, pp. 11-14.

20. *Tletvornyi dukh*. Bakhtin embeds here the title of chapter 1 ("The Odor of Corruption") of Book Seven (Alyosha) in *The Brothers Karamazov*. Reference is to the malodorous decay of Father Zosima's body after his death, when believers were expecting miracles.

21. Reference is to Tatyana Larina, heroine of Pushkin's *Eugene Onegin* (1823-31).

22. See *The Brothers Karamazov*, Book Six, ch. 2 (Notes of the Life in God of the Elder Zosima), (d) "The Mysterious Visitor." In one of his discussions with the young Zosima, the visitor (soon to confess his secret murder) promises that "paradise lies hidden within all of us—here it lies hidden in me now, and if I will it, it will be revealed to me tomorrow and for all time."

23. See *The Brothers Karamazov*, Book Two, ch. 6 (Why is Such a Man Alive?). [A/B] This passage is discussed in this volume, ch. 3, "The Idea in Dostoevsky, pp. 86-87.

24. The theme of the "accidental family" is well developed in Dostoevsky's journalistic writings, but Averintsev/Bocharov refer the reader specifically to *The Adolescent*, Part III, ch. 13 [The Epilogue], where Nikolai Semyonovich comments on Arkady's notes.

Glossary of Proper Names and Works

Glossary of Proper Names and Works

Items starred [*] in the text are listed here alphabetically. If Bakhtin gives both the work and its author, the item appears under the author only; otherwise the work is listed separately.

AESCHINES Socraticus [4th c. B.C.]
One of Socrates' most devoted followers, present at his master's condemnation and death. Aeschines was the author of Socratic dialogues in his own right, which were highly regarded as faithful to Socrates' style and personal manner.

ALEXAMENOS of Teos
According to Aristotle, the first person to write dialogues in the Socratic style before the time of Plato. Most likely he was a contemporary and acquaintance of Socrates.

ANTISTHENES of Cyrene [c. 455-c. 360 B.C.]
Athenian philosopher, pupil of Socrates. Considered by some to be the founder of the School of the Cynics, he exercised considerable influence on Stoic philosophy. He led a life of severe asceticism. His motto "I do not possess, in order not to be possessed" is said to have elicited from Socrates the rejoinder, "I can see your vanity, Antisthenes, through the holes of your cloak." Diogenes was one of his pupils.

In the realm of the word, Antisthenes taught that virtue and happiness were based on knowledge, and that knowledge could be attained through the proper study of words and their definitions. He was the author of several dialogues, fictive orations, and interpretations of Homer.

APULEIUS, Lucius [fl. A.D. 150]

Latin writer born in North Africa, most famous for his prose romance *Metamorphoses, or The Golden Ass*, one of the few Latin novels surviving in its entirety. It is the tale of a man transformed into an ass who wanders about the lands of the Mediterranean, observing human folly and undergoing countless adventures. Apuleius is also the author of *Apologia* (a self-defense against accusations that he had won the love of a woman by the use of magic, with interesting commentary on local superstitions), *De Dogmata Platonis, De Mundo, De Deo Socratis*, and numerous translations.

ARIOSTO, Lodovico [1474-1533]

Italian poet and satirist, famous for his romantic epic *Orlando Furioso* (1532) in 46 cantos. It is a continuation of Matteo Boiardo's *Orlando Innamorato* (1472-94, unfinished), but while Boiardo's *Orlando* is a robust and rather naive chivalric epic, Ariosto's sequel is more ironic, at places even a burlesque. Bakhtin finds the *Orlando* a congenial text for several reasons: it is, first, an example of a later author "re-accenting" a hero by passing him through a different voice; and secondly, Ariosto plays with his own image in the text, using the opening octaves of each canto to expound his own personal views and comments.

ASKOL'DOV, S. [Sergei Alekseevich Kozlov, 1870-1945]

Philosopher, chemist, and theoretician of ethics and religious psychology, publishing under the names Alekseev, Askoldov and S. Askol'dov. In the 1920s he founded a religious discussion group, The Brotherhood of St. Seraphim of Sarov, with which Bakhtin was associated; membership in the Brotherhood was in fact one accusation against Bakhtin after his arrest in 1929. Askoldov also attended, along with Bakhtin, meetings of the Voskresenie [Resurrection] Circle in Leningrad in the 1920s. Askoldov's early works include "Osnovnye problemy teorii poznaniia i ontologii" [Basic problems in the Theory of Knowledge and Ontology] (1900); "Khristianstvo i politika" [Christianity and Politics] (1906); "O sviazi dobra i zla" [On the Connection between Good and Evil] (1916); "Soznanie kak tseloe" [Consciousness as a Whole Entity] (1918). Bakhtin mentions two of Askoldov's articles that attempt to apply these ethical and psychological concerns to Dostoevsky's art: "Religiozno-eticheskoe znachenie Dostoevskogo" [The Religious and Ethical Significance of Dostoevsky] (1922), and "Psikhologiia kharakterov u Dostoevskogo" [The Psychology of Characters in Dostoevsky] (1924). In these works Askoldov constructs a kinship system for Dostoevsky's heroes based on psychological traits, giving a central place to Stavrogin. While Bakhtin appreciates the "multi-voicedness" of this approach, he still considers it monologic.

BARBIER, Auguste [1805-82]

Minor French poet and satirist on social themes. His best known works are *La Curée* (1830), written against the opportunists in the 1830 Revolution, *L'Idole* (1832), a denunciation of Napoleon, and numerous pieces critical of the social and economic realities of early industrialization.

BELINSKY, Vissarion Grigorievich (1811-48)

Enormously influential critic and journalist, whose annual surveys of new literary developments helped to establish Russian literature as a self-conscious artistic and social force in the first half of the nineteenth century. Belinsky's interpretations of Gogol and the early Dostoevsky became as famous as the works themselves. Due to the "progressive" and social bias of much of his work, Belinsky's critical writings have become canonical in the Soviet Union.

BELKIN, Abram Aleksandrovich [1907-70]
Soviet Dostoevsky scholar, editor, and compiler. When Bakhtin mentions the upswing in Dostoevsky studies in the 1950s he has in mind, among other works, Belkin's "Dostoevskii v otsenke russkoi kritiki" [Dostoevsky as Evaluated in Russian Criticism], in *F. M. Dostoevskii v russkoi kritike: sbornik statei*, introduced and annotated by Belkin (Moscow: GIKhL, 1956).

BILINKIS, Yakov Semyonovich [b. 1926]
Soviet literary scholar specializing in Tolstoy (*O tvorchestve L. N. Tolstogo*, 1959) and Dostoevsky.

BION BORYSTHENES [c. 325-c. 255 B.C.]
Greek philosopher, son of a freedman and a former hetaera and himself a freed slave, strongly influenced by the Cynics. Like his predecessor Crates the Cynic, Bion preached poverty, the simple life, and the doctrine that happiness is achieved only through an acceptance of human limits and an adjustment to circumstances. He belonged to no specific philosophical school, and spread his word wandering from town to town, lecturing for alms.

The form most closely associated with Bion is the diatribe, or "conversation." Bionic diatribes contain two or more voices, usually unfolding as a dialogue between a wise man and a nameless, less virtuous second party. Bion's language is forceful, inventive, and frequently obscene, characterized by a caustic humor and merciless in its criticism of social conventions. His style was later one of the formative influences on Roman satire.

BOETHIUS [c. 480-524]
Roman philosopher best known for his *De Consolatione Philosophiae* [The Consolation of Philosophy], c. 524, written by him in prison while awaiting execution for treason. The *Consolation* is a dialogue, in alternating prose and verse, between the author and the Spirit of Philosophy—who urges on him a Stoic attitude toward the injustices of the world.

Boethius' translations and commentaries on ancient thinkers became a major source of information for Medieval Europe, and the *Consolation* itself inspired many translations and imitations. Bakhtin sees the work as a Christian adaptation of Menippean principles—filtered, to be sure, through the Greek diatribe, which traditionally despised fortune and sang the virtues of poverty and slavery.

BOILEAU's *Dialogue des héros de romans*
Nicholas Boileau [1636-1711], French poet and critic, was one of the earliest representatives of the neoclassicist movement in France. His *Dialogue des héros de romans* [1713; written c. 1665] is a dialogue on the Lucianic model satirizing the pseudo-heroic novels in vogue in the early seventeenth century (the novels of La Calprenède, Mille. de Scudéry, etc.). The *Dialogue* opens on Pluto's complaint that the dead are no longer what they once were: they have

neither elegance of expression nor common sense. When Pluto attempts to summon up real historical heroes to prove his point, he is greeted by a series of mincing shepherds and shepherdesses.

Bouvard et Pécuchet
Unfinished novel by Gustave Flaubert [1821-80], published in 1881. Two copying clerks systematically set out to master all the disciplines contained in the encyclopedia by buying a farm and attempting to develop it scientifically. The clerks fail miserably as each field of knowledge reveals itself to be complex, contradictory, or simply unable to account for real experience. In his projected scenarios for the end of the book, Flaubert has his two clerks again reduced to copying—but this time their project is simply to copy out anything that comes to hand: tobacco pouches, old newspapers, maxims from the many books they had consulted for their various disastrous experiments. Faith in the "totalized vision" is replaced by a passion for taxonomy, and the result is a grotesque *encyclopédie-manquée*.

"Catechism of a Revolutionary"
Political manifesto of the Russian nihilist revolutionary Sergei Nechaev [1847-82], which called on revolutionaries to practice violence, self-abnegation, and sacrifice for the cause. Nechaev's most famous exploit was the murder of a Russian student in 1869, designed to cement the loyalty of his "revolutionary cell." For this murder Nechaev was arrested in 1872, and he died ten years later in Peter and Paul Fortress in Petersburg.
    Dostoevsky was keenly interested in the Nechaev case, and incorporated its murder into the plot of *The Possessed*. For the connection between Nechaev and that novel, see Konstantin Mochulsky, *Dostoevsky: His Life and Work*, trans. Michael A. Minihan (Princeton, 1967), pp. 417-23.

CERVANTES' *Novelas ejemplares*
Cervantes' third book (1613), written between the two parts of *Quixote*. It consists of twelve short stories in the style of an Italian novella, but with perhaps a stronger overall ethical orientation. The style of the stories is mixed: some are picaresque episodes, others realistic accounts of criminal life; still others are entertaining love triangles or philosophical tales.

CHAADAEV, Pyotr Yakovlevich [1794-1856]
Russian philosopher and social critic, author of a series of "Philosophical Letters" in the 1820s and '30s which earned him immediate fame and the honor of being declared officially insane under the repressive reign of Nicholas I. In the "Letters" he laments Russia's isolation from Europe and exclusion from Divine History, but sees in that isolation both a hope for salvation and a divine mission. Although Chaadaev himself was a religious thinker and not a public activist, his writings were influential on both Slavophiles and Westernizers in Russian intellectual history. Dostoevsky chose Chaadaev as one of the prototypes for Versilov in *The Adolescent*.

CHERNYSHEVSKY, Nikolai Gavrilovich [1828-99]
Russian radical critic and publicist, a leading representative of Russian utilitarianism in the 1850s and '60s. He edited the influential progressive journal *Sovremennik* [The Contemporary] from 1853 until his arrest in 1862 for revolutionary activities; while in prison he wrote his didactic-utopian novel

Chto Delat' [What is To Be Done?] (1863). Chernyshevsky's martyrdom (seven years hard labor and twenty years exile in Siberia), plus the phenomenal popularity of his novel among Russian social activists, made him a great mythologized hero in the postrevolutionary search for nineteenth-century precursors to Bolshevism.

In 1855 Chernyshevsky wrote "The Aesthetic Relation of Art to Reality," an essay that has since become canonical for official Soviet literature. In it he defends mimetic, representational, utilitarian art—to the extent of insisting that emotion is art's prime ingredient, and that in art "feeling and form are opposites." Bakhtin's use of Chernyshevsky here, as the prototype of a novelist who seeks an objective, deliberately de-centered novel (*The Pearl of Creation*), is thus characteristically eccentric.

CHRISTIANSEN, Broder [b. 1869, last publication 1940s]
German aesthetician and philosopher of language, influential on the early Russian Formalists. In his *Philosophie der Kunst* (1909) he developed the idea of a *Differenzqualität* or "quality of divergence" between literary and nonliterary discourse, and introduced the term *dominant* into literary studies.

CRITIAS [460-403 B.C.]
Author of elegies and tragedies, and one of the Thirty Tyrants appointed by Sparta to rule Athens after the Peloponnesian Wars. His *Homiliae*, to which Bakhtin is probably referring here, having come down to us only in fragments ("discussions"). Critias was an early associate of Socrates, and—despite his reputation for unscrupulousness and extreme pro-Spartan sympathies—is remembered not unkindly by Plato in his dialogues.

CRITO [fl. 400 B.C.]
Athenian friend and follower of Socrates, referred to by Plato in the *Apology*, *Phaedo*, and *Euthydemus*. In the *Crito* he visits Socrates in prison and tries to persuade him to escape.

Crito also wrote dialogues, but the seventeen lost dialogues ascribed to him by Diogenes Laertius are not authenticated.

CYRANO DE BERGERAC's *Histoire comique des états et empires de la Lune* (1643-48, published 1657)
Cyrano de Bergerac (1619-55), French author, soldier, and duelist, wrote two fantasy-romances, one taking place on the moon and the other on the sun. Such fantasies were conventional vehicles in the seventeenth century for social and political satire. In this work, *Comical History of the States and Empires of the Moon*, the author visits the moon and describes its people and its institutions, with estranged and therefore devastating clarity.

DES PÉRIERS' *Cymbalum mundi* (1538)
Bonaventure des Périers (d. 1544), Burgundian classicist and satirist, directed his *Cymbalum mundi* against Christian liturgy and discipline. A prose work in four dialogues, it is very much in the style of Lucian, involving, for example, scandals between heavenly messengers and earthly rogues. The work was quickly suppressed and survived only in a single copy.

DOLGUSHIN Circle
A group of Russian political radicals, brought to trial in July 1874 for disseminating propaganda and fomenting revolution. Dostoevsky followed the case

carefully in the newspapers, and modeled Dergachev (in *The Adolescent*) on Dolgushin.

In the early drafts of *The Adolescent*, the Dolgushin affair was to be as central to that novel as the Nechaev scandal was to *The Possessed*. But this role was later reduced and modified; Dergachev's "revolutionaries" are more reminiscent of the Russian utopian socialists of the 1840s.

DOLININ, A. S. [Arkady Semyonovich Iskoz, 1883/8-1968]
Great Dostoevsky textual scholar, editor, and compiler. When archival materials first became available in the 1920s, Dolinin began a complete edition of Dostoevsky's correspondence, and the careful commentary he provided to the notebooks and manuscripts made possible a whole generation of scholarship. His 1947 work on *The Adolescent*, "V tvorcheskoi laboratorii Dostoevskogo" [In Dostoevsky's Creative Laboratory], is a model study of a Dostoevskian novel seen in genesis through its successive drafts. Dolinin maintained that there never was a radical split in Dostoevsky's political allegiances, by demonstrating in his work the continuity of the novelist's lifelong progressive sympathies. It was Dolinin, for example, who first traced Dolgushin's presence in *The Adolescent* (see above entry), and who juxtaposed Nechaev and Dolgushin.

Dolinin's edition of Dostoevsky's letters, and the new image that emerged of Dostoevsky as a correspondent and "dialogist," was indispensable to Bakhtin in his scholarship.

ENGELHARDT, Boris Mikhailovich [1887-1942]
Prolific and incisive Russian literary scholar, active on both sides of the Revolution. In addition to his work on Dostoevsky, Engelhardt wrote on Pushkin, translated Stendhal and Maupassant into Russian, produced children's editions of Swift and Cervantes, and was a well-known translator of Wilhelm Wundt, the German philosopher and physiologist whose work was also of interest to Bakhtin.

EPICTETUS [c. A.D. 55-c. 135]
Stoic philosopher and freed slave, who preached in Rome and later in Nicopolis to a large and devoted following. His lectures in eight books were collected by his pupils and later published; these writings had a great influence on Marcus Aurelius, Roman emperor (161-180) and Stoic philosopher.

Epictetus involved himself less with the theoretical sides of philosophy than with the dissemination of Stoic teachings among the ordinary and humble multitude. He counseled moderation of appetites, serenity in the face of death, and abandonment of all desires whose fulfillment was not under man's control.

ERMILOV, Vladimir Vladimirovich [1904-66]
Soviet literary scholar and critic, whose conventionally politicized studies of Dostoevsky, Gorky, Tolstoy and Chekhov exemplify respectable party-line scholarship in the 1940s and '50s. During the most difficult years for Dostoevsky's survival in Soviet Russia, Ermilov's role was not especially commendable: he was the first to proclaim that "we don't need Dostoevsky's *Devils*" [Russian title of *The Possessed*], and it was on his initiative that a 1930 reissuing of *The Possessed*, already typeset and ready to roll, was canceled and the plates dismantled.

When times improved, so did Ermilov's tolerance. In 1964 he signed an open letter in defense of Bakhtin, during the controversy surrounding publication of the second edition of *Problems of Dostoevsky's Poetics*.

EUCLID [450-380 B.C.]
Bakhtin clearly has in mind not the famous geometer but rather Euclid of Megara, called "Euclid the Socratic," one of the oldest and most faithful of Socrates' disciples. After the death of his master, he founded the Megarian School, a blend of Socratic ideas and the teaching of the Eleatic philosophers. Euclid wrote dialogues, none of which are extant.

EVNIN, Fyodor Isakovich [b. 1901]
Soviet Dostoevsky scholar, with studies on *The Possessed, Crime and Punishment*, and on Dostoevsky's pictorial imagery. In his essays in the 1959 anthology *Tvorchestvo F. M. Dostoevskogo*, Evnin censures Dostoevsky for his "tendentious typization" in the more socially regressive novels, which, Evnin claims, turned real-life prototypes into vulgar caricatures.

FÉNELON, François [1651-1715]
French prelate and writer, tutor to the duc de Bourgogne, grandson of Louis XIV. For his royal pupil's edification Fénelon wrote *Dialogues des morts* (1712-30), conversations on moral themes among famous heroes and statesmen of the past.

FONTENELLE, Bernard [1657-1757]
The *Dialogues des morts* (1683), to which Bakhtin refers, are a series of witty dialogues on philosophical themes conducted by historical figures beyond the grave. Fontenelle was one of the earliest proponents of science against religious orthodoxy and the claims of Providence. He often employed the dialogue as a vehicle for a more "open-ended" universe, as in his *Entretiens sur la pluralité des mondes* (1685), conversations between himself and a lady of his acquaintance on the insignificance of man in the solar system. The work served to popularize both scientific inquiry and the advances in astronomy.

FRIDLENDER, Georgy Mikhailovich [b. 1915]
Major Soviet Dostoevsky scholar, with works on the individual novels and on Dostoevsky's links with world literature. In his full-length study *Dostoevsky's Realism* [*Realizm Dostoevskogo*, Moscow-Leningrad, Nauka, 1964], Fridlender takes issue with Bakhtin's understanding of Dostoevskian "polyphony" (pp. 188-91). Fridlender admits that Dostoevsky does present his characters through their eyes and not the author's, but he claims that the place and moral purpose of the character is nevertheless carefully calculated by the author. "Authorial point of view," Fridlender writes (p. 190), "is not only expressed in direct authorial value judgments but in the grouping of characters, their interrelationships, the logic of their development and fates . . ." The freedom Dostoevsky grants his characters is only relative, he insists. Raskolnikov and the others are not "independently developing musical themes" but characters carefully correlated with one another. Outside this authorial correlation they lose all their meaning, and therefore their place in the novels is of necessity predetermined to a certain extent. The *whole* of a Dostoevskian novel, he argues, is a finished entity [*zakonchennost'*], and inevitably somewhat monologic.

Fridlender voices here a frequent criticism against Bakhtin, one which Bakhtin himself freely admitted was a difficult area in his thought (the nature of the "whole" in a polyphonic novel). The Dostoevsky book insufficiently explores this area. A more complete discussion can be found in his extensive essay from the 1920s, "Avtor i geroi v esteticheskoi deiatel'nosti" [Author and Hero in Aesthetic Activity] in *Estetika slovesnogo tvorchestva*, pp. 7-180.

GASSENDI's materialism
Pierre Gassendi (1596-1655), French mathematician and philosopher, advocated the atomistic theory of Epicurus in opposition to the mechanistic worldview of Descartes. Gassendi had considerable influence on the literary figures of his time, including Molière.

GLAUCON
Frequent speaker in Plato's dialogues (*The Republic, Parmenides, Symposium*) and most probably a brother of Plato's. Glaucon was an Athenian philosopher in his own right and the author of a book containing nine dialogues; thirty-two other dialogues have been ascribed to him but are not authenticated.

GOETHE's *Götter, Helden und Wieland* [1774]
A short farcical play in which Goethe satirizes the classical style of Wieland's play *Alceste* (1773). Wieland is spirited from his bed to confront the real protagonists in the Greek Alcestis story, along with their dramatist Euripides, and is astonished at their vigor and immense proportions. Wieland, apparently, was gracious enough not to be offended by the satire, and developed a friendly relationship with Goethe in Weimar.

GRIMMELSHAUSEN, Hans Jakob [1610?-76]
German novelist, strongly influenced by the French and Spanish picaresque novel. His major work *Simplicissimus* (1668) tells of the survival and education of a simple hero during the horrors of the Thirty Years' War.
   Der fliegende Wandersmann nach dem Monde (1659), mentioned by Bakhtin in chapter 4 as a carnivalized menippea, is apparently a translation from the French attributed to Grimmelshausen. Scholars are not agreed on its authorship.

GROSSMAN, Leonid Petrovich [1888-1965]
Dostoevsky scholar, whose works from the 1920s, *Put' Dostoevskogo* [Dostoevsky's Path] and *Poetika Dostoevskogo* [Dostoevsky's Poetics] examine the moral implications of the novelist's rejection of absolute truths. Grossman has been one of the most prolific students of Dostoevsky's ties with western literature, with studies on Dostoevsky and Balzac, Hoffmann, Voltaire, and the writer's relationship to the Gothic horror tale and boulevard novel.

HERACLIDES PONTICUS [4th c. B.C.]
Academic philosopher and pupil in Plato's Academy in Athens. Only fragments of his writings have survived, mostly dialogues, on a wide variety of subjects in the humanistic and physical sciences. His dialogues were famous for their vivid portrayal of personalities and rich use of myth, and influenced both Cicero and Plutarch.

HERZEN, Alexander [1812-70]
Russian publicist, essayist, and author of philosophical dialogues, in the form

of "letters" and "conversations" (*From the Other Shore, Letters from France and Italy*). Herzen emigrated from Russia in 1847. In London he started the first Russian Free Press, whose publications (*The Bell, Polar Star, Voices from Russia*) found their way back to Russia and there became a major factor in the morale and even the politics of the country. As Dolinin has shown, the philosophical and dialogic prose of Herzen was a profound influence on Dostoevsky from 1862 to the novelist's death.

"HIPPOCRATIC NOVEL"

More accurately, the Hippocratic (or Pseudo-Hippocratic) Letters. The fictive letter was a favorite genre of the Greek Cynics, and the twenty-seven letters in this collection were probably composed by a Cynic in the first century. They purport to be the correspondence exchanged between Hippocrates and various citizens of the Thracian city of Abdera concerning, among other things, the supposed laughing madness of the philosopher Democritus and the visit of Hippocrates to cure him. After hearing him account for his laughter at the follies and vanities of his fellow Abderites, Hippocrates pronounces Democritus both sane and wise.

The Hippocratic Letters are considered to be the first extended fiction in Western literature in epistolary form. Though recognized as apocryphal in antiquity, they were included in Renaissance editions of the Hippocratic corpus, insuring the continued currency of the story. See Holland, pp. 70-77.

ION OF CHIOS [490-421 B.C.]

Greek poet. His memoirs have not survived, but are quoted at length by Athenaeus (f. 200 A.D.) in his compendium *Deipnosophistai* [Doctors at Dinner]. Ion of Chios was the author of anywhere from 12 to 40 plays, in addition to elegiac poems, epigrams, paeans and encomia, all in a faultless, polished, and witty style. He had a legendary fondness for wine and other pleasures, and is reported to have said that both virtue and tragedy needed the satyric element to make them complete.

IVANOV, Vyacheslav Ivanovich [1866-1949]

Russian poet, critic, literary scholar, and the most prominent representative of the second-generation Symbolists. He celebrated the concept of *sobornost'* [religious communality], and advocated overcoming the individualism of the West with a new syncretic art based on medieval Byzantium. Dostoevsky, in Ivanov's opinion, was one of the great creators of new myths for future *sobornost'* art. For all his attention to theme, Ivanov was among the first major critics to analyze the formal structure of Dostoevsky's novels; this, and his perception of Dostoevsky's "philosophical realism" (realism based not on cognition but on insight) is appreciated by Bakhtin in his survey of "Dostoevsky and the Novel-Tragedy" in chapter 1.

JULIAN THE APOSTATE [332-63]

Roman Emperor, 361-63. Despite his pious Christian upbringing, Julian developed a passion for the classics and the old gods. On becoming emperor he reinstituted the pagan cult, proclaimed general toleration for all religions, and restored land to the temples. His reforms did not long outlast his reign.

Julian's surviving work includes orations, a large number of letters, and the menippean work to which Bakhtin refers in chapter 4: the *Convivium* or *Caesares*, a comic account of Constantine's reception on Olympus.

KAUS, Otto [b. 1891]

German playwright and literary scholar who wrote on Gogol and Dostoevsky. According to Kaus, Dostoevsky's novels were products of the "spirit of capitalism" which forced hitherto isolated worlds to interact; capitalism, in his view, was not only an economic principle but also a structural principle in artistic works.

In addition to *Dostojewski und sein Schicksal* (1923), Kaus wrote *Der Fall Gogol* (1912), *Dostoejewski: zur Kritik der Persönlichkeit, ein Versuch* (1916), and *Die Träume in Dostojewski's "Raskolnikoff"* (1926).

KIRPOTIN, Valery Yakovlevich [b. 1900]

One of the better "official party critics" writing on Dostoevsky. From 1932 to 1936 Kirpotin was head of the Literary Section of the Central Committee, and during the critical years in the formulation of the doctrine of Socialist Realism he was secretary of the Organizational Committee of the Writers' Union (1932-34). He was ever the obedient party spokesman in literary matters. In the brief 1946-48 "spring" occasioned by the 125th anniversary of Dostoevsky's birth, Kirpotin actively participated by sponsoring new critical anthologies and reissuings of the novels. His task was to integrate nineteenth-century masters such as Pushkin and Dostoevsky into Soviet culture; his approach was to make Dostoevsky respectable by saturating him with quotes from Marx and Lenin. Kirpotin encouraged a tolerance for Dostoevsky's conservative ideology on the same grounds Lenin had defended Tolstoy: both great novelists "mirrored the contradictions of their epoch." By Bakhtin's standards, however, Kirpotin is still very much a monologic critic, insisting as he does on Dostoevsky's ultimate endorsement of social revolution and virtue through suffering.

It should be noted that Kirpotin was among those party functionaries most violently opposed to awarding Bakhtin a doctorate for his dissertation on Rabelais, defended in 1947.

KOCK, Paul de [1794-1871]

Prolific and extremely popular French novelist of the first half of the nineteenth century, whose sentimental and often crudely risqué works (*Georgette* [1820], *Mon voisin Raymond* [1822], *L'Amant de la lune* [1847]) provide a good picture of everyday life in France of the time. In Dostoevsky's *Village of Stepanchikovo*, the tyrannical and fraudulent hero Foma Fomich pretends to be occupied with philosophy and weighty social problems, but in reality he is reading the novels of Paul de Kock.

KOMAROVICH, Vasily Leonidovich [1894-1942]

A productive member of that generation of Soviet literary scholars that greatly benefited by the opening of the Dostoevsky archives after the Revolution. Komarovich utilized correspondence, memoirs, diaries, and manuscripts to research Dostoevsky's early years, his pre-prison utopian idealism and relations with Belinsky and Pleshcheev. Among his more important studies are "Mirovaia garmoniia" [World Harmony], "Dostoevskii i shestidesiatniki" [Dostoevsky and the Men of the Sixties], "Dostoevsky and Heine," and various essays on the effect of the early years on the later novels, especially *The Adolescent*.

Komarovich was apparently active in religious circles in Leningrad during the 1920s, and joined The Brotherhood of St. Seraphim of Sarov.

KORNFELD, Paul (1889-1942]

German Expressionist playwright. Bakhtin probably has in mind such early plays as "Die Verführung" [The Seduction, 1913], in which the hero, Bitterlich, kills everyone who offends his aesthetic or ethical sense; and "Der Grosse Traum" [The Great Dream, 1923], a satire on the idealism of the revolutionaries.

LESAGE's *Gil Blas* [1715-35]

Alain-René Lesage (1668-1747) worked on his four-volume picaresque novel *Gil Blas* for 25 years; the work later became one of the models for the more "moral" *Bildungsroman*. In it, a young man leaves home at 17 and encounters the dishonest and honorable from all levels of society; he rises to a position of wealth, falls into disgrace, is imprisoned, recovers his position, and repents in his quiet old age.

The novel was enormously influential on Fielding, Sterne, and Smollett (who translated it into English). The open, easy-going character of Gil Blas, as well as the elegance and good humor with which Lesage depicted life's adversities, made a deep impression on Dostoevsky — who in his plan for the unwritten *Life of a Great Sinner* noted to himself that "the dryness of the narration [should] sometimes border on Gil Blas."

LUCIAN [c. 120-180]

Prolific Greek satirist and Sophist, perhaps the wittiest and least reverent Greek writer under the Roman Empire. He is credited with inventing the satirical dialogue as a literary form. Most of his famous works are mocking counterparts of traditionally serious genres: his mock travel narrative *A True Story*, his Dialogues of the Dead (one of which portrays the early Cynics Diogenes, Crates, and Antisthenes ridiculing newcomers to the underworld), and his attack on the Atticists in *Lexiphanes*. Lucian's influence on his own time has been compared (perhaps too generously) to Swift and Voltaire in theirs; like them he was a freethinker who criticized the reality of his society by "carnivalizing" its straightforward forms.

LUNACHARSKY, Anatoly Vasilievich [1875-1933]

Old-guard party intellectual, who survived the Revolution to become one of the most influential of Bolshevik scholar-bureaucrats. An editor of the Soviet Literary Encyclopedia and member of the Academy of Sciences, Lunacharsky served as People's Commissar of Education from 1917 to 1929. He was thus in a position to intercede for intellectuals threatened by the political excesses of the regime. He was not, however, very active on their behalf; on the contrary, evidence suggests that Lunacharsky frequently cooperated in the purging of academics.

Lunacharsky's favorable review of Bakhtin's Dostoevsky book ("O 'mnogogolosnosti' Dostoevskogo") appeared in 1929, when Bakhtin was already under arrest. It was not sufficient to prevent Bakhtin's exile to Siberia, but was probably instrumental in preventing a worse fate. Lunacharsky's review praises Bakhtin for his astute separation of ideological and artistic factors, and counsels the Russian reader to know Dostoevsky but not to live by him, to learn *through* him but not from him.

MARTIAL [42?-102?]
Latin epigrammist famous for his elegant and often grotesque sketches of everyday life in 1st-century Rome. In contrast to his more high-minded satiric contemporary Juvenal, Martial valued less an exposure of moral evils than wit, precision, and a polished style.

MENIPPUS of Gadara [first half of 3rd c. B.C.]
A slave who became a pupil of the Cynic Metrocles, purchased his freedom, settled in Thebes, and proceeded to satirize all formal schools of philosophy and all philosophical elites. Any form that pretended to be a vehicle for learned discourse—the treatise, the cosmography, the epistle, symposium, or dialogue—was fair game for his ridicule. Thirteen titles are attributed to him by Diogenes Laertius, but that list and some fragments are all that survive. The titles suggest considerable variety and invention: satires on philosophers and grammarians, parodies of epics and tragedies, a descent into Hell, and pieces ridiculing superstition and the presumptuousness of last wills and testaments. We know Menippus largely (and perhaps fictionally) through Lucian's dialogues; it would be very much in the spirit of Menippean satire to stylize or mythologize even its founder.

Menippean satire as a genre is characterized by its mockery of serious forms, its digression and exaggeration, and its mixture of prose and verse (lofty quoted verse "novelized" by the less reverent prose surrounding it).

MEREZHKOVSKY, Dmitri Sergeevich [1865-1941]
Major pre-Symbolist poet and literary philosopher, one of the first to contrast extensively the worldviews and creative logic of Tolstoy and Dostoevsky [*L. Tolstoi i Dostoevskii*, 1902; in English as *Tolstoy as Man and Artist, with an Essay on Dostoevsky* (New York, 1902)]. It was Merezhkovsky who coined the phrases "seer of the flesh" for Tolstoy and "seer of the soul" for Dostoevsky. His obsession with defining Dostoevsky as "the poet of evangelical love" earns him a place in Bakhtin's list of philosophical monologizers.

MIKHAILOVSKY, Nikolai Konstantinovich [1842-1904]
Populist activist and literary critic. His monograph on Dostoevsky, *A Cruel Talent* [Zhestokii talant] was published in 1882, amid the adulation that followed the novelist's death. It was a major attack on Dostoevsky's reactionary views and passion for suffering ("the world of beasts at prey"), and can be said to have founded the tradition, very productive in Soviet times, of condemning Dostoevsky's work on political grounds. In English, see Nikolai K. Mikhailovsky, *A Cruel Talent*, trans. Spencer V. Cadmus, Jr. (Ardis, 1978).

MAIKOV, Apollon Nikolaevich [1821-97]
Russian poet, one of Dostoevsky's closest friends and most active correspondents. Against the trends of the 1850s and '60s Maikov espoused a politically neutral "art for art's sake."

NEMIROVICH-DANCHENKO, Vladimir Ivanovich [1859-1943]
Russian dramatist and director who founded, together with Konstantin

Stanislavsky, the Moscow Art Theatre (1898). The theatre was closely associated with Anton Chekhov and later with Maksim Gorky.

PEREGRINUS of Parium [c. A.D. 100-165]
Cynic, of a rather eccentric sort. We know of him largely through Lucian, who admired his colorful character but had some doubts about his integrity. Peregrinus was suspected of murdering his father, fled to Palestine and became a Christian, was imprisoned for this, quarreled with the Christian community and then wandered about Egypt, Italy, and Greece as an itinerant preacher. In 165 he committed suicide by throwing himself on the flames at the Olympic Games.

PETRONIUS, Gaius [d. A.D. 66]
Presumed author of the *Satyricon*, a racy, realistic, and irreverent depiction of the Roman Empire of Nero's time. With its mixed form (prose and verse) and sardonic attitude toward contemporary issues, the *Satyricon* is for Bakhtin a classic menippea—and a major landmark in the development of the novelistic line to which Dostoevsky belongs.

PHAEDO (Phaidon) (4th c. B.C.)
Friend and disciple of Socrates, author of dialogues, and prominent participant in Plato's dialogue *Phaedo* (on the death of Socrates).

PHILOSTRATUS (fl. c. A.D. 210)
Greek author, also known as "The Athenian." He was a pioneer in fictionalized biography, and his best-known works in this genre include *Lives of the Sophists* and the *Life of Apollonius of Tyana*, based on a mystic philosopher of the first century. He also wrote dialogues.

PISEMSKY, Aleksei Feofilaktovich [1820-81]
Russian novelist, dramatist, and short story writer, well-known for his somber and objective descriptions of the hardships of village life (the novel *Tysiacha dush* [A Thousand Souls, 1858], and the drama *Gor'kaia sud'bina* [A Bitter Lot]). Pisemsky is something of an historical anomaly—with his pessimism, misanthropy, and absolute lack of idealism he resembled more the French naturalists than his own Russian compatriots of the 1860s.

POBEDONOSTSEV, Konstantin Petrovich [1827-1907]
Russian jurist, government administrator, and Procurator of the Holy Synod (lay head of the Orthodox Church) under the last two tsars, Alexander III and Nicholas II. He was immensely influential as a supporter of absolutism, and as a bulwark against liberal tendencies in Russian government and society. Dostoevsky was one of his friends and correspondents.

PONSON DU TERRAIL, Pierre-Alexis [1829-71]
One of the most prolific of the *roman-feuilletonistes* (novelists publishing in installments in daily papers or periodicals). Perhaps his most famous work is *Les exploits de Rocambole* (1859), which takes the hapless hero through 22 volumes of adventures.

QUEVEDO, Francisco [1580-1645]
Great Spanish poet, satirist, and novelist. Bakhtin probably has in mind his viciously satirical *El buscón* (1603-08), and his five "visions" or dreams (*Los*

sueños, 1606-22), which indict the hypocrisy of the age. Quevedo was a master stylist and exploiter of language, ingeniously deforming his Castilian prose to the delight of sophisticated readers.

ROZANOV, Vasily Vasilievich [1856-1919]
Russian philosopher and literary critic, whose major work on the Legend of the Grand Inquisitor (1890) was among the first to point out the central role of the Underground Man in Dostoevsky's art (in English, see Vasily Rozanov, *Dostoevsky and the Legend of the Grand Inquisitor*, trans. Spencer E. Roberts [Cornell University Press, 1972]). Heavily influenced by Nietzsche, Rozanov espoused the view that sexuality was central to man's coordination of his biological and spiritual planes. He was a passionate admirer of Dostoevsky all his life, which caused him much personal misery: as a very young man he married Dostoevsky's faded former mistress, who treated him as callously as she had Dostoevsky twenty years earlier.

ST. SIMEON THE NEW THEOLOGIAN [d. 1032]
Eleventh-century Byzantine mystic and theologian, raised in Constantinople and an intimate of the Emperors Basil and Constantine. The major tenets of his teaching (embodied in "discourses" or *slova*) concern the actual application of theoretical Christian doctrine to the Christian life ("Discourse on Faith," "Discourse on Three Forms of Prayer"). His prose is remarkable for its simplicity, earnestness and persuasive manner; his contemporaries, accustomed to a more artificial elegance, considered the "discourses" unscholarly and insufficiently rhetorical.

St. Nilus Sorsky, fifteenth-century spiritual leader of the Russian trans-Volga hermits, drew heavily on the works of St. Simeon, whom he considered an inspirational expression of the mystic love possible in a personal union with Jesus through spiritual prayer. With the revival of interest in Hesychast teachings in nineteenth-century Russia, both St. Simeon and Nilus Sorsky enjoyed a special popularity in philosophical and religious circles. According to a catalogue compiled by Leonid Grossman in the early 1920s, Dostoevsky's library contained several works by St. Simeon.

SATYRE MÉNIPÉE DE LA VERTU DU CATHOLICON D'ESPAGNE (1594)
A satirical pamphlet in mixed verse and prose, parodying the assembly of the États généraux and supporting the cause of Henri IV. The work was apparently a joint effort by various middle-class functionaries, lawyers, clerics, and scholars, with general authorship credited to Jean Leroy, a canon of Rouen. It contains a burlesque description of the opening of the assembly, imaginary speeches by real personages, and various appended satires and epigrams. Its mocking brilliance and topical relevance made it enormously popular, and its appearance coincided with the Ligue's defeat.

SCARRON, Paul [1610-60]
French author whose writings helped discredit the mythological and heroic "grand style" of seventeenth-century prose and poetry. Bakhtin probably has in mind *Le Roman comique* (1651-57), an account of life among itinerant actors, and Scarron's popular parody on Virgil in seven books, *Virgile travesti* (1648-52).

SENECA, Lucius Annaeus [4 B.C.-A.D. 65]
Roman scholar, tragedian and Stoic philosopher, tutor to Nero. Of Seneca's wide and varied output, Bakhtin singles out his *Apocolocyntosis* or "Pumpkinification," also entitled "A Trifle upon the Death of Claudius." It is authentic Menippean satire, a fantasy on the journeys of the soul of the Emperor Claudius, who was poisoned by his wife Agrippina in A.D. 54. The work is thinly veiled political criticism of the corrupt court patronized by the late Emperor, and contains much bitter personal invective as well.

SIMIAS of Thebes
Member of Socrates' inner circle and one of the disciples willing to put up money for his escape. He was among those present at the master's death. In the *Phaedo* he argues against the soul's immortality. Simias apparently also wrote dialogues; Diogenes Laertius ascribes twenty-three to him, but none are extant.

SHESTOV, Lev [Lev Isakovich Schwartzmann, 1866-1938]
Russian-Jewish religious philosopher and literary critic. In his *Dostoevskii i Nitsshe: filosofiia tragedii* (1903) Shestov portrayed Dostoevsky as a great mystic, one who rejected human morality and sought God in irrationality and subjectivity. Shestov did not deal with individual novels, but rather enlarged on Dostoevsky's mysticism as a philosophical creed, contrasting it with Tolstoy's very different identification of morality with God. For the above work in English, see Lev Shestov, *Dostoevsky, Tolstoy & Nietzsche*, trans. Spencer Roberts (Ohio University Press, 1969), pp. 143-322.

SHKLOVSKY, Viktor [1893–1985]
One of the most prolific and visible founders of the Russian Formalist movement in the 1920s, whose creative activity now stretches over half a century. In *Za i protiv* [Pro and Contra], Shklovsky argued against Bakhtin's polyphony; later Shklovsky contentiously reviewed Bakhtin's book on Rabelais in "Fransua Rable i kniga M. Bakhtina" [in *Tetiva: o neskhodstve skhodnogo* (Moscow, 1970), pp. 267–73]. There he took issue with several points: with Bakhtin's apparent willingness to see every conflict as "carnivalized," and with his insufficient attention to the historical aspect. Both Rabelais' satire and his carnival are historical, Shklovsky insisted. History might repeat but it also moves forward; "Bakhtin tends to merge the repeats into an immobility" (p. 272).

SOPHRON [fl. 5th c. B.C.]
Syracusan writer of mimes. He is generally considered the founder of the literary mime, and was highly respected by Plato. Sophron's mimes, written in a sort of rhythmic prose, took as their subject matter the events of everyday life.

SOREL, Charles [1599-1674]
French author whose most famous works ridicule the seventeenth-century passion for pastoral romances. Bakhtin probably has in mind his "carnivalized" works, the early picaresque novel *La vraie histoire comique de Francion* (1623), and *Le berger extravagant* (1627). In the latter novel, the hero loses his sanity by reading too many pastoral romances, and sets out in the dress of

a shepherd to experience a number of ludicrous adventures. *Le berger* was a satire on the immensely popular prose romance by d'Urfé, *L'Astrée* (1607-27).

SOULIÉ, Frédéric [1800-47]
French novelist, one of the earliest writers of *roman-feuilletons*. His forty best-sellers, on macabre and sensational themes, include *Les deux cadavres* (1832), and *Les mémoires du diable* (1837-38)

STIRNER, Max [Johann Kaspar Schmidt, 1806-56]
German individualist philosopher, whose *Der Einzige und sein Eigentum* [The Individual and his Property, 1845] is a defense of philosophical egoism and one of the earliest reactions against Hegelian philosophy. In it Stirner argues that the ego is a law unto itself and the human individual is the only ultimate value; all systematic philosophies are therefore fraudulent, as are all doctrines espousing a "common humanity." The work is permeated by a passionate anti-intellectualism and exalts the will and the instincts. Not surprisingly, Stirner is seen as a precursor to Nietzsche, although he also shares something with the anarchists. He did not, however, preach revolution; he preached rebellion. "Revolution is a social or political act; rebellion is an individual act."

For Stirner, the goal was not so much freedom as "ownness," the right to possess and practice one's own unique vision. In true rebellion, he claimed, the use of force is inevitable, but the end goal is not violence or conflict. The goal is a "balance among strong wills," since true security in one's uniqueness would remove all reason to be hostile toward another. Stirner in fact hoped for a "Union of Egoists" to replace the state.

Elements of Stirner's philosophy are clearly reflected in Raskolnikov, and the bankruptcy of a "Union of Egoists" in Raskolnikov's final dream.

SUE, Eugène [1804-75]
Enormously successful author of *romans-feuilletons*. His most popular is probably *Les mystères de Paris* (1842-43), a sensational picture of Parisian low life mixed with colorful characters and then-current ideas of social and political reform.

THE SYMPOSIASTS
Symposium literature (i.e., descriptions of conversations at dinner table or drinking party) was a whole genre in ancient Greece. Its masterpiece is Plato's *Symposium*, but symposia were also written by Xenophon and Aristotle. The genre became a vehicle for serious philosophical discussion (as in Epicurus), as well as a repository for various unconnected anecdotes and lore. Not surprisingly, the serious philosophical symposium was parodied by Menippus and Lucian, and the depiction of crude and vulgar banquets became a major theme of Roman satire. In late antiquity, the Symposiast tradition was exemplified by Athenaeus, and then by the *Saturnalia* of Macrobius (ca. 400), a vast compendium of poetics, philosophy, and various commentary on the ancients.

TELES of Megara [fl. c. 235 B.C.]
Cynic philosopher. Teles was one of the earliest writers of diatribes (short ethical discussions), which were not in themselves especially distinguished but were successful in communicating the Cynic teachings in simple and popular

language. Teles is also important for his quotations and portraits of earlier writers (Bion Borysthenes, Crates the Cynic).

TIECK, Ludwig [1773-1853]
Prolific representative of early Romanticism, accomplished in lyric poetry, drama and translation. Bakhtin perhaps has in mind his early tale of horror, "Der Runenberg" (1804), or his huge and eccentric drama "Kaiser Oktavianus" (1804).

VARRO, Marcus Terentius [116-27 B.C.]
Roman politician, prolific scholar and linguist. Of him Augustine said: "His reading was so wide, it was a wonder he ever wrote anything; his writing so numerous that no one could ever read it through." He left 490 volumes in all genres and on all topics.

His *Saturae Menippearum Libri* have survived only in the form of 95 titles and 591 fragments. The satires were usually cast as dramatic dialogues, of mixed prose and verse in the seriocomic style, and they exploited a variety of "estrangement" techniques to make their point: playing with point of view (the view from above), treating the reader as tourist and the satire as guidebook, recording impressions of an author after a 50-year sleep, etc. These satires were probably originally published as pamphlets intended for a general audience. The language was, however, extremely complex and erudite, full of neologisms, puns, and extravagant constructions.

VINOGRADOV, Viktor Vladimirovich [1895-1969]
Linguist and theoretician of literary style, friendly critic of the Formalists, and persistent opponent of Bakhtin's discourse-utterance theory. The relevant major difference between Vinogradov and Bakhtin involves what Vinogradov calls the "rhetorical quality" [*retorichnost'*] of artistic prose. Vinogradov was much interested in the interplay of oral and written forms—the traces of the oratorical in prose, and the literariness of oratorical speech—and investigated their interaction in terms of "rhetorical" and "poetic" categories. His apparent relegation of the novel to the category of rhetoric (*On Artistic Prose*, 1929) evoked a somewhat polemical response from Bakhtin in his essay "Discourse in the Novel" (see *The Dialogic Imagination, Four Essays by M. M. Bakhtin* [Austin: Univ. of Texas Press, 1981], p. 268). For more background on the dialogue between Vinogradov and Bakhtin, see Chudakov's commentary to "On Artistic Prose," in V. V. Vinogradov, *O jazyke khudozhestvennoi prozy* (Moscow: Nauka, 1980), pp. 338-39.

VOGÜÉ, Eugène-Melchior [1848-1910]
French man of letters, one of the first to popularize in his homeland the great Russian novelists of the second half of the nineteenth century. His *Le roman russe* was published in 1906.

VOLYNSKY, Akim Lvovich [A. L. Flekser, 1863-1926]
Symbolist literary critic, whose *F. M. Dostoevskii: kriticheskie stat'i* (1906) attacked the positivism and utilitarianism of the nineteenth-century radical critics. Volynsky insisted that social and political questions were irrelevant to Dostoevsky's art, and concentrated instead on aesthetic considerations—as they influenced both Dostoevsky himself and his created characters. He credited Dostoevsky with the first thorough and penetrating examination of

the human psyche confronted with the phenomenon of Beauty. Dostoevsky was, in Volynsky's opinion, one of the first Russian writers to challenge the naive association of the Beautiful with the Good and the True. The Beautiful was, on the contrary, dangerous; in his analysis of *The Idiot*, Volynsky shows how the miracle of Beauty creates the desire for possession, and unleashes the most terrible forces of violence and egoism.

WERFEL, Franz [1890-1945]

Austrian poet, novelist and playwright. His Expressionist drama "Spiegel-mensch" [The Mirror Man, 1920], to which Bakhtin refers, is a variant on the Faust theme: the hero Thamal releases his lower self by shooting into the mirror, and is then in thrall to this double. At last Thamal turns himself in to the authorities, drinks poison (which returns Spiegelmensch to the mirror) and redeems himself in a monastery.

XENOPHON [c. 430-c. 355 B.C.]

Athenian historian and philosopher, later exiled to Sparta and Corinth for his military activity against Athens. In his *Hellenica* he continued Thucydides' history of Greece; his *Memorabilia of Socrates* was a popular exposition of philosophy. The *Cyropedia*, to which Bakhtin often refers, is Xenophon's didactic and highly subjective biography of Cyrus the Great.

XENOPHON of Ephesus

Author of Greek romances, about whom so little is known that he has been assigned anywhere from the second to the fifth century A.D. His *Ephesian Tales* (or *Ephesiaca*) are generically exemplary material of the Greek romance, with separated lovers, shipwrecks, enslavement, seductions, and the inevitable fidelity and happy ending. Plot development and characterization are so poor that some scholars have considered the novel (extant in five books) to be a bad abridgment of a longer work. This judgment could be due, however, to an insufficient appreciation of the generic characteristics of the Greek romance. For Bakhtin's discussion of the genre, see his essay "Forms of Time and Chronotrope in the Novel," in *The Dialogic Imagination*, pp. 86-110.

Index

Index

Mikhail Bakhtin (1895-1975) was a leading Soviet critic and literary theorist whose work was first published in the 1920s and who, for political reasons, had to withdraw from an active literary life. Rediscovered by young Russian literary scholars in his lifetime, Bakhtin is now recognized in the West as a major philosopher of language and theoretician of the novel.

Caryl Emerson is an assistant professor of Russian literature at Cornell University and co-translator (with Michael Holquist) of *The Dialogic Imagination: Four Essays by M. M. Bakhtin.*

Wayne Booth is professor of English at the University of Chicago and the author of, among much other work, *The Rhetoric of Fiction.*